Witchcraft, Intimacy, and Trust

WITCHCRAFT, INTIMACY, *and* TRUST

Africa in Comparison

✳

Peter Geschiere

The University of Chicago Press   •   Chicago and London

Peter Geschiere is professor of African anthropology at the University of Amsterdam. He is the author of many books, including, most recently, *The Perils of Belonging: Autochthony, Citizenship, and Exclusion in Africa and Europe*, also published by the University of Chicago Press.

The University of Chicago Press, Chicago 60637
The University of Chicago Press, Ltd., London
© 2013 by The University of Chicago
All rights reserved. Published 2013.
Printed in the United States of America

22 21 20 19 18 17 16 15 14 13   1 2 3 4 5

ISBN-13: 978-0-226-04758-4 (cloth)
ISBN-13: 978-0-226-04761-4 (paper)
ISBN-13: 978-0-226-04775-1 (e-book)

Library of Congress Cataloging-in-Publication Data

Geschiere, Peter, author.
   Witchcraft, intimacy, and trust : Africa in comparison / Peter Geschiere.
      pages ; cm
   Includes bibliographical references and index.
   ISBN 978-0-226-04758-4 (cloth : alkaline paper) — ISBN 978-0-226-04761-4 (paperback : alkaline paper) — ISBN 978-0-226-04775-1 (e-book)   1. Witchcraft—Africa.   2. Witchcraft—Social aspects.   3. Witchcraft—Psychological aspects.   4. Intimacy (Psychology)   5. Trust—Africa.   I. Title.
   BF1584.A35G47 2013
   133.4'309—dc23

                                                                2013007997

   ♾ This paper meets the requirements of ANSI/NISO z39.48-1992 (Permanence of Paper).

To Eric de Rosny
and to Peter me-Meke and Hans Mempouila Meke
for their courage, in different times and different moments

Contents

Acknowledgments

Witchcraft is a terrible word—elusive, but all the more powerful for being so. Its messiness drives to despair not only the people who fear it but also academics, even those who believe they can keep their distance when studying it. Terribly destructive, it is also productive in a transgressive way that makes it utterly fascinating. It nestles at the inner core of social relations, yet is as capable of globalization as the most modern ideas or practices. This book is an attempt to deal with its paradoxes by focusing on this amazing ability to be both intimate and global. The chapters do so not so much via theoretical or conceptual reflection as by juxtapositions of apparently quite different situations and moments, in the hope that some recurrent patterns will emerge. The challenge is especially to understand the consequences for trust: if witchcraft is the unsettling realization that intimacy can be terribly dangerous, how is it possible to build nonetheless the degree of trust necessary to live and work with one's intimates? It will be clear that there are no definitive answers. The very ambiguity of intimacy—comforting yet at the same time inherently dangerous—means that trust can never be an ontological certainty. For Georg Simmel, trust depended, next to knowledge, on "a further element of . . . quasi-religious faith." This applies most strongly to the struggle over trust as a counterpoint to the inherent link between witchcraft and intimacy. In this configuration, trust is emphatically situational. All we can hope is to highlight certain factors and relations that make the "suspension of doubt," as a precarious base for trust, possible despite the dangers hidden in intimacy.

✳

Approaching such uncertainties through a juxtaposition of different situations and processes means that for this book I am in debt to many, many people for helping me to understand these different settings. So the list of acknowledgments here is particularly long. Yet all this assistance has been equally valuable for me.

Birgit Meyer, even though she is a lot younger, acted as my insightful and patient guru for this book. Without her inspiration and rigorous thinking I would have long been lost in juggling these ambiguous notions of witchcraft, intimacy, and trust. Jim Siegel became a new friend, and a most inspiring one, during this struggle for clarity; I only regret that I could never attain the elegance of his writing, evident even in the comments he sent me. The spirit of *père* Eric de Rosny, a very old friend, is everywhere in this book. Unfortunately he died in 2011. I dedicate this book to him—to his courage in his quest for healing and reconciliation in unorthodox corners.

A very different source of inspiration was my ongoing contact with my Maka friends from the region in Southeast Cameroon where I have done fieldwork since 1971. If I understand anything about the working of witchcraft, its ideas and practices, it is due to their patience in introducing me to the ambiguities of their visions of the *djambe*. I owe special thanks to Meke Blaise, my assistant now for over forty years, and to his two sons, Peter me-Meke and Hans Mempouila—both are medical doctors now. I include them in the dedication in admiration for their courage in working for the healing of their people—differently from Eric de Rosny, yet under equally difficult circumstances.

Academia has brought its own kind of challenges and stimulations—of course in a theoretical sense, but also (and for me much more importantly) through personal inspiration. Jean-François Bayart and Achille Mbembe remain leading lights for me, constantly renewing themselves. For this book Jean and John Comaroff's explorations and comments were especially exciting and rich, again and again opening up new directions to think through; and so were Arjun Appadurai's challenging perspectives on unexpected aspects of globalization. I owe special thanks to Gyanendra Pandey and Clifton Crais, since it was they who insisted on the link with intimacy as particularly intriguing in my ramblings about witchcraft during a presentation at Emory. Subsequent panels on drafts for this book, organized by Kate Luongo (at the ASA in San Francisco), Mike McGovern (at Yale), Jean-François Bayart (at the REASOPO network in Paris), and Jacinthe Mazzocchetti (at Louvain-la-neuve), and a marathon discussion at the Johannesburg Workshop for Critical Theory, were also most stimulating.

Over recent years it became increasingly clear to me how much I have learned from my PhD students (most of whom have now luckily passed the threshold and reached prominent positions). This applies especially to Cyprian Fisiy, my comrade-in-arms from the first steps we took to struggle for greater clarity in all this clamor over witchcraft in the Cameroonian set-tings where we both worked. I am particularly grateful that even though he now has a leading position at the World Bank, he continues to be inter-ested in my scribblings on the topic. But it applies as well to the many PhD students from Cameroon and other parts of Africa who followed him—for this book notably to Antoine Socpa, Margaret Niger-Thomas, Basile Ndjio, Robert Akoko, Ibrahim Mouiche, Timothée Tabapssi, Grace Fisiy, Rogers Orock, Abdou Salam Fall, Francisco Mucanheia, Abdoulaye Kane, and Graeme Reid. This book also bears the traces of collaboration with many PhD students from elsewhere, notably Karin Willemse, Jan Jansen, Dmitri van den Bersselaar, Marloes Janson, Adri van den Berg, Michel Doortmont, Amber Gemmeke, Jan Bart Gewalt, Rachel Spronk, Martijn Oosterbaan, Marleen de Witte, Jacqueline de Vries, Jill Alpes, Naomi van Stapele, Apos-tolos Andrikopoulos, and my "younger brother" Francio Guadeloupe.

Working in Cameroon was most stimulating because of all the contact with colleagues there: first Paul Nkwi, a pillar in all the consecutive proj-ects we undertook over the last thirty years; but also Francis Nyamnjoh—I hope we will write many more articles together; Jacqueline Ekambi, Luc Mebenga, Edjenguèlè Mbonji, and Thierno Bah; also many Camer-oonologists from elsewhere: Miriam Goheen, Janet Roitman, Dominique Malaquais, Piet Konings, Roberto Beneduce, Simona Taliani, Jane Guyer, Michael Rowlands, Jean-Pierre Warnier, Nicolas Argenti, Philip Burnham, Alec Leonhardt, Roberto Moise, and José van Santen.

Special thanks to Rafael Sanchez for guiding me through Mauss and Sie-gel, and to Susan van Zeyl, Laia de Soto, and Roberto Beneduce for showing me the way through Freud. Also to my guides in Brazil, notably Livio San-sone, Jocélio Teles dos Santos, Mattijs van de Port, and Luis Nicolau Parés; and to my most inspiring colleagues in South Africa: Isak Niehaus, Caro-lyn Hamilton, Deborah Posel, Pamela Reynolds, Sarah Nuttal, and Shamil Jeppie.

Many colleagues in Leiden offered me encouragement and breathing space in the midst of battles for survival—especially Gerti Hesseling, who left us far too soon, Reimar Schefold, Mineke Schipper, Jarich Oosten, Wasif Shadid, Sabine Luning, Peter Pels, and Patricia Spyer. But this book was mostly conceived after my passage to Amsterdam, under the benevolent eyes of Peter van der Veer, Hans Sonneveld, Jan Breman, Annelies Moors, Anita Hardon, José Komen, Niko Besnier, Jan Willem Duyvendak, and Eve-lien Tonkens, with Robert Pool and Vinh-Kim Nguyen as most welcome newcomers.

Many thanks also to all the colleagues in other settings (forgive me for this long and rambling list with too many omissions): Adam Ashforth,

Richard Banégas, Karin Barber, Heike Behrendt, Alice Bellagamba, Florence Bernault, Thomas Blom Hansen, Filip de Boeck, Nils Bubandt, Andrea Ceriana Mayneri, Bambi Ceupens, John Cinnamon, Fred Cooper, Kate Crehan, Armando Cutolo, Veena Das, Mamadou Diawara, Mamadou Diouf, Andreas Eckert, Harri Englund, James Ferguson, Mariane Ferme, Alcinda Honwana, Béatrice Hibou, Gudrun Lachenmann, Ruby Lal, Murray Last, Carola Lentz, Liisa Malkki, Adeline Masquelier, Annemarie Mol, Achim von Oppen, Pierre Petit, Charles Piot, David Pratten, Ute Röschenthaler, Oscar di Simplicio, Inger Sjørslev, Daniel Smith, Shalini Randeria, Vyjayanthi Rao, Dorothea Schultz, Sharika Thiranagama, Joseph Tonda . . . and many, many more! Special thanks to Ruth Marshall and Juan Obarrio for the way they mix stern criticism with friendship and fun. And a very special thanks this time to David Brent from University of Chicago Press with Priya Nelson for being such particularly stimulating editors.

✳

A final word about my changing position toward this thorny topic. Why a second book on witchcraft after almost twenty years? (My earlier book on the topic, *The Modernity of Witchcraft*, was published in 1997, but the earlier French version, *Politique et sorcellerie: La viande des autres*, had come out in 1995.)

There are many reasons for this, but the main one is a gradual shift in my own position. My first confrontations with the world of "witchcraft"—first through the literature on early-modern Europe and then, much more intensively, during my fieldwork among the Maka—were colored by a certain fascination. The stories my Maka friends told me in 1971 were full of excitement, opening up a secret, adventurous world in which anything seemed to be possible. Over time, however, the ugly effects of this preoccupation with the invisible became ever more difficult to ignore. The endless gossip about witchcraft machinations in politics or behind new forms of entrepreneurship and enrichment is a source of great unrest, mixed with fear. But for me it was even more worrying to see how witchcraft worked from the inside—how even apparently close families were eventually destroyed by horrible insinuations and accusations, sometimes leading to direct violence. Hence the focus in this book on the link with intimacy. Moreover, such internal suspicions were often grafted onto people's struggles to get access to new forms of consumption and enrichments ("modernity"?). No wonder so many friends complain that they cannot understand why modernity in Africa brings a reinforcement of witchcraft rather than a weakening of it, as in the West.

Of course, such opposing of Africa to the West is problematic. The present-day obsession with witchcraft dangers is deeply marked by Africa's confrontation with the West. Witchcraft is not a traditional given but a historical phenomenon; the particular and highly varying forms it takes in the African continent are shaped by deep historical changes in which colonization and the ensuing global power relations are central. Yet the longer I know people, the more difficult it becomes to ignore such complaints about how modernity in Africa has reinforced witchcraft, poisoning personal relations by omnipresent suspicions. It may be naive to hope for an effective *didactique contre la sorcellerie* (a pedagogy against witchcraft), as my missionary friends in the region did, asking me to contribute to this (see the last pages of this book). Yet I feel bad that I disappointed them miserably—and again in the present book—because many Africans clearly feel the need for such a *didactique* to liberate them from witchcraft's horrors. I doubt, though, whether the solution can be so radical, precisely because it is the inherent link with intimacy—the focus of this book—that makes it impossible to try to erase these fears from people's minds by just a *didactique*. Nonetheless, I still think that academic explorations can help, if not to eradicate these tenacious ideas, at least to relativize them. After all, people do manage to establish trust, even though one's intimate relations are heavily charged with danger. Given this danger, trust is always precarious and situational (never "ontological"). Yet focusing on such struggles over trust may help to historicize "witchcraft" and its visions, bring out their situationality, and rob them of their apparent inevitability.

Prologue

THE FOCUS OF THIS BOOK is on the close and mesmerizing link between witchcraft and intimacy in present-day Africa but also in other times and places. It is more specifically on the problems this link raises for establishing trust despite imminent danger between people who are close (in whatever sense). To some readers this theme of witchcraft, intimacy, and trust may appear to be an exotic topic. And it is true that the very notion of witchcraft—I will come back to problems with the term—has exoticizing implications. However, I hope to show that witchcraft discourse because of its recurrent link with closeness addresses issues that are quite general, maybe even universally human. In many societies and at quite different moments in world history, witchcraft has been seen as particularly frightening since it conjures up the danger of treacherous attacks from close by—from inside a social core where peace and harmony should reign. The implicit message of this type of discourse might be generalized even further. It conveys the warning that seeds of destruction are hidden inside social relations as such, even though these are vital for any human undertaking. This implies quite a different view of human sociality from the one that prevails in much anthropological work, or even in social science more broadly. One of the aims of this book, then, is to show that the continuing preoccupation in many parts of Africa with witchcraft is not a sign of the continent's "otherness." It reflects, rather, one way of addressing issues that are crucial to human sociality. It is in this perspective that this book opts for a comparative outlook that can help to trace different trajectories in the link between intimacy and danger, often imagined as "witchcraft," and the implications of these historical trajectories for the struggle to establish trust in the face of lurking danger.

Questions concerning the link between witchcraft and intimacy have intrigued me ever since the start of my fieldwork among the Maka in the forest of Southeast Cameroon in 1971. My new friends soon made it clear that I would never understand anything of their politics and views on power (the original topic of my research) if I did not take seriously their notion of *djambe*—a term they always translated as "sorcellerie" or "witchcraft." The world of *djambe* turned out to be full of surprises. This occult force could be used for all sorts of purposes, including healing and accumulating riches and power. But a core element that remained a somber refrain was the close link between *djambe* and *ndjaw* (house, family). It seemed to be self-evident to my Maka friends that "witchcraft from inside the house" (*djambe le ndjaw*) was the most dangerous kind. Witches were supposed to have a special hold over their relatives, betraying them to their fellow witches during their weird nightly meetings. New forms of *djambe* might graft themselves onto modern changes, taking on a global allure, adorned with airplanes and new forms of consumption, yet even these innovative *djambe* versions always seemed to emanate from the intimate circles of home and family. The horror of the *djambe* seemed to be condensed in the realization that the people with whom one has to live and work—whom one has to trust—can become particularly dangerous.

I found the self-evidence with which the Maka linked this *djambe* to kinship quite disconcerting. But another surprise was how people "worked" with kinship. They turned out to be true masters in using kinship terms—and the claims, obligations, and emotions they implied—to interpret and reinterpret their social contacts, thus ordering networks that were growing ever wider due to urbanization and new forms of migration. In everyday life both kinship (*bjel*) and witchcraft (*djambe*) proved to be highly dynamic notions, lending themselves to creative reinterpretations. Subsequently I found also that their mutual articulation—the idea of witchcraft as betrayal from the inside—is surprisingly general. Not only among the Maka but indeed throughout Africa "witchcraft" is linked to the family in one way or another. This is why I came to refer to it as "the dark side of kinship" (Geschiere 1997). On other continents as well, the basic image of "witches" as people who have acquired the ability to transform themselves, leave their bodies at night, and fly off to nocturnal meetings in order to engage in horrible conspiracies is surprisingly general. And a fixed correlate of such images is the emphasis that witches most often find their victims in their close surroundings. The exact form of proximity may vary—in some settings it may concern, for instance, neighbors rather than relatives; or the sorcerer may be an outsider who works through an ally within—but there is almost always a link with intimacy in some form. And though nowadays many see witchcraft as "globalizing," apparently reflecting the increase in scale of social relations, it is still seen as rooted in people's close environment. This ongoing nexus with intimacy becomes all the more striking since at the same time it seems to "go global."

Of course, the close link between occult aggression and intimacy is an old theme in social science. We may think of Freud's vision of *das Unheimliche* (the uncanny) as the familiar turned against us—*das Heimliche* (the homely) suddenly taking on threatening proportions—and Simmel's vision of *der Fremde* (the stranger) as seminal leads that, as we shall see below, have received surprisingly little attention in the wave of recent literature on the topic of intimacy.[1] Indeed, a witchcraft view of intimacy as riddled with danger seems to be at loggerheads with the tenacious anthropological vision of the inner circle of home and family as a haven of reciprocity.

Issues

Despite this book's wider ambitions, it may be wise to start from more modest points of departure: the issues that plague witchcraft studies and their recent revival in anthropology. Exploring the implications of the link of this elusive notion to intimacy in a comparative perspective may be rewarding in this context for several reasons. A central question to this book is to what extent this recurrent but variable nexus helps to illuminate some common element—a beacon?—in the wild proliferation of uses for the term *witchcraft*. In present-day Africa, for instance, people seem to be so obsessed with the supposed exuberance of new forms of occult aggression that they use the term *witchcraft* as a sort of passe-partout for any perceived danger. Such loose terminology helps to confirm the feeling that witchcraft is indeed omnipresent. Therefore, some effort toward trying to contain the term may be most welcome.

Another advantage is that characterizing witchcraft as *the danger inside* offers openings for wider comparison. As noted above, it makes areas that are nowadays beset with fears of witchcraft—like present-day Africa—not that exceptional. The realization that intimacy can be extremely dangerous is not unique to Africa. The ways in which intimacy is delimited may vary, along with the ways it is related to danger, but making the link is not a mark of a radical alterity.

Moreover, as noted, linking witchcraft to intimacy will automatically raise the issue of trust. If the witch is not an absolute other but a person hidden in your close surroundings, it becomes an urgent and immediate question how you can put your trust in the people with whom you have to live and work. Again, highly different answers can be imagined, depending on the historical setting, but the challenge is a general one.

Before further exploring these different lines of argumentation, it is high time to address obvious problems of terminology. A major difficulty for focusing on the link between witchcraft and intimacy is, of course, that both terms are extremely slippery: they are used in all sorts of ways, becoming the kind of "floating signifiers" against which Lévi-Strauss warned us so strongly.[2] Adopting such everyday notions has tricky implications for academics. This will be clear for *witchcraft*—a term that triggered long debates among anthropologists and others, some colleagues even charging academics that they, by their indiscriminate use of a term like *witchcraft*, encourage the popular obsession in Africa with the omnipresence of occult aggression (see below). But the same critique can apply to *intimacy*, a term that has become quite fashionable in recent decades among social scientists and others and has been used with so many meanings that it verges on becoming emptied of sense. Linking the two might appear, therefore, a dangerous undertaking.

The reader may be familiar with the problems of the term *witchcraft*. As Malcolm Crick warned us as early as 1979, it is a Western term that has implications of its own—especially pejorative ones—and thus distorts when used to translate local notions that often have a much wider array of meanings. The problem is, however, that in many parts of the world—certainly in Africa but also elsewhere—this Western term has been eagerly appropriated by the public. Especially when used to describe a perceived crisis—such as the popular alarm, already mentioned for Africa, over a supposed proliferation of new forms of "witchcraft" against which older sanctions are of no avail—it acquires an urgency that is difficult for academics to ignore. In the African contexts where I have worked, people used the term—or its French equivalent *sorcellerie*—to address an all-pervasive presence that covered all sorts of occult dangers and fears, surpassing local distinctions and demarcations.[3]

However, despite this often frightening diffuseness—in everyday life people tend to apply this label to every disconcerting phenomenon—the witchcraft imaginary has a common core: the figure of "the witch" flying off through the night to a witches' meeting that returns in widely different parts of the world.[4] Of course this basic core is elaborated in highly different ways: witches' transformations can take all sorts of forms, along with the ways they execute their nefarious plans. Yet, as said, almost everywhere they are believed to strike from close by: witchcraft is a form of aggression that is most dangerous because it comes from inside.[5]

However, already this basic image of the witch betrays a primary ambiguity. Witches may hide inside, but they are oriented toward the *outside* world. Flying off to betray kin to outsiders, the witch makes a hidden breach in the enclosed space of the family or the community, through which its very life force can be drained, siphoned off to the outside world. This ambiguous position at the interface of the in- and the outside is vital for understanding the continuing resilience of these ideas despite enormous social changes during colonial and postcolonial times. I titled an earlier book *The Modernity of Witchcraft* (1997) in order to address this surprising capacity of an imaginary that is deeply rooted in the familiar realities of the house or the village to graft itself onto new technologies—for instance, airplanes (consider the common image of flying in witchcraft constructs)—and the new inequalities brought by global changes.[6] The challenge is to further understand this discourse's capacity to invest the global in the familiar, and vice versa.

The term *intimacy* is almost as slippery. In the chapters below I will start from African examples where witchcraft is often explicitly linked to kinship—the intimacy of the family, summarized as "the house." It will be clear that in such contexts kinship has to be taken not as a biological given but as an eminently social notion. In African contexts, family and "the house"[7] are highly dynamic notions, assuming ever new forms and bridging considerable distances with the increase of scale of personal relations. However, the family is certainly not the only form of intimacy that may make people vulnerable to hidden dangers. When examples from other parts of the world are compared, quite different frameworks of intimacy come to the fore—in Europe it is the neighborhood, more than the family, that is seen as a hotbed of witchcraft; in Bahia, the main Candomblé region of Brazil, such rumors are rather centered on the prestigious temples of this "African" religion, as places of a special intimacy.

In view of such variations it may be wise for clarity's sake to contextualize the terms people use for such special relations—*kinship, proximity, intimacy*—and to study them in relation to each other. In the African contexts where I worked, the family was and is an important pole for intimacy, but it is certainly not the only one. Proximity (in a localist sense) is very important as well; indeed, due to the many ways in which people can "work with" kinship terms, often proximity seems to create kinship and thus become expressed in kinship terms. Elsewhere, as noted, other forms of intimacy may have central place. The question is then whether, for instance, the heavy emphasis on kinship, in the sense of consanguinity and descent as in many parts of Africa, has certain implications for the way notions of family and the house (and therefore also of the "witchcraft of the house") graft themselves onto new forms of global mobility. Is there a link with the impressive elasticity of African notions of the family, now bridging transcontinental distances? Is there a difference with, for instance, the way European notions of the house have become intertwined with new forms of mobility?

In any case, for both terms, *intimacy* and *witchcraft*, the best solution for dealing with such overlaps and differences may not be to try to impose strict definitions. For intimacy as well, the challenge is to follow what people themselves define as intimate—what is "inside." Rather than referring to a similar substance, the term *intimacy* may focus attention upon what people mark as a separate domain: "What makes for intimacy is the refusal of generality—what applies between those intimate is privileged and to a degree immune for general understanding."[8] Clearly, this demarcation can take on very different forms. All this risks leading to some sort of methodological circularity: witchcraft rumors serve as indicators of what people see as intimacy; and vice versa, intimacy as a criterion of when fears of hidden aggression can be labeled "witchcraft." However, I hope to show that focusing on the nexus between the two poles, despite all variations and ambiguities, can help to highlight different historical trajectories in their mutual articulation that are of direct consequence for present-day relations.

❋

Let me return to the three directions sketched above for exploring the link between witchcraft and intimacy. Some elaboration may help to set the parameters for the lines of argument pursued in this book. First of all, the recurrent link with intimacy as a core element may help to contain the notion of "witchcraft." This has some urgency, especially in African settings where, as said, the term *witchcraft* has become so generalized in everyday language that its meaning becomes increasingly vague and limitless. People seem to define witchcraft mostly in a negative way, as the antithesis of religion or moral order in general. And it is precisely this emptiness that seems to turn it into an all-pervasive and omnipresent threat. A relevant point is academics' role in this generalizing. As said, in the wake of the sudden comeback of witchcraft in academic studies in the 1990s, some authors have warned anthropologists in particular that their indiscriminate use of the term is reinforcing this popular image of witchcraft as an all-pervasive danger. All the more reason to explore whether the link with intimacy—not as a fixed beacon but as a constantly reinterpreted notion—can serve to arrive at least at some sort of containment of the very fluid and open concept of witchcraft.

Second is the idea that the "witchcraft view" of intimacy as inherently dangerous implies a different outlook on sociality—that is, different from the view that classical anthropology propagated with considerable success of the family as a safe core within the broader social organization. For example, consider Marshall Sahlins's classical model of "primitive exchange" based on a set of concentric circles. The model shows an arrow that starts in the inner core ("household") and moves through outer circles (from "lineage sector" to "village" to "tribal sector" to "intertribal sector"). The arrow goes from "generalized reciprocity" in the inner circle, via "balanced reciprocity" in the middle, to "negative reciprocity" in the outer circles (Sahlins [1965] 1974:199). The message is clear: in the center core trust reigns, but this diminishes the wider the circle becomes.

Of course, since then many anthropologists—notably feminists—have pointed out the tensions that may also exist within this "inner core" (see further Broch-Due and Ystanes 2012). Still, it is striking how widespread the use of a notion like "reciprocity" remains in our discipline, especially in relation to forms of personal exchange. Below (chap. 1) I will link this to a particular reading of Marcel Mauss's classic *Essai sur le don* (1923–24), based on a problematic translation of *rendre le don*, Mauss's central notion, as "to reciprocate the gift" (even though Mauss himself hardly used terms like *réciproque* and clearly had a much more ambivalent view of what *rendre le don* implied). The tenacity of the *reciprocity* notion in anthropology seems to reproduce an implicit equation of an "inner circle"—family or community—with self-evident solidarity and trust. This vision has also had great impact in other academic fields and even more outside academia: consider, for instance, the celebration of "the" local community or the firm belief in the family as a safety network in much development discourse, of particular relevance for Africa.[9] The emphasis on the dangers of intimacy that dominates many discourses on witchcraft—in Africa as elsewhere—conveys a completely opposite view. As the Maka notion of the "witchcraft of the house" suggests so powerfully, the main danger lurks in the very core of sociality; it is the attacks "from within" that are most frightening.

Finally, my third point is the comparative potential of focusing on the link between witchcraft and intimacy. The main reason I think it important to follow this link into more detail is that it helps to *désenclaver l'Afrique*, as Achille Mbembe challenged us most forcefully to do already twenty years ago.[10] One of the dangers in writing about witchcraft is that it can be read as "primitivizing Africa," confirming stubborn prejudices in the North about a "backward" continent. To avoid confirming such stereotypes, it may be tempting to try to ignore the popular obsession with witchcraft in many parts of the continent. Yet the force of these preoccupations makes it increasingly difficult to disregard the witchcraft conundrum and its modern dynamics. The solution might rather be to try to show that the fears behind such obsessions reflect more general tensions. Viewing witchcraft as the terrible realization that the most dangerous aggression comes from inside may highlight that it reflects human fears that are certainly not particular to the African continent. As said, the link with intimacy is recurrent in discourses on occult aggression in many parts of the world. And the feeling that intimacy brings not only protection but also danger may be familiar to people everywhere. Exploring the nexus with intimacy can therefore help to show that Africans with their worries about a proliferation of new forms of witchcraft are not at all unique.

Indeed, a profound ambivalence about intimacy—as desirable yet at the same time frightening—haunts human forms of sociality all over the world. Thus, present-day preoccupations with witchcraft in African societies can be studied in a broader comparative framework that treats developments in Africa as one trajectory of a general human struggle. The challenge is, then, to look for concepts and parameters that can help to explain different patterns in the articulation of witchcraft, intimacy, and trust—all three studied as highly fluid notions—in different parts of the world. This challenge is all the more pressing since comparing variations in people's notions and practices regarding witchcraft (or intimacy or trust) seems to make it very tempting to resort to radical cultural differences as final explanations—a view that seems to be making a comeback in anthropology with the renewed interest in notions of ontology.[11] A question central to this book is how a more historical approach—referring to divergent historical configurations that have a considerable time span and specific implications up to the present day—can serve as an antidote to the culturalist temptations that continue to plague anthropology. But let me first outline the topics of this book's chapters, and from there return to the question of comparison.

Chapters

The first chapter, confronting theory with ethnography and experience, will seek to trace the notions of witchcraft and intimacy in their precarious relation with the book's third key notion, trust. Equally slippery—and equally popular among social scientists recently—the notion of trust is the inescapable third pole of our conceptual triangle: as said, the link between witchcraft and intimacy automatically raises the question of how one can nonetheless build trust with people with whom one has to live and work. Both intimacy and trust may be in vogue nowadays, yet recent theorizing about these notions does not offer much support for understanding their implications for witchcraft. The best guides may still be Freud's interpretations of the uncanny as close to home (*heimlich*) and Simmel's emphasis on "a further, quasi-religious element" as essential to trust. Yet the open way in which these classical authors used these notions—in contrast to more recent tendencies to fix them—suggests that rather than from theoretical explorations at a conceptual level, insight may come from historical studies of the varying trajectories of these three notions in their changing articulations.

Following this lead, chapters 2 and 3 will be historical. Rather than striving for an analytical delimitation of the central notions of witchcraft, intimacy, and trust, I will try to follow them through a series of examples from my fieldwork among the Maka (Southeast Cameroon) over the last forty years; these will be set against examples from elsewhere in Africa. The aim will be to show how the link between witchcraft and intimacy changed over time, and with it people's efforts to establish trust nonetheless. The historical shifts in people's demarcations of family and intimacy in dramatically changing settings—from colonial labor levies to urbanization to transcontinental migration—provide a map for shifting patterns in witchcraft rumors and the ways people managed (or did not manage) to affirm trust despite nagging doubts. The constant innovation is striking: links that were hardly imaginable in earlier periods become self-evident in more recent times. Yet witchcraft rumors remain rooted in intimate relations, now covering growing distances and unprecedented forms of inequality.

Next I will compare these African trajectories with patterns in other settings in space and time—in chapter 4 with early modern and present-day Europe; in chapter 5 with Candomblé in present-day Bahia; and in a short interlude with two studies of Melanesia and Java that raise conceptual challenges. This enumeration may give the impression of a somewhat Frazerian style of haphazardly comparing, but I hope to show that each case offers seminal starting points for comparison, both in regard to specific historical trajectories and for the more analytical approaches they inspired.

For Europe, both the by now impressive library of historians' publications on the witch trials in early modern times and the less numerous studies of present-day beliefs and practices show that here witches are sought among neighbors, rather than among relatives. Chapter 4 seeks to show that this difference might be related to different contours of what is understood by "the house"—more closed in a spatial sense in Europe, more stretchable in Africa. Thus this comparison can serve in particular to highlight the impressive elasticity of the African idea of the house, in the present-day context even becoming transcontinental, so that the dangers of intimacy pursue migrants across the ocean.

An interesting conceptual framework to understand such differences is provided by Jack Goody's old contrast between Africa and Eurasia as being marked by opposing trends in the realm of production and especially reproduction (1976; see also Goody 1973). No doubt Goody's oppositions—which he deduced from different articulations between, on the one hand, material circumstances (the contrast between agriculture with the hoe and with the plow) and, on the other, the organization of kinship, marriage, and inheritance—have to be nuanced in many respects. Yet his short and highly exploratory study helped to give more body to the well-known opposition between "wealth-in-people" as characteristic of patterns of accumulation in Africa and "wealth-in-things" as typical for Eurasia.[12] It might be worthwhile to pursue to what extent such divergences can help to explain specificities in people's conceptions of "the house," particularly in relation to the scope of occult dangers. The striking elasticity of the house, and kinship relations in general, that continues to mark patterns of social organization in many parts of the African continent, still bridging new inequalities and new distances, fits in very well with the old "wealth-in-people" concept.

The subject of chapter 5, the rise of Candomblé in the Bahia area of Northwest Brazil into a respected religion, which has fascinated so many anthropologists, offers a very different contrast to developments in Africa. While the encapsulation of African societies in broader (post)colonial frameworks seem to have made local ideas and practices around occult powers ever more disreputable, related ideas transplanted from Africa to Brazil through the horrors of the Middle Passage seem to have followed an opposite trend. Up to the first decades of the twentieth century in Brazil, these African notions and practices were generally—by both authorities and commoners—regarded as *feitiçaria* (fetish-cult). But from the 1930s on, the Candomblé temples succeeded in emancipating themselves from associations with disreputable witchcraft and imposing themselves as prestigious centers of a Brazilian religion with authentic roots in Africa. The link between occult power and intimacy returns here as well, but in a somewhat different setting: as spaces for "African" cults the new temples—called *terreiros* since they gave these cults a fixed local base—provided an alternative to the family after the destruction wrought by the Middle Passage. Rumors of witchcraft (*feitiçaria*) focused (and still focus) on the new spaces of intimacy of these *terreiros*. A major difference is, however, that these temples also provided a new basis of trust, built not on a denial of the occult forces or a frontal attack against them but on the recognition of these powers and their (partial) canalization through the priests and (increasingly) priestesses. Again, a special historical context can explain this spectacular transformation from witchcraft into a prestigious religion. However, this transformation may be temporary. More recently the Pentecostal wave has led—as in Africa—to virulent attacks on Candomblé. The Pentecostal pastors, able to mobilize huge followings, have no hesitation whatsoever in equating the powers of the Candomblé priests again with witchcraft that comes straight from the devil and therefore must be eradicated at all costs. Still, the flowering of Candomblé offers a seminal example of how the belief in occult forces can be turned into a religion, inspiring new forms of trust—even if this trust remains mixed with fear.

The subsequent interlude provides two shorter comparisons with Melanesia and Java. Both likewise offer intriguing contrasts with the African examples. In witchcraft studies Melanesia is often cited as the classic other to Africa: its "outside sorcerer" would be the opposite to the "inside witch" in many African contexts. Yet this contrast is clearly too simple: in Melanesian societies as well the relation between hidden aggression and proximity is complex. More important might be a contrast in approach. While, especially lately, African studies of witchcraft relate local tensions to shifts in broader constellations of power, academics in Melanesian studies remain interested in notions of ontology, often used in a culturalist sense and implying radical cultural differences that are taken as given and more or less outside history. Andrew Lattas's vivid study (2010) of the ongoing ebullition of so-called cargo cults in Melanesian contexts—centered on millenarian dreams of untold riches that have been confiscated by the whites but will ultimately become available for the Melanesians—raises questions in this respect. Precisely because of the vitality with which he highlights the fascinating dynamics of these cults and the hybridization of local and foreign elements in their imaginary, the question is why he sticks to the ontology notion that so easily acquires culturalist overtones among anthropologists.

A very different theoretical approach inspired James Siegel's sensitive effort to do full justice to the horror of witch hunts that were suddenly unleashed in East Java after the collapse of President Suharto's New Order (1998). Siegel presents his book (2006) as a challenge to the anthropological study of witchcraft in general. Rather than relating these outbursts to the sociocultural context as anthropologists tend to do, he focuses on people's search for words—"naming the witch"—to try to bring closure to an experience of the uncanny. The focus on the uncanny—in the Freudian sense of "the familiar" turned against us—corresponds to my linking witchcraft to intimacy. So does Siegel's emphasis that the notion of the witch is not sufficient to close off uncanny experiences, since it brings in "the unknown," thus creating a primal uncertainty that easily leads to violence. A difference from the other examples below—Africa but also Europe and Brazil—might be that there it is not a lack of words but rather their exuberance that is striking. But such differences raise interesting questions.

Such insights, developed for various regions, are followed up in my concluding chapter by a return to the central issue of the book—the possibility of establishing trust despite intimate dangers. The focus in this chapter is on new patterns emerging with the rapid increase in scale of social relations. The important role that new media of communication—notably visual ones like TV and video—have come to play in people's perceptions of the occult in Africa (as elsewhere) raises important questions in relation to trust. The media give the relation to intimacy new aspects—witchcraft on TV offers viewers a direct sight into people's intimacy, but it adds distance at the same time. This implies certain shifts in the way truth and, therefore, trust is established.

✳

A final remark about this book's approach to comparison relates to the role of modernity in a comparative view on witchcraft—lately a hot issue in debates among Africanists. From the above it may be clear that my comparisons will be in historical rather than in cultural terms. It may not be superfluous to insist on this since, as said, among anthropologists topics like witchcraft, intimacy, and trust seem to readily inspire an approach in terms of cultural contrasts—ontological differences between cultural areas—seen more or less as givens. I hope to show that precisely for a theme like witchcraft that is notoriously hybrid and mobile—its representations constantly traveling and being borrowed, mixed, and innovated—such a culturalist approach is difficult to maintain. In this sense our theme may raise more general challenges to anthropology in today's globalizing world that is so deeply marked by cultural borrowing. As said, what instead is needed is to relate specific trajectories, like the intense obsession with witchcraft in Africa, and its implications for present-day relations, to broader historical trends in the reproduction of societies and their articulations with outside influences. Such an approach is in line with what will be the leitmotif of this study: the surprising capacity of witchcraft discourses to combine an obsession with secret mobility—witches' ability to fly off to unknown places—with a firm rootedness in familiar realities of village and kin.

This articulation of the local with wider horizons seems to be crucial to the resilience of these discourses in the present-day world, despite deep changes. Witchcraft's peculiar articulation of the local and the global offers also a strategic vantage point for confronting a question that runs through all the examples from Africa in this book: the special relation many Africans construe nowadays between witchcraft and the modern. One of the aims of the book is to show that their preoccupations with witchcraft are not exceptional but can be read as dealing with basic issues that haunt every society—including so-called modern societies. Yet it is difficult to deny that in many parts of the continent people's obsession with witchcraft remains particularly intense, despite all modern change. Indeed, many Africans believe that the witchcraft obsession is *reinforced by* these changes. As mentioned above, many of my friends from Cameroon and elsewhere in the continent keep complaining that in Africa witchcraft seems to get stronger with the impact of modernity. Why does it not disappear, as in the West? How come it seems to thrive with every change?

Such complaints have to be taken seriously, even though they seem to ignore how strongly present-day witchcraft conundrums are shaped by the confrontation with the West. These complaints show that the theme of witchcraft and modernity is not just an anthropological paradigm that is now in for some debunking in academic debate.[13] Of course, such debunking is always welcome. Yet it may be good to underline that this linking of modernity and witchcraft—as in the very title of my 1997 book on *The Modernity of Witchcraft* and in many other recent studies (see chap. 1)—is also an urgent issue coming up with particular force in everyday life in many African contexts. Of course, *witchcraft* is about much more than modernity—it is indeed becoming an almost empty signifier that seems to apply to almost anything—just as there are other discourses available in African contexts to address modernity's confusing impact. But the link people make between witchcraft and modern changes baffles many and creates great unrest in many parts of the continent.

Why do people relate to modernity in a way that makes it seem closely linked to witchcraft? It's a challenging question. A possible answer, pursued in this book and in line with the emphasis on the link with intimacy, may be sought by focusing on the immediacy with which in many parts of Africa the forces of modernity—the world market, state formation, and the development industry, but also education, modern health care, and new religious movements—affect the private sphere of the family and the home. Intermediate institutions that could mitigate the impact of such global forces seem to be relatively ephemeral and little developed in most African contexts. Is this also why the family—of course not as a traditional core but in constantly renewed and especially extended forms—remains so central, grafting itself onto new social elements? This is certainly not determined by cultural specifics—kinship as a typically "African trait." It may be more rewarding to look at the particular dynamics of African family patterns—and their capacity to bridge ever deeper inequalities and ever greater distances—as historically circumscribed aspects. Yet in present-day circumstances this elasticity often seems to be stretched to a breaking point.

The challenge is, again, to relate such specificities in the impact of modern changes to long-term historical processes in the production and reproduction of society in ways suggested above.[14] Or to put it in more concrete terms: this book seeks to understand the intensity of people's obsession with witchcraft in present-day Africa against a wider background of struggles with the dangers of intimacy but also in relation to specific ways that modern changes have been grafted onto local realities.

1

THE DANGERS OF HOME
Ethnographical and Conceptual Explorations

THE PROLOGUE SKETCHED A DILEMMA. *Witchcraft*—like *intimacy*—is an extremely slippery term. Indeed, its strength—the secret of its resilience in so many different contexts—may precisely be its diffuseness, making it a panacea that seems to apply to almost anything, an empty signifier that because of its very emptiness seems to be omnipresent. This makes it a dangerous term—including when it is used by academics. Yet precisely because of its remarkable resilience and capacity to graft itself upon modern changes, the solution can hardly be to ignore it. A somewhat unsettling question—unsettling at least to me—raised after a presentation I recently gave at a conference in Yaoundé showed most graphically how far the term *witchcraft*'s generalizing tendency goes and why academics might be careful in taking the notion on board.

> The conference took place in 2009 at the Université catholique de l'Afrique centrale in honor of Eric de Rosny, a Jesuit who wrote beautiful books about his initiation as a healer in Douala (de Rosny 1981 and 1992). The topic was medical pluralism. I presented a paper on witchcraft and healing. In order to save time, the audience—mostly students from the Catholic University—was asked to put questions on little pieces of paper. After my talk I was pleased to get a pile of these. Yet the first one I opened came as a shock; it was brief but pointed: "When will you Europeans stop exporting your forms of *sorcellerie* to Africa: Freemasonry, Rosicrucianism, and homosexuality?"[1]
>
> Of course I should not have been surprised. I knew that witches are believed to indulge in same-sex bacchanals during their nocturnal meetings. I knew also of the crucial role Freemasonry and Rosicrucianism play among the Cameroonian political elite (their rituals are supposed to determine political in-fighting among the president and his cronies); and I had become all too familiar with people's association of Freemasons

with homosexual practices and thus with witchcraft.[2] Moreover, it was clear that the questioner had linked *sorcellerie* not by accident to highly controversial topics in present-day Cameroonian society: since 2005, "witch hunts" have been unleashed by both the government and the population against supposed homosexuals, and for a longer time there have been furious popular protests (with support of notably the Catholic Church) against the elite's involvement in Freemasonry and Rosicrucianism. Still, the little note surprised me since it showed so graphically how all-encompassing the notion of *sorcellerie* had become. And the increasing attacks on homosexuals show how such generalizing can help to victimize people.

In Cameroon, as elsewhere, this generalizing tendency acquired new scope over recent decades. In the 1970s witchcraft was hardly a topic for public debate. These were the hopeful days when "modernization" still seemed to be a clear and quick route—when the "young states of Africa" still hoped to modernize rapidly, unencumbered by a heavy traditional load. In those days, talking openly about witchcraft was frowned upon by many—not only by the government but also by more educated people in society—as an attempt to "traditionalize" Africa and deny its progress. However, all this changed in the 1980s when there was growing disappointment in "development." At the same time it became increasingly clear that the view of witchcraft as a traditional relic automatically disappearing with modernization was untenable. In 1971 my Maka assistant would still say, "Where there is electric light, witchcraft will disappear." Now there is electric light, even in some Maka villages, yet nobody would dare to say that this led to the disappearance or even the decrease of witchcraft. On the contrary, witchcraft rumors have come to abound precisely in the more modern sectors of society. Witchcraft as a topic came out increasingly into the open, and newspapers, TV, and other media started to pay ever more attention to it. Its increased presence in public debate seemed to go together with the generalizing trend noted already, and this made it seem, indeed, all-pervasive: witchcraft "running wild" and lurking everywhere in society.[3]

No wonder that also in academic language the notion made a spectacular return. After independence—for most African countries around 1960—many scholars tended to avoid topics like witchcraft for fear of "primitivizing" Africa and ignoring modern developments. Yet the dynamics of these notions precisely in more modern sectors of society became too powerful to be ignored in the long run. Since the early 1990s a wave of studies on "witchcraft" has emerged, especially by anthropologists and historians, focusing on all sorts of aspects and settings.[4] There is, as said, a real danger that this new tendency to adopt highly fuzzy notions from everyday language will confirm popular concerns that witchcraft has in fact become an omnipresent danger.

This confronts academics with the basic dilemma sketched above. Ignoring the presence of what people call witchcraft in everyday life is hardly possible, but the very term threatens to suck academic studies into all the inconsistencies and shifts that seem to be characteristic of this field. The solution might not be to try to impose an analytical delimitation of notions that have acquired such presence in everyday life—this might lead to a quixotic struggle to control a notion that is so powerful because of its slipperiness. An ethnographical approach might be more useful. Below I shall first sketch how I was confronted by these notions—both witchcraft and intimacy—during my forty years of fieldwork in Cameroon. Then I shall try to relate their changing contours in the field to more general, theoretical discussions. The aim is to show how the link between witchcraft and intimacy emerged from the interaction between ethnography and theory as a possible beacon to bring some clarity in this marshy field.[5]

Witchcraft: The Pitfalls of a Notion

When I set out in 1971 to do fieldwork in Southeast Cameroon for my PhD project, I did not intend at all to study "witchcraft." On the contrary. I wanted to be a "modern" anthropologist focusing on new developments in Africa. As I've said, these were the days of great but simplistic optimism about the ability of the "young states" of Africa to rapidly "modernize," since they were supposed to be less encumbered by the load of tradition than, for instance, older civilizations in Asia. My intention was to study local effects of state formation (local-level politics) and to avoid hobbyhorses of classical anthropology like kinship and witchcraft. The first problem I was confronted with was that openly discussing politics—that is, anything related to national or regional politics—turned out to be quite dangerous under the authoritarian one-party state of Cameroun's first president, Ahmadou Ahidjo. A second problem emerged once I was settled in a village. I soon found that whenever I wanted to talk about local politics with the villagers—this at least was more or less permitted—my spokespersons invariably began to refer to the powers of the *djambe*. Clearly to them, any form of power—whether of the village chief and the old notables in the village council, or the authority of family elders (women included) within their own household—was related to the *djambe*. They translated this term as *sorcellerie* in French (or even used the word *sorcellerie* while speaking

Maka, the local language). The *djambe* evoked a fascinating shadow world behind any event in the everyday world; it proved to be also an extremely polyvalent notion.

Elsewhere I have extensively described the Maka imaginary around *djambe* (Geschiere 1997), so a short sketch must suffice here. People describe the *djambe* as a nasty creature living in someone's belly which gives its owner (*djindjamb*—a person who took the trouble to develop his or her *djambe*) special powers. The main power is the capacity to transform oneself into an animal or a spirit. Especially at night when the owl calls, the *djindjamb* will leave his or her body and fly off into the night—"along the cobwebs of the *djambe*"—to the *shumbu*, the nightly meeting of witches. There terrible cannibalistic banquets are staged. Stories of the debaucheries of these nightly meetings—marked by shocking transgressions, violent encounters, and devious victories—are many.[6] But one element recurs in them all: each *djindjamb* has to offer a relative to be devoured by the other witches; in daily life the victim of this nightly treason will fall ill and die unless people call in the *nganga* (healer)[7] to "see" the guilty witches and force them to lift their spell. Basic to Maka discourse on the *djambe* is that it is about the betrayal of one's kin to outsiders. In many respects *djambe* is positioned at the interface of the private and the public: between the intimate world of kinship or the house, on the one hand, and the outer world and its fascinating opportunities for self-enhancement, on the other. Witches are supposed to have a special hold over their relatives, but they use this in order to hand over their victims to outsiders.

However, this is only the dark core of the *djambe* notion. Apparently it can be used in many other ways as well. It is noteworthy, for instance, that *nganga* (healers) are also supposed to have a *djambe*. They are even supposed to have developed an exceptionally strong *djambe*—this is why they can "see" the witches, "fall upon them," and force them to deliver their victims. To my surprise, I myself turned out to have a *djambe* that permitted me to drive my modest Citroen 2CV without causing an accident. *Djambe* can be channeled for constructive purposes: to heal, to accumulate wealth and power. However, there is always the danger that the basic instinct—that of betraying and cannibalizing one's relatives—will break through. For this reason the *nganga* remains a dangerous and potentially suspect person. *Nganga* will always insist that their "professor" has bound them with heavy interdictions to use their *djambe* powers only to heal and not to kill; but people are not altogether sure about this—as said, there is always the risk that the basic instinct of the *djambe* will manifest itself.

Another surprise for me was how deeply the *djambe* notion turned out to be affected by all sorts of modern technologies. Rumors about the nightly escapades of the *mindjindjamb* (witches) referred to their use of planes and airstrips, and the *miedou* (medicines) that were most sought after were those bought from mail-order firms in Europe. Moreover, *djambe* was not at all limited to the village. On the contrary, it was constantly referred to in more modern settings—in the city, in education, health care, and sport, and most of all in national politics and new forms of entrepreneurship. *Djambe* in fact offered a seductive discourse to address the riddles of modern development: the rapid emergence of shocking new inequalities, the enigmatic enrichment of a happy few, and the ongoing poverty of the many. This capacity of the discourse to graft itself onto new developments might be the secret of its surprising resilience despite deep changes, in Africa as elsewhere.[8]

Yet all this innovation notwithstanding, the *djambe* remains closely linked to the familiar realities of village and family. This capacity of a local discourse to graft itself onto modern changes is certainly not special to the Maka area. On the contrary, everywhere in Africa local notions that people now generally translate with terms like *witchcraft* or *sorcellerie* seem to provide tempting discourses to interpret modern developments that are baffling to many. It is this ambiguity that I tried to catch in the perhaps too adventurous title of my 1997 book *The Modernity of Witchcraft*.

The choice of the term *witchcraft* was the fruit of long discussions with a Cameroonian colleague, Cyprian Fisiy. I met Fisiy in 1987 in Yaoundé, the capital of Cameroon, where he worked at the Institute of Human Sciences, then the country's central institute for social science research. As a student of law he had become interested in issues of witchcraft—notably in how state courts should deal with the popular pressure to intervene against the supposed proliferation of new forms of witchcraft. Moreover, he had been officially assigned to participate in a larger research project initiated by the Ministry of Scientific Research, called Sorcellerie et Développement (Witchcraft and Development). We decided to work together on the impact of these local notions. Together we published on changes in jurisprudence in regard to witchcraft affairs, particularly the growing inclination of some courts to condemn "witches" on the basis of the testimony of *nganga* healers who had "seen" that the accused had gone out; we published also on the impact of witchcraft ideas on development projects and forms of accumulation (see further Fisiy and Geschiere 1990, 1991, 1996, and 2001).[9]

One of the first decisions we had to make concerned the terminology. For me as an anthropologist, an obvious option was to stick to local terms like *djambe*. However, for Fisiy as a lawyer, this was hardly attractive; Cameroon has over two hundred languages, and he argued that our work had to be of a more general applicability.[10] I agreed; after all, I had learned quickly that the representations concerned do not respect language demarcations or ethnic borders. On the contrary, it was striking how ideas on occult aggression traveled and intermingled. Even in the relatively inaccessible Maka area there were constant rumors about new forces introduced from somewhere else, and people mixed all sorts of languages when discussing these issues. In general, there is no search for purity or respect for authenticity in this field. Even people like the *nganga* have to constantly reinvent themselves in order to show that they are in touch with the changes.

One possibility was to adopt a more neutral notion—for instance, "occult forces." But this would mean that we were isolating ourselves from intense discussions going on in society that were couched in terms like *witchcraft* or *sorcellerie* (cf. Fisiy's role in the ministry's program Sorcellerie et Développement).[11] The modern dynamics of these local notions—the ease with which they are grafted onto new forms of technology and inequality—have given rise to an expanding regional discourse, one that overflows the limits of local terminologies and in which terms like *sorcellerie* and *witchcraft* are central. It was especially this hybrid and fluid interregional conglomerate that we wanted to address, since it seemed to have such an increasing hold on people's minds. The considerations above led us to choose to retain the term *witchcraft*—but with misgivings. The problem remains that the term gives only a very partial translation of local notions.[12] Yet, as said, it has acquired a presence of its own in many parts of Africa, and therefore it seems to merit being called by its name. Avoiding the term risks isolating social scientists from the very processes they want to study.[13]

Fisiy and I had these discussions at the end of the 1990s. Since then there seems to be only increasing reason to focus on a term that is so central in wider societal discussions. Returning to a term in the local language becomes ever less of an option. Many youngsters hardly speak this language anymore. The crystallization of an interregional culture (one could use the term *civil society* here) of the occult, mixing elements from all over—from different local cultures but also Christian and Asian borrowings, thus truly global in outlook—defies any preference of researchers for looking for an authentic core. In such a context they have little choice but to follow the terms people themselves use, diffuse and constantly changing as they are.

Nevertheless, the increasing currency and generalization of a term like *witchcraft* reinforce its allure as an omnipresent and all-pervasive threat in popular perception. There is a dilemma here that may defy any ultimate solution.

Academic Discourse and the Dangers of a Panacea Notion

How should academics deal with such a conundrum: notions like witchcraft can hardly be avoided, yet using them might reinforce their self-evidence? There is good reason for such a question especially for anthropologists, now that they again write so much about the topic. The suddenness of the "return" of witchcraft in academic studies was quite striking after anthropologists' relative silence on the topic during the first decades after decolonization (for most African countries around 1960). Witchcraft, sorcery, and magic may have been favorite topics in anthropology during colonial times, but with independence and the emergence of "the young states of Africa" anthropologists became increasingly reluctant to address such "traditional" issues. Thus when Cyprian Fisiy and I started to work on the modern dynamics these representations were assuming, we found that hardly anything had been written on such topics by anthropologists (see Fisiy and Geschiere 1990). Only a few years later, however, the topic enjoyed a sudden comeback (cf. Comaroff and Comaroff 1993; Geschiere 1997). Since the mid-1990s, witchcraft, and especially its relevance for people's conceptions of the modern, seems to become an almost obligatory topic—or at least a sideline—for any anthropological fieldwork in Africa.[14] Some even speak of a new paradigm of "witchcraft and modernity."[15] A common focus in the stream of witchcraft studies since the 1990s was, indeed, that many address manifestations of these occult powers in more modern settings: in relation to new forms of wealth and enterprise; as a dark undercurrent in politics and the functioning of the state; in modern forms of health care, sports, and education. Clearly there was a common project to study witchcraft not as a traditional relic but rather as a dynamic set of notions that graft themselves also upon modern changes.[16] But is it appropriate to speak of a "paradigm"?

In more recent years it has become almost commonplace in the constantly growing literature on witchcraft in African contexts for authors to distance themselves from this supposed paradigm of "witchcraft and modernity." Often Jean and John Comaroff's notion of "occult economies" as crucial by-products of "millennial capitalism" (Comaroff 2000) is singled out for criticism, with my 1997 book on *The Modernity of Witchcraft* mentioned as a secondary target.[17] The aim of the present book is certainly not to try and save such a "witchcraft and modernity paradigm," if only because I feel such a paradigm never existed. One should never object to serving as a punching bag for subsequent authors if this helps academic debate to progress. This is what the ever more popular notion of "paradigm" seems to serve for. However, I am not sure that in this case this notion is very helpful. Of course, none of the authors who are supposed to have launched this paradigm would ever claim that witchcraft in present-day African contexts is only about modernity; as said, the term is increasingly becoming an empty signifier that seems to refer to almost anything. Nor would these authors ever claim that the recent dynamics of these notions can be understood without taking into account their long and variable histories. Even if these dynamics make people evoke airplanes, magical airstrips, and notions of debt that easily intertwine with capitalist logic, it is clear that these haunting images have their own history that for each regional context has acquired special aspects (cf. Geschiere 2000). The Comaroffs may emphasize the generality of occult economies as an inherent by-product of millennial capitalism all over the world—which to me still seems to be quite an effective attack on the image of Africa as the great exception—yet it is quite clear from their texts that for them as well, these occult economies have their own historicity, making for highly variable forms of expressions.[18]

Luckily there are also nuanced and therefore much more fertile critiques of what was at stake in the return of witchcraft studies in the 1990s. Already in 2003 Tod Sanders warned against a "vulgarization" of the link with modernity, so that anthropologists risked analyzing witchcraft as only a popular protest against neoliberal developments. There is certainly a danger here of an automatism that is not very rewarding. Sanders's formulation that "African witchcraft may well be part *of* modernity, but by no means needs to be *about* modernity" is a very balanced and useful one (2003:338). In the 1990s it was, indeed, most topical—in reaction against widespread views of witchcraft as a traditional relic—to emphasize the ongoing dynamics of witchcraft ideas, especially in modernizing sectors of society (see Bernault 2009). Moreover, I think it is still a challenge to understand how exactly—in different contexts and in different ways—these local ideas could graft themselves so easily onto very rapid and deep changes (it is in this sense that I think convergences between, for instance, witchcraft and capitalist logics remain seminal). But such interest should never limit our view of what Ceriana Mayneri calls most evocatively *l'imaginaire grouillant* (teeming imaginary) expressed in constantly shifting discourses of *sorcellerie*.[19]

Loose use of the central notions is for me another reason to doubt whether the heterogeneous conglomerate of studies on witchcraft and modernity can be seen as sprouting from a "paradigm." Most of these authors were very careful not to even try to define the terms they used—neither the local ones nor their translations. Instead, they seemed to prefer to follow the use of these notions and the shifting ways people employ them to address changing situations. This turn in academic discourse, clearly influenced by the prevailing "postmodern" trend in anthropology in the 1990s, may have been most beneficial for following the shifting character and the resilience of these discourses under rapidly changing circumstances. Yet this increasing looseness in academic terminology coincided with a generalizing trend in people's deployment of terms like *witchcraft*, and this can have confusing implications—as may be illustrated by my being caught off guard by the question at the Yaoundé conference about Europeans exporting their forms of *sorcellerie* to Africa. Thus we are back at the question that was the starting point of this chapter: how can we counter the tendency of concepts like witchcraft or *sorcellerie* to become panacea notions—a tendency that risks confirming people's worries about the omnipresence of the dangers evoked? The increasing readiness since the 1990s of academics—and notably anthropologists—to use these terms quite loosely can have unfortunate implications in such a context.[20]

An obvious way out might be to try to force ourselves to control our terms, impose clear definitions and categorizations, and thus create more clarity. Yet this would imply imposing a grid on conceptions that seem to challenge our understanding precisely because they are so fluid. The consequence might be that we evacuate precisely what we want to understand: the fluidity and ambiguity that seems to be the secret to the resilience of these ideas. Another brief digression about my struggle with *djambe* while in the field may illustrate why I think the solution has to be sought elsewhere.

The loose terminology of recent witchcraft studies contrasts strongly with earlier studies from classical anthropology, in which authors seem to be much more intent on categorizing the local notions and proposing unequivocal distinctions.[21] However, I became quite skeptical of such clarity when I made my first efforts in the field to explore this secret world of the *djambe* that kept emerging in discussions of power and political confrontations. Forcing myself to be systematic, I created a small archive of little cards (this was long before the computer era) on which I noted each scrap of information on different manifestations of *djambe*. However, in no time I had three drawers full of cards that seemed impossible to sort into any order—which made me feel like a Don Quixote who believed he should stop the windmills. I seemed to be attempting to freeze a domain that was in constant movement. Not only were informants contradicting each other, but the same informants might flatly contradict their own statements from yesterday—without being in the least concerned when I tried to point out inconsistencies in what they said. I came to realize that precisely this elasticity of people's discourse on *djambe*—always allowing for a whole array of interpretations—might be the secret of its surprising capacity to graft itself onto deep changes. I soon concluded that there was a danger of oversystemization in older academic studies of witchcraft and that these discourses remained resilient because of their loose and flexible character (see Geschiere 2000 and 2011). Maybe Kapferer (2002:22) hints at the same issue when he concludes that "the potential [of phenomena of magic and sorcery] is much greater when released from the prison of reason."[22]

Another aspect of the same dilemma: of course, it is the very first task of academics to try to create some clarity in the marshy domain of occult forces—that is, at least try to work with clear definitions and unequivocal classification. Yet if one wants to understand the surprising resilience of these ideas and their "modern" dynamics, it might be wise to heed Michael Jackson's warning that this very search for academic clarity can make anthropologists (and other academics) vulnerable to what Niels Bohr called *das Abtötungsprinzip* ("the killing-off principle"—Jackson 2009:15). Bohr, a Danish physicist, warned that methodological rigor may destroy the very subject of our investigations. Witchcraft is a preeminent example of a phenomenon whose very strength is that it defies all classification and distinction. The diffuseness of the discourse seems to be the secret of its power.

The challenge is how to deal with the power of unclarity—always difficult for academics. Of course, this challenge arises with other topics as well. Because social scientists, and anthropologists in particular, have to work with concepts that are often in the center of debates in the societies concerned, they are constantly confronted with a dilemma between academic clarity and shifting realities. The demands of the academy may force us to try to fix terms, yet in practice these are constantly shifting and full off ambiguities. Maybe one of the reasons why witchcraft studies continue to attract particular interest is that this topic raises such problems in very pregnant forms.[23] Witchcraft often presents itself as the very opposite of science, as the archetype of everything that is secret and opposed to transparency.[24] This makes it all the more problematic to try and catch it in a fixed formula. The only choice is to opt for a loose terminology that can do full justice to the constant shifts and ambiguities of the central notions.[25]

Yet how does this relate to the predicament, outlined above, that academics' loose use of notions like witchcraft may reinforce the popular use of the term as a panacea so that it seems in fact to be lurking everywhere in society? Isn't there a way out? Cannot we find a more nuanced way in which academic terminology would help to limit this fluid notion, thus relativizing its apparent omnipresence? A recent debate that surprises by its vehemence can help to explore the options available. Such different authors as Stephen Ellis, Gerrie ter Haar, and Terence Ranger have criticized the return of witchcraft in anthropological studies of Africa and especially the vagueness of the notions used, but they have arrived at quite different solutions.

Ranger (2007) warned for a tendency toward " a conflation of the African occult into one sinister phenomenon"; he added quite critical comments on the recent wave of anthropological studies mentioned above.[26] For him the most urgent task is "disaggregating the African occult." In an earlier article he emphasized especially the continuing need to sharply distinguish religion and witchcraft (or "the occult"), which for him are opposites. In the same article he attacked Ellis and Ter Haar's 2004 book *Words of Power* as an example of "accounts of African 'religion' which are largely accounts of 'witchcraft' and other occult practices" (Ranger 2006:353). Indeed, in that book and other publications Ellis and ter Haar defended the opposite solution to counter what they see as anthropologists' deplorable tendency to portray witchcraft (or "the occult") as an all-pervading category in African societies. They insist that academics would do better to avoid such terms altogether. For them, what anthropologists tend to label "witchcraft" is rather part of a larger vision of spiritual power that marks African society and can better be studied as "religion."[27]

Both critiques address the worrying generalizing of notions like witchcraft or sorcery that make them appear as omnipresent forces, not only to the population but also in academic publications. But it is clear that both solutions for achieving more terminological clarity entail problems as well. Ellis and Ter Haar's emphasis on a wide imaginary of "spiritual power" that can best be studied as "religion" leaves open the question how then to address people's insistence that there are important distinctions in this field. The horrifying threat of witches trying to kill their own relatives and the more novel fear of people who try to get rich by "selling" their victims as some sort of zombies are most definitely not seen as part of religion. On the contrary. So it is hard to ignore Ranger's warning that distinctions be-

tween religion and witchcraft are extremely important to people in practice—and therefore have to be taken seriously by academics as well.[28]

Yet the problem with Ranger's solution of retaining clear distinctions is
the subversive quality that seems to characterize this field. Notions of "the
occult," "magic," "witchcraft," or whatever term one uses seem to have
one thing in common: a deep subversive tendency diffusing and confusing
any conceptual distinction. Even Ranger's own examples are marked by
this shifting quality. The famous Zimbabwe spirit mediums (for Ranger a
classic example of "religion"—and therefore *not* of witchcraft) seem to be
in practice under constant risk of being denounced for using their powers
in their own interest, in which case they could become associated with
witchcraft.[29] In many other contexts as well, making a categorical distinction between religion and witchcraft as proposed by some academics can
hardly do justice to the continuing struggle of the people to keep the two
apart. In Ranger's 2006 article "religion" seems to be equated with "good"
and "witchcraft" with "evil." It *would* be wonderful if the two could be
separated so clearly. In practice all such distinctions seems to be constantly
confused by the ambiguity of power (see further Geschiere 1997).

It is certainly not only in Africa that apparent evil can suddenly turn
out to be good while trusted leaders are shown to have indulged in the
most vicious kind of evil within the very heart of the community. The
discourse on witchcraft seems to be one effort to try and deal with such
basic confusions. No wonder that all conceptual distinctions in this field
are relative and ambiguous.[30] Studying witchcraft may therefore involve
following people's struggle for clarity in a minefield of ambiguities and
slippages. Ranger is certainly right that distinctions in this field have to be
taken very seriously. But rather than taking the distinction between religion and witchcraft as self-evident and given, it may be more rewarding to
try and follow how oppositions are affirmed or contested in a continuing
engagement.[31]

Of crucial importance in Ranger's articles is another aspect: his highlighting of the historical context in which witchcraft could become a passe-
partout term affirming its omnipresence. In colonial days, missionaries
included everything that had to be combated, "traditional religion" fore-
most, under the category of despicable "witchcraft." Present-day Pentecostals and other currents in popular Christianity continue this with their
equation of tradition and an omnipresent devil. One could add that the
ways in which "witchcraft" has recently become a public issue—openly
and most emphatically discussed on TV and in newspapers and other media—have further reinforced this trend. If anthropologists want to address
the spectacular dynamic of representations of occult forces in many parts

of the African continent (as elsewhere), it is important not to be taken along by this generalizing tide.

Thus we return to the dilemma of how to reconcile, on the one hand, the need for a loose terminology—so as not to freeze the shifting quality of witchcraft discourse that is so important to its power—with, on the other, the need to contain the term in order to avoid confirming sweeping generalizations about witchcraft's omnipresence. Is it possible to define a substantive core in these kaleidoscopic representations so that witchcraft becomes more than just religion's other and acquires a meaning of its own?

The question is whether the link with intimacy, highlighted above, can offer a solution that at least gives some grip on witchcraft's constantly shifting manifestations. We saw already that this link recurs in widely different settings—certainly not only in Africa—and in widely different forms. Such a starting point seems sufficiently open to chart not only the constant shifts and ambiguities in witchcraft discourse but also its varying trajectories in different historical settings. All the more so since the other pole—intimacy, whether of the family or the neighborhood or other forms of proximity[32]—is also constantly shifting.

Witchcraft and the Dangers Within

Another brief ethnographic digression can indicate why the link with the intimacy of the family came across so very vividly from my research among the Maka. It may also help to outline what questions arise from this link.

As said, one of the first regularities I noted in the endless stream of rumors about the *djambe* was that my Maka informants seemed to take the close link between *djambe* and kinship (the *djambe le ndjaw*, witchcraft of the house) as a self-evident truth. Rumors of witchcraft attacks—which in this region only rarely translated into public accusations—always pointed to people of the same compound or from within the same family. Urban elites complained that despite all their commitment to the village of origin, they were really afraid to go back since "these people will eat us." Initially I thought such statements referred to the kind of sponging in which Maka villagers excel, as I knew only too well from personal experience, but I soon discovered that there was a deeper reference here to witches, who are supposed to "eat" their own kin. *Nganga* (healers) would emphasize that they could heal only if the family wanted to cooperate, and indeed they always discovered that the main source of danger lay inside "the house." My anthropological training had made me see kinship and witchcraft as opposites—witchcraft as an attack on the order imposed by kinship—but to my interlocutors they seemed closely intertwined: witchcraft as the flip side of kinship rather than its opposite. Thus I came to characterize the *djambe* already in my first book (1982) as "the dark side of kinship."

The inherent link with kinship is cogently conveyed by a recurrent trope in witchcraft stories, a kind of condensation of this basic truth: the figure of the witch as a martyr who sacrifices himself or herself rather than betray another relative. The sad example of Eba's death was the first time I stumbled upon this kind of interpretation—a motif I was to encounter many more times. During one of the first months of my fieldwork in the village of Logbood (1971), Eba (pseudonym), a man in the strength of his life, suddenly succumbed to a heavy attack of malaria. His family was in shock: one day Eba seemed to be still in good health and the next he was dying! So they made furious but as yet unspecific hints at witchcraft: they clearly were looking for someone to blame. However, other people said the very suddenness of his death showed that he must have been himself a witch. After all, everyone knows that when an "innocent"—that is, someone who does not "go out" in the *djambe*—is attacked, she or he will die slowly. Only an altercation between witches leads to a sudden death: they can "see" who is attacking them, and then it becomes a battle of life and death. Therefore, some people whispered that Eba must have been a witch who had gotten the worst of the eternal fights among the witches—to put it differently: he got what he deserved.

But friends of Eba opted for another interpretation. Maybe he was a witch—after all, he had been very successful in the outlay of cacao and coffee plantations, and that suggested he knew how to defend himself against jealousy. However, it was more probable that he had sacrificed himself because he did not want to offer yet another relative to his witch companions. This image of the witch as a person of special courage returns in proverbs about the terrible loneliness of the witch, who has "brother nor sister, father nor mother." The idea is that if a witch refuses to give yet another relative, he has to face the wild crowd of witches all alone; people shudder before such an image. In this interpretation Eba might have been a witch but he was also a martyr who, despite earlier betrayals, had made a final stand by refusing to give up yet another kinsman.[33] All these various interpretations converge on one point. Even to those who emphasized Eba's tragic courage, the close link between witches and relatives—witchcraft as the betrayal of kinship—was self-evident.

My characterization of *djambe* as "the dark side of kinship" expressed my puzzlement or even shock that the family (*ndjaw boud*—people of one house), which is always celebrated by the Maka as one's last line of protection, was so closely associated with the treacherous *djambe*. When, after my first stint of fieldwork, I started reading more widely in the vast anthropological literature on magic/sorcery/witchcraft—as noted, at the outset I had not foreseen that the topic would loom so large in my research, since my plan was to study *modern* politics—I learned that I should not have been so surprised. The close link with kinship is very present in the classical studies on Africa and Melanesia.[34] Yet in these contexts the link was not so striking, because these studies focused on witchcraft or magic in small local communities where everybody was related to one another anyhow.

However, the Maka villages where I worked could most clearly not be studied in isolation. Village society turned out to be deeply marked by wider processes—profoundly restructured by colonial rule and subsequent postcolonial state formation, by "development" and the impact of the market economy. This made it all the more striking that despite continuous increase of scale in social relations, the *djambe* continued to be so closely linked to the family and the house.[35] Yet equally striking was that rumors about *djambe/sorcellerie* had at the same time also undergone a sort of "globalization." We saw that the basic imaginary of *djambe*—and this applies to witchcraft imaginary in general—emphasized both its being rooted in proximity *and* its opening to the outer world. Crucial in the core image of the *shumbu*—the witches' nocturnal meetings—is that there they betray their relatives to outsiders. However, this opening to the outer world seems to have undergone a dramatic increase in scale.[36]

One of my Maka spokesmen told me already in 1973: "We have our own planes, much quicker than yours—our witches fly to Paris and back within a single night." The zombie spirits who once were supposed to be put to work on "invisible plantations" on Mount Kupe in West Cameroon by the nouveaux riches with their novel kind of witchcraft are now said to be sold to the mafia—Mount Kupe has become only a relay station in global circuits of labor exploitation (see de Rosny 1981; Geschiere 1997). But even such vertiginous speculations about dark global conspiracies are linked to the familiar, though ever-shifting, theme of the betrayal of kin to outsiders.

This new zombie witchcraft highlights the paradoxical combining of the global and the local in a particularly pregnant way. People tend to emphasize its novelty, opposing it to older forms of witchcraft in which the witches would cannibalize their victims. Now they are believed to turn them into zombies to exploit their labor or even, as people put it, "sell" them. Eric de Rosny (1981) traces the obvious link to traumatic memories of the slave trade, but he also relates all the excitement over this new form of witchcraft to people's bewilderment by the capriciousness of the new inequalities and the vagaries of the world market—why do a few people become so rich while all the others invariably fail in their plans? Rumors about zombies provide at least a possible explanation for the shocking wealth of the new elites.

Yet even this "modern" form of witchcraft is linked to the Maka obsession with the *djambe le ndjaw* (witchcraft of the house). Focusing on how the *nganga* (healers) try to deal with this new threat, de Rosny (1981) shows also that they always insist that the whole family has to be reunited. Often this involves urbanites who have lived in the city for generations and must now search for their kin in the faraway countryside. Despite all novelty and increase of scale, the most dangerous attack is still supposed to come from inside.[37] This ambiguous position of the *djambe*—at the interface of intimate relations within the house and the outside world, dangerous but also promising—seems to be a leitmotif in witchcraft stories, in Africa but also elsewhere.

The link with intimacy becomes ever more salient with this increase in scale of both social relations and witchcraft rumors in recent periods. It is not by accident that among earlier anthropologists the one who formulated this link most succinctly was Philip Mayer, who mainly worked in a budding urban center in South Africa: "Witches and their accusers are people who ought to like each other, but in reality refuse to do so" (1954/1970:55). One can wonder whether Mayer's statement leaves enough room for the full ambivalence of these ideas. An accusation of witchcraft does not necessarily mean that the relationship is discontinued: supposed attacks can be covered up and forgotten, at least for some time. But he did sum up most effectively the confusing combination of closeness and aggression that makes witchcraft so deeply uncomfortable.[38]

Again, this paradoxical link is certainly not an African specialty. It returns in different forms but with the same intensity in different places and moments. Above I have already noted some variations. In Europe witchcraft rumors focus on the neighborhood as a source of danger—both in early modern Europe at the time of the epidemic of witch hunts (consider the title of Briggs's overview *Witches and Neighbours* [1996])[39] and in Favret-Saada's well-known study (1977) of twentieth-century French peasants' constant fears of covert attacks by their neighbors (see chap. 4). In some areas in the Pacific a large role is attributed to an outside sorcerer, but this figure is always believed to work through an ally inside—so here again witchcraft thrives at the interface of the in- and the outside (see interlude, below). In the Candomblé world of Northeastern Brazil, rumors of witchcraft (*feitiçaria*) swarm, as noted, around the *terreiros*, the temples that in many respects replaced the family for the (ex-)slaves (see chap. 5). Again witchcraft is situated on a precarious interface of an intimate inner circle and an uncertain outside.

Continuity and New Beginnings

Relating witchcraft to intimacy—and in many African contexts this means the family—raises another problem that has long vexed the domain of African studies: the issue of continuity, and especially of how to escape from a culturalist image of "African tradition." Recently two social scientists—Ruth Marshall, a Canadian political scientist who worked for a long time in Nigeria, and sociologist Joseph Tonda from Congo-Brazza, who now works in Gabon—offered challenging contributions to this old question. Both insist that the idea of religion as a separate domain was shaped by the colonial encounter and that this applied equally to witchcraft as religion's "other." This is certainly not a new insight. However, these two authors succeed in bringing across most vividly the urgency of this conceptual shift—away from any idea of a continuous African tradition—by the powerful ways in which they relate this idea to the present-day realities in the parts of Africa they study. Noteworthy are also their attacks on anthropologists who neglect this because of the discipline's supposed obsession with continuity.[40]

In her book on the Pentecostal "revolution" in Nigeria (2009) Marshall objects to any idea of continuity: "Witchcraft and Christianity are not eternal objects, but historical, rare. . . . There are no lines of continuity in an objective or material sense; such lines are only analytical abstractions or forms of representation objectified through practices, whether practices of ethnographic inscription or real political struggles" (Marshall 2009:26). She takes Foucault's idea of the event as her starting point, as a precarious *rapport de forces* (relation of forces) that can always be inverted (35). One of the great charms of Marshall's book is that even her more abstract and theoretical passages remain deeply grounded in her experience of the everyday life of Pentecostals in Lagos. This gives her general explorations all the more power and impact. And indeed, her interpretation of the Foucauldian notion of event comes remarkably close to "her" Pentecostals' view of conversion as a crucial moment bringing "a complete break with the past"[41]—of which Paul's dramatic experience on his way to Damascus is, of course, the archetype. For Marshall, "the [colonial] encounter was in every sense, a situation of beginnings" (63). And she deals quite severely with a whole range of distinguished anthropologists for neglecting this.[42]

In many respects Marshall continues John Peel's influential work on religious innovation in Yorubaland during colonial times (see, for instance, Peel 1969). But she is also strongly influenced by the Congolese sociologist Joseph Tonda, already mentioned, who is even more outspoken about the novelty of *la sorcellerie* in (post)colonial contexts, and equally critical of at least some anthropologists.[43] Tonda's *Le Souverain moderne* (2005) is one of the most original and powerful books coming from Africa in recent years. From it the figure of the Modern Sovereign—*le corps du pouvoir* (the body of power) in Congo and Gabon—emerges with haunting force. Tonda describes this sombre figure as "the power that, since the colonial encounter, rules, from inside, the African masses, both the subjects and the mighty" (book jacket). Crucial for him is that this particular *dispositif* of power does not emerge from an opposition between, on the one hand, mission, market, and state and, on the other, local ideas of occult forms of power (*l'esprit sorcellaire*). On the contrary, *le Souverain moderne* is created by the magmalike fusion of all of this. Tonda's main target is scholars—anthropologists and others—who believe in "the Great Divide": "African culture" as some sort of antipode to external influences like development, liberal reform, and especially *le travail de Dieu* (the missionary impact).

For Tonda, it is a complete fallacy to blame the continuing crisis in Africa on a tenacious "traditional" African culture—a "pagan spirit" obsessed with witchcraft. On the contrary, for him "the workers of God," as much as the politicians, the businessmen, and the consumers with their greed for Western products are deeply implicated, since it is from the amalgam of all these elements that the fetishization of power and consumption was born that is the very hallmark of *le Souverain moderne* (2002:39, 180; 2005:182). Only by recognizing the deep imbrications of witchcraft, missionary impact, state performance, and new forms of entrepreneurship and consumerism can we finally get rid of the tenacious opposition of tradition and modernity.[44] For Tonda—as for Marshall—the colonial encounter is an incisive turning point that has to be taken as the starting point for understanding new beginnings (2005:258). It brought a *déparentélisation* (dissolving of kinship) of society by creating *des lieux non-lignagers*, places outside the logic of the lineage (think of the missionary posts, the administrative centers, the trading posts) where a completely different logic "of the camp" emerged (2005:11, 77, 121). The consequence is not a disappearance of witchcraft but on the contrary the rapid expansion of completely novel forms of *sorcellerie*, now also "deparentalized"—that is, no longer linked to the lineage but tuned to wider horizons of global circuits (2005:77, 213; 2002:27). "Indeed, the colonial moment frees the constitutive imaginary of witchcraft ideology, since this moment undermines the ideological configuration of the lineage. . . . The work of the imagination that is set loose by this moment is the same that continues in our time in ever more intensified forms under the impact of globalization" (2005:258).[45] These are powerful warnings for an anthropologist trying to look for some recurrent element in witchcraft representations and practices.

Marshall and Tonda certainly show how much any idea of "African culture" hinges upon unwarranted assumptions of continuity. Moreover, it is quite clear how decisive the colonial encounter has been in delimiting religion as a separate field, and hence also in objectifying witchcraft as some sort of counterdomain. These are deep conceptual changes.[46] Yet it may also be important to point out that the colonial encounter has a history of its own—it has lasted far too long to be seen as a more or less abrupt "moment." I would rather see it—and maybe also the emergence of Tonda's "modern sovereign"—as a long-term *articulation* in which different elements are combined in highly precarious and accidental ways.[47] The question is whether Marshall's notion of event, along the lines of Foucault, is not too abrupt—maybe due to the influence of her Pentecostals and their obsession with abrupt conversion? Tonda and Marshall rightly warn against any tendency to look for an essence of witchcraft—or of religion—as a given of human nature that since time immemorial reproduces itself in different forms but retains some core essence. Yet seeing it as just a product of the colonial moment—however innovating that moment may have been—seems to turn history into a kind of roller coaster and may underrate determined attempts by people involved to maintain some sort of continuity.

It might be interesting to place Manduhai Buyandelger's book (i.p.) on the return of shamanism in Mongolia next to Tonda's and Marshall's attacks on anthropology. The focus of Buyandelger's fascinating book is on the quite desperate search of people in Western Mongolia for shamans who can put them again in contact with neglected spirits of their ancestors. In Mongolia, shamanism had been almost eradicated by the terror of a Stalinist government in the 1960s and 1970s. However, the dramatic impoverishment of a large part of the population under postsocialism—in this particular area because of a quaint experiment with a "neoliberal shock therapy" that went wrong—brought a comeback of "origin spirits," neglected under socialism and therefore embittered and vengeful. Shamans are the only mediators who through trance can contact these roaming spirits. Thus, recent years brought an unexpected restoration of sha-manism, with all sorts of novel elements. Buyandelger's moving accounts of people's anxious attempts to enlist the help of new shamans to find and address their dead—who often had been anonymously buried and seemed to be forgotten—are certainly reminiscent of Marshall's and Tonda's em-phasis on new events. In many respects the return of shamanism after its dramatic destruction under socialism is a new beginning. Yet Buyandelger conveys powerfully how deeply important it is to her people to relink to their lost past.[48] Apparently anthropologists are not the only ones who are looking for continuity. Even the most mythical form of constructing such continuity can become a very real force for people in everyday life.

An effective and even elegant way to avoid getting stuck in the old stale-mate of change versus continuity is suggested by Jean-François Bayart's theorizing around the state. In the footsteps of Deleuze, he goes to great length to show that any essential definition of the state (for instance, by invoking the "Weberian" model so dear to liberals—but is it really Webe-rian?) leads to serious distortions. Instead Bayart proposes seeing the state as a constantly emerging "event" in the Deleuzian sense—that is, in op-position to "essence." In this view, which also takes inspiration from Fou-cault, *event* is a creative moment in which the state is constantly assuming new forms. Representations and practices around occult aggression can be grasped in a similar way. Witchcraft, both as a notion and as a set of prac-tices, certainly has a history, but it clearly has to be seen as an event that constantly produces new forms. It is not part of a given *durée* but rather an uncertain articulation of different *durées*. It must be possible, then, to look for recurrent elements in this process that can help us surpass a view of witchcraft as only a counterpoint to something else (for instance, religion). As said, it is precisely such a negative delimitation—as just the opposite of religion—that seems to turn witchcraft into a diffuse threat lurking every-where in society.

It may be tempting to look for such recurrent elements in similar im-ages of the witch that return all over the world (the image of witches leav-ing their bodies at night, flying off to meetings with fellow witches, and plotting mischief—and so on).[49] Yet if the idea of witchcraft as an event is to be taken seriously, it may be good to remember Foucault's insistence that an event is always relational (*un rapport de forces*). Then it is not so much the images themselves that set the terms for new beginnings—after all, their manifestations can vary endlessly—but rather the social configu-rations. Thus, notably he relation to intimate settings—family or other forms of proximity—emerges as a possible anchoring point for the witch-craft notion in its many appearances. Just as the state may be as seen as an event taking on new forms in a context of unstable relations, so the nexus between witchcraft and intimacy may be studied as an unstable relation that constantly produces new avatars—as I know only too well from the now more than forty years that I have followed the turmoil of witchcraft rumors in "my" village in East Cameroon.

Examples from my Maka research and elsewhere in Cameroon can serve again to make this understanding more concrete. Here the link with intimacy, so strongly emphasized above, is certainly not an invariable, continuous given. On the contrary, there are many tendencies that seem to override it. For instance, at first sight the role of the *nganga* (healer) with the Maka and elsewhere in the forest of southern Cameroon seems to contradict this link, since these healers' powers appear to surpass kinship. *Nganga* are supposed to use their *djambe* force against witches and to be able to attack them regardless of social (or spatial) distance. People say also that *nganga* should not live with their family, since their powers are so frightening that they would be a danger for their own kin.[50] In several respects, therefore, they seem to be beyond the framework of family. However, at a deeper level kinship is an essential condition for enhancing their occult powers. People will whisper that in order to be initiated into all this dangerous knowledge, *nganga* had to sacrifice a close relative, offering him or her to their "professor" as a reward for all the lessons.[51] Thus, ultimately also the *nganga* role is firmly rooted in kinship.

To be noted is also the recent trend throughout the African continent to complain that witchcraft is breaking through the boundaries of kinship—supposedly it has lost its moorings in the family. This is one of the reasons why people worry about witchcraft "running wild." The link between witchcraft and kinship seems to become ever more stretched with modern changes and a constant increase of scale. New forms of witchcraft are seen as particularly shocking because they seem to be effective against anybody, kin or no kin. For instance, in Basile Ndjio's ([2006] 2011) fascinating study of *feymen* (Cameroon's equivalents to the Nigerian 419s as experts in global computer fraud, false money schemes, and other illicit practices) he emphasizes that the current association of the mysterious success of these swindlers—and some of them do become amazingly rich—with particular forms of witchcraft is no longer linked to kinship. Their *mokoagne moni* (magical money) helps them to find their victims—mostly credulous businessmen and politicians—on a much broader, even global scale: their "fronts" are in Europe, South Asia, and the Gulf states. This is indeed a far cry from the idea that "witchcraft never crosses the water" (that is, the sea) as people used to say in earlier decades.[52]

Still, when one follows Ndjio's rich case studies in detail, one finds that even these references to *feymen* witchcraft eventually point back to the close environment of kin and locality: the helpers of a *feyman* are suddenly bewitched when they accompany him to the village that takes revenge for the unwillingness of their "ungrateful son" to share his new wealth; a local community in Douala raises a magical barrier to another *feyman*'s activities by closing its ranks. This is symptomatic. Witchcraft may be supposed to work now on a much wider scale. Yet in most of these global witchcraft stories there is ultimately a pointer back to local realities of neighborhood and family.[53] The village and its emotional intimacy may, at least in some respects, become an almost virtual reality to many Cameroonians in the city, but it is still deeply engraved in witchcraft visions.[54] However, intimacy has no fixed shape in such obsessions. On the contrary, it can take on all sorts of new forms, be extended in space, and even become multilocal, as we will see below.

As said, Joseph Tonda insists that since the colonial encounter *la sorcellerie* largely surpasses the old lineage order ("beyond what is thinkable and possible in the lineage order," Tonda 2002:237). Yet in his very vivid books the link with the family is still everywhere. Even *Mammywata*—the beautiful lady, often white, with blond hair, who captures young men with evil promises of untold riches—asks her followers to sacrifice a close parent, often a child (Tonda 2002:85; 2005:177). *Mammywata* may be the very symbol of modernity and its promises of unlimited consumerism, but she is apparently not completely outside kinship. One might wonder whether Tonda's insistence on a complete *déparentélisation* of society as a logical outcome of the colonial moment is not too sweeping.[55] In many parts of Africa it is rather the remarkable elasticity of kinship claims—bridging completely novel inequalities and distances, albeit precariously—that remains quite striking (not too say worrying). We shall see that even African migrants in Europe and America fear the telephone calls from home with their endless demands undergirded with hidden threats. The association of family with witchcraft as a serious threat for migrants far away from home shows the impressive stretching capacity of the family-witchcraft complex. Tonda is certainly right that in such novel contexts witchcraft takes on new guises, but its precarious yet inherent link with kinship and the family is frequently reaffirmed despite unprecedented distances. Apparently the map of intimacy can constantly be redrawn, sometimes stretching the witchcraft-family complex almost to a breaking point, yet without destroying its grasp.[56]

✳

The above may suggest some caveats regarding my conceptual triangle of witchcraft, intimacy, and trust. It can work only with a relational view of all three the poles: of witchcraft as an event shaped by its ambiguous and volatile relation with intimacy—also seen as constantly shifting[57]—resulting in a continuous and uncertain struggle for establishing or maintaining trust. Clearly it is only when the three poles are seen as constantly shifting that this triangle can serve to outline recurrent patterns in the mutual articulations. This may sound somewhat disheartening—a triad of uncertainty! Yet by following different historical trajectories I hope to show that the three concepts, in their shifting connections, offer at least some footing in the marshy world of witchcraft.

But let us first consider to what extent theoretical explorations around the notions of intimacy and trust, both undergoing a recent *hausse* in social sciences, can provide leads on how to study their precarious and shifting relation with occult aggression.

Intimacy as the Uncanny

One of the reasons I became ever more interested in the link between witchcraft and intimacy was my irritation that Western audiences often show signs of being shocked when I speak about African ideas on witchcraft—and especially when I emphasize how central the idea of a betrayal of kin, even of a father or a mother, is in this imaginary. Often I cannot help wondering how many of my listeners have been on the couch with a shrink. Did not Freud warn us already that the intimacy of the family is not just a happy enclave in society but also a primal hotbed of aggression? How then can African notions about the link between witchcraft and kinship come across as amazing? Such parallels confirm that the deep worries of Africans (and many others) about witchcraft relate to a universal issue: how to deal with aggression from close by—with the realization that intimacy is not just a haven of peace but also a lethal source of threat and betrayal.

It might be worthwhile, therefore, to have a closer look at the notion of intimacy. Can the close link with intimacy highlight what shapes witchcraft in its ongoing transformations? Can it serve to contain the tendency of the latter notion to be applied to almost anything so that it appears to be omnipresent? The concept of intimacy itself has become so fashionable among anthropologists and other social scientists that it risks being emptied of substance. Apparently its currency does not stop it from being used in widely differing ways. Yet there is a common tendency: a positive view of intimacy. References to potential dangers are conspicuously absent from recent explorations around this notion.

This positive trend remains implicit in the current, but also somewhat facile, use of the term *intimacy* as a euphemism for sexual relations, whether or not in a conjugal setting. A good example is American anthropologist William Jankowiak's 2008 collection *Intimacies: Love and Sex across Cultures*. The notion of intimacy is not problematized in this voluminous book.[58] It seems mainly to function as a buzzword. Precisely because its meaning is taken for granted—no need to analyze it—it takes on quite happy implications: a comfortable niche, a domain of trust in a hostile society.

However, the prize for the most paradisaical version of the notion goes without a doubt to British sociologist Anthony Giddens. In his *On Intimacy* (1992) Giddens analyzes intimacy between partners as the pinnacle of modernity, marking the transition from "romantic" to "confluent" love. He closely relates intimacy to autonomy and trust: in his version, intimacy expresses the ideal of two adult persons who respect each other's differences and leave scope for each other's autonomy so that they can trust each other. Heavily leaning on psychotherapeutic literature, he poses intimacy cum autonomy as the opposite pole of addiction cum dependency—a view that is in marked contrast with basic elements of witchcraft discourse. Any idea that intimacy can be fraught with special dangers and lead to stifling dependency is lacking here; the notion has only positive overtones, evoking a safe haven of trust.[59]

A completely different view has been forwarded by British-American anthropologist Michael Herzfeld in his publications on "cultural intimacy" (1997).[60] For him this is certainly not the highest stage of modernity; it is rather the counterpoint to official nationalism. Herzfeld's main point seems to be that the formal symbols of Benedict Anderson's "imagined community" are complemented by more hidden everyday truths—he speaks of "rueful self-recognition" (6)—that are at least as important to the reproduction of national sentiments. Examples are Greek jokes about Greek machismo (and probably Dutch ironies about Dutch stinginess), which create an informal or even ironic acceptance of one's identity. For anthropologists, this version of intimacy is much more promising. In Herzfeld's use of the notion there is clear interest in its ambiguities—like the tension between formal denial and implicit recognition of certain disreputable truths. Moreover, Herzfeld places his notion on the threshold between the private and the public: he refers to sentiments that are quite private yet nonetheless halfheartedly publicized. There is indeed an interesting link to witchcraft as a discourse that brings out into the open what should remain private—the hidden tensions within the family or community, now exposed to the public gaze—and this is already a step away from the vision of intimacy as a cozy, protected sphere. Yet until now the debate on Herzfeld's seminal notion has hardly explored this direction. It was mainly hijacked for discussions of anthropologists' ethical problems with the intimacy that builds up during fieldwork. [61]

Even anthropologists working on Africa have tended to neglect the close link between intimacy and treacherous attacks from the inside. To mention just one example: Parker Shipton's beautiful book (2007)—winner of the prestigious Herskovits Award—on "entrustment" among the Luo (Kenya) has "intimacy" in its subtitle but again hardly problematizes the notion. Toward the end of the book we learn that intimacy "means potential rivalry too." Here Shipton finally recognizes that sharing does not exclude rivalry (219–20). Yet this is still a far cry from awareness of a deep fear of kin with whom one must collaborate but who have at the same time a most dangerous hold over one.

Clearly we need other versions of the intimacy notion if we want to consider why to people in Africa—and elsewhere as well—it is quite evident that intimacy is closely linked to witchcraft and (hidden) aggression from inside. Interesting impulses come from outside anthropology, for instance from the American literary critic Lauren Berlant, who launched a whole project on the notion in *Critical Inquiry* (1998). For her, intimacy is full of ambiguity. It seems to belong to the private, but it is always on the border of the public: "the inwardness of the intimate is met by a corresponding publicness" (281). Intimacy is in her view not necessarily a small-scale phenomenon. On the contrary, she speaks of the "modern, mass-mediated sense of intimacy" and adds that "intimacy builds worlds: it creates spaces and usurps places meant for other kinds of relations" (282). She sees it as a highly mobile notion: "liberal society was founded on the migration of intimacy expectations between the public and the domestic" (284).

All this may not seem to relate directly to the witchcraft examples I have offered. Yet below we will see that Berlant's emphasis on intimacy's "usurping places meant for other kinds of relation" becomes quite unexpectedly relevant for the new dynamics of witchcraft notions—its penetration into new public spaces, for instance through the production of videos. Even more relevant is Berlant's argument that "in its expression through language, intimacy relies heavily on the shifting registers of unspoken ambivalence"(286). This is much closer to the witchcraft vision of intimacy as a sphere of life that relates to different spaces and is full of deep tensions and ambiguities.

The question remains how to understand that for people the notion of intimacy can apparently evoke feelings of both safety and danger. As so often, it may be revealing to go back to the root of the term, the Latin *intimus*. In the classical context the word was not linked at all to sex or conjugal relations. An *intimus* is a person's best friend and adviser. But the adjective has the additional meaning of "particularly effective"—and there is a current association here with *vis* (violence): *intimus vis* means particularly effective violence! Here we get very close to Maka ideas about *djambe* and kinship.

One can wonder, moreover, how so many recent authors with a quite positive—not to say idealized—view of intimacy manage to completely ignore Sigmund Freud. After all, Freud, much criticized as he is now, had things to say on this point that are still highly relevant. He hardly used the term *intimacy*. Still, his insistence that the family is a hotbed of aggression and guilt remains crucial to the present discussion. In particular Freud's essay on *das Unheimliche* (The Uncanny; 1919/2003) offers inspiring starting points for exploring the tension between intimacy, trust, and aggression.[62] It is, however, largely ignored in recent writings on intimacy; so it may be all the more worthwhile to give some attention to this short but challenging essay.

The text can be seen as part of Freud's ongoing project to prove the relevance of psychoanalysis for gaining a deeper understanding of works of art. Indeed, his main purpose seems to be to prove that his approach allows him to discover a deeper meaning in the fairly enigmatic story "The Sandman" (1816–17) by E. T. A. Hoffman, the king of storytellers of the German *Romantik*. Elements of "The Sandman" made it into Offenbach's equally exuberant opera *Hoffman's Erzählungen*. Freud focuses on the role in the story of *das Unheimliche* (the uncanny), in the figure of Coppelius, alias Coppola (the Sandman), who keeps appearing at unexpected moments and thus drives Nathaniel, the young man who is the story's main actor, to madness and suicide—a fate that befell so many unhappy torchbearers of the *Sturm und Drang* that haunted the German *Romantik*. However, Freud does not start with the story but rather—in line with his general focus on language as a main tool for riddle-solving—with an extensive analysis of the central terms *heimlich* (homely) and *unheimlich* (unhomely—that is, ghastly, uncanny). A major part of the text consists of a very long quote from a dictionary of the German language (by a certain Daniel Sanders, 1860) summing up all the different meanings of both terms. At the beginning this is quite boring—until one notes that the consecutive meanings of *heimlich* gradually verge toward their opposite, *unheimlich*! Indeed, the ambiguous meanings of *heimlich* emerging from Freud's long enumeration are quite intriguing. The term seems to have strong positive notions since it is closely related to *Heim* (home), but these more positive implications are balanced by another array of meanings centered around secretive implications (*Heim* as a place where things remain hidden, withdrawn from sight). Freud is not bothered by the fact that German is about the only language where this strange trend of *heimlich* switching into its very opposite gets linguistic expression. He does note that equivalents in English, French, Italian, Portuguese, Arabic, and Hebrew do not show this tendency, but apparently he feels that German expresses here a basic ambiguity, and it is on this ambiguity that he bases his further analysis.[63]

The central theme in Freud's analysis is that *das Unheimliche* (the uncanny)—in this case the figure of Coppelius/Coppola—is so frightening because it is about repressed memories that come back with a vengeance. It is repression that turns the familiar (*das Heimliche*) into the uncanny (*das Unheimliche*). When Coppola, an optician, unexpectedly emerges from a crowd, Nathaniel is no longer capable of containing the fears that have plagued him from childhood. He panics when he thinks Coppola is actually an old friend of his father, Dr. Coppelius, who may be also his father's murderer. As a young boy Nathaniel associated Dr. Coppelius with "the Sandman," mentioned by his mother when she wanted the children to be off to bed, and later explained by a nursemaid as "a man who comes to children and throws a handful of sand in their eyes, so that their eyes jump out of their heads, all bleeding. He then throws their eyes in his bag and takes them off to the half-moon as food for his children. These children sit up there in their nest; they have hooked beaks like owls and use them to peck up the eyes of the naughty little boys and girls" (Hoffmann 1816–17, quoted in Freud 1919/2003).

For little Nathaniel, Dr. Coppelius's heavy footsteps on the stairs when he came to visit his father in the evening were a sure sign that he was no one else than the Sandman. Hoffmann weaves various episodes in his fantastic story that seem to confirm that Nathaniel's early and later fears are not based on fantasy alone: for example, the poor boy overhears a horrible discussion between Dr. Coppelius and his father in which the latter beseeches the doctor not to take his son's eyes; later on Coppola, the itinerant optician, tries to sell him "eyes, lovely eyes." Freud deftly relates Nathaniel's fantasies to his fear of castration (being blinded stands for being castrated—remember Oedipus). But most of all he focuses on Coppola as *das Unheimliche* since he is out of place: he prompts the return of memories that had been repressed as all too frightening. *Das Heimliche* becomes *unheimlich* when it is out of place.

Hoffmann's haunting story and Freud's ambitious analysis have many more layers that are of interest. But of special importance in the present context is that Freud offers clear starting points for studying the uncomfortable link between intimacy and the uncanny. His leading question is how to understand the switch of *das Heimliche* into its very opposite, *das Unheimliche*; and even more how to understand the reverse: how *das Unheimliche* can be turned again into *das Heimliche*—or, to relate this directly to witchcraft discourse, when closeness breeds fears of hidden aggression, and how the threat of hidden aggression can be neutralized so that trust can be established. Of course Freud himself wants to go a lot further than this. He wants to offer a definitive explanation of such transitions, which in this case are seen as caused by repression: *das Heimliche*—in Nathaniel's case, a horrible childhood memory that was repressed—becomes *unheimlich* when it turns up later and is experienced as completely out of place. It remains to be seen to what extent this specific explanation holds for witchcraft fears. The great merit of Freud in any case is that he leaves behind the view of intimacy as a domain of harmony, and even more that he suggests steps for understanding the complex intertwinement of security and fear in people's experience of intimacy. Which, of course, makes it all the more strange that so many present-day authors tend to ignore this old insight and seem determined to cling to a positive image of intimacy as a harmonious sphere of security. [64]

The Struggle over Trust

The above may already suggest that recent theorizing around the other pole of our triangle, trust, sketches an equally positive image of proximity. To optimistic authors like Giddens and the psychotherapists he quotes with such enthusiasm, it seems self-evident that intimacy and trust are complementary. Both inside and outside anthropology, the general idea that intimacy breeds trust remains very influential: trust in the inner circle as a prepolitical, even ontological given.

Yet in witchcraft discourse it is a continuous challenge to combine the two. This is why the struggle over trust is an inevitable complement to the link between witchcraft and intimacy. To my Maka friends, the particular dangers of the *djambe le ndjaw* (the witchcraft inside the house) meant that there was good reason to distrust one's intimates. Indeed, in many parts of the world a key word in the discourse about how to protect oneself against witches seems to be *closure*. Among the Maka a central notion is *bouima*, always translated as "blinder" (to armor oneself). To them a good armory is essential, preferably supplied by a specialist (*nganga*)—even though contacting a *nganga* implies that one is entering the *djambe* domain. Again, the Maka are certainly not exceptional in this. Favret-Saada (1977/1980) describes farmers in the French countryside as obsessed with the need to magically close off their compounds against attacks by jealous or simply evil neighbors.

The question all this raises is how one can ever fence oneself off from one´s intimates, with whom one shares so much, but who may turn out to be deadly dangerous. The more general implication seems to be that trust is never a given, not even in kinship societies (or, rather, especially not there)—this in telling contrast to current stereotypes of what are sometimes called "anthropological societies." Clearly, even within small-scale communities trust is constantly tested, and, therefore, it is of vital importance that it be repeatedly reaffirmed. To the Maka the family is essential—it is highly questionable whether one can survive without it—yet at the same time it is a source of mortal threats. It may be precisely *because* to humans kinship appears as a primal necessity in one's life that it is seen as fraught with dangers. The Duala, a group on the Cameroonian coast—the "autochthons" of the huge city of the same name—have a saying, "You have to learn to live with your witch" (see de Rosny 1992:114). This may be a much more common problem, even in so-called modern societies, than Giddens and company are prepared to admit.

What has the general literature to say about such predicaments around trust in zones of intimacy? As with intimacy, the very popularity of the notion of trust bids fair to turn it into another buzzword across the disciplines, cropping up in the most unexpected places.[65] Not only anthropologists evoke trust as crucial to the quality of relations. Representatives of the "harder" social sciences have also become fond of the term. For many economists trust has become a black box invoked when the gap between their computer simulations and everyday developments becomes too great. Organizational sociologists and management experts follow suit. When I decided to explore the notion of trust, I expected to encounter the tenacious tendency of economists and others to stick to a rational choice model, explaining trust or the refusal of trust as stemming from the well-understood self-interest of the actors involved: trust as based on knowledge. Of course such starting points raise problems in a field like witchcraft that is so strongly characterized by secrecy and ambiguous interpretations.

Yet, somewhat to my surprise, certain anthropological ideas—or even premises—about trust were as much a hindrance, notably the tendency of many anthropologists to simply equate kinship with solidarity and reciprocity and therefore with trust. This may surprise in view of the discipline's long-standing interest in witchcraft, magic, and such. However, these later aspects tended (and still tend) to be seen as exceptional moments of crisis after which reciprocity is restored.[66] Indeed, reciprocity—which in its more simplistic versions seems to imply automatic trust—has attained an almost sacred status in anthropology. In a critical essay, Chris Gregory (1994) discusses gift-giving with its obligation for reciprocity as the anthropological answer to theories of wealth based on commodities and capital (like the Marxian vision).

Of course, one cannot generalize for anthropology as a whole. Interpretations departing from these assumptions have come to the fore as well. As said, feminist anthropology in particular emphasized the tensions, often hidden but sometimes erupting in fierce violence, within the inner circle of the family. Unfortunately these countervoices have not succeeded in seriously undermining the almost self-evident status in the discipline of reciprocity as a fixed corollary of exchange in smaller settings. Precisely because this link is often left implicit, it is seen as self-evident (see Broch-Due and Ystanes 2012). This anthropological view of the local community has had considerable impact outside the discipline—notably in development studies.

It would be quite interesting to follow the genealogy of the notion of reciprocity and find out how it acquired such a central place in the discipline. Probably it would be necessary to go back to the very founders of the discipline and even beyond. Apparently Edward Tylor simply linked *kindred* to *kindness*, "two words whose common derivation expresses in the happiest way one of the main principles of social life."[67] But beyond him looms Tönnies—with his sympathy for a disappearing *Gemeinschaft* that was in everything the opposite of the *Gesellschaft*—and beyond this the German *Romantiker* with their nostalgia for an innocence that had been lost due to progress and rationalism.

However, rather than go so far back, it may be more clarifying for our argument to briefly dwell on the shadowy role of the reciprocity notion in the work of Marcel Mauss, still a towering figure in debates on exchange. Mauss's classic essay on *le Don* (the Gift)[68] is a recurrent source of inspiration in these debates—constantly undergoing new revivals. The recent resurgence of interest in his work may make it all the more important to highlight the quite precarious way in which it was linked to the notion of reciprocity. As signaled above, severe doubts can be raised about the translation of Mauss's central notion *rendre le don* as "to reciprocate the gift" in the 1990 English edition of his essay. *Rendre* is a much more neutral term than "reciprocate"; a more correct translation migh be simply "to return the gift."[69] This is not just a technical quibble, since the translation "to reciprocate" tends to obfuscate Mauss's considerable attention to the ambiguities and even dangers of the gift, including in "archaic" societies: he noted that if the given thing was not properly returned in due time, it could even kill the original receiver.[70] This darker side of the gift is difficult to reconcile with Sahlins's image, cited above, of "generalized reciprocity" as characteristic of intimate forms of "primitive exchange."

In fact, Sahlins's interpretations seem to have played a key role in the all too easy linking of Mauss to reciprocity. Sahlins's by now equally classic text "On the Sociology of Primitive Exchange" ([1965] 1974) offers a convenient—if somewhat misleading—landmark for situating the increasing centrality of the reciprocity notion in anthropology.[71] The core of Sahlins's text, which has been summarized in the prologue, is the concentric circles model he was so fond of for understanding "segmentary" (sometimes "tribal") society. The main message was that "generalized reciprocity" prevails in the inner circle but such exchange gradually becomes more restricted, finally becoming "negative reciprocity" in the wider circles. This is neatly summed up by Sahlins himself: "It follows that close kin tend to share, to enter into generalized exchanges, and distant and non-kin to deal in equivalents and guile" (Sahlins [1965] 1974:198). Family is trust, haggling is outside.

In his *Stone Age Economics* (1974) Sahlins presented his text together with a chapter called "The Spirit of the Gift" in which he elaborated upon Mauss's *Essai sur le Don*. In the latter text, he does pay attention to Mauss's explorations of the ambiguities of the gift. But in the more general text on "primitive exchange" nothing remains of this ([1965] 1974). Indeed, the dark side of Mauss's model sits uneasily with Sahlins's positive image of "generalized reciprocity" in the core sector, "the house."[72] This image can accommodate witchcraft and its link to intimacy only as an exception, as an opposite of kinship—as many anthropologists still tend to do. Allowing for the inherent link between witchcraft and intimacy—that is, witchcraft as part and parcel of the kinship order—may require a less unequivocal vision.

More recent commentators tried to give reciprocity a more ambivalent meaning by pointing to different trends in exchange, even within the inner circles.[73] Yet rather than trying to save the reciprocity notion, it may be judicious to emphasize that Mauss's version of exchange was much more layered and that the notion of reciprocity itself was smuggled into the English translation of his classical text. The implicitness with which many anthropologists continue to equate closeness with reciprocity and trust[74] makes the notion and its assumptions a hindrance for arriving at a more nuanced view of sociality—or in concrete terms, for understanding the broader implications of the link between intimacy and witchcraft for struggles over trust.[75]

The general literature seems to leave us with an unenviable choice between, on the one hand, a rational-choice approach of economists and others who see trust as following from relevant knowledge and, on the other, a tenacious current in anthropology that seems to see reciprocity and hence trust as an essence of "anthropological societies." Neither option is very helpful for showing how witchcraft flowers on the interface of the intimate and the public. Yet here as well, a seminal lead comes from an older social scientist whose work on trust seems seems unjustly neglected in present-day debates on the concept—at least by anthropologists. Already in 1900, Georg Simmel—more or less Freud's contemporary—published his challenging reflections on trust as not only being based on knowledge but also stemming from "a further element, difficult to describe, that in its most pure form is embodied in religious faith" (Simmel [1900] 1990:174). This element is so hard to describe since it concerns "a state of mind which is both less and more than knowledge"; yet it is—still according to Simmel—crucial for understanding trust.

In a seminal contribution Guido Möllering, a German organizational sociologist, tried to capture the complex interplay Simmel construed between knowledge, ignorance, and trust by insisting on a "suspension of doubt" as crucial to any form of trust: "Suspension can be defined as the mechanism that brackets out uncertainty and ignorance, thus making interpretative knowledge momentarily 'certain' and enabling the leap to favourable (or unfavourable) expectation" (Möllering 2001:414).[76] This perspective of "a suspension of doubt" that requires "a leap of trust"— reminiscent of Kierkegaard's famous "leap of faith" as vital to any form of belief—can serve to bypass both the rational-choice and the anthropological visions of trust. To put it in more general terms: to go beyond the tendency either to understand trust as just "good" knowledge or to see it as an essence that is more or less given with small-scale relations and broken only in exceptional circumstances.

Simmel's focus on this crucial but uncertain "further element" (even "almost religious"!)—just like Möllering's notion of "suspension of doubt" as a possibility, but never as a certainty—seems to speak directly to the Duala proverb quoted above about learning to live with one's sorcerer. If witchcraft discourse expresses the alarming realization that the most dangerous form of aggression comes from inside, the main challenge it raises might be to discern when one should suspend the doubt that stems from this knowledge, so as still to be able to collaborate. What "leap of faith" might help to reestablish trust in one's relatives? From the examples below different answers will emerge for dealing with this terrible challenge, varying from desperate attempts to expel the threatening elements from the inner circle to efforts toward neutralizing the dangerous forces or to assuage jealousy via a just redistribution of new forms of wealth (but when is redistribution "just"?). The conclusion might be that, like intimacy, trust is never self-evident.[77] It has to be studied as a product of specific historical circumstances, as a continuously new "event." All we can hope for is to indicate certain factors or settings that make for a possible suspension of doubt as a condition for a trust that is never a given.

✳

It appears that recent theoretical explorations of the notions of intimacy and trust are of little avail for bringing analytical clarity to the witchcraft conundrum. In the above, general insights emerged rather from following the opposite direction: a view from witchcraft on both intimacy and trust served to highlight certain blind spots in much of the literature on these notions—notably the all too easy equation of intimacy with trust, underrating the tensions that can originate from closeness and their destructive implications.

It might be wise to repeat the caveat emphasized before: the conceptual triangle of witchcraft, intimacy, and trust can work only if all three notions are seen as strictly relational; the poles of the triangle are themselves constantly shifting, and so do their mutual articulations. It is only by following in detail the shifting connections of these three poles that recurrent patterns can be traced, depending on historical settings that are variable and changing. Attempts to fix these notions analytically may indeed, be of little help in such a context. History, more than generalizing theory, might be the best guide for untangling the kaleidoscopic articulations between occult aggression, intimacy, and the (im)possibility of establishing trust. The following chapters will therefore seek to follow specific trajectories of witchcraft, intimacy, and trust—all three in constant movement—depending on historical changes in the societies concerned but also on processes of mutual articulation, borrowing, and readaptation.

Yet for following such historical trajectories and the articulations of witchcraft, intimacy, and trust they produced, some analytical leads especially from the older literature discussed above could be helpful. Notably, Freud's emphasis on the ease with which *das Heimliche* (the homely) can switch into something terribly *unheimliches* (uncanny), and his focus on the particular moments when such switches occurr, offers seminal points of orientation. Further, Simmel's stress on the "religious element" in trust that allows for a "suspension of doubt" suggests focusing on the particular circumstances under which such suspension succeeds (or does not succeed). These insights do not provide definitive explanations, but they may point to patterns—special ways of linking intimacy and witchcraft, or the (im)possibilities for trust in certain historical situations. This indeterminacy is precisely the force of these conceptual approaches.

2

WITCHCRAFT, INTIMACY, AND CHANGING PERCEPTIONS OF DISTANCE

African Examples

WITCHCRAFT MAY BE ANCHORED IN INTIMACY. But the confused theoretical state of the latter notion—as explained in the preceding chapter—seems to be of little help for getting firmer footing in an effort to understand this link. An alternative, to be explored in this chapter, might be history—that is, to follow intimacy in its varying historical trajectories. Can people's references to witchcraft and its changing contours be elucidated by relating them to shifting perceptions of intimacy and distance over time? In this chapter I want to follow the changing parameters in various parts of Cameroon of what is intimate and what is distant in direct interaction with the enunciation of witchcraft. This will be complemented with examples from elsewhere in the continent.

One of the recurrent trends in the recent explosion of studies on witchcraft in Africa is an emphasis on the need to historicize people's ideas and practices on occult aggression—which corresponds to the view of witchcraft, developed above, as an *event*. Far from constituting a timeless "traditional" element, these representations are now studied as having their own dynamics. In my earlier book *The Modernity of Witchcraft* (1997) I tried to show that restless changeability is inherent to these notions. People talk about witchcraft as a constant battlefield, where it is a matter of life and death to surprise one's opponents—to outmaneuver them, if possible, with new ruses. No wonder the world of the witches seems beset by constant outbreaks of new forms that appear to bring uncanny danger precisely because they are unknown (one could almost speak of "fashions," but then deadly ones). This trend toward constant innovation is crucial for understanding how witchcraft images can graft themselves so easily onto modern developments. To the people concerned there is often not the slightest incongruence in rumors—now recurrent throughout the continent—about witches using airplanes and nocturnal airstrips: were these riders of the night not always up to new tricks?

This changeability also marks the link between witchcraft and intimacy, which likewise is not a timeless element. People's shifting interpretations of this link directly affect their imaginary of the occult. In many parts of Africa—and elsewhere—witchcraft representations seem subject to a continuous increase of scale: as said, people insist nowadays that witchcraft is "globalizing." This does not keep witchcraft discourse—and concomitant practices—from continuing to refer ultimately to the familiar realities of kin and the local. Yet the ways in which witchcraft manages to articulate the global with the local are many and constantly changing. This chapter will try to follow these changes over time in a few empirical settings.

Changing Parameters of Intimacy and Distance

In 1971, when I started my fieldwork in a few villages in the Maka area in Southeast Cameroon, witchcraft rumors and accusations were increasingly focused on the ambiguous relation between the village and an emerging elite of more prosperous "sons of the soil" who had made their career in the city. The rise of these new elites—whom the villagers mostly called *nos évolués*, having no qualms about retaining colonial terminology from the days of French rule—was a relatively new phenomenon. All elites owed their success to the fact that they were the first—most of them in the 1940s and 1950s—to have obtained some schooling. Thus they could profit from the rapid Africanization of the public services after the country's independence (1960) and get access to relatively well-paid jobs within the government. Those were the days when a primary school certificate could suffice for being appointed ambassador or obtaining another high post in the government hierarchies. In the Maka area—in the dense forest of the East Province, of difficult access, and generally seen as one of the more backward areas of the country—the emergence of a new, educated elite came later than in the country's more dynamic zones, like the West Province (Bamileke land), around Douala (the main port), or around Yaoundé (the capital, in the land of the Beti). Yet at the end of the 1960s several young Maka men from the village where I lived had succeeded in gaining salaried positions as well. Even if these were still quite modest (e.g., school director in an urban center in East Province; *sous-préfet* [assistant district officer]), the very fact that they were now in government service created new inequalities that deeply impressed the villagers. The consequence was that the new elites' relations with their village of origin—with their "brothers," as they invariably put it—were beset by deep ambivalences.

Everyday life in the Maka area is still marked by a powerful egalitarian ideology. Before colonial conquest (1905–10) the Maka social order was expressed in kinship terms. People lived in small hamlets formed around a patrilineal segment. There was no central authority above the village level.[1] At most, closely related villages could work together in the eternal *dombe* (hostilities) between different groups, but such collaboration was always temporal. Moreover, hamlets were constantly splitting up because of internal conflicts. This fluid setup did certainly not mean that relations within the village were egalitarian in practice. In many respects the Maka order was (and still is) a gerontocracy: old men had far-reaching authority over "their" young men and women. Maka leaders were "big men" trying to attract as many women and dependents as possible to their compound— thus outdoing their rivals in neighboring settlements.

Yet such ascendancy was circumscribed by an egalitarian ideology that is still quite powerful. In this respect as well, the Maka leaders can be seen as true "big men": their leadership depends on personal performance and has to be constantly reaffirmed in the face of strong leveling mechanisms. Most important leveling forces were the segmentary implications of the kinship order, allowing dissatisfied segments to split off, and the discourse of *djambe* (witchcraft) that makes it very dangerous—not to say fatal—to incur the jealousy of relatives. However, the forceful imposition of colonial state authority—in this area realized by two waves of extreme violence by the Germans in 1905 and then again in 1910[2]—introduced a completely new element into this configuration. The stories I could still get from the elders in 1971 of how they had seen the Germans march into the village resounded with their utter amazement at the kind of authority these new conquerors claimed as self-evidently theirs: without referring to any personal relation—as Maka big men would do—the new authorities just claimed the right to command in most brutal ways. It came as a great shock that, apparently, the Germans and their African auxiliaries pretended to have the right to give orders to complete strangers, something unheard of in Maka society.

In 1914–15 the French conquered this part of the German colony, and they continued to rule with a most emphatic show of authority. Elderly people told me long stories about the horrors of *les travaux forcés* and the utter capriciousness of the French *commandants*. Independence in 1960 did not change much in this respect: the postcolonial state continued to claim unconditional authority. The new civil servants—even if they were now Cameroonians—practiced the same rituals of domination and humiliation they had inherited from their colonial predecessors, and their equally emphatic show of authority continued to be confirmed by harsh forms of violence by the *gendarmes* against any subject who dared to talk back to the *sous-préfet*. In my book *Village Communities and the State* (1982), I analyzed the present-day relations of authority in the Maka area as based on an unstable mixture of quite opposite conceptions of power: on the one hand, personal power of the village leaders, constantly circumscribed by a powerful egalitarian discourse; and on the other, the unconditional obedience claimed by a highly authoritarian state that made itself felt down to the village level.

This rapid historical sketch may help to clarify the deep ambiguity of the position of the new Maka *évolués* and their special vulnerability to the local *djambe* discourse. They were born in the village, and people addressed them emphatically as "brothers" or "fathers," depending on the generation. Thus their position was embedded in the old discourse of kinship with its leveling implications. Yet at the same time they were representatives of the authoritarian state. Most of them worked in public service, and in the 1960s they had been rapidly recruited for regional political positions in the UNC (Union nationale camerounaise), the emerging single party that in no uncertain terms supported the high-handed authoritarianism of the state and its servants. This gave these *évolués* both formal and, even more importantly, informal access to the new opportunities for advancement in the urban sectors. The villagers were adamant that these new leaders, as "sons of the village," had to support them in getting jobs in the city, scholarships for their children, and protection in case of problems with the *gendarmes*. Their new positions made these *évolués* far richer than anybody staying in the village could ever hope to become. The hot issue became, therefore, to what extent these new figures of success were willing to share with their former "brothers" in the village. Such tensions, marking the emergence of a new elite, are documented all over Africa (and elsewhere). But in the forest area of Cameroon they were particularly sharp because of the absence of any well-institutionalized hierarchy in the old order and the persistence of a powerful egalitarian ideology.

These tensions came to play a central role in my fieldwork. When I arrived in 1971, my aim was, as noted, to study the interaction between state formation and authority relations at the local level. However, it soon became a major problem to me that the two spheres seemed to be completely separated: they seemed to exist side by side, with people switching from one register to another across the divide, but without clear links between the two. This was the heyday of one-party dictatorship and state authoritarianism in Cameroon—as elsewhere in Africa. In a view "from below," there hardly seemed to be any interaction between village politics and the new forms of authority so forcefully imposed by the state. Every Sunday at the village palaver, where the chief and his elderly notables (*lessje kande*—lit. speakers in council) were supposed to solve the village's *milesu* (affairs), people acted out the local order with much sense of drama. Everybody had the right to speak, and people—including women—did so with ostentatious prowess. Elders periodically tried to calm the din by telling an old story or singing a song that was supposed to bring reconciliation, but they often had great trouble in ruling the crowd. I enthusiastically wrote in my notebooks that this was "tribal democracy" in optima forma.

However, whenever the *sous-préfet* came to visit the village there was a complete change of behavior. The same man who had dared to contradict the most respected elder with much gusto and verbal violence stood with his head bowed, cap in hand, in front of the *sous-préfet*, hardly daring to utter a word. And indeed, this very authoritarian official would admonish him in no uncertain ways to be brief. The omnipresence of the *gendarmes* with their handcuffs and their *bâtons* (sticks) was enough to smother any expression of discontent. The refrain of the villagers whenever they were summoned to appear before the *sous-préfet* in town—*je vais au pays des blancs* (I am going to white man's country)[3]–seemed to sum up the complete failure of my research plan. Apparently there was as much distance as in the colonial days. In my research reports I compared the state to a balloon filled with power that seemed to float over society, inspiring deep fear[4] without being anchored in it.[5]

An Urban Elite Attacked by Village Witchcraft

The first indication that there actually was a link between the two worlds came via rumors about witchcraft—in retrospect not surprisingly. The rumors concerned the most important elite figure from Logbood,[6] a village that due to the early founding of a school by a Presbyterian mission (until the 1970s run by American missionaries) could boast of a significant number of *évolués*.

In the late 1960s this man, Jean Eba, had succeeded in accumulating a number of quite important administrative and political positions.[7] In the hierarchy of state schools he had gradually climbed to the rank of inspector. More important, he had become one of the mainstays of the one-party hierarchy in the region, *président de la sous-section* and, linked to this, *adjoint au maire* (deputy mayor). But Eba hardly seemed to enjoy his success. In contrast to another *évolué*, his cousin Simon Mbang, he hardly participated in village life when he was there on holidays and weekends. He remained mostly within his compound at the village edge. Whenever he had to appear in the village, his behavior was almost a caricature of that of a *fonctionnaire*: stiff, authoritarian, and impatient. Several friends told me later that there were specific reasons for his reserve. At the end of the 1960s Eba had chosen to return to the village, according to some because he had run into "difficulties" in his job elsewhere in the East Province (people hinted at financial irregularities). But this soon became a painful intermezzo: Eba fell ill, his complaints were quite mysterious (general fatigue), and no doctor succeeded in curing him. So people soon started to whisper about witchcraft. Apparently Eba himself shared this view, despite his Western education: after some hesitation he told me that he had begun to frequent one *nganga* after another. Finally a *nganga* from Djem country (some sixty miles away) succeeded in helping him, but insisted that he had to leave the village and return to one of the urban centers of the East.

At first the story did not surprise me very much. I was already familiar with the deep involvement of educated elites—even if they saw themselves as *les nouveaux Blancs*—with the *djambe*, a term the Maka now invariably translate as *sorcellerie*. One of my new friends was Ms. Mendouga, who had the reputation of being the most powerful *nganga* of the area and who regularly boasted to me about her high-placed clients: hadn't I seen the big black Mercedes parked in front of her house yesterday?[8] That belonged to the *préfet* (senior district officer), who had come to ask her for help with his political troubles. Indeed, the sight of such an imposing car in front of her poor house was striking. My assistant had explained to me that elites competed for Mendouga's favors—she was so powerful that she could make or break a man's career. However, those stories were all about infighting among the elites— murderous attacks on rivals in order to promote one's own chances in the fierce competition for posts.

Eba's story was different. It made no reference at all to political rivals; the attack was supposed to come "from below." People—both other *évolués* and villagers—consistently explained it in reference to Eba's unusual step of settling again in the village after having made a career in the urban centers. Everybody agreed that the reason for his plight was jealousy and that the source of the attack had come from inside "the house." According to some, his cousins had been furious because they were refused entry when Eba received the *sous-préfet* in his house for a sumptuous meal; others said the people of his own lineage felt he had neglected the interests of his kin when, as chairman of the party's subsection, he presided over the election of a new village chief. Whatever the real reason, it was clear to my informants that his relatives had attacked him with a mixture of herbs and liquid that they had buried under the path to his house; he had unknowingly stepped on it and thus the *miedou* (medicine) had entered his body.

The story of Eba's misfortune reflected a basic pattern in Maka conceptions of witchcraft: the *shumbu*, the nightly meeting of witches where each witch offers in turn a relative to be eaten by their horrible companions. This was what they had done to Eba, who would surely have died if the Djem *nganga* had not managed to "see" them and then "fallen upon them" and forced them to lift their spell. Eba still complained about the huge sum of money he had to pay the *nganga* for this.

This powerful knot of ideas—witches leaving their bodies at night and flying off to meet with witches from elsewhere in order to betray and eat their relatives—can explain why to everybody, Eba himself included, it was clear that the attack had come from inside. For other *évolués*, moreover, the story had a clear moral: one should be very careful about venturing back into the intimacy of the village—if one came too close, sooner or later the villagers' jealousy would ensnare you. Thus the *djambe* imaginary had (and still has) paradoxical implications for relations between villagers and "their" elites. *Djambe* may be one of the most powerful leveling elements within the village, as a constant reminder to overambitious leaders how dangerous it can be to disrespect the egalitarian ideology by refusing to share with their relatives. However, with the urban elites who had profited from novel opportunities to make a career in the outer world, it had in practice an opposite effect, leading them to keep their distance from the village—which (and this was new) they could in fact do since they lived now in town.

This was certainly not what the villagers wanted. On the contrary, especially in the early decades after independence the "sons of the village" who had made their career in the city were the villagers' only access to the power of the state and the promises of public service. As noted, people tried in all possible ways to remind their successful "brothers" that they were close relatives, that they should help them when they were in trouble with the *gendarmes* or get scholarships and jobs for their children. The elites felt swamped by all these requests. Hence their complaint that they were "eaten" by their "brothers"—a direct reference to the "eating" of the witches at the nightly *shumbu*.

The consequence was a kind of catch-22. On the one hand, the villagers were complaining about their *evolués'* apparent reluctance to bring development to the village—as my neighbor exclaimed, "They do not even build a house in the village; how do they think we will ever get progress here?" On the other, the new elites insisted that they had to keep their distance because of the *djambe* and its dangers. In retrospect it is quite striking that in these days the relatively small distances between village and urban centers—the capital, Yaoundé, is at 150 miles distance, the centers in the East only at 20 to 60 miles away—were still seen as offering real protection. In the 1970s it was only when *évolués* returned to the village that they were supposed to be in real danger. This would soon change.

Urban Witchcraft Attacks the Village

More than twenty years later, village history seemed to repeat itself. Another *évolué* from the same village, Simon Mbang (the cousin of Eba mentioned above), decided also to return to the village, but his reason was that he had reached retirement age. For a few years he lived there without problems, but then it was his turn to become involved in nasty witchcraft rumors. Yet besides apparent parallels with the earlier events, there were also interesting differences. Significantly, Mbang was not seen as a victim who had to be protected but rather as a perpetrator who had to be punished. Clearly, the witchcraft imaginary allows for highly different interpretations of intimacy and aggression.

It all started in early 1994 with the unexpected return to the village of a certain Jeanne, daughter of Jean Mpoam. The latter had left the village more than thirty years earlier. People from his *grande famille* in the village had bitterly complained that he seemed to have forgotten about his brothers. Apparently he was doing reasonably well in Douala, where he worked in a pharmacy. But he did not seem prepared to invest any of his wealth in the village. He let the house he had inherited fall into ruins, and it was only rarely that people managed to persuade him to come and attend a social function in the village. Yet when he died, his children brought his body back to the village, and it was buried there. In earlier years his children had been to the village once or twice during school holidays. So when Jeanne quite abruptly reappeared in the village, she did find relatives with whom she could stay.

Soon it turned out that her return had a special purpose. Only a few days after her arrival, she announced that she could heal people through "exorcism and clairvoyance." Apparently people were impressed by her knowledge. Some days more than eighty persons came to be blessed by her. Her popularity grew all the more when it became clear that one did not have to pay her—this was in sharp contrast to the practice of other healers. All people had to bring was a new candle. During her sessions she would invoke God; then she made her clients drink water she had consecrated, rubbed them with a special oil, and finally spoke a benediction over them. However, after only a week her performance took a new turn: she started to accuse several prominent people in the village, notably including Mr. Mbang, of dabbling in new forms of witchcraft. People were shocked to hear this, but many believed her. One argument—often heard in similar tense situations—was that Mbang had never been afraid of the *djambe* in the village. Wasn't this the reason he had dared to return and live again with his brothers? He must have his own occult support; how else was it possible that he had braved the *djambe* without being hurt?

Such vague suspicions were suddenly concretized when Jeanne announced a new revelation: Mbang had brought the terrible *kong* into the village—a new form of witchcraft about which the villagers had been whispering already for some time, and which was especially related to the *nouveaux riches* and their enviable styles of consumption (see below). However, Mbang was determined to impose his own truth. Almost immediately after he had heard the rumors the woman was spreading, he lodged a complaint for defamation with the *tribunal de première instance* in Abong-Mbang, the administrative center of the subdivision. Clearly Jeanne had underrated the powerful contacts Mbang still had in the region—probably she had been away too long. Within two months (an amazingly short period for Cameroonian justice) the court judged the affair: Jeanne was sentenced to a heavy fine (45,000 FCFA = $200 at the time) and a three-month probation. The last clause was quite threatening: it meant that she would be in jail as soon as she hinted again at Mbang's secret powers. So she disappeared the next day.

Yet to the villagers the whole affair was not over. For many, the *kong* accusation against Mbang still stuck. His resounding victory before the court did impress people. They may not all have been convinced of the veracity of the court's decision; however, no one was left with any doubt that Mbang's support "up there" was still strong. But the whole affair had dramatic consequences for Mbang's relation with Eba, his cousin and the other main *évolué* of the village. Eba's people had been the first to believe Jeanne's denunciation of Mbang. Indeed, they hinted to have known all along that Mbang must have used special powers to advance his own children but block the others in his family. Jeanne's accusation of *kong* witchcraft had only substantiated these previous suspicions. Even after the court took the edge of Jeanne's denunciations, all relations between the two branches of the family were cut.

Both Eba's and Mbang's stories circle around the relation between urban elites and the village as a focus for witchcraft rumors—that is, both concern the precarious way in which a discourse on intimacy bridges new social and spatial distances. However, the course of events was quite different. One reason is that the political context had changed drastically. The early 1990s brought a dramatic switch from an extremely stiff and authoritarian one-party state to a formal situation of democracy and multipartyism in which political debate was suddenly allowed again and people were no longer afraid to speak up against the authorities. An unexpected side effect of the new law of freedom of association—until 1990 all forms of association that were not approved by the one-party had been strictly forbidden—was the sudden blooming of all sorts of independent churches and religious cults, many of which had a more or less explicit Pentecostal flavor. In the 1970s the activities of some Baha'i missionaries in the region had led to swift and drastic interventions by the DO.[9] But after 1990 a religious healer like Jeanne could proceed unhindered. Apparently she had felt that her gifts were not enough appreciated in Douala, where she lived; she may have hoped that the village of her father would offer virgin territory for her missionary fervor. But she clearly underrated the strength of the old elite networks. Mbang might have given up all his former positions, but he proved to still have some pull within the government's hierarchies.

It is noteworthy that he immediately took the accusation to the *tribunal*. This was a quite daring step, since beginning in the early 1980s the courts, especially in the East Province, had begun to take accusations of witchcraft seriously. In a dramatic switch of existing jurisprudence, the courts had begun to show their willingness to take the allegations of local *nganga* (healers) as evidence for convicting witches and imposing serious punishments (up to ten years in jail, heavy fines—see Fisiy and Geschiere 1990). In former days the *nganga* had good reason to fear the courts, since they could be accused of defamation if they tried to denounce a witch—in the 1970s people still complained to me that these white-man courts protected the witches by pursuing the *nganga*. But in the 1980s several judges, clearly under heavy pressure from the population to do something about the proliferation of new forms of witchcraft, were ready to accept *nganga* as expert witnesses. How else was it possible to constitute proof against the witches? Therefore, Mbang took a real risk in taking the matter immediately to the court. However, the remarkable swiftness with which the court reacted—normally witchcraft cases drag on for years and years—indicated that he knew what he was doing. His contacts were still powerful enough to make the court shut up the woman—at least in the open.

Another difference was Mbang's jovial personality. Unlike Eba, he was very much "a man of the people," clearly enjoying his popularity among villagers. They were impressed by the career he had made, and even more by the fact that this did not stop him from being friendly with them. All this somewhat covered up people's continuing doubts about Mbang's dabbling with the terrible *kong*. Yet the suspicion remained in the air, and it was reinforced by the breach with Eba and his family. But in contrast to Eba, and despite these serious rumors, Mbang did not feel forced to leave the village in order to create distance. He kept on living in his big house at the outskirts of the village, and he died more than ten years later without running into further difficulties with the populace. He was buried in front of his house with great pomp.

Even more relevant to our theme might be another difference between the two cases: the changing contours of intimacy/distance in relation to witchcraft. While in Eba's case witchcraft—the fearsome *miedou*—was seen as a local force ambushing the urbanite upon his return in the village, Mbang's *kong* is seen as an *urban* form of witchcraft. The latter story therefore exemplifies the closing of the gap between city and village. Witchcraft was no longer a local emanation to be used against urbanites, but it was imported from the city to the village.

A most vivid picture of this *kong*—the new zombie witchcraft mentioned in chaper 1, also called *ekong*, *famla*, or *kupe* elsewhere in Cameroon—is to be found in Eric de Rosny's seminal books about his initiation as a *nganga* in Douala in the 1960s, when there was a mounting panic about *ekong* in this city. It was the novelty of *ekong/famla* that made it so frightening. People saw it as a form of witchcraft particular to the new rich who had emerged with surprising rapidity in the first decades after independence. *Ekong* witches would no longer eat their victims but put them to work on invisible plantations on Mt. Kupe. This would be the secret of their amazing accumulation of wealth, which transgressed the old order of things.[10] Around 1960 *ekong* witches were still to be recognized by their ostentatious display of new luxury goods, like fridges, cars, and modern houses. Nowadays it takes more to make someone "smell" of *ekong*.

In the rumors about Mbang's *kong*, city and village had become hard to distinguish: Jeanne, his accuser, was even more of an urbanite than he himself. She imported the idea of an urban witchcraft that was supposed to be particularly strong in the more developed southwestern parts of the country. But the effect was that both she and Mbang became enmeshed in the vicious circles of intimacy drawn by witchcraft discourse. This discourse may have bridged the distance between city and village—apparently with relative ease—but in the end it referred back to the small-scale intimacy of the family. The main effect of the story seemed to have been a definitive rupture between Mbang and his cousin Eba, even though they lived across from each other in the part of the village that belonged to their lineage. For her part, Jeanne may have returned to her familial village in the hope that her gifts would prove to be particularly powerful there, but she had not counted on Mbang's ability to bring in the support of outside authorities. This confusion of levels—the ease with which novel socioeconomic developments are linked to old forms of familial discord—may be one of the secrets of the remarkable resilience of this discourse and its practices.[11]

Developments in a very different part of the country—the Southwest, its economic heartland—show how witchcraft can also bring the village to the city, an even further imbrication of the two poles.

Witchcraft Brings the Village to the City

Francis Nyamnjoh, a Cameroonian anthropologist who most vividly describes witchcraft vicissitudes in both his novels and his scientific publications, refers to an affair that in some respects resembled the stories of Eba and Mbang but illustrated yet another pattern. Nyamnjoh (1998) relates how in 1998 the *fon* (chief) of Bum, a village far up in the Northwest, traveled south to Tiko and Douala, two urban centers on the coast—both more than five hundred miles from Bum—in order to put a stop to a proliferation of witchcraft among his "sons" in this faraway region. This audacious step put him in an open confrontation with the forces of order of the state, but it was most effective in reestablishing his authority over his subjects in diaspora. It seems telling that witchcraft was again at the heart of this novel effort to bridge the distance between village and city.

In the northwestern Grassfields, notions like village and chief have different meanings, compared to social frameworks in the Maka region. The Northwest, in the formerly British part of Cameroon,[12] is the province where chieftaincy has retained its most condensed form up till the present day. While in the forest area chieftaincy is mostly a colonial creation—as said, before colonial conquest small patrilineal groups had formed independent hamlets with no fixed positions of authority at a higher level—the chiefs of the Grassfields are traditional figures whose authority continues to be supported by a complex set of institutions. The relatively small size of these chieftaincies—the biggest ones still count only a few hundred thousands of subjects, and most are much smaller—goes together with a particularly heavy control of the chiefs and the associations around their courts over everyday life. In these societies the chief and notably the *kwifon*—described by Nyamnjoh (1998:75) as a "more or less secret police association"—are the obvious authorities to control witchcraft. Indeed, Grassfielders often express some contempt for forest people who have no chiefs and who seem ready to submit even highly private affairs, like witchcraft problems, to the authority of the state.

The northwestern Grassfields was and still is also one of the most densely populated areas of present-day Cameroon, from where large numbers of migrants moved to the emerging centers of the (post)colonial economy near the coast.[13] When, around 1900, the Germans created a big plantation complex on the fertile slopes of Mt. Cameroon, a volcano that rises straight from the coast to an imposing four thousand meters, it was Grassfielders who met the new demand for labor. Together with the Bamileke, their neighbors from the West Province in Francophone Cameroon, they migrated in large numbers to the newly emerging cities, especially Douala, Cameroon's economic center on the coast, and later also Yaoundé, the country's capital. As in the Maka area, the relations of these migrants with their village of origin soon became a focal point for rumors and accusations of witchcraft.

Nyamnjoh relates how in the 1990s the community of Bum migrants in the coastal area—Bum is one of the bigger chieftaincies of the Northwest but has been mostly bypassed by development because of its remote location—was shaken by ever more worrying rumors about witchcraft. These soon centered on a man called Msame who worked as a foreman in a plantation of Del Monte Bananas (a fairly modest position but one that assured him a regular salary). The rumors were triggered by a series of sudden and inexplicable deaths among his close relatives both in the village up in the Northwest and in Tiko, the coastal town where he worked. First Msame's mother suddenly died in the village; then a niece from Douala who came to offer her condolences to him in Tiko fell ill and died also. This was too much of a coincidence for the cousin's husband. So he went to consult a diviner in Bum, who saw that Msame had the terrible *nyongo*.[14] This particular diviner was very graphic in his explanations: he had "seen" that Msame's mother was now splitting wood in the invisible world, while his niece was selling *puff-puffs* (pastries) and picking coffee there, all to the enrichment of Msame, who would even have agreed to "sell" more than seven others to his *nyongo* association because he wanted to become very rich. This triggered other accusations against supposed acolytes of Msame. The whole Bum community in the coastal area risked being torn apart by rumors about internal witchcraft.

This was reason enough for the chief to take a surprising step. Though it is a contested point whether a Grassfields chief is even allowed to leave his realm—according to custom he should sit at home and grow fat while receiving the homage of his subjects there[15]—the Bum chief suddenly descended upon Tiko, accompanied by several of his subchiefs. They had Msame arrested on the spot and also two of his acolytes in Douala; all three were bundled off to Bum, where they were to be judged by the terrifying *kwifon*. However, the chief was clearly overstepping his mandate. His right to arrest subjects within his own realm is already relative (under the Cameroonian constitution the prerogatives of "customary chiefs" are defined only vaguely), and he was certainly not entitled to make an arrest so far outside his boundaries. So Msame's wife went immediately to the *gendarmes*, who had the *nji*, the Bum's chief representative in Tiko, arrested for unlawful detention of Msame. This triggered a large-scale effort among all Bum migrants in the area; after two weeks they succeeded in bringing together enough money to corrupt the *gendarmes* and liberate the *nji*. In Bum, the *kwifon* decided that all three accused had to pass the frightening sasswood ordeal. However, Msame managed to escape and went into hiding. Of the other two detainees, one took the poisoned drink, but he did not die, so he was innocent. The other, a woman, drank and did not die either. Yet the diviner decided that she was guilty nonetheless. So she was held in custody, pending a final decision by the *kwifon*.

Nyamnjoh's story stopped here, leaving an open ending. But his conclusions are quite firm. He emphasizes that the whole maneuver did serve to confirm the authority of the chief, even over his subjects in the faraway coastal area. Yet the chief clearly made a risky gamble: his arrest of Msame and his acolytes could have brought him into an open confrontation with the authorities of the state. Indeed, he was saved only by the readiness of the Bum community in the area to contribute lavishly in order to corrupt the *gendarmes* and save the chief the loss of face of seeing his own representative in jail. Nyamnjoh provides an interesting answer to the question of why the Bum chief was willing to take such a risk, by pointing out the increasing involvement of the chiefs in what he calls "the politics of belonging" (see also Geschiere and Nyamnjoh 2000). As elsewhere on the continent, the sudden breakthrough of democratization brought a comeback of the "traditional chiefs" in Cameroonian politics—especially because they could play a crucial role in legitimizing the belonging of their subjects.

In Cameroon the switch from authoritarian one-party rule to multipartyism was particularly dramatic—on the one hand because of the extreme authoritarianism of the preceding one-party regime, first under

President Ahmadou Ahidjo and then under Paul Biya, his successor, and on the other because of the tenacity with which the latter has succeeded in holding on to power up to the present day. As elsewhere, an important factor behind Biya's unexpected success in hanging on was the effectiveness of the regime's "politics of belonging" in dividing the opposition and thus neutralizing the impact of multipartyism. In the Cameroonian case, the regime's defensive actions had two prongs. One was the restoration of chiefs. Before democratization Biya may have marked the chiefs as potential obstacles for development, but in the new configuration they were rediscovered as potential vote-banks, assuring the regime—which pays their salaries—of votes that failing one-party control could no longer guarantee.[16] The other measure, equally effective and novel, was the encouragement of regional elite associations. Civil servants, also dependent on the regime for their salaries, were quite abruptly ordered to create regional associations and thus capture the votes of "their" people for the president's party. The latter policy was even more of an innovation since until 1989, under the extreme centralism of Cameroon's one-party rule, all associations outside the party had been strictly forbidden; this applied especially to regional groupings, which were supposed to undermine national unity, the much-celebrated ideal of Ahidjo, and of Biya in his early years. After 1990, on the contrary, chiefs and elite associations became mainstays of the regime's survival (see also Geschiere 2009b).

In the new order of things, the relations between chiefs and urban elites became a crucial issue. Until then, this relation had often been a strained one. The elites felt they represented a modern kind of leadership, even vis-à-vis the village, and were therefore impatient with the chiefs' traditional claims. No wonder many chiefs tended to see their successful subjects in the cities as potential rivals. However, with the new emphasis on belonging as a crucial issue in national politics, some form of cooperation became crucial if both the chiefs and the elites were to play the roles the regime expected of them. The rash action of the chief of Bum very clearly fit in this pattern. Before descending on the coast, he had gone to great length to reconcile himself with Bum's urban elites. In earlier days he had seen the new Bum Development Association, created by these elites, as a potential threat. But when this association, profiting from the new law on freedom of association, could assume a higher profile, the chief showed himself suddenly willing to put his moral authority behind its initiatives at the local level. Nyamnjoh analyzes his descent upon the coast as the finishing touch in this respect. The chief showed in no uncertain terms that even Bum people living elsewhere were still his subjects and still depended upon him to keep things in order. For this he was apparently even willing to risk a dangerous confrontation with the judicial authorities of the state, who are normally very jealous in guarding their prerogatives.

It is characteristic that his intervention hinged, again, on witchcraft. The recurrent rumors about occult aggression from inside that threatened to tear apart the Bum community in Tiko and Douala offered an ideal entry point for the chief to reaffirm his authority over the elites in diaspora. They clearly needed him to put a stop to the witchcraft lurking inside. Further, this discourse proved to be capable of bridging new distances with apparent self-evidence, relating the village to the city while still sticking to the maxim that aggression from within is the most dangerous. To be noted is also that Msame and his acolytes, thoroughly urbanized as they were, exercised their frightful powers only on their relatives from Bum: apparently even in the new setting witchcraft still remained closely linked to intimacy. But Nyamnjoh's final conclusion is that the whole affair showed how both autochthony and witchcraft were now "reproduced on an increasing scale" (1998:81).

Witchcraft, Distance and the Post–Cold War Moment

The brief ethnographic vignettes above illustrate how that the incisive changes in the relation between village and city over the last fifty years have affected the content of witchcraft imaginary and the ways in which people deal with it. For Eba the city was still far enough away to offer protection against village witchcraft; in Mbang's case the *kong*, an urban form of witchcraft, penetrated the village; the chief of Bum felt obliged to leave his realm and arrest witches in the city. Relations of intimacy are being reproduced on a wider, supralocal scale, and this allows for new applications of witchcraft conceptions.

Clearly such changes are not unique to Cameroon; they fit into a wider configuration with global dimensions. In his recent book on Togo, Charles Piot (2010) focuses on the "post–cold war crisis" to capture this broader moment. He uses the notion to analyze the convergence of a series of quite unexpected changes in Togo in the 1990s: the whirlwind of NGOs pervading the country; major changes in the performance of the state, which to a certain extent seems to go underground (while remaining omnipresent at the same time); the wave of Pentecostalism; but also new concerns of urban elites over witchcraft in the village (and elsewhere). Clearly this emphasis on a post--cold war crisis as a turning point has broader relevance, certainly for Africa—all the more so since Piot launches it as a further focusing of the notion of "the postcolonial," which lately has become so common that it risks losing its meaning and impact (2010:2, 15). Piot rightly insists that the 1990s brought changes that in many respects were more radical than independence around 1960. The notion of the postcolonial state, for instance, applied very well to the first decades of independence, when the state very much continued the policies of its colonial predecessor, just as the new development industry continued colonial interventions. In this sense my Maka friends were quite perspicacious in speaking of Cameroonian civil servants as *les (nouveaux) Blancs* and the government post as *le pays des Blancs*. But the notion of postcolonial may be less directly relevant for understanding the changes of the 1990s. The forms taken on by the state in its struggle with structural adjustment after the end of the 1980s—aptly summarized by Béatrice Hibou's notion of the "privatization of the state" (1999/2004)—seem to be quite different from the postcolonial state of earlier decades, notably in the ways in which authority has come to be exercised at the local level. Is it still useful to bring all this together under the label of "the" postcolonial?[17]

Piot's emphasis on the wider implications of the post–cold war crisis is helpful in pointing out that new and indeterminate articulations of the global and the local are being acted out in which the state is more informally involved, while other forms of belonging (and exclusion) acquire a dynamics of their own; of course the latter were always present, but they now invade the public domain with unprecedented force. This may be one of the reasons why this moment is so saturated with witchcraft—which after all can be seen as the flip side of belonging, precisely because of its close link to intimacy and inequality. The challenge is to see to what extent witchcraft discourses and practices take on new expressions under these changing circumstances. The emphasis on a post–cold war crisis can also help to show that the "the politics of belonging" highlighted by Nyamnjoh and others are not just inspired by cunning Cameroonian politicians but fit into a much broader configuration that emerged in the 1990s.

The immediate causes for the explosion of struggles over belonging and exclusion that shook many African regions after 1990 are clear. An important factor is certainly the new policy of the development establishment, which—especially since the World Bank report on Africa of 1989—switched from myopic reliance on the state to an equally myopic celebration of decentralization and bypassing the state as *the* solution. As noted earlier, this implied in practice that neoliberal developers, looking for an alternative for the state, came to put their faith in "traditional chiefs" and even more in "the" community, taken as a unitary given. These may be quite surprising hobbyhorses for liberals, but they brought a *retour en force* of localist forms of belonging. Equally important for this explosion of belonging was democratization, which automatically raised the thorny issue of who can vote where—and with it a growing resentment of "strangers," who were accused of trying to dominate politics in the land of their "hosts." Such resentment was gratefully used by former one-party regimes to neutralize the effect of open elections (see Geschiere 2009b and, for Cameroon, Socpa 2002).

Yet, clear as these backgrounds may be, it remains important to underline that the neoliberal appeal to tradition produced new effects: it promoted neotraditional ways of affirming one's belonging within new spatial boundaries and new scales of intimacy—for instance, bridging the rift between village and city or even striving for more global forms of belonging (see below). No wonder there was a direct link to changing contours of witchcraft. Piot (2010) shows most graphically in his last chapter how this post–cold war crisis set the stage for new and much more direct interventions by the urban elite to deal with witchcraft in the village.

In my own encounters with the new vigor of elite associations in Makaland, I was similarly confronted with the quite unexpected force with which witchcraft emerged as a central issue. In 1995, after an academic conference we organized in Yaoundé, I received an invitation from the Association des Elites Maka Mboans to come and address their next Yaoundé meeting, since they wanted very much to hear my advice on how to bring development to their region and finally break, as they put it, "the stagnation for which the Maka area was unfortunately known." I felt honored. In the days of the one-party regime prior to 1989, the Maka elites in Yaoundé had been quite cool to my research; they felt that I was too much influenced by the villagers' perspective, and they were also worried about my efforts to try and discuss politics with them—in those days this was *not* done. Apparently things had changed. Indeed, the very existence of this association was a sign of change. As said, the changes around 1990 led to a volte-face of the regime in its attitude toward such *associations des originaires*, the apt Francophone name for elites organizing themselves in relation to their home village or region.

One of my Maka friends—an important *fonctionnaire*—told me later how utterly surprised he had been when in 1992, at the approach of the first open elections for the presidency, he was suddenly asked to get organized and create an association for his region in order to promote the campaign of Paul Biya, the ruling president. What used to be strictly forbidden under one-party rule—in those days any effort by an ambitious politician to organize his own constituency would put him at risk of being accused of subversion and trying to undermine the unity of

Cameroonians under the aegis of the party[18]—was now encouraged and even made obligatory. Clearly the job of my Maka friend would be in danger if he did not heed the request. All this had evident reasons. The regime was nervous about these crucial elections, since the opposition was very vocal in those days. The once-so-suspect institute of elite associations now offered unexpected possibilities for paralyzing the opposition: since these *fonctionnaires* depended on their government salaries, they could easily be obligated to go home and use their moral authority among "their" people to make these vote for Biya.[19] But my Maka friend was quite bitter about his experiences with campaigning. A female *fonctionnaire* from a neighboring village had received a lot more money for the purpose, so she could regale villagers with many crates of beer and appetizing food. Therefore "his" villagers had immediately accused him of keeping some of the money for himself—"you know how these villagers react . . ." Moreover, he complained that it had been impossible to bring some coordination to the elites' activities in their home village. For him, this proved again that Maka people were simply not capable of keeping such an organization intact. Indeed, after 1992 the new Maka elite associations had been splitting constantly.

On a visit in 1991 I had already noticed that things had changed. The clearest sign was that in most Maka villages imposing buildings were being erected along the mud road where I did my main research. These turned out to be new mansions built by urban elites. For my friends as well, this was a huge change. The Maka elites, who had always been scared of the village and reluctant to really invest there, were suddenly building houses! And it was evident that these were going to be showy buildings, clear status symbols. One elite, a civil servant from Yaoundé, had erected a palace with an imposing portico surrounded by pillars, a clear imitation of the palaces of the Islamic emirs from North Cameroon.

Throughout Cameroon—as elsewhere in the continent—elite associations seemed to own the future. The regime no longer tried to curtail them—on the contrary. In addition, the new NGO wave opened up new possibilities. Many civil servants actually took early retirement in order to found their own NGOs. While the real value of government salaries was falling lower and lower, founding an NGO promised to bring access to new sources of funding from development agencies. The new development credo of bypassing the state, decentralizing, and reaching out to society were certainly not lost on these brokers. While still using their contacts in government circles, they hoped to profit from their base in their region of origin to get their own development projects going. As in other regions, the Maka elite now had powerful reasons—both economic and political—to take their belonging more seriously.

> The reception I got at the meeting of the Association des Elites Maka Mboans was, indeed, quite impressive. It took place at the stately house of the chairman, a medical doctor of considerable renown. The elites—men and women—were sitting in luxurious fauteuils. The chairman made a friendly speech to welcome me. He elaborated on the need to finally bring development to the villages I knew so well. As he explained it, the elites were now more than ever intent on helping their "brothers" down there, they felt genuinely involved with the region of their ancestors, and they were eager to hear how I felt about their initiatives to get things going. I replied that I was impressed by their enthusiasm and was certain their participation would bring a new élan to the villages. But before I could go on, an excited discussion started about what would be the central topic for the rest of the afternoon: witchcraft and the need to overcome it if ever things were going to change in the villages.
>
> In itself it was not such a surprise that witchcraft proved to be the issue that would dominate the whole meeting. After all, the main topic was supposed to be how to bring development to the village, and for some time already elites had been insisting that the villagers were wrecking everything with their jealousy and their witchcraft (cf. Fisiy and Geschiere 2001). Yet I heard a new note: the elites now clearly voiced a conviction that *they* were the ones who had to put a stop to this—*they* had to make sure that one way or another witchcraft was again contained. My imprudent remark that many of them were themselves consulting *nganga* was swept aside: this was very different, for they were consulting *nganga* for healing and protection, not to kill and to destroy.
>
> The elites no longer saw it as a solution for themselves to simply maintain a safe distance, as their predecessors did in earlier decades. Clearly they realized that they now had to take their belonging more seriously. As said, there were important economic reasons for this, such as the prospect of running NGO development projects and, in this area, the possibility of participating in communal exploitation of the forest, opened up by the new forest law.[20] Political reasons were even more pressing: the regime now required anybody with political ambitions to bring in the votes of his or her constituency. Another new element was that the elites no longer put their faith in the state and its juridical ap-

paratus to deal with the witchcraft challenge. The dominant opinion was rather that they themselves had to do something. If they had to take their belonging to the village seriously, there was no escape anymore—one way or another they had to confront witchcraft themselves. There was also an emerging agreement that this solution had to be sought in the restoration of traditional—or rather neotraditional?—checks. The chiefs (who, as noted, in Makaland were mainly a colonial creation) had to take their responsibilities more seriously, and the *nganga* had to work for containing occult aggression as they had in the olden days. Only such supports within village society itself could restore the order so that elites could feel safe in their own village and keep their development initiatives going.

The parallels with the confrontations Piot describes for villages in north Togo as characteristic effects of the post–cold war crisis are striking (Piot 2010, chap. 5). There as well, urban elites were no longer satisfied with sending money home. On the contrary, they wanted to get involved directly in village affairs. Moreover, like the Maka elites, they no longer seemed intent on hiding behind the authoritarianism of the postcolonial state, which was undergoing dramatic transformations.[21] And to Togo elites as well, the main stumbling block became witchcraft. During a dramatic session Piot attended in 2006, when representatives of the urban elite came down to a village, the excitement over witchcraft ran so high that people finally decided to appoint a committee to look into the issue. A year later, the committee reported and, here as well, its solutions were mainly of a (neo)traditional tenor: it blamed, amongst other factors, "the neglect of local shrines" and "the lack of strong local diviners"—another telling illustration of how the neoliberal setting is very conducive for bringing back, in one way or another, "tradition" (Piot 2010:152, 159. 183n17).

Feymen and Their Magic Money: Beyond Kinship?

The neoliberal approach to development and the politics of belonging propagated by the regime brought a reaffirmation of the village as a crucial beacon for urbanites (even though the latter in practice have often no intention at all of going back there).[22] But younger Cameroonians were already experimenting with new conceptions of space, claiming a global citizenship. This was accompanied by concomitant changes in the scope attributed to witchcraft. For the Bum and Maka elites in the examples above, witchcraft still expressed itself within the grid of kinship and village. But there are now increasing rumors in Cameroon about more modern magicians who in their relentless pursuit of wealth transgress all customary boundaries, including the link between witchcraft and kinship.[23]

In the 1990s the country was in the grip of *feymen*, young men, briefly mentioned in chapter 1, who became experts in all sorts of confidence tricks—counterfeit money, loaded casino games, secondhand car trade, and many others shady practices—some of them with great success.[24] In those days my Cameroonian colleagues would complain, for instance, that it had become impossible for them to get a visa for Kenya because that country had been inundated by Cameroonian *feymen* who had had considerable success in cheating wealthy businessmen and politicians. Dominique Malaquais starts her pioneering article on the group by briefly summarizing the short but eventful career of Donatien Koagne, seen by many as the arch-*feyman*: after successfully cheating several African heads of state—the *feyman* expression is *faire un coup*, and their hallmark is that they look for new "fronts" all over the globe—this expert at cheating was arrested in Yemen, where he preferred to stay since the French secret service was after him and his *carnet*, which was undoubtedly bulging with important secrets. [25]

The rapid emergence of these *feymen* expressed new conceptions of space and distance. While in the 1970s the distance between village and city was still seen as a major rift, *feymen* claimed the world as their terrain. Yet for most Cameroonians they are also closely related to witchcraft. How did this increase of scale affect the imaginary of the occult? In his captivating study of these new global tricksters, Basile Ndjio (2006) shows that inside Cameroon they seemed to become a new role model. As in so many other African countries, the old role model of the *fonctionnaire*, who due to his school certificates had made a rapid career in public service, appeared to become outdated in the 1990s. With structural adjustment and the shrinking of the state, many lost their jobs or were relegated to lower positions. Government salaries became less and less attractive and were often not paid for months on end. The final blow was a 1994 devaluation by 50 percent of the franc CFA (the money of all former French colonies and until then strongly supported by France). In that year the purchasing power of official salaries was diminished by no less than 60 percent. Soon a new nickname began to circulate for the *fonctionnaire: long crayon* (long pencil—the implication being that the power of the pencil no longer did them any good). Ndjio shows that young people especially became ever more enthralled with completely different figures of success: the *feymen*, who were often illiterate and of very humble origins but by their courage and wit succeeded in outclassing the ponderous *fonctionnaires*. Ndjio tells of how young *feymen* would humiliate important *fonctionnaires* by visiting their nightclubs, ordering more expansive brands of champagne, and on top of that leaving with *la petite* who for that night had clearly been destined for the minister.

Yet Ndjio emphasizes also that people's perceptions of these young rascals were highly ambivalent. On the one hand they were admired and envied for their recklessness in cheating the rich, and even more for the carelessness with which they flaunted their riches. driving around in the most expensive cars, dressed in clothes of the most sophisticated brands, often renting an entire floor in a Hilton hotel, and so on. However, at the same time people were worried about the mysterious source of all this money. A recurrent trope in *feymen* stories—next to the descriptions of extravagant consumption—is the term *mekoagne money*, bewitched money (Ndjio 2006:62–68). Anyone who touched such money would end up badly, including the *feymen* themselves. Thus these *feymen* were linked to witchcraft in all sorts of ways. Yet Ndjio is very insistent that this was seen as a new form of witchcraft that transgressed the old boundaries, since it was no longer related to kinship. Indeed, people in Cameroon often cite the *feymen* to demonstrate that nowadays witchcraft is more frightening since the new witches seem capable of attacking *anybody*, not only their own relatives.

Feymen emphatically want to be global people, plying their tricks not only inside Cameroon but even more in the world at large: other African countries but also West Europe and the Gulf, and some have tried to open up new fronts in Southeast Asia and Eastern Europe. They seem to revel in ostentatiously transgressing the old rules of conduct. Especially in the early 1990s, many *feymen* showed a marked inclination for girlfriends from outside their own ethnic group, and, even more shocking, they refused to use their new wealth to build a house in their village of origin; on the contrary, they preferred to construct lavish villas in the city.[26] Their propensity for flaunting their wealth—dazzling cars and clothes, orgies of champagne in exclusive clubs—was even more of a transgression.

Most *feymen*, certainly the most successful ones, come from the Bamileke group. In some respects they follow in the footsteps of successful Bamileke entrepreneurs of earlier generations, who gave this group the reputation of having a special economic prowess.[27] Yet Ndjio (2006, chap 2) highlights these older entrepreneurs' deep disapproval of the youngsters' outrageous behavior. Parsimony and respect for hierarchies within the Bamileke order had always been the secret of entrepreneurs from this group. So how could the *feymen* flaunt their riches with such utter lack of respect for their chiefs and their elders? The rapid emergence of these *nouveaux riches* seemed to mark a breach of ethnic codes. Completely in line with this transgressive behavior, their deployment of occult forces seemed to go beyond kinship. The magic that was assumed to make their deceit so successful was deployed in novel contexts—often against foreigners, notably non-Cameroonians. Thus *feymen* played an important role in the globalization of representations of the occult.

Yet, as noted before, when one follows their life stories more closely—and Ndjio's study provides very rich case studies—kinship seems to return through the back door. Especially when witchcraft is involved, the cases ultimately refer to the intimate background of these new figures of success. Apparently the link between witchcraft and the intimacy of the family is not that easy to undo.

> One of Ndjio's most interesting case studies concerns Claude Le Parisien, a very successful *feyman*, to whom the author had special access (Ndjio 2006:75–89, 155–63). A dramatic switch in Le Parisien's career occurred when, in the municipal elections of 1996, he agreed to run for office for the government party, President Biya's CPDM. Of course, the party leadership asked him to seek votes within his own constituency—which in Cameroonian politics means his region of origin. So Le Parisien started his campaign by returning to "his" village. However, as soon as he arrived there things took a dramatic turn. Suddenly several of his helpers felt completely paralyzed and beset with a fierce panic. Soon the whole gang left in disarray. But this story had a sequel. By the time of the next elections (2002,this time for Parliament), Le Parisien seemed to have learned his lesson. He had established a regular presence in the village, divorced his Beti wife, and become engaged with a Bamileke girl from his own village; he had even begun to build a house there. This time the villagers were more receptive: Le Parisien was very well received, and he was elected without any problem.

The story fits into a wider context, since Le Parisien's reintegration into his village coincided with a determined offensive by the government to co-opt the more successful *feymen*. In the early 1990s politicians, especially those of the governing CPDM (the former one party that had succeeded in holding on to power), had seen the emergence of the *feymen* as a serious threat to their power. No wonder, in light of Ndjio's descriptions of how *feymen* reveled in openly humiliating higher politicians by offering rounds of expensive champagne and stealing their *filles*. However in the course of the 1990s the government clearly changed its policies, deciding to co-opt the *feymen* rather than continue to attack them. It created a special association for "young entrepreneurs" (ASSOJAC) and even offered some *feymen*—

like Le Parisien—important political positions in the party (Ndjio 2006, chap. 6). The main condition was that they be willing to use their riches and their personal contacts to support the party's political campaigns, especially during election times. In Cameroonian politics, this meant they had to return to the village and build up support there—another example of how the regime used issues of belonging to circumvent multipartyism in the marshaling of votes.

Indeed, one of the strongest points of Ndjio's analysis is that he shows with a wealth of ethnographic details how at least some *feymen* were thus recaptured by the joint action of village and state. In order to be received within the administrative-political elite they had to accept the basic rules of the game—that is, to go back to the village and use their support there for helping President Biya and his CPDM win elections. But this meant that the village now had leverage to impose its demands on these young rascals: construct a house there, marry a local girl, and so on. In several of Ndjio's cases, witchcraft acted as a powerful leverage for this. One can wonder which disciplining *dispositif* was more powerful—the state or the village (I would bet on the latter); but the combined force of the two was in any case most effective.

In certain respects this taming of the *feymen* had its tragic aspects. At first their wild energy seemed to make them break out of the straitjacket of ethnicity. But a red line through Ndjio's masterful study is how at least some of them were brought to heel by the politics of belonging that helped the Biya regime survive all opposition. However, Ndjio shows also that not all *feymen* permitted themselves to be co-opted within the existing parameters of power. Some refused to run for office and remained aloof to the village. They went even more global than before, leaving for new *fronts*—virgin territories for new *coups*.[28]

"Bushfallers," Transcontinental Migration, and the Stretching of Kinship/Witchcraft

The same paradox—witchcraft discourse being applied to novel forms of globalization and yet remaining related to the familiar realities of kinship and locality—comes to the fore with new and highly adventurous forms of transcontinental migration, a global drama in which African young men and women have become very visible as actors.

Around the turn of the twenty-first century a new term emerged in Cameroon, especially in the coastal areas where Pidgin English is the lingua franca: the word *bushfalling*, expressing a new and quite special view on transcontinental migration. *Bush* stands for Europe or any more affluent part of the world—in itself a surprising transformation, since calling someone a *bushman* used to be seen as insulting, mocking someone for coarse behavior. However, present-day *bushfallers* are persons who are top-notch since they have succeeded in getting out. The image seems to be of a hunter who ventures into the bush and "falls" into luck—that is, returns with rich booty. The term and its popularity aptly sum up the now increasingly general idea among young people, both men and women, that they must leave since there is no future in Cameroon. The risky ways people try to make the passage—through the desert, across the sea, paying important sums of money to "travel agents" of dubious reliability—betray deep disappointment with the situation at home.[29]

In a pioneering article, the Cameroonian journalist Julius Nyamkimah Fondong (2008) compares earlier generations of migrants from the Anglophone Northwest Province to present-day *bushfallers*. The earlier Anglophone emigrants mainly went to North America, hence their nickname in local pidgin, *America Wandas*. Fondong emphasizes the deep differences between them and the bushfallers. The *America Wandas* were well-educated young people who obtained scholarships to study abroad, where they were well received. They all planned to return after completing their studies: their diplomas would guarantee them well-paid jobs in public service. However, with the shrinking of the government after 1987 and the general context of crisis, many chose to remain in America and find a job there. Yet they maintained good relations with the family at home, sending regular remittances and participating in or even initiating developments projects at home. The profile of today's bushfallers is totally different. They are often only barely educated, and even if they have a diploma, they do not find it useful in their efforts to get out.[30] They mostly just take their chances without any contacts in the country they plan to reach (and if they succeed at all "crossing over," they often end up in another country than originally planned). Yet even in such cases, families will emphasize that they heavily contributed to their son's or daughter's migration project. The problem is, of course, that the adventurous nature of the bushfaller's undertaking makes it quite uncertain whether she or he will return or even maintain any links with the family at home. The metaphor of the hunter who ventures into the bush and returns with rich booty has a flipside: many stories about hunters tell how they found greener pastures in the bush and decided to found a new settlement there. So the family will redouble its efforts to bind the migrant and make sure that he or she will not "forget," even when at a considerable distance (Alpes 2011). More research on the ways in which families try to "bind" their bushfallers will be of great interest. But there are some indications.

In an earlier chapter I quoted a saying that was common in Anglophone Cameroon in the 1980s: "Witchcraft will not cross the water."[31] I emphasized that with the rapid intensification of oversea migration, people are no longer so sure of this. Consider, for instance, the stories told to the police by young Nigerian women who enter Europe, some as minors, and then quickly disappear into prostitution networks. In these stories *vodun* plays a central role—apparently it is supposed to "cross the ocean" without any problem. In the declarations of the Nigerian girls the trafficker and the family at home seem to be closely intertwined. The references to *vodun* raise questions, since the term seems to be less common in Nigeria (even in the country's western parts—it rather comes from Benin and Togo), but the girls are aware that it rings a bell with the European police (van Dijk 2001). The police often tend to see *vodun* oaths as key to understanding why the girls are so reluctant to speak up against their traffickers.[32] But the details of their stories about these oaths are complex. They refer to bodily parts (nails, tufts of hair, scratches of skin) assembled before departure to confirm the pact that the trafficker makes with the family. The girls clearly feel deeply worried about their family when they break the pact and talk to the police—also in the sense that the family will be angry with them (Taliani 2012; Andrikopoulos 2011). The Nigerian popular press adds other aspects to these stories. Articles with impressive photos of sumptuous houses and Mercedes cars explain that in certain villages in southwest Nigeria young women working in the sex industry in Europe have brought great wealth to their families.[33] Clearly the girls are under heavy pressure from the family at home. In this context also, the exact relation between traffickers and family in the stories about *vodun* oaths may require closer study.

A striking example of how families try to maintain their grip over even faraway migrants comes from Galia Sabar's study (2010) of Ghanaian Pentecostals in Tel Aviv and their recent fears. Especially after the start of the intifada in Palestine at the end of the 1980s, when Israeli employers had less opportunity to profit from cheap Palestinian labor, the number of African immigrants into Israel increased rapidly. From 1998 on, Sabar, an anthropologist at Tel Aviv University who worked in several parts of the African continent, could study African churches that Ghanaian immigrants created in Israel. In 2000 she noted a sudden change in her informants' stories. There were ever more references to witchcraft and evil spirits. One informant told her that "the witches are now in Israel. . . . The Jewish rabbis have stopped protecting us . . . they stop closing this area to protect it and then the bad witches from home enter. They come from home. . . . Our families from Ghana send them" (Sabar 2010:111, 127). Church members began complaining of vague, psychosomatic afflictions. Sabar sees a direct link to their increasingly difficult situation in Israel: police clamping down on immigrants, many losing their jobs or having to satisfy themselves with less well-paid ones.[34] People increasingly complained about their relatives at home, who did not seem to understand how difficult it was to gratify all their demands and keep sending money.[35] Many dreaded making calls home, and even more receiving phone calls from home. Of course it had become increasingly easy (and cheap) to call each other. But this seemed to augment the pressure. As another of Sabar's informants complained:

> I lost much of my work . . . but my family keeps calling . . . every week . . . they want more and more . . . when I say I have nothing they get angry with me . . . their voice is changing and they start talking badly to me . . . Now it is hard for me even to walk . . . I am praying to God to protect me from the bad spirits they send me. . . . They send very, very bad spirits on me. . . . Oh God, please help me.[36]

The wider importance of these examples will be clear. The general perception in affluent countries of the North of transcontinental immigrants as individual actors is highly misleading. Even if they did come by themselves, they are carrying a heavy load of expectations from the family members who claim to have "sent" them (even if they hardly contributed to the risky passage) and expect to profit from their success. This stretching of intimacy dramatically increases the scope of witchcraft fears.[37] Disappointing the family remains extremely dangerous, even if one is a great distance from home.[38]

Intimacy and New Distances

It may seem a long way from Eba—the Maka évolué who got in trouble by his return to the village—to feymen handling their "magic money" on a global scale or migrants in Europe who fear that the spirits from home may cross the ocean after all. Yet some elements of what the Maka call the djambe le ndjaw (witchcraft of the house) seem to develop along with this constant increase of scale. Despite growing distance, there seems to be a recurrent and somber refrain that people "at home"—even if this home has become an almost virtual one—have dangerous powers and must therefore be respected. The latter examples above indicate that the idea of home is stretching ever more: even phone calls across huge distances can re-create the intimacy that is both highly valued and feared. Yet there are also increasing signs that kinship relations become strained to a breaking point by new distances and even more by new inequalities. Some migrants insist that they have broken off all relations with the family at home—but it is quite frightening to stick to this when one falls ill in a new country.

The comparison with Freud might be interesting here. His solution for escaping from the tensions inherent in family life is the most individualistic conceivable: the analyst helps the individual through deep introspection and a highly personal journey to liberate himself from past traumas and thus leave behind the aggression hidden inside the family. In the cases above, people instead sought a solution by creating distance—which time and again proved to be of little avail. The Maka *évolués* in the 1970s still thought that withdrawing into city life could create enough distance. In those days the very possibility of making a life outside the village was completely novel, at least in Makaland, where an urban elite emerged quite late. No wonder that relations with "sons of the village" who lived in the city became a hotbed of witchcraft allusions and rumors. But in the following decades, such a distancing proved to be of less and less avail: city and village became interlocked in translocal witchcraft intrigues. In the 1980s people still could say that "witchcraft cannot cross the water." But Sabar's Ghanaians in Tel Aviv seem to accept now that "the rabbis can no longer close the area" and that spirits do cross the distance from the home country.

The constantly changing axis of distance and intimacy seems to be a red line in the dynamic metamorphosis of witchcraft imaginaries. From Eba's *nganga* simply telling him to go back to town in order to keep his distance from the village to the *feymen* with their *mekoagne money* or the rabbis who have to close their country against spirits from Ghana, constantly different ideas and figures emerge from witchcraft imaginaries. But behind this kaleidoscopic chaos emerge the changing contours of distance and intimacy as a leitmotif, inspiring a constant struggle to effect closure despite increasing mobility. Indeed, this tension between mobility and closure seems to be a basic one in witchcraft imaginaries in general. Central is the reference to special kinds of mobility—mostly nocturnal and therefore secret. Maka witches are said to fly away at night along "the cobwebs of the *djambe*," just as in European folklore witches are still depicted as flying on broomsticks; the *nganga* (healers) in Douala have to make a nocturnal journey to dangerous Mt. Kupe to fetch back the spirits of their clients, put to work there on invisible plantations (de Rosny 1981), just as the *Benandanti* in early modern Friuli (Italy) went off at night to battle with the magicians in another valley (Ginsburg 1966).

In view of this heavy stress on mobility, it is hardly surprising that the present-day witchcraft imaginary in Africa is so full of airplanes. In the short Cameroonian documentary on a child witch in a village near Yaoundé, mentioned before, the girl starts her revelations by announcing that the witches of her group take their victims away in their plane. When the old man whom she says is their pilot denies all this, she laughs in his face and insists: "Yesterday I sat next to him, his left hand was on the controls and his right hand between my breasts."[39] A *nganga* in a Maka village discovers a nightly landing spot behind someone's house and boasts about how difficult it was to destroy it. Among the Kabre (north Togo) a witches' coven sells its victims in order to have enough money to buy its own airplane (Piot 2010, chap. 5). Yet all this traveling remains anchored locally, in the intimacy of family and neighborhood: the planes are linked to specific landing spots behind the houses of a village, and the noise they make when landing makes people wake up; the *nganga* on his dangerous journey to distant Mt. Kupe needs the support of the client's relatives in order to be able to return safely. All these examples may reflect the recent globalization of witchcraft, but they seem to improvise also on an older view of witchcraft as the betrayal of kinship—though now on a dazzling scale. A basic tendency of kinship/family may be to create a more or less closed community, while witchcraft constitutes a secret opening through which the community's life force is drained—flowing away to wider horizons. Elsewhere I argued that there is a striking convergence with people's experience of the growing impact of the market on local communities. The often quite abrupt penetration of the world market in many parts of the African continent also brought a drain of life force in the most literal sense: slave trade, colonial forced labor, the attraction of wage labor elsewhere. No wonder witchcraft offers such a tempting discourse for trying to deal with modern changes (see Geschiere 2000:25 and 2011).

✱

The recent wave of anthropological studies on this topic offers telling examples of this inherent tension between mobility and local rootedness. In one of the more historical monographs of the new harvest of witchcraft studies on Africa, Isak Niehaus shows how the increase of migrant labor in the South African Lowveld, especially since the 1950s, has been accompanied by new images of witchcraft: the *tolokotsi*, male and female baboonlike creatures with weird sexual powers over their victims; the *manlambo*, a snake that brings wealth but feeds on the owners' relatives; the night train that does not make a sound but takes people to unknown destinations (2001:50, 56, 72). Niehaus's overview of witchcraft cases—going back to 1943(!)—shows that accusations used to focus on conjugal relations and, especially after 1960, when "betterment schemes" for the new Bantustans imposed villagization, on neighbors (chap. 5). But in his second book (Niehaus 2012) he points to increasing accusations against cognates, especially against the father, who is becoming the object of fierce jealousy in a context of deindustrialization. In the present setting, younger people have diminished chances to find reliable jobs in the mines and elsewhere. Fathers have often more experience of the wider world than their sons, and this shrinking of horizons goes with an inward turning of witchcraft accusations, now affecting patrilineal descent, the very core of the family in many African contexts.[40]

Harry West's monograph (2005) on the Mueda plateau in North Mozambique is equally historical in its outlook but deals with very different sequences. West vividly shows how Muedans' *uwavi* imaginary—as dynamic and fluid as the Maka *djambe*—allowed the people to confront particularly dramatic transitions: from very intensive Portuguese colonialism through Frelimo's scientific socialism to an equally ideological neoliberalism. The severity of socialism had particularly confusing implications: on the one hand a stern refusal by the regime of any idea of occult powers, on the other a more pragmatic but very firm conviction that sorcery was out of hand. *Uwavi* (sorcery) always "festered in the intimate spaces among kin," but under socialism people were forced to live together in larger "modern" villages. According to the elders, this meant that "the sorcerers of different matrilineages danced together at night in the village center." And no "father" was capable of controlling this turmoil (West 2005:178–79). Later, neoliberalism in Mozambique meant—as elsewhere, yet still somewhat surprising—determined efforts to bring back "tradition," here propagated as an ostentatious break with socialism. But many people interpret such a return in terms of *uwavi*, meaning that the new big men—politicians and businessmen—neglect the "governance of the night" for the sorcery of self-enrichment (248).

James Smith's *Bewitching Development* (2008) deals with surprising articulations of neoliberal development and witchcraft in the Taita hills of southeastern Kenya. For Smith, changing witchcraft images play a crucial role in people's appropriation of development. The very idea of development may seem outdated to some Western intellectuals, but Smith emphasizes that it is still cherished by the Taita through local reinterpretations. Central in this are new "spatiotemporal distinctions" within witchcraft imaginary. The Taita refer not only to African but also to Arabic and even American witchcraft. Within African witchcraft people distinguish between "more and less advanced forms," but both mainly affect kin and neighbors—this in contrast to the more recently imported Arabic and American forms (Smith 2008:99–101).

In all of these examples a recurrent element seems to be the by now familiar but still gruesome notion that witches have to take their turn in offering close ones (relatives, neighbors) to their nightly companions. As Clifton Crais formulates it so well in his study of the Eastern Cape (South Africa), *Politics of Evil*: "Witches are especially evil because they use some intimate knowledge of their victims to sow tragedy, *as if those who know us best are most capable of doing harm*" (Crais 2002:4, emphasis added).[41] Madumo, the hero of Adam Ashforth's book on Soweto ("a story, particular and personal, drawn from life," 2000:vii), endures a true ordeal that shows how resilient the link with kinship can be, even in places like Johannesburg townships, where it has become almost "virtual." Plagued by constant fears and ailments, Madumo visits a *sangoma*, who tells him his bewitchment comes from ancestors who are angry about his neglect. But it turns out to be very difficult to locate these ancestors. Like many South African urbanites, Madumo has lost trace of his kin, who are scattered all over the country. In the end he quite arbitrarily goes to a village where some of his father's relatives are supposed to live. He arrives, and the villagers are indeed eager to organize a big party for the ancestors—of course at Madumo's expense. But until the very end of the book it remains unclear whether he has tried to reconcile the right ancestors (see also Ashforth's monograph, 2005). As Bond and Ciekawy conclude in the introduction to their 2002 collection *Witchcraft Dialogues*: "[witchcraft] . . . is liberated from its parochial moorings," yet it "remains embedded in kinship and community" (2001:324).

There is a powerful logic here that keeps cropping up with different implications. The story of the witch as martyr, sacrificing him- or herself, cited above as a most powerful expression of the link between witchcraft and kinship among the Maka, comes back in many gradations elsewhere. Simon Bockie records an account from his own grandfather from Lower Congo, who was reminiscing about his days as a *ndoki* (witch):

When no family volunteers to provide a victim, we draw lots. . . . However my most frustrating experience as *ndoki* comes when I have no alternative but to provide my closest relative such as son, daughter, brother, sister, or parent. Doubtless this is the most devastating period for any *ndoki*. There are those who decline to comply with the demand, but by doing so they endanger their own lives. Therefore we appreciate a *ndoki* (but by no means do we encourage him) who sacrifices his own life in order to save that of his beloved kin. (1993:65)[42]

Elsewhere this logic is supposed to have different consequences. Birgit Meyer (oral communication) mentions that among the Ewe in southeastern Ghana, known throughout the country for their secret powers, a witch who no longer can offer a relative (or no longer wants to do this) is believed to go mad. Isak Niehaus (oral communication) cites cases from the South African Lowveld in which, confronted with a similar dilemma, people are supposed to have committed suicide to save their kin. But everywhere the merciless logic seems to prevail that witches have to go on sacrificing their kin (van Binsbergen 2001:243).

Striking is that this representation is so easily commodified: witches are supposed to "sell" their kin, usually to gain access to new forms of wealth. In a perverse way these rumors seemed to express efforts to retain the intimacy of the local group in a context of constantly increasing mobility and new opportunities for enrichment. Of course there is good reason to remain wary of romanticizing witchcraft in the past as having been more in equilibrium—a recurrent tendency that marks witchcraft studies all over the world. Yet it is clear that the coming in of new and often highly coveted commodities has given new momentum to witchcraft imagination.[43] Commodification may seem to be opposed to intimacy, but in practice it seems to trigger a search for new intimacies.

Such re-creating of intimacy amidst ever-intensifying mobility generates new challenges. It raises to a new level the issue of trust in expanding and uncertain settings. If intimacy is capable of covering ever greater distances—which makes futile any hope of employing new technologies to create physical distance and find definitive protection against its dangerous implications (by leaving for the city, going overseas, or whatever)—how then can trust be established? It is tempting to return here to Freud's challenging analysis of how *das Heimliche* (the homely) can turn into its very opposite, *das Unheimliche* (the uncanny). For him the answer was repression, and the solution was to return to these repressed childhood memories that became so *unheimlich* when they turned up much later and clearly out of place. The notion of repression might need a further thinking through to make it relevant for the witchcraft conundrum. But Freud's emphasis on things from home becoming *unheimlich* when they turn up "out of place" speaks most directly to the the disarray of persons described above who thought they had created distance—the Maka *évolués* who believed themselves safe in the city, the *feymen* who tried to go global, the migrants overseas—but met *das Heimliche* in unexpected forms and settings nonetheless. A recurrent element is noteworthy: in all these circumstances witchcraft rumors and accusations turned on the vital question of how to come to terms with new inequalities, and thus with jealousy within the group taking on unprecedented range and expression. The dynamics of witchcraft notions in articulation with the increase of scale of intimate relations—summoning up ever new images of inherent dangers—require a search for new ways of establishing trust.

3

TO TRUST A WITCH

THIS CHAPTER CONCERNS the third pole of this book's conceptual triangle: trust. In the prologue I noted that lately this concept has been as much in vogue in the social sciences as intimacy, but that in this case as well, its popularity has not resulted in more clarity. Below I will make some further introductory comments on recent debates on the notion of trust, elaborating on ideas set out in chapter 1. Then I will try to follow, along similar lines as in the preceding chapter, different historical trajectories in the articulation of trust with witchcraft and intimacy on the basis of examples from my Maka research and from other African settings.

Trust: Rational, Ontological, or Historical?

It is hardly surprising that the notion of trust has experienced a new boost of life since the 1990s. This was the time of an unprecedented flowering of "management studies," a new shoot of organization sociology which used "trust" as a sort of magical wand. Moreover, the growing insecurities of capitalism as a supposedly rational system—the increasing dominance of finance capitalism, which according to some rapidly deteriorated into a kind of "casino capitalism"[1]—seemed to require an ever wider stretching of current forms of trust—in hindsight, after the dramatic collapse of 2008–9, a clear overstretching. Urgent reasons, even for economists, to take the concept of trust seriously.[2]

The challenge of the concept in these present-day contexts will be clear: it marks the limits of the rational choice approach so dear to economics and related disciplines. As a long line of thinkers from Georg Simmel through Niklas Luhmann, Herbert Frankel, and Anthony Giddens has highlighted, trust is based on a complex mixture of knowledge and uncertainty (Simmel's *Wissen und Nicht-wissen*), but it always also contains an element of affect that gives it—even in situations of very weak knowledge—particular force, possibly stronger than purely rational choice would. Here one therefore has to enter a zone where it becomes inevitable to include culture, affect, emotion, or morality—whatever term one prefers—in the analysis in one way or another.[3] For many of the leading authors in trust studies, this seems to result in uncomfortable compromises.[4] Yet as Guido Möllering notes in the seminal article (2001) quoted above, the impact of rational choice remains strong: there is a constant tendency in trust studies to return to a mapping of "good reasons" as the main strategy to understand why in a given situation people do, or do not, trust.

It is of particular interest therefore that, as noted above, Georg Simmel emphasized so strongly—in both his study of money and his essay on secret societies—the key role in trust relations of a "further element" beyond knowledge and calculation. Even more striking is his term for this mysterious element: he called it *Glauben*, equating it to religious faith.[5] For Simmel, trust had to be understood first of all as combining sound reasons with faith. We saw as well that Möllering condenses this "further element" into the notion of a "suspension" (*Aufhebung*) of doubt. He speaks also of "a leap over the gorge" that separates "the land of interpretation" from "the land of expectation": "despite precarious knowledge and uncertain interpretation this suspension lifts a person by a 'mental leap' into the land of firm expectation (whether positive or negative)" (Möllering 2001:412–14).[6]

However, as noted earlier, Simmel's approach to trust in terms of a leap of faith is not only a good cure for rational choice addicts when they have to understand, for instance, the vagaries of casino capitalism. It may be as salutary for anthropologists, many of whom still have a tendency to entrench themselves in a bastion of gift-giving and reciprocity when addressing trust in kinship contexts. It is important not to underestimate the continuing power of such a view despite all criticisms. Especially noteworthy is the self-evidence this paradisiacal view of some sort of pristine situation still has outside the discipline building on a commonsense assumption that kinship is synonymous with trust. This assumption returns, for instance, even in the work of a sophisticated author with a keen historical sense like Charles Tilly. In his book *Trust and Rule* (2005), kinship figures as some sort of primal example of trust networks.[7] This may be understandable in the context of Tilly's large-scale historical project, which aims at understanding the global processes through which restricted networks of trust—"kinlike solidarity"—were integrated into broader "public politics" (Tilly 2005:7–9). Yet the confidence with which he declares that "participants in kinship and other trust networks usually take them for granted" is striking (Tilly 2005:6). This runs exactly counter to the obsession in many parts of Africa (and elsewhere) with witchcraft as festering within the family. And even in Tilly's own society there are such long traditions of violent strife and deep hatred *within* the family that the premise of kinship as the cradle of trust requires nuancing.[8]

These are not mere academic quibbles. Consider, for instance, the central role this image of the family as a safe haven of solidarity and trust continues to play in development sociology, notably for Africa. In the 1980s Goran Hyden's notion of an "economy of affection" that allowed Africa's "uncaptured peasantry" to take an "exit option" into the "economy of affection" was hailed by many as the key to understanding Africa's crisis[9] (Hyden 1980; see also Geschiere 1984 for an early critique). And the role family and village economy continue to play in many development schemes for the continent indicates that neoliberal experts as well still tend to see the sector as some sort of safe refuge—indeed, an economy where only affection reigns. The combination of a firm belief in the blessings of the market with an assumption of a community still dominated by reciprocity can only lead to a precariously split position.

A view of trust as an inherently uncertain issue because of the close link between intimacy and witchcraft can help to bridge such apparent discontinuities. It is precisely the permanent struggle over trust—never an ontological given, not even in "primitive" kinship societies—that links the sphere of (supposed) reciprocity to the market, the local to the global, or the traditional to the modern. In this sense Simmel's emphasis on a "leap of trust" seems to be highly relevant for anthropological studies as well. A great advantage of Simmel's approach is, moreover, that—like Freud on "the Uncanny"—he suggests concrete questions rather than fixed answers; these questions can be addressed ethnographically and historically in order to tackle the complicated knot of witchcraft, intimacy, and trust. When are people willing to suspend their doubts in the face of omnipresent danger? What encourages such a "leap of faith," and when it is bound to fail? In the rest of this chapter I propose to follow such questions for the Maka and other societies discussed in chapter 2. A leading question there was how people cope with new distances in space, and even more with new and much steeper inequalities. Here I will focus on how this increase in scale, both spatially and socially, puts the issue of trust to a major test: can the scope of trust-making be expanded concomitantly with the extension of "the house" over new distances and new inequalities?

Trust and Doubt: Recourse to the *Nganga* (Healer)

In the 1970s the obvious option for my Maka friends—as for most Cameroonians—in a case of growing distrust within "the house" was to visit the *nganga* (healer). This is logical, since such healers are supposed to be experts at "seeing" what the witches are plotting. They all acquired a "second pair of eyes" (*miesj meba*) as the first step in their laborious initiation. This allows them to "surprise" these evildoers and force them to lift their spell. All this is supposed to make the *nganga* experts at reconciling tensions within the family. Compare the following account.

A few weeks after I had started my fieldwork in "my" Maka village, I heard that Mbili was ill. I had taken quite a liking to him because of the way he played his guitar and sang little songs he heard on the radio. Clearly he wanted to be "modern" in some artistic way. *Mbili*, "arrow," was his nickname because of his impressive rushes on the football field, and he loved to be called by it. The next day people said he was still ill, so I decided to go and see how he was doing. But on the way to his family's house we met Mendouga, who had been pointed out to me already several times as the greatest *nganga* of the whole district. She was accompanied, as always, by her dog—a yellowish hairy animal, quite friendly—and a little boy. She seemed quite happy to see us— earlier on she had tried to contact the "new *ntangue* [white man]" of the village. So we walked down together, Mendouga explaining to me with her somewhat mocking smile that Mbili's people had called her in to "resolve things." When we got to the house—a rambling complex of poto-poto houses[10] and kitchens, some of them in a state of approaching collapse—Mendouga was offered a big rooster. She told the little boy who accompanied her to hold the animal. Then we entered Mbili's room. Clearly Mendouga had no problems with my going in with her.

Mbili was in bed, looking a bit weak and upset. She sat down at his bedside, held his hand, and stroked his head. Then she started to talk in a low voice. The main message seemed to be that everything was going to be all right. But there was also a note of warning: she had "seen" that some people were plotting evil things, but they should know now that she had spotted them so they had better turn back. Clearly the warning was addressed to "someone" inside the house, but no further details were given. After delivering this warning, Mendouga chuckled—by now I had come to dread her giggling—and stood up to leave. On the way out she explained to me that this was the way to put an end to evil: now the witches would think twice, because they knew that she would be after them if they did not refrain from further mischief. After one more giggle—clearly very satisfied that I had seen her demonstration of good intentions—she left with her dog, the boy running after her, dragging the protesting rooster by the neck.

This little sketch gives an image of how a healer should behave. *Nganga* can be men or women. They are supposed to have learned their secrets through a long initiation with the "professor" who taught them to "see" (the famous second pair of eyes) and also to "tie up the witches" and rob their *djambe* (witchcraft) of its power.[11] Thus *nganga* can nip dangerous threats in the bud and reestablish trust within a family that risks being torn by hatred and jealousy. But this, of course, depends on people's willingness to trust the *nganga*. I soon was to understand that precisely this is a big issue.

Ambiguities of the *Nganga*

Mendouga's small performance in my presence—it was evident that she welcomed the opportunity to show me that any nasty rumors about her were unfounded—indicated why people should trust a *nganga*: she had the capacity to "see." The reputation of her "professor" (to whom she kept referring without ever specifying his identity) should further guarantee that she had "the power." All this impressed the villagers. Yet to the Maka it is self-evident that the *nganga* themselves must be deeply involved in the very *djambe* they are supposed to combat. How else could they be able to heal? In the beginning I was a bit disconcerted that my friends would insist with such assurance that "of course" a *nganga* like Mendouga was a *djin-djamb* (someone who has the *djambe*—that is, a witch). A big *nganga* of her caliber would actually have a *djambe* that "beats all records." And indeed, the other *nganga* I was to talk to later all confirmed that their "professor" had helped them to develop the *djambe* in their belly in order to give them exceptional powers. But they would always add that of course the professor had bound them with heavy oaths—the *itsi* (interdictions) that will kill someone immediately if she or he transgresses them—to use their powers only to heal and never to kill. However, the Maka are never sure of that. After all, a *djambe* is a *djambe*, and its basic instinct is to betray and kill people. There are, indeed, persistent rumors (as noted above) that *nganga* have to offer a close relative to their professor in order to fulfill their initiation. On top of that there are all sorts of sayings that an ambitious pupil will end up killing his *nganga*-professor. This is why a pupil always has to go away once his or her initiation has been completed.[12]

To put it more succinctly, one has to kill in order to be able to heal. *Nganga* are deeply respected as long as they seem to have the power, but they are at the same time seen as highly dangerous persons who can at any time direct their formidable power against you. This vicious circle—the main protection against the *djambe* is to be sought in the very field of this *djambe* itself—makes any form of trust highly uncertain and situational. The *nganga* can heal and restore trust only if people are willing to trust him or her. But complete trust is very difficult, since the *nganga* are such ambiguous and potentially dangerous figures. It is on this point—central to the conundrum of witchcraft, intimacy, and trust—that my earlier book on witchcraft (Geschiere 1997) has been severely criticized.[13] For instance, the French-Togolese political scientist Comi Toulabor—whose publications on humor as the flipside of West African politics I greatly value—reproached me sternly for not making a clear distinction between the "witch" and the "magician" (the first being unequivocally evil, the second capable to use his or her special powers only in a more positive way—Toulabor 1999). John Hund (now at the University of the North in South Africa) attacked me even more forcefully, making me an outstanding example of the fact that "academic writers are . . . unfortunately some of the worst perpetrators of confusion." He is clearly shocked that I repeated my informants' view of the *nganga* as a kind of super-witch who can heal only by using the same powers as witches do. For Hund this is an "overwhelming misunderstanding" (Hund 2000:369–70). He insists instead that healers (for him especially the *sangoma* of South Africa) should be radically kept distinct from witches.

Of course the whole witchcraft conundrum would be a lot easier to solve if such a separation could be applied so simply. The problem is, again, the subversive character of witchcraft discourse, which easily erodes all such nice conceptual distinctions—in Africa just as elsewhere in the world.[14] It is clear that there are wide differences in how African societies view central actors in the occult domain—the healers, the chiefs—and to what extent they try to separate these leaders from the hidden powers. It is also true that in the forest societies in Cameroon where I did my main fieldwork, the central notions (*djambe* among the Maka and *evu* among the Beti) are extremely broad and fluid, covering a wide array of expressions of the occult, from highly negative to fairly positive ones—*djambe/evu* being potentially lethal but also essential for healing, exercising authority, or accumulating wealth. Elsewhere in Cameroon, for instance in the more hierarchical societies of the country's western highlands (Bamileke, Bamenda), there is a determined effort to compartmentalize the sphere of the occult through terminological distinctions between more negative and more positive forms. In these societies the chief may be associated with occult powers, but he is normally rigidly separated from the darker manifestations of these powers. However, such distinctions are always precarious and never self-evident. Maintaining them against the inherent fluidity of any discourse on the occult seems to require a constant struggle. For instance, in the 1990s, when many chiefs from the Cameroonian highlands got into trouble with their subjects for continuing to support the hated regime of President Biya, people were quick to accuse them of being real witches, set fire to their palaces, and damage their Pajeros—all things that had been assumed to be impossible only a few years before, but that were now seen as legitimate since the chiefs had obviously strayed off the right path and begun making alliances with the witches.

There are also good reasons to take the distinctions that are often emphasized in, for instance, the literature on South Africa between witch and *sangoma*—or between the *sangoma* as a "priest-diviner" and the *inyanga* as his disreputable colleague—not too easily for granted. Even Hund (2000:373) emphasizes that they all use "the same occult forces," but he insists that there is an "ontological" difference. One can sympathize with his effort to distinguish the *sangoma* as a reliable ally in these dark struggles. But who makes this "ontological difference" between actors that are so closely involved with the same forces? And how can such a distinction be maintained in practice? Widely different views of the *sangoma* pertain in daily life. In the famous Ralushai report (1996) on the bloody witch hunts unleashed by young men who called themselves "ANC comrades" during the last years of the Apartheid regime in Transvaal, people say quite nasty things about *sangoma* ("with a lust for blood and easy money," 268). Indeed, the young comrades put the healers in an impossible bind. They were the first to be suspected of being involved with the horrible *muti* murders (the practice of maiming victims, especially children—preferably while still alive—in order to use their vital organs for "medicine"). Often the healers could escape being lynched in their turn only if they were willing to use their powers to "smell out" other witches. Thus the notorious diviner Ramaredi Shaba in Sekhukuneland would give drugs to the comrades and then install a big screen—which she called "African Television"—on which the dazed comrades would recognize the faces of "witches" who had to be necklaced (Delius 1996:195).[15]

Rather than taking such terminological distinctions—between witch and *sangoma*, or between "bona-fide" and "mala-fide" healers—as givens, the question might be how exactly such compartmentalization is maintained, through which struggles, and by what means. For it is obvious that maintaining such distinctions will always entail a precarious struggle against the blurring tenor of discourses on the occult. And, as noted, this subversive charge, undermining any clear-cut distinction between good and evil, may be the secret behind the impressive resilience of these discourses in the face of modern changes.[16]

In Cameroon, examples abound of this constant struggle against such ambiguities. The efforts by Father Eric de Rosny to involve his *nganga* friends in a kind of united front against *la sorcellerie* can serve as a striking example. De Rosny's admirable career was referred to above. He arrived in the 1950s as priest in Douala. In the 1960s he started his initiation as a *nganga*. His courageous explorations while working both as a priest and as a *nganga* are most vividly described in his *Les yeux de ma chèvre* (1981; see also de Rosny 1992).[17] One of the strong points of his books—and more generally of his work in Cameroon—is that he takes people's worries about rampant witchcraft most seriously. He argues that a common front is necessary against this threat—not only a judicial offensive but a collaboration of judicial authorities with theologians, psychiatrists, medical doctors, botanists, and, not in the last place, *nganga*. Thus already in the 1990s he founded a working group with people in all these fields—a very enthusiastic group that regularly meets and in which *nganga* work closely with highly trained scientists.

In 2005, de Rosny organized a large-scale conference at the Catholic University of Central Africa (Yaoundé), called Justice et Sorcellerie, that became a true event. Almost one thousand people turned up to listen to a medley of speakers—anthropologists, theologians, but also people from the Ministry of Justice, judges, lawyers, and *nganga*. De Rosny's group was very present throughout the meeting. Yet time and again this raised particular problems of terminology. De Rosny set great value on the distinction between *sorcier* (witch) and *contre-sorcier* (healer), arguing that it is only on the basis of such distinction that it may be possible to overcome doubts about the *nganga* and involve them in a positive way in the struggle against witchcraft.[18] But regularly one of his *nganga*, when taking the floor during the conference, would introduce himself as Mr. So-and-so, *sorcier* (which is how *nganga* normally introduce themselves, especially in the forest region). Some healers quickly corrected themselves and said *contre-sorcier*, but others did not even bother.

When an older and very experienced *nganga* was asked after his presentation how he managed to keep the witches at bay, his reply was revealing: "Eh bien, je retourne le mal" (Well, I send the evil back).[19] This reflects the current idea that *nganga* condense their powers in a "mirror," which they use not only to shield their clients but also to reflect any evil back to the witch from whom it came. *Retourner le mal* means that the witch will be attacked by his or her own evil. This expression also illustrates most graphically the ambiguity of the *nganga* position. To the client who asks for protection, the *nganga* is of course a healer. But the supposed witch against whom all sorts of evil is released will protest that the *nganga* himself is an evil witch attacking innocent people in order to earn his fee.[20]

It might be tempting to ascribe such ambiguities to new developments around the *nganga*—notably the impact of money and new opportunities for enrichment. Indeed, below we will see that the *nganga* profession has been deeply affected by the wave of consumerism that has overrun post-colonial Africa (see also Tonda 2005). But people's preoccupation—not to say fascination—with *nganga* treachery seems to have a very long history. In my research the theme emerged quite unexpectedly from my efforts to get some idea of the forms of organization that shaped Maka society before the colonial conquest (1905–10). The elders often responded to my questions with dramatic stories, of an epic quality, about the old warlords—how they confused their opponents with spectacular magical tricks. No wonder *nganga* played a key role in these stories. The most famous warlord was Nkal Selek, who towards the end of the nineteenth century led his people, the Mvang, out of servitude to the Yebekolo and then went east to terrorize the Maka villages on the north side of the Nyong River. Many elders told me stories about Nkal Selek's exploits, but the best version came from the old chief of Zoumé, on the border between what are now the land of the Maka and that of the Mvang. This tale is of special interest here since it centers on the treacherous role of a *nganga*, an old woman, who helped Nkal Selek to get the better of his patron (or even "father") Evina, the cruel Yebekolo chief.

> The full version of the story is to be found in Geschiere 1997. Here a short overview of the elements of special interest to the entanglement of intimacy, witchcraft, and (dis)trust must suffice. Recurrent tropes in the old chief's story were Nkal Selek's beauty ("his hands were white like yours, Pierre"—that is, me) and his arrogance. All the men of Nkal's family were killed when Evina and his Yebekolo overran their village. But Evina looked at Nkal and his brother Viang, saw how beautiful they were, and said: "No, I am not going to kill these boys; they will be my *boane mpanze* [children of the house, now mostly translated 'pages']." Nkal became Evina's special favorite. The latter even took Nkal along on what would turn out to be a fatal expedition for Evina himself: a search for the powerful *bubuwa* (war medicine) that an old woman in the land of the Mpele was supposed to have.
>
> As the Zoume chief told me:

They marched for a long time through the forest: *via, via, via.* Finally they found the woman sitting in front of an old hut. She was alone; her man had died. She sat there, dirty and hungry since no one looked after her. But she had the basket with *bubuwa* that her husband had left her. The basket was full—full of *bubuwa.*

The old woman saw them coming. She said, "No, don't come further, you beautiful men. I am too dirty. What did I do that you come to see me in this state? My husband is dead. He left me to die here as well. You have come to kill me? Let me wait here for my death by myself."

But Evina said, "Mother."

She asked, "What is this? Am I your mother?"

He said, "We did not come to kill you, we came to see you."

She refused. "Do you want to see me like this, all dirty?"

But he insisted, "If you are dirty, I feel dirty as well. It is you who brought me into this world."

She still did not trust him: "If it is like this, if you are my son, don't you see my shame? Don't you see my misery? Let me see what you can do."

The Zoumé chief then described in detail what Evina did for her: his pages built her a house, his women bathed and powdered her skin, they prepared food and drink for her. Finally she relented and showed Evina the basket with *bubuwa.* Then she spoke the magical formula: "Give me."

Evina told Nkal to go quickly to the neighboring village and collect eight boys and eight girls. Nkal ran off through the forest (*bou, bou, bou*) and collected ten boys and ten girls. Just before arriving at the woman's place he hid two boys and two girls in the bush along the path. Evina offered the eight boys and girls to the old woman, and she accepted. She made Evina the *bubuwa* as promised.

But as the Zoumé chief added with a mischievous smile: "Yet Nkal sat through all this. He may have been a slave, but this allowed him to see what happened."

On the way back, Evina preferred to spend the night with his crowd in the next village. But Nkal got up in the middle of night. He said to himself, "*Itombang* [cry of rage]! Will I return empty-handed? This will not happen. I will go back to see the old woman."

He went to try his luck. (It is like you, Pierre: you come to us and then you leave, taking the stories we tell you with you.)

Nkal found the woman, who was surprised: "Young man, why do you come back? You were here already with your father."

He said, "That is true, but I came back. *Sague me dombe* [make me the war]—for me also."

She replied, "But I did make the war already for you and your father."

But he refused. "No, you did it for my father. I want you to do it for me."

She said, "*Ho.* Is it like this?"

"Yes, it is like this. Don't talk to me anymore, just make me the war now. It is me, Nkal Selek, who speaks to you."

The woman accepted. She went again through her ritual preparations with the basket, burning little sticks of bamboo; then she placed the horns and her basket in front of him, and again uttered the key formula: "So give me."

Nkal produced the two boys and two girls he had hidden in the bush.

But she was not satisfied, "You have to add."

Then Nkal said, "I give you my father Evina."

After this crucial moment, the chief concluded the story briskly:

The woman accepted, gave Nkal her blessing with saliva, and told him, "Go, the war will be yours."

Nkal became a great warrior. He went from left to right, destroying all the villages. But Evina became ever weaker and stayed at home. Throughout the region people cried Nkal's name. Sometime later, death took Evina.

This old story—in the 1970s still the main epos in this region because of the fearful memory of Nkal Selek—confirms many of the elements discussed above. First of all, the close link of witchcraft with intimacy: the danger for Evina came from close by. But it should be noted that then already intimacy proved to be quite elastic. Evina had killed Nkal's family, but—since he had adopted him subsequently as his favorite page—their relation was apparently considered so intimate that both the old woman and Nkal himself felt he could sacrifice Evina as his "father." The most glaring element is the treachery of the old *nganga*—first she accepted Evina as her son, since she was moved by all he had been doing for her (new house, staff of servants), but then she was ready to betray him first chance she got. Clearly her *djambe* was so greedy that it could not resist getting hold of a new victim. The most powerful lesson of the story as a whole is of course that in witchcraft nothing is certain: it seemed to offer Evina unparalleled power, but ultimately it became the cause of his weakening and untimely death.

There is a striking parallel here with the rise and fall of Raymond Malouma, the all-powerful politician in Makaland during the 1970s. In the early 1970s all my friends agreed that there was a hidden cause behind Malouma's victories over his many rivals in the region and his meteoric rise to the very top of national politics (for some time he was even a member of the Bureau politique national): he had used his money to buy the support of the most powerful *nganga*, deep in the forest beyond Lomie. Typically, nobody could disclose the identity of this *nganga*—people really did not seem to know his name—but everybody agreed about his special power. The end of Malouma's career came as abruptly as his rise: in 1981 he was sacked from all his positions and went into hiding. Clearly he had fallen in disgrace with the leadership of the one party. Nobody in the region knew why—though there were many speculations—but again everybody agreed about the "real" reason: his own *nganga* had "sold" him. This is a recurrent pattern in people's speculations about power and the *djambe*: its specialists, like the *nganga*, can give people enormous power, but sooner or later they will betray them in the most heinous ways.

In other respects also the role of the *nganga* is marked by great uncertainties that make the vital issue of trust most precarious. A related problem is that one is never sure whether *nganga* still have their special power. There are many examples of how it can suddenly break down.

A spectacular example of this was Mendouga's sudden fall when defeated by the frightening *gbati*. As said, when I arrived in Makaland in the beginning of 1971, Mendouga's reputation as the most powerful *nganga* of the district seemed unassailable. People were especially impressed that she seemed to have prestigious *fonctionnaires* (*sous-préfets* and even the *préfet* himself) among her clientele: as said, regularly a big black Mercedes would be seen parked in front of her modest house. Then people would whisper that, again, one of the *Grands* had come to ask for her help against his political rivals. Yet her reputation collapsed as abruptly as the star of a rival *nganga* went up.

When I arrived, excited rumors were already circulating about a new form of witchcraft, the *gbati*, that had spread suddenly from the Northwest (land of the Mvele).[21] Its particularity was that only young boys who had not yet slept with a woman could hold it in their belly. Normally the elders rule the roost in the occult world, but with the *gbati* young boys would suddenly be stronger! No wonder this new form of the *djambe* raised great fears. After a few months, things came to a crisis in the village where I lived, two villages down the road from Mendouga's village. A group of young boys started to hint that they indeed did have the *gbati*. They had attacked several women of their families—stopping the water on their fires from boiling and the food from cooking, making the women's fields and maybe even their wombs infertile, and the like.[22] Moreover, there were rumors that they had a list of people they planned to kill. So the village chiefs and his elders decided to invoke Mendouga's help. After all, she had told everybody that she had done a course with a great *nganga* in the land of the Mvele to be ready when the *gbati* would enter her area. A big palaver was organized where Mendouga would publicly exorcise the boys' *gbati*.

However, things took an unexpected turn. As Mendouga interrogated the boys, her dog suddenly started to bark ferociously. She herself turned very pale and seemed to collapse on the spot. But she pulled herself together and rushed off with the dog. Later she explained to me that her dog had warned her. Apparently she had not been enough on her guard; maybe she had underrated how dangerous these young boys were. This meant she had not foreseen their sudden attack (of course an invisible one; other people had not seen anything). They had almost "bound" her, but she was saved by the dog. She was so weakened, though, by this treacherous attack that all she could do was leave immediately; else she would have certainly succumbed to them. The villagers mainly noted that she had already been paid (2,000 CFA—about $7) but seemed unwilling to return that money despite her blatant failure. Later on, a *nganga* from a few villages away was brought in and succeeded in nipping the *gbati* in the bud.[23]

After this, people seemed to have less and less confidence in Mendouga's powers. My neighbor would insist that the witches, during one of their nightly meetings, had decided to take the power away from her. This was why she had failed so lamentably with the *gbati* boys in our village. Mendouga went to great length to enlist people's attention. She spread rumors that she was pregnant, although everybody knew she was far beyond childbearing age. Later on she said that she had ended her pregnancy because she had seen the child was a *mongolien*.[24] Moreover, she kept talking about her elite clients—implying that she would soon have to make a trip since her friend the *préfet* was in trouble and needed her. However, people seemed little impressed by all this; the general opinion remained that "the power" had not come back to her. She died at the end of the 1970s, almost forgotten by all her former clients. When I asked how she died, people would only comment that witches tend to settle their scores amongst themselves. Other people would quote a Maka proverb about *mindjindjamb* (witches) who want to "take without sweat": Mendouga's poor ending showed again that the *djambe* may bring prestige and wealth for some time, yet all this does not stay.

Modern *Nganga* and the Fear of Charlatans

Such uncertainties surrounding healers are certainly not exceptional. Throughout Africa people seem to be obsessed with the question as to how separate "charlatans" from "bona fide" healers. Such charlatans might just be ineffective people intent on taking your money, but—much more worrying—they could as well be dangerous figures intent to harm you and draw you into the circles of witchcraft. In her dissertation on the surprising success of female *marabouts* in Dakar, Amber Gemmeke (2008) shows that how to recognize charlatans has become a major preoccupation for many. It keeps coming up, not only in private conversations but also in debates in the media. For orthodox Muslims these female *marabouts* are a *contradictio in terminis*, since women can hardly legitimate their expertise with an appeal to the Koran. Yet they are quite popular, even more than many of their male colleagues. This does not stop clients from testing their knowledge in all sorts of ways—the clients' expectations run high, but their fear of being stuck with a charlatan who is just faking and has no real knowledge is almost as high.

Another telling example of how confusing the proliferation of healers is comes from the other end of the continent, South Africa, from the Ralushai report, already mentioned.[25] No less than a quarter of this voluminous report (88 pages) is dedicated to a "Proposed Draft Legislation to Control the Practice of Traditional Healers" (Ralushai 1996:64–87). The authors' concerns are clear. The general tenor of the report is that witchcraft as a deadly danger has to be taken seriously. In order to combat it they propose, therefore, an adaptation of existing legislation and the founding of a National Traditional Healers Association, following the Zimbabwe example (which by now has parallels in many African countries). Such an association would have to guarantee that only "bona fide" healers will be mobilized in the fight against witchcraft. However, this immediately poses the problem of how to separate the latter from "mala fide" elements. As mentioned above, the report itself cites numerous examples from *inyanga* and *sangoma* who were deeply implicated in the horrible witch hunts by self-styled ANC "comrades"—either by helping the young men to "sniff out" witches through very special procedures or by being in fact involved in the gruesome *muti* murders that had unleashed these hunts. Reading the long series of articles of the committee's draft of a constitution for this healers' association, one realizes how difficult it is, indeed, to "control the practice of traditional healers," though this is what the report sets out to do. The healers' invisible expertise is marked by such deep ambiguities that any attempt to separate mala fide and bona fide reminds of Don Quixote's tilting at windmills.

Still, throughout Africa people continue to put their trust in *nganga*, *marabouts*, *tradipracticiens*, "traditional healers," or whatever term is used. Everywhere people are very worried about the proliferation of charlatans, yet they are willing to suspend their doubts and put their fate in the hands of people they often hardly know. There seem to be good reasons here to talk, à la Simmel, of a "leap of trust" that is "almost religious." However, this open-endedness unfortunately makes it impossible to give a definitive answer to the question of when and why people are prepared to make this leap. The basis for trust in this treacherous field seems to shift constantly. Below I seek to highlight historical changes and recurrent patterns in the ways in which *nganga* try to affirm their trustworthiness, on the one hand, and clients try to distinguish and avoid "charlatans," on the other.

In the Maka area, the general profile of *nganga* changed quite dramatically around 1980. This had important implications for the way trust could be established. The *nganga* I came to know in the 1970s maintained a fairly low profile. They had good reasons for this, since in those days *nganga* were regularly in trouble with the government for creating unrest; they could easily be accused of defamation. Most politicians did regularly consult *nganga*, but this was a private matter; formally they had to denounce witchcraft as a major obstacle to development and as a form of sabotage of the government's efforts for the population. In the official view the *nganga* were the main representatives of this dark world, so they had to be watched carefully (see further Fisiy and Geschiere 2001). Most *nganga* tended, therefore, to remain somewhat in the shadows. They lived in fairly modest *poto-poto* structures, often at the margins of the village, and tried to behave as normal locals. Most of them did not speak French and could neither read nor write.

Their ways of establishing trustworthiness varied greatly. All of them constantly made references to their own "professor" who had taught them so many things and bound them with heavy *itsi* (interdictions) to use this

secret knowledge to heal and not destroy. But all of them also had distinctive ways to make their secret knowledge public—guardedly.[26]

Mendouga wore a striking ring, a huge iron one with a nondescript orna-
ment on it. She told me that this was her secret hiding place where she
could take refuge when the witches had ambushed her. But the main
proof of her expertise was her "mirror," in which she could see whether
her client spoke the truth. She described the mirror to me (but I was
never allowed to see it) as a narrow bottle containing a bundle of sticks
and a viscous liquid. When interrogating a client, she would let the
liquid pass between the sticks. If one drop remained, she was sure that
the client was lying.[27] This was crucial, since invariably her first question
would be "Did you go out [ouas] yourself?"[28] If she saw in her mirror
that the client had lied to her—saying that he had not gone out while
in fact the mirror showed he had done so—the case was hopeless. She
could only tell the client to go home and fight his struggle alone.

Mendouga's practice of healing was very private. Most of her curing—
and her show of extraordinary powers—took place inside her house in
private with her clients. Other nganga—especially many of her male
colleagues—enhanced their power by more spectacular performances in
public. In the same village where Mendouga lived, a younger nganga,
Mezing Merlin, began to establish his reputation in the early 1970s by
the impressive dance performances he staged—in principle from sunset
to sunrise—in order to invoke the help of the mindjim (spirits of both
the deceased and the witches) for his cures. When he announced he
would dance, people came from the whole canton to attend this special
occasion. And indeed, Merlin's performances were spectacular: he would
dance with his impressive torso naked, adorned only with belts of the
skin of the panther or the genet (just like the old warriors) and a small
skirt around his waist,[29] shaking his hips ferociously at the deafening
thunder of drums, making complicated circles and turns while singing
in the interludes with a moaning, throaty voice. Often his performance
would be made even more exciting when a little girl, his pupil, would
dance in front of him, similarly attired, proudly shaking her hips with
Merlin's body towering behind her. However, public as his performance
might be, his ceremonies to cure his patients, who sometimes lived for
weeks in his compound, was done in private, similarly to how Mendouga
organized her practice. Different as their performance was in many respects, they both addressed their patients in a reassuring way (at least
initially), avoiding direct accusations and preferring to talk vaguely
about hidden threats and how they would be able to defeat these.

The villagers, from their side, were certainly not ready to take things for granted. On the contrary, they were constantly watching for proofs that a *nganga* still had the power to defeat "the" witches; they often compared different *nganga* and their interpretations. In some respects the limited scale on which *nganga* operated could facilitate trust. On the one hand, these *nganga* knew many of the people they were treating; on the other, the villagers were familiar with all the rumors on how these *nganga* worked. They knew about their successes but also heard very quickly about their failures, and the latter could easily lead to a complete breakdown of trust, as when Mendouga was unexpectedly defeated by the *gbati* boys.

However, in all the examples above there was also a countervailing tendency to seek out a *nganga* farther away: Eba (the Maka *évolué* who returned to the village but fell ill) went all the way to the land of the Djem when his illness did not subside. Mendouga boasted that she had to follow "her" *préfet* on many of his trips since he was afraid to travel alone. Evina, the Yebekolo chief, and Nkal Selek, his slave-"son," sought the *bubuwa* far out in the land of the Mvele. There seems to be a recurrent principle that in one's choice of the *nganga*, the unknown or at least the faraway inspire trust. Even in earlier days, closeness/distance seems to have had an ambiguous impact on people's reasons for putting their trust in a *nganga*.

The 1980s brought important changes, notably the emergence of a new type of *nganga* who experimented with novel ways of creating trust. These *nganga* were much more in the open, aggressively enhancing their presence and insistently offering their services to anybody who could pay. For them there was little reason to keep a low profile as their predecessors used to do. Indeed, now government officials were prepared to give them an official role in the intensification of their campaign against witchcraft. Elsewhere (Fisiy and Geschiere 2001) we have shown that, at least in the East, the government became increasingly obsessed with witchcraft as a most dangerous form of *subversion*. As one *sous-préfet* would invariably thunder at the villagers whenever he arrived for a visit: "When will you stop sabotaging all government plans with this d— witchcraft of yours?" The irony was that thus village witchcraft increasingly appeared to be, indeed, an action against the state, even though it was not clear that it was intended that way.

Another irony was that in the ensuing judicial actions against the witches the judges felt obliged to allow the *nganga* and their expertise to play a crucial role as witnesses for the prosecution. Beginning in 1980, courts in the East began to condemn witches" without asking for tangible proof of aggression as had been required in jurisprudence until then. However, this made the question of how to establish definitive proof of invisible aggression extremely urgent. The expertise of the *nganga* seemed to be the only alternative the judges could base their verdicts on. Indeed, in many of the court files we consulted, the testimony of a *nganga* proved to have been the final reason for convicting the accused (Fisiy and Geschiere 1990). The problem is, of course, that to the Maka the *nganga* is the obvious representative of the *djambe* world. So by engaging the *nganga* in their offensive against witchcraft, the judges and the other officials confirmed the very ideas they wanted to combat. The position of *nganga* was strongly reinforced by this official recognition.

In particular, the *nganga* who were asked to perform for the tribunals in the towns—typically all of them were men: in these more modern contexts women seem to recede to the background in witchcraft affairs—behaved very differently from the healers I knew in the 1970s. Often they had returned from a stay in the city. They emphasized in any way they could that they were modern figures—they dressed European style, often sporting huge sunglasses; they built their "hospitals" right in the center of the village, trying to attract attention with big signs; they boasted of their medical knowledge, claiming to apply their "science," and were prepared to work closely with the *gendarmes* to have unrepentant "witches" locked up and dragged before the courts.

> The change in the *nganga*'s profile was a big surprise to me when I returned to the village in 1989 after an absence of eight years. A memorable event was meeting a new *nganga*, Baba Denis, in a village very close to the one where I mostly stay. I knew Baba's name already, since I had seen it in files of the court cases against witches that my colleague Cyprian Fisiy had managed to get from a former colleague at the Court of Appeal in Bertoua, the capital of East Province. As described in the files, Baba's performance was markedly different from that of *nganga* like Mendouga and Merlin. Apparently, after his return from Yaoundé a few years earlier, Baba had made his name with large-scale "purifications" of several villages. He would approach the village chief, pointing out that his village was beset by aggressive witches and offering his services to combat the evil. On a given day he would come to "apply my science," as he said. All villagers would be admonished to bring out their *miedou* (medicine). Most people would comply, bringing amulets of various kinds and throwing them on a heap. But invariably some people would not comply. Then Baba would go to that house with the village's

notables, invade it, and emerge with various contraptions said to have been hidden under the roof or in the walls (the accused would often imply that the healer had planted them himself). Thereupon Baba would hand the culprits over to the village chief and alert the *gendarmes*, who would come to arrest them. Later, when the case came before the court (often after the accused spent several years in jail), Baba would be the main witness, testifying that he had found evil things in their house and also that he had "seen" them "going out at night."

When I finally had the chance to visit Baba myself, he turned out to be, indeed, quite different from Mendouga or the other *nganga* I had known earlier. The house itself—he called it his "hospital"—was markedly different. It was an impressive structure right in the middle of the village, at an important crossing of two throughways. It was adorned by three big signs. One said "Docteur Baba Denis guérisseur [healer]"; the next one "astrologue" (astrologist—a new notion for most villagers); the third "Rosecrucien" (Rosicrucian—Cameroon's President Paul Biya is supposed to be a staunch adherent of this secret association). Baba received us dressed in a European costume that was somewhat shabby but included a tie.[30] He took off his big sunglasses, asking us to come into his "consultation room"—an officelike room with a big desk, a shelf of books (some from Western medicine but also a few books on "Eastern magic"), and, in contrast to the formal, almost bureaucratic atmosphere, several burning candles.

Clearly Baba did not like the idea of being interviewed. So he did most of the talking himself, explaining to us how he used his "science" to bring peace to the villages. He emphasized his important contacts in Yaoundé, mentioning that his brother still worked at the Presidency, and insisted on showing me how well he kept records on his patients, dutifully noting the dates of their visits and other details. In other aspects as well he imitated the style of a *fonctionnaire* (civil servant) with a dry, bureaucratic air. The villagers often commented that he had learned this formal style in the army, where had served for quite some time. According to some, he had been sacked because of financial irregularities, even spending some time in jail. Yet this served only to further enhance his prestige as a *nganga*, since everybody knows that the prison is the place to learn the really dangerous secrets.

Baba's ways of enhancing his credibility had other new aspects. He emphasized the scientific nature of his expertise, styling himself as a *docteur* with his books, his hospital, and his files. But even more striking was that he spoke about his patients as *les coupables* (the guilty ones). In other respects as well his approach was quite far from Mendouga's reassuring behavior. *Nganga* like Baba become threatening figures, working closely with the *gendarmes*, ready to hand over witches to *la Justice*. In Baba's case this was clearly related to his privileged role as one of the *nganga* who were regularly asked to testify in court. But in the 1980s many *nganga* with a lesser profile than Baba, especially younger ones, similarly became much more aggressive in their quest for potential clients. People often told me how they would be approached by a *nganga* they hardly knew who would warn them that their compound was mined with evil and assure them that he knew how to purify it—of course for a handsome fee. The *nganga* were obviously not exempt from the general trend toward increasing commercialization, and this made them all the more aggressive in their search for clients.[31]

People's worries about charlatans invading their area are also strengthened by the greater mobility of the *nganga*. It is no longer exceptional for healers from the West and even the Northwest Provinces—"Grafi-people" (Grassfielders), feared and envied for their talent for entrepreneurship—to come to the region. People even whisper that Nigerian healers are active, and, as everywhere, Nigerians are seen as the preeminent charlatans.[32] Yet the practical implications of this greater mobility for trust are, again, double-edged. In the case of figures like Mendouga and Merlin, who belonged to the area, people knew about their successes but also their failures and all the gossip about them. Being more familiar with the healer gave some certainty. The new type of *nganga* nearly always comes from outside. Sometimes they are completely new to the area; more often they are *originaires* who spent an extended time in the city and then unexpectedly returned to the village.[33] So it is more difficult to check on them. However, at the same time their status as a partial outsider gives their expertise novel aspects—always appreciated among those who seek help in witchcraft—which makes it all the more difficult for people to resist their insistent warnings that something has to be done in order to protect one's compound.[34] The new *nganga*, in their frenzied search for clients, often seem to bet on inspiring fear in order to push people to suspend their doubts—a quite negative form of trust.[35]

Clearly, the ongoing increase of scale of social relations—the increasing intertwinement of village life and city life—directly affects the ways in which trust is created between the *nganga* and the people. The greater mobility of *nganga*, the modernization of their practices, and their collaboration with the new elites make the villagers more uncertain about how one can distinguish charlatans from "real" healers. However, this does not decrease the need for healers. And, again, *nganga*'s increasing mobility can be an asset, since novelty often works as an advantage in witchcraft. Despite all this variability, the changing context seems to have some general implications: *nganga* are becoming more aggressive in their search for clients, and fear seems to become ever more important in making people put their trust in a *nganga*, despite significant doubts.

Another general aspect is that *nganga* seem forced to become ever more visible. Their greater public role—as, for instance, before the courts—along with the need to advertise themselves as modern figures, in close touch with the new elite, and the increasing competition for clients, makes it ever more difficult to keep a low profile in daily life. The *nganga* have had to step out of the shadows, shedding at least some of their secrecy. One can wonder whether their increasing public profile can become a danger for their role as healers[36]—a topic we will return to.

A New Solution: God's Work as the Basis for Ultimate Trust

The 1980s brought in many parts of Africa a new approach to witchcraft and the conundrum of intimacy and (dis)trust: Pentecostalism. One of the great attractions of Pentecostalism in Africa is that it promises a radical break with both witchcraft and family.

Of course Pentecostal missionaries, especially American ones, had already long been active in Africa. But the 1980s brought a sudden proliferation of Pentecostal churches, sects, and movements all over Africa. The switch in Pentecostal preaching around that time from "asceticism to accumulation," as Robert Akoko calls it in his book *Pentecostalism and the Economic Crisis in Cameroon* (2007), was very important for the rapidly increasingly popularity of the Pentecostal message throughout the continent. The new "gospel of prosperity," to which most churches shifted, preached that true believers did not have to wait until the hereafter; they would get rich here and now.

In Cameroon, Pentecostalism's impact initially remained quite limited. As noted above, one of the riddles of Cameroonian history is why since colonial times there had been so little scope for the independent religious movements that proliferated throughout Africa next to the mainline mission churches. In Cameroon a few prophets did emerge under colonial rule.[37] But their following remained fairly limited, certainly compared to the religious ferment in neighboring countries. It was only after the one-party ban on freedom of association was lifted (1989) that the Pentecostal movement really took off in Cameroon, especially in Anglophone regions (Northwest and, even more, Southwest Province), and in the big cities, Yaoundé and Douala. In the faraway East Province its impact still remains fairly limited.[38] In neighboring countries—particularly Nigeria (see Marshall 2009), the Congo, and Gabon (see Tonda 2002 and 2005), but also the Central African Republic (see Fancello 2012)—Pentecostalism had already been very much alive, and this has inevitably had an impact in Cameroon.

Even before the switch to the "prosperity gospel," Pentecostalism had brought a completely new approach for the struggle against witchcraft (see Meyer 1999). While the established churches—to which most Pentecostal converts belonged earlier in their lives—tended to deny the reality of witches, the Pentecostals have always taken witchcraft most seriously, equating it with the devil. Thus the struggle against witchcraft, as a major manifestation of Satan himself, became the basic theme in their version of Christianity. No wonder that in Africa the public confessions that form the climax of Pentecostal services mostly center on former escapades in witchcraft, from which the speaker was saved by a dramatic conversion. While the older churches, established by missionaries in colonial times, cannot promise a cure for witchcraft (since they tend to deny its very existence), the Pentecostals offer definitive certainty that they are able not only to protect against witchcraft but also to take this evil away from anybody who does not stray from the right path (or openly repents of having strayed from it). Their cure is simple: the moment of conversion—the archetype of which is Paul's shattering experience on the road to Damascus, when God spoke to him and turned him from an unbeliever into the new church's most zealous apostle will save the true believer from witchcraft.

Of special interest to our topic is that the Pentecostal solution for witchcraft differed not only from that of the missionary churches but also from the approach of the *nganga*. The latter mostly see it as their task to repair relations, particularly inside the family; even if their increasingly direct accusations now seem to poison relations, they pretend at least to work toward restoring peace within the house.[39] In contrast, the Pentecostals advocate "a complete break with the past" (Meyer 1998). In practice this means a break with the extended family, since the devil is seen to operate via blood ties. Indeed, many authors emphasize that central to Pentecostalism in Africa is a determination to liberate the believer from the pressures of kinship.[40] Thus the new message seems to bring a decisive turn, exploding the coherence of the triangle of witchcraft, intimacy, and (dis)trust. The solution seems to be as simple as it is drastic: the believer must leave the family behind and will thus be liberated from its witchcraft-infested intimacy. Then he will enter a new intimacy, that of the global Pentecostal community, in which trust is guaranteed since it is based on faith.[41] The question is of course whether this radically new approach succeeds in puncturing the witchcraft issue in practice.

Has the Pentecostals' principled attack on the family and its intimacy, now equated with the devil, really broken open the conundrum of "the witchcraft of the house" and the concomitant struggle to maintain trust nonetheless? The answer is far from clear yet. First of all, it seems that there are great variations in the degree to which people are admonished to keep their distance from the family. In Ghana this seems to be a major theme, even in everyday life (see Meyer 1999 and de Witte 2008). But in Malawi, Harri Englund does not see a similar tension—on the contrary, he notes that "*mudzi*, the term for both 'home' and 'village.' had deep moral connotations among born-again Christians no less than other residents of the township" (Englund and Leach 2000:235; see also Englund 2002 and 2007b). For Congo-Brazzaville, Joseph Tonda (2002) notes Pentecostals' distrust of the family; yet this does not seem to lead to a dramatic break—maybe because in this area more extensive kinship links had already been quite reduced. My Pentecostal friends in Cameroon seem to hardly see a problem in reconciling their faith with intense preoccupation with family issues—including active participation in huge funeral rituals.[42]

Another complicating factor is the constantly contested position of the pastor, who is, of course, vital for the establishment of new forms of trust that would surpass the old predicaments. One thing that Pentecostals throughout Africa—and probably not only there[43]—seem to have in common is that preachers are constantly scrutinized regarding whether they live up to their own preaching. Of course this raises endless rumors that they have been found wanting. Already in 1999 I could buy at Ekok, the Cameroonian border station with Nigeria, far out in the bush, one of these eloquent Nigerian posters showing a short strip of images: a successful Pentecostal preacher arriving in his own plane, with his Mercedes waiting for him. His driver takes the road, but he is stopped at a police checkpoint. The policemen open the boot and find it full of cranes! Clearly the reverend himself is a witch!

Yet common as such rumors are, there are many regional variations in how *le travail de Dieu* (as Tonda 2005 calls it) relates to witchcraft.

In the ethnography on Ghana, local equivalents to the *nganga* seem to be almost smothered by the sheer weight of huge Pentecostal churches. Marleen de Witte (2008) makes a seminal comparison of one of these churches to Afrikania, a religious movement that seeks to revive "traditional religion." She emphasizes the limited success that Afrikania has enjoyed.[44] A big problem for this alternative movement is that it is constantly vilified by the media—which in Ghana seem to be under complete Pentecostal control—as a true tool of the devil. Another problem is that the "traditional" priests involved tend to shy away from the wider publicity that seems necessary for working together in a churchlike movement like Afrikania (one of de Witte's perceptive conclusions is that this movement is forced to organize itself more or less as a church, precisely because it is in constant confrontation with the Pentecostal churches).

Joseph Tonda gives a completely different picture for Congo Brazzaville and Gabon, where there seems to be a continuous articulation of *nganga* and *travailleurs de Dieu*, who are often quite hard to distinguish from each other. There is certainly much antagonism: he even speaks of *nganga dépasséss* (*nganga* who are overtaken), who have lost much of their "therapeutic capital" to new healers who are literate and invoke scientific knowledge or the Christian God as proof of their superiority (Tonda 2002). However, he shows that in practice neither the victory of the new healers nor the distinction between the two is clear in the Congolese context. Tonda quotes several *travailleurs de Dieu* who claim to have definitively vanquished the formidable *ndjobi* fetish, the most powerful of all since it had "eaten" all earlier fetishes. Yet the *ndjobi* association keeps reappearing. Many considered it the real secret behind President Omar Bongo's longevity (Tonda 2002, chaps. 4–5). Pentecostal healers who claim to be empowered by God are accused by their own relatives of working for the God of the Rosicrucians (Tonda 2005:79). Indeed, as said, Tonda's general thesis is that *le travail de Dieu*—and certainly Pentecostalism—is deeply intertwined with *l'esprit sorcellaire*, resulting in a "magma" (one of his favorite terms) from which *le Souverain moderne* is emerging This is a very different view of Pentecostalism and its relation to witchcraft. A full "break with the past" seems to be excluded here.[45]

Pentecostalism and its claim to replace the dangerous intimacy of the family with a global community of true believers certainly open new perspectives: despite variations, there is a clear promise here of surpassing kinship, which may appear to be a self-evident base of trust but is in practice marked by fatal distrust. Instead, Pentecostalism offers a vision of new forms of trust based on a new morality. For Nigeria, Marshall (2009) takes this new vision very seriously, but she is also skeptical: 'In particular the rise of the prosperity movement and the emphasis on miracles, increasingly realized through pastoral charisma, give the Born Again moral economy an increasingly occult form" (Marshall 2009:177). Marshall emphasizes that to the Pentecostals sovereign power depends on revelation. Therefore a definitive institutionalization of power, let alone a theocracy, remains impossible. But this implies also "the impossibility of securing authoritative knowledge that could provide the grounds for trust"—while the establishment of new forms of trust is, in her view as well, badly needed by Nigerians who have to face "the ordeal of urban life" in a context of continuously increasing uncertainty and insecurity (Marshall 2009:195).

Yet the short but vivid conclusion to Marshall's book, on a manifesto by a rebellious young pastor defending new insights into the relation between religion and politics, testifies to the continuing dynamism of Pentecostalism in African contexts. Whatever their differences, Pentecostal churches have at least opened up a vision of new forms of trust that offer an alternative to the intimacy of the family and its dangers. In this sense they doubtless brought a new phase in the struggles over intimacy and trust, even if they did not resolve these. The question remains whether their frontal attack on witchcraft does offer any chance of a decisive breakthrough. Or does it—like similar frontal attacks in other places and times—reinforce people's belief in such dangerous forces? Of special interest to our theme is many African Pentecostals' direct equation of the devil with the family. Thus the devil as the impersonation of cosmic evil is reduced to the dangers of kinship—which, of course, has special implications for the general theme of witchcraft, intimacy, and trust in Africa. I will return to this in this book's last chapter.

Everyday Ways of Coping

An appeal to a *nganga* and converting to Pentecostalism are the more dramatic options in the struggles over witchcraft and trust. But in everyday life more low-key ways of coping with intimate dangers may be more common—and more effective. The Duala saying quoted already, "You have to learn to live with your witch," is a constant refrain when people discuss witchcraft: the main thing is to avoid jealousy within "the house." It is jealousy from within that breeds occult aggression, so the point is to avoid making your intimates too jealous. Recently, a Cameroonian friend of mine announced his plan to "construct" in the village, and we discussed the dangers such a project might entail—building a house "back home" is what villagers expect from an elite, yet it means venturing back into the intimacy of the village. But he cut the discussion short by saying: "If my brother wants to kill me, what can I do?" The answer was, of course, already implied by the rhetorical question: he had to make his brother fully participate in the project in order to avoid dangerous jealousy.

Yet such somber warnings collide frontally with the consumerism that in recent decades has attained such spectacular levels throughout postcolonial Africa.[46] In Cameroon, a favorite saying—often spoken between men over drinks—is *Oui, oui, un Grand n'est pas un petit* (You see, a Grand is not a little one). The saying is often used ironically, to mock people who do everything to show that they have to be taken for a Grand. Yet its implications are very real: one has to show constantly that one is, indeed, a Grand, and the best way is to employ the usual signs: expensive housing, elegant clothing, flashy cars. One day I had to pick up a colleague, one of my oldest friends in Cameroon, at the airport in Amsterdam, but immediately after landing he mysteriously disappeared. As a younger Cameroonian colleague pointed out to me with sly humor, the reason should not have been mysterious to me: of course a *Grand* like the professor would do anything to avoid being spotted getting into my Volkswagen Beetle. Indeed, the professor turned out to have rushed outside immediately after retrieving his luggage to catch a cab.

Consuming is deeply serious in Africa. It expresses a constant struggle for affirming one's status. And because the lines of stratification are unclear—the inexplicable enrichment of some, their equally sudden fall—it seems all the more important to underline success with ostentatious spending. But how to reconcile this with people's deep worry about jealousy from close by? The answer is, of course, "just redistribution." A key point in witchcraft imaginary all over the world is that it reminds the rich and the powerful to share.[47] But what is "just"? In a context where new inequalities seem to break through "traditional" frameworks, such a question becomes particularly delicate. In all the examples above, such new inequalities—an *évolué* against the village, a chief redisciplining his elites in the city, families struggling to keep a hold on migrants across the sea, elite associations blaming witchcraft for blocking development of their village[48]—gave novel implications to issues of intimacy, danger, and trust. In all these examples, kinship links are so resilient that they still manage to bridge new geographical and social distances. But this certainly does not mean that trust is a given in these new contexts. On the contrary, with such an increase of scale, the everyday struggle to strike a balance between just redistribution and rampant jealousy takes on new forms, often putting the elasticity of kinship relations to a heavy test.

A sad example of such struggles—showing how difficult it is to keep out of witchcraft's vicious circles—is offered by a Maka family I have known well since 1971. I came to know the family after it was cited to me as one of the last examples of a *ndjaw boud* (extended family, lit. people of one house) that had retained its cohesion. The family lived in a sprawling compound with a constantly growing array of houses and kitchens inhabited by seventeen adults with a much larger number of children: an elderly couple, their five sons (four of them were married and with children), and two sons of the deceased brother of the elder, who had also left behind three widows, each with her own kitchen. I knew other families of a similar size, but over time they all split up due to various reasons. This family seemed to keep its cohesion—at least until quite recently. The sons all took their schooling quite seriously, and several of them managed to get salaried jobs (as driver, nurse, and bookkeeper in government service). But all of them returned to the village and the compound.

My main contact with the family was my friend Franklin (pseudonym), who was exceptionally conscious of the need to share. Indeed, to me he seemed a living incarnation of what anthropologists term *reciprocity*. Traveling with him was a very time-consuming affair, since in each and every village he seemed to have a relative or a friend at whose home we should stop, offer a small present, and chat a little. Often these were very indirect relations; once he insisted on making a big detour to meet a man who had been married with the bride-wealth Franklin had paid for his present wife—that is, Franklin had paid bride-wealth to his bride's father, who had used the money to pay for a bride for his own son. For Franklin it was unthinkable to pass through the region without going to pay his respects to the young couple—else they might think he wished them harm.

Through his work as a nurse in various places, Franklin had made many new friends, including expatriates and Cameroonians from other regions who worked for development programs. Even after he returned to his own village, many of them came to visit him. These were invariably quite demanding events. He certainly enjoyed the visits—it showed how much people respected him—but he was always struggling to cope financially. Of course the guests did bring presents and contributed food and drinks. However, Franklin insisted on inviting almost the whole village for the party that had to follow each person's arrival. When his wife or his older children protested—why did he have to invite everybody? would they invite him in return?—his answer was always the same: "How can I refuse people? They are my people, so I have to share with them." In this he was supported by his brothers, who had fewer visitors but completely agreed that one had to share.

However, over time the solidarity within this impressive family bulwark came increasingly under stress, and Franklin began to speak of threatening witchcraft attacks. In the beginning he was very vague about where such attacks were coming from. But over time it became clear that he thought the danger was coming from inside. Moreover, apparently a switch took place. At first Franklin, and even more his wife, had feared a treacherous attack from close by. But later they became ever more worried about insistent whispers that they themselves were using witchcraft. The main focus for such rumors was the success of two of Franklin's sons at the university. Expatriate friends of his had paid for the schooling of his first two sons (after a long series of daughters with his first wife, who died quite young, he had two sons with a second wife). The rumors started when the two boys had almost finished university, so that soon they would be able to apply for lucrative positions. Their father and his brothers had also done quite well for their generation, holding lower-salaried jobs; however, the boys' success at the university would introduce a new kind of inequality within the family.

The witchcraft rumors took shape only gradually. It all started when Franklin's wife planted "medicine" around their house, trying to block out bad influences. Then Franklin invited a *nganga* (a relative stranger who was passing through the area) to purify the place. In 2005 his wife insisted that they build a new house at a little distance from the family compound, and another *nganga* was invited to come and "seal" this place. Apparently they still saw themselves as potential victims of others' jealousy. But later the rumors turned around: Franklin and his eldest daughter were accused of using *kong* to block the progress of children from other branches of the family. Franklin's two boys were said to be enjoying such success because they were fortified by Franklin's *kong*. Of course everybody knew where the money for the boys' schooling had come from. Moreover, Franklin had gone to great lengths to let others profit from this boon: for example, his sons lived with their cousins in the city so that the latter could study as well. Yet his continued drive toward reciprocity seemed of little avail against the jealousy raised by the young men's success.

As is typical in such cases, the accusations were not directed against the sons—everybody continued to praise them as the hope for the whole family—but against Franklin, who was by now an aging man. The main accusations came from other *originaires*, notably from his brother who had worked as a bookkeeper for the government and had returned after he was pensioned. He brought along his own son: a handsome boy, quite well dressed, who was clearly out of place in the village, yet seemed to be trapped there. The contrast with Franklin's sons, who came for short visits and then returned to the city, was glaring.

Up to the time of this writing, the whole affair has not yet surpassed the rumor stage. Nobody has taken concrete actions, and the accusations remain vague. Still, it is clear that the original solidarity within the family has been deeply affected. Franklin and his wife withdraw ever more in their own house outside the family compound, or with the children in the city. For Franklin it is especially sad that his talent for sharing is apparently no longer effective against the threat of jealousy. Once he complained bitterly that "people become too jealous these days." The reason is clear: with the success of his sons, inequalities of a novel caliber are emerging.

In this case it is possible to identify a definite turning point when people in this family ceased being willing to "suspend their doubt" (as Simmel might put it). For as long as I have known the family, there have been internal conflicts: the old mother complaining with the sons about her husband and his rough behavior, sometimes trying to set her favorites up against the father; jealousy between the brothers, and even more between their wives. But such discord was always covered up by constant sharing and shows of solidarity. However, the bigger the stakes became—Franklin's sons approaching truly elite status—the more difficult it became to contain the jealousy. Typical is the ambiguous way in which witchcraft rumors took shape. First Franklin and his wife saw themselves as victims, but then they suddenly were marked as culprits.[49] Another factor to be noted is that this example does not conform at all to the stereotype of witchcraft as a conservative force—as a reaction from a supposedly static local community against dynamic elements brought in from the outside. Rather, all persons involved seem to be in movement. The main accusations came from people who had been away themselves, and the main cause for jealousy seemed to be access to new opportunities—other returnees had tasted these opportunities but were now back in the village without much support outside, in contrast to Franklin. In a certain sense witchcraft here has a progressive tenor, pushing people to struggle for their own access to the new riches.[50] In such a context, the age-old strategy of "just" redistribution that Franklin had always applied with so much energy became more and more difficult.

However, there are also cases where striking a balance between new ambitions and "just" redistributions seems to work, at least to a certain degree. Benoit (pseudonym), a Cameroonian friend from the Grassfields (Western Province), is planning to opt for early retirement after an exceptionally successful career with a development organization in Europe. Recently he started to lay out an impressive property—people in the area speak about *une ferme* (a ranch)—close to his village of birth. Until now, when home for holidays, he lodged with his elder brother, who took care of the family compound; but when he returns more definitively after retirement, he wants to live in his own house. The project became ever more ambitious, and so the first question became who should supervise the work on site.

> Benoit explained to me that he had had a long discussion about this with his older (and only) brother, and the latter understood that a younger man should be in charge. After some deliberation, Benoit entrusted this crucial role to a young teacher in the village who was not of his own family. But he hastily explained that, of course, he had instructed the young man that in all the stages of the project's execution his close family had to be involved. Moreover, he went to great length to point out to his brother how he—and his children—would profit from the project.
>
> As yet the project is in its first phase. But it is worth noting in view of the impressive investments at stake, that until now no discord has arisen—no rumors about threatening dangers and no accusations of foul play. Benoit is a very prudent person, highly conscious of possible dangers. The very fact that he dares to start such a large-scale project shows that he feels sure that he will be able to keep the dangers at bay. As he puts it: "The villagers are so happy that now they will have also a successful son of the soil in their midst. They know it will work to their advantage. So I feel quite safe."

Different factors can explain why in this case, even though inequalities of a much larger scale are involved than in Franklin's case, success and trust seem to go together (at least until now). First of all, the Grassfields, in western Cameroon, is a very different area from Makaland, in the southern forest zone. A difference Grassfielders never tire of emphasizing is that they have "real" chiefs while "these forest people" did not know chieftaincy until colonial conquest. Indeed, chieftaincy has a long history in the Grassfields, which makes for highly hierarchical forms of organization that contrast with the emphatically egalitarian ideology marking social life in forest societies.[51] Elsewhere (Fisiy and Geschiere 1991; see also Geschiere 1997) Fisiy and I have shown how important the continuing moral authority of these chiefs is for legitimizing and protecting new forms of wealth.[52] Benoit was always very careful in his relations with "his" chief—paying his respects on every possible occasion and dedicating the whole project to him. He realizes that the support of the chief is crucial for legitimizing his new riches in the eyes of the population.

There are also other factors that make relations inside the triangle of intimacy, witchcraft, and trust in this area quite different. Recall that Benoit entrusted the crucial role of supervising his entire project to a relative outsider: a young teacher who was not really family. For Jean-Pierre Warnier, in his seminal study of "the spirit of enterprise in Cameroon" (1993—unfortunately still not translated into English), this is one of the basic strategies with which the rising bourgeoisie from these parts of the country protect themselves against the "disaccumulation" that so often results from the pressures of kinship. Warnier addresses current stereotypes, which can be summarized as "Beti contra Bamileke," that poison present-day politics in Cameroon. These stereotypes are not without interest for the discussion here, since the theme of kinship-witchcraft is central to them. After 1982, when Paul Biya became president, "his" Beti succeeded in gaining ever more control over the state apparatus. However, economic power is rather in the hands of the Grassfields people (Anglophone Bamenda and Francophone Bamileke) who became strong supporters of the opposition after the return of multipartyism in the 1990s. This stalemate makes the stereotypes all the more venomous. Grassfields supporters of the opposition will reproach the ruling Beti politicians for "eating the state" since they prove unable to resist endless familial pressures for redistribution, while Beti people, from the southern forest area, tend to see the Bamileke as unscrupulous entrepreneurs who would "sell their own mother in order to get rich."[53]

The great merit of Warnier's 1993 analysis is that he gets beyond such culturalist stereotypes and points out certain sociohistorical factors that can explain entrepreneurship's greater scope in the western parts of the country. Businessmen from these areas play a dominant role throughout the country; in contrast, strong leveling mechanisms seem to undermine any form of entrepreneurship in the forest societies. Central to Warnier's argument are a series of strategies that he attributes to Bamileke entrepreneurs in their struggle against the forces of *désaccumulation* that remain so powerful in other societies. Most of these strategies have to do with kinship. Warnier emphasizes, for instance, "the practice of solidarity according to merit" that allows entrepreneurs to ignore requests of notoriously incapable relatives. Another recurring theme is "the containment of family." As an example of this strategy Warnier describes a very successful Bamileke businessmen who created an independent firm, strictly separated from his main business and of minor importance, where he could park family members in need of work (significantly, he called these relatives *les delinquants*). A somewhat different strategy but with similar effects is to offer young kinsmen only underpaid jobs; thus the entrepreneur manifestly respects kinship obligations and profits at the same time from access to cheap labor. However, for key positions where absolute trust is necessary, for instance for the bookkeeper position in a firm, someone from outside the family is recruited—just like the young teacher (also nonkin) whom Benoit chose to supervise his "ranch."[54]

The strategies Warnier attributes to successful Bamileke entrepreneurs show that kinship as such is never a sufficient basis for trust—to the contrary. It is true that in the Grassfields, people's conceptions of new inequalities are definitely not outside the triangle of kinship, witchcraft, and (dis)trust. Warnier (1993:74) notes that many successful businessmen from the area are the object of dark rumors of *famla* (the new witchcraft of the wealthy, the regional equivalent to the *kong* mentioned above). There is a rather weird link with kinship here, since everybody knows that one can be initiated into this *famla* only by "selling" one's kin. However, according to Warnier, these dark rumors have little effect on the position of these successful people in everyday life, and certainly do not force them to redistribute more of their new wealth among the family than they were planning to do. Such accusations hardly have the leveling effect they attain all too often in the forest societies.

The emergence of the new Grassfields bourgeoisie creates inequalities of a completely unprecedented order. It is obvious that these can no longer be reconciled with any idea of "just" redistribution among relatives in order to avoid jealousy and threatening witchcraft attacks. But here other reasons for trust emerged that are clearly beyond kinship: first of all the ongoing moral authority of the chief, and second (certainly not less important), special possibilities of limiting the demands of the family. Other criteria—proven merit, a practice of long-standing collaboration—can play a role and supersede considerations of kinship when one is selecting "really" trustworthy collaborators (see Warnier 1993:231–33). This may explain why, at least for the time being, witchcraft is kept at bay in Benoit's project, in contrast to the accusations surrounding the recent successes of Franklin's sons. To put it in more general terms, kinship as a basis of trust—that is, the willingness to suspend one's doubt about possible attacks from within the family—seems to be put to a heavy test when relations are stretched over ever greater social or spatial distances. Additional reasons for trust are then needed to ease "the leap of trust." Else witchcraft threatens to become all-pervasive and "run wild," as my Maka friends complain so often nowadays.

✳

The leitmotif in this chapter, as in the preceding one, is a constant increase of scale, kinship relations bridging ever greater distances and ever deeper inequalities. This raises new challenges within the old dilemma of how to create trust despite the dangers of intimacy. There is certainly not a uni-linear pattern here of trust becoming ever more difficult the greater the distance. For instance for the *nganga*, as we have seen a central but ambiguous beacon in people's search for trust, distance in relation to propinquity can have variable implications. *Nganga* from the region—like Mendouga and Merlin—are easier to trust in some respects: people know them and what they have done. But such familiarity can also raise doubts due to the unrelenting stream of rumors and gossip that affects every reputation. In this sense it can be easier to put trust in someone from outside. Moreover, we saw that the preference for *nganga* from farther away is nothing new: in the past as well these were believed to bring new forms of empowerment and protection, unknown to one's rivals. Recall how Evina and Nkal Selek, the famous warlords of precolonial days, went all the way to Mveleland to get the *bubuwa* of the old woman. However, increase of scale also raises new issues of trust: the basic idea of "just redistribution" to forestall the dangerous jealousy of kin becomes ever more difficult to retain. This goes together with a search for new supports for trust: modern *nganga* who claim to work on the basis of "scientific" knowledge, or the Pentecostal promise of a definitive break with family and witchcraft. Yet, like the appeal in the Grassfields to the moral authority of the chiefs for legitimating new forms of wealth, these new supports do not offer definitive reasons to suspend one's doubts.[55] These additional supports can do no better than kinship in offering a basis for self-evident—"ontological"—trust. People's willingness to suspend their doubts remains situational and circumscribed by a wide array of factors.

The question is then, of course, whether it is possible to identify key factors that do play a role in this suspending (or not suspending) of people's doubts. I will return to this in the final chapter. Here it may be important to emphasize that, clearly, the triangle of intimacy-witchcraft-(dis)trust retains much of its coherence even with the increasing distances and inequalities that mark present-day life in many parts of Africa. In modern contexts as well, everyday life is still haunted by the tension between, on the one hand, the fear of an intimacy that can give the ones who are close a dangerous hold over you and, on the other, the need to establish at least some form of trust with one's intimates in order to collaborate. In the examples above, intimacy, with its dangers, could still be equated with kinship.

Yet it is clear that the relations within this triangle are stretched to a breaking point. For Joseph Tonda, in his books on Gabon and Congo, this breaking point has been reached already (Tonda 2002 and 2005). In his view, as mentioned above, the old kinship order and its complement, *la sorcellerie* are ruptured by the colonial moment, which opens space for a new *logique du camp* in *des non-lieux lignagers*. In the examples above from Cameroon and elsewhere, it rather seems as if kinship is ever more stretched, which creates ever deeper tensions, but still retains some hold over people, imposing obligations that are seen as "traditional" but have become completely "neotraditional" both in form and in content. Through all these changes kinship remains closely linked to witchcraft; in some respects the link seems even to be fortified.

This resilience of the link with kinship and the often surprising emergence of witchcraft in novel settings call to mind Michel de Certeau's visionary formulations regarding the role of *l'étrange* as a furtive but all-pervasive force (in the introduction to his seminal study of devil exorcisms among the nuns of Loudun in seventeenth-century France). He sees "l'étrange . . . [comme] une force d'affût dans les tensions de la société" (de Certeau 1970:7). The literal translation of this evocative phrase would be "the strange as a power that is lurking in the tensions of society." But in this context it is tempting to translate *l'étrange*—the notion that fascinated de Certeau so much—not as "the unusual" but rather as "the uncanny."[56] De Certeau's vision of it, as a force working deep but often hardly perceptible changes *from the inside*, may be very relevant to the issues at stake here. It summons up a vista—somewhat related to Freud's vision of the uncanny and its return—in which Africans' obsessions with witchcraft fit within a broader configuration. How is this struggle for trust against the dangers from close by—*das Heimliche* becoming *unheimlich* because it seems to be "out of place"—expressed in other times and other places?

4

COMPARATIVE PERSPECTIVES I

Witches, Neighbors, and the
Closure of "the House" in Europe

CAN THE CONCEPTUAL TRIANGLE of witchcraft, intimacy, and (dis)trust be generalized? Can it serve to follow the vicissitudes of notions of occult aggression in other parts of the world, beyond Africa? As noted above, the idea of witchcraft as a transcultural notion has been the subject of fierce debates, especially between historians and anthropologists—the former showing some impatience with the latter for being so reluctant to generalize (see chap. 1, n49). Therefore it may be logical to begin comparative explorations with the rich and ever-growing corpus of studies by historians of witch hunts and witchcraft in early modern Europe (sixteenth and seventeenth centuries). After all, several of them looked explicitly for inspiration to studies by anthropologists of witchcraft in Africa. However, the topic led not only to rapprochement but also to distancing between the two disciplines in somewhat capricious alternations. In the 1970s historians were interested in comparisons with anthropological data, while anthropologists were more reserved. Lately the balance seems to be somewhat reversed, with at least some historians venting their disappointment in comparative possibilities with anthropological studies, while anthropologists increasingly emphasize the need to historicize the subject. We shall see that the ambiguous positioning of witchcraft imaginaries at the interface of local relations and wider frameworks, strongly emphasized in the preceding chapters on Africa, is also central to such reversals in the interactions between the two disciplines.

This chapter will explore in what sense the linking of witchcraft to intimacy and (dis)trust is relevant for Europe, not only for historical studies of the witch trials in early modern times but also for studies of more recent manifestations of witch beliefs in this continent. To what extent is it possible to perceive distinctive patterns in the ways European societies related proximity to witchcraft? There is an apparent difference here since, as said, both the abundant historical studies about the witch hunts in early modern Europe and the much scarcer academic literature on witchcraft in present-day Europe—especially Jeanne Favret-Saada's seminal studies (1977, 2009) on witchcraft in the French countryside in the 1970s—emphasize that in Europe witches are neighbors rather than kin. It will be worthwhile to follow this contrast in more detail, also in connection with another aspect where there might be a difference: the shifting character of conceptual distinctions and the ease with which one role fades into another (healer into witch, or vice versa)—an aspect that was highlighted in the African examples above but stringently denied in some European studies. The question is whether specific trends in the way intimacy is defined and articulated with an idea of occult danger can explain such correspondences and differences.

However, first a short overview of some of the reversals in the dialogue between historians and anthropologists on the topic will be helpful.

Historians and Anthropologists on Witchcraft— Rapprochements and Distancing

In the 1970s historians of witchcraft in early modern Europe became interested in anthropological studies of apparently comparable phenomena in Africa. This led to some debate between the two disciplines regarding whether it was at all possible to apply a notion like "witchcraft" cross-culturally. Symptomatic for problems in this context was that the two disciplines seemed to have quite different perceptions of these phenomena. Mary Douglas's ironic statement in her 1970 introduction, quoted earlier, to a collection of papers by historians and anthropologists[1] suggests, indeed, a wide gap between the two disciplines on this topic: "The anthropologists of the 1950's developed insights into the functioning of witch beliefs which seemed about as relevant to the European experience as if they came from another planet. Dangerous in Europe, the same beliefs in Melanesia or Africa appeared to be tame, even domesticated; they served useful functions and were not expected to run amuck" (Douglas 1970:xiii).

Since then things have changed on both sides. For anthropology, Douglas was mainly referring to witchcraft studies from the heyday of structural-functionalism (1950s) which—in accordance with Max Gluckmann's oft-cited notion of conflict as a kind of outlet that served to reinforce the existing social order—analyzed witchcraft accusations and fears mainly as serving to confirm the status quo. Hence Douglas's quite surprising characterization—no doubt mixed with irony—of witchcraft in Africa and Melanesia as "tame, even domesticated." Since then anthropologists have had ample reason to realize that these "beliefs" could most definitely "run amuck" in Africa and Melanesia.[2]

On the side of historians there have been incisive changes as well. In his seminal overview of the debate between the two disciplines on witchcraft, the British historian Ronald Hutton (2004) signals a series of rapid shifts. He notes that around 1970 many historians seemed interested to fit their studies of witchcraft in early modern Europe into a global approach by comparing to older anthropological studies of similar phenomena. However, Hutton notes as well that already in the 1970s disappointment set in. American historians in particular maintained that the "primitive" societies studied by anthropologists in Africa and elsewhere could hardly be compared to the "much more complex" societies of early modern Europe.[3] But according to Hutton, the main reason for historians' disappointment with anthropological parallels was the insistence by many anthropologists that notions of occult aggression were so specific to each culture that comparisons, certainly on a global scale, would be most precarious. For some anthropologists this emphasis on cultural specificity was reason enough to eschew the use of the term *witchcraft* altogether, as too laden with ethnocentric connotations (cf. prologue above, and Crick 1979). And, as mentioned, Douglas's 1970 collection closed with a contribution by Thomas Beidelman which opened with a stern statement that "witchcraft and sorcery . . . seem labels for social phenomena that differ radically from society to society" (Beidelman 1970:351)—hardly an encouragement for efforts toward comparisons! Any idea that these concepts circulate and influence each other across borders was absent from statements like Beidelmann's.

However, among historians the interest in a global perspective on witchcraft phenomena continued to grow. In 2004, the German historian Wolfgang Behringer published a "truly global history of witchcraft."[4] Based on impressively wide reading—including much work by anthropologists on Africa—Behringer's book offers, indeed, a fascinating overview of a huge span in both time and space. Resolutely refusing "any narrow definition of witchcraft," he proposes to blur "neatly drawn boundaries" (2004:3). This enabled him to sketch a complex of practices and ideas of enormous variety, yet circling around similar preoccupations.[5] In the same year, Ronald Hutton published the article cited above that suggested concrete starting points for a fruitful collaboration between historians and anthropologists on witchcraft, despite the earlier disappointments. Hutton, for his part, did try to formulate a more specific definition that had to be global at the same time. Basing himself on an impressive overview of studies on 148 extra-European societies, he set out to overcome anthropological squeamishness about using the term *witchcraft* as a transcultural notion. For him witchcraft is certainly not a *universal* phenomenon, as Behringer suggested. Hutton noted that, for instance, in most of Siberia shamanism seemed to offer an alternative to witchcraft in the explanation of misfortune; thus these societies fall outside his global definition. But for other societies, where the notion of the witch was and is present, Hutton formulated a "global model" of five characteristics (see below) that should allow for broad comparisons between historical and anthropological data.

At the same time it became increasingly difficult for anthropologists to refuse any comparison by withdrawing into a celebration of the specificity of each society and its witchcraft ideas.[6] One of the reasons was that in Africa and elsewhere they were increasingly confronted with unmistakable signs that witchcraft ideas and practices show a dynamic of their own in interaction with modern changes. In this process ideas travel, for the occult is an optimal field for hybridization and constant borrowings from elsewhere—on a regional or even global scale. Of course, there are good grounds for the reticence of anthropologists like Crick (1979) to generalize a notion like witchcraft. As said, missionaries (and subsequently anthropologists) played a crucial role in choosing this Western term as a generalizing translation for local notions, and in the process these notions were severely distorted. The digressions above on the notion of *djambe* among the Maka in Cameroon showed that translating it as *sorcellerie* (witchcraft) limits the notion in a pejorative sense by neglecting all sorts of more positive implications. The problem, however, as signaled in chapter 1, is that the Maka will now invariably use this translation. Indeed, all over the world people seem to have eagerly appropriated Western terms like *witchcraft*, *sorcery*, *magic*. This is not a process that can be ignored. It reflects a particularity of the field of the occult, which is especially open to borrowings and influences from outside. There is a basic logic at work here that may be universal: if witchcraft is about overwhelming the other—a victim or a rival—surprise is a great asset. New weapons may more easily vanquish the other's protections. Indeed, few fields seem to be so innovative as the realm of speculations on occult forces.

In the preceding chapters I have noted that in African contexts—especially after independence—it became increasingly impossible to study witchcraft as something local, as most anthropologists had tended to do. Yet anthropological respect for the specificity of each culture seemed to form an obstacle for following these processes of borrowing, traveling, and increase of scale of what appeared to be highly esoteric notions. To give just one more example: I vividly remember my shock when, at the beginning of my fieldwork in Cameroon in the early 1970s, my neighbor in a fairly remote village explained to me that the most powerful weapon in the *djambe*—not only to defend oneself but also to attack—had become "the ring of Madam Mylla," which people bought from this "lady" in Paris by mail order through the post office in the district headquarters. Notions of the occult are certainly not impervious to globalization—on the contrary. This is the crucial problem for statements, like Beidelman's quoted above, that ideas "differ radically from society to society" (Beidelman 1970:351); or for Hutton's demonstration that many societies do not know witchcraft even though their neighbors do (Hutton 2004:424). Can these ideas be so nicely classified in accordance with boundaries between societies as perceived by the historian or the anthropologist? To give just one concrete example to the contrary: the Baka ("Pygmies") of Southeast Cameroon are assumed not to have "witchcraft beliefs" (van Beek 2007:309). Yet their healers are now actively sought out by the Cameroonian elite, including the president's wife, as the most effective *nganga* in the country. The rapid enrichment of these healers, often living deep in the forest, who are regularly picked up in big Pajeros and escorted to Yaoundé, makes the assertion that witchcraft beliefs do not exist among these people difficult to maintain. Or consider the rapidity with which the panic over magical "penis-snatchers" (you shake hands with a stranger and your penis is gone) spread across the whole of West Africa in the 1990s (Bonhomme 2009).

For some decades anthropologists were reluctant to confront these dynamics of witchcraft imaginaries. As said, there were particular reasons for this—anthropology's struggle to overcome the opprobrium of having been "colonialism's handmaiden," and the general emphasis on Africa's need to rapidly "modernize" itself. Such reluctance might offer an additional explanation for the fact that the witchcraft debate with historians more or less stagnated in the course of the 1970s. However, all this changed in the 1990s with the sudden return of witchcraft as a central topic in anthropology, especially for Africa. Anthropologists were finally realizing that witchcraft could no longer be studied as something purely local or "traditional."

Witchcraft and State Formation: Europe and Africa

The growing interest among anthropologists in the dynamics of witchcraft, seen in a wider setting, forced them to take work by historians more seriously. In my 1997 book *The Modernity of Witchcraft: Politics and the Occult in Postcolonial Africa* I noted that for anthropologists one of the lessons of historical studies on Europe could be the importance of the broader context. Historians may envy anthropologists that they can study witchcraft in action. Yet the main sources for historians—files on witchcraft processes before state and ecclesiastical courts—forced them from the start to acknowledge the impact of broader processes like state formation and religious change (notably the role of the church). At the time I was fascinated by the way Robert Muchembled studied these files as an articulation of two discourses: the old discourse of the peasants who accused witches in their midst of harming their harvests, livestock, and persons (*maleficium*, as it was called in the court files), and a new one on Satan as the central figure in the witches' sabbath, introduced by the ecclesiastic and worldly authorities. Indeed, Muchembled's analysis of the witch trials as part of a "civilizing offensive" of the budding absolutist state—aimed at nothing less than "the political and religious conquest of the countryside" and a definitive repression of popular culture—seemed to correspond to dramatic changes in the very area where I was working, southeast Cameroon.[7] From the 1980s on, courts in Cameroon, like those in other African countries, started to condemn "witches" on quite flimsy evidence and in a complete reversal of existing jurisprudence. It was tempting to see parallels with the "civilizing offensive" and the "subjection of bodies and souls" that Muchembled views as the main reason behind the European witchcraft trials. In Cameroon—as elsewhere in Africa—the one-party state developed extremely authoritarian tendencies, and in this context witchcraft was regularly marked as one of the most dangerous forms of "subversion." Here again, there seemed to be a concerted drive by the government behind the witch trials (Geschiere 1997, chap. 6).

The irony was that at the time I wrote the 1997 book, historians were moving away from interpretations à la Muchembled. In his 1996 survey *Witches and Neighbours: The Social and Cultural Context of European Witchcraft*, Oxford historian Robin Briggs concluded, for instance, that "none of the stronger, more centralized states of early modern period ever undertook a major nationally organized campaign against witches" (Briggs 1996:325). Along similar lines, German historian Wolfgang Behringer (2004, chap. 4) emphasized that more extensive witch hunts were a corollary not of emerging absolutism but rather of failing state formation, notably in parts of the German empire where rulers like the prince-bishops, sometimes nicknamed by their contemporaries "witch bishops,"[8] had great difficulty in maintaining their authority.

> Behringer emphasizes that in such contexts state authorities could not withstand heavy pressure from the peasants to persecute witches; often they seemed tempted to cede to such pressure in order to resolidify their hold over their subjects. More successful rulers in the stronger absolutist states—like France, England, the Palatinate, and Bavaria—were weary of witchcraft accusations, especially because of their uncontrolled proliferation. Behringer pays particular attention to a terrible witch hunt

in the 1580s in Trier, where Prince-Bishop Peter Binsfeld, together with a newly established Jesuit college, unleashed a persecution that would make over one thousand victims. The Jesuits used young boys in their custody as a kind of spirit mediums, sending them out to attend witches' sabbaths so they could report on whom they had "seen" there. The boys proved ideal weapons for the Jesuit fathers to intervene in local politics by directing their accusations where they saw fit. Thus the persecution, though it started with the usual suspects (poor women and to a lesser degree men), began to involve ever more important persons. It climaxed with the trial and execution of Dr. Dietrich Fade, one of the richest and most respected citizen of the town (Behringer 2004:93–97).

Such examples made the authorities in more absolutist states reluctant to get involved with local witch hunts. For instance, already from the 1580s on the Parliament of Paris was highly critical of witchcraft persecutions (Behringer 2004:128; cf. also 105). In a similar vein, Brian Levack concluded that the witch-trial zeal of local courts was more and more held in check by central authorities. The latter may not necessarily have been against the persecution of witchcraft, but they were firm "advocates of what has come to be called the rule of the law." This often implied "adherence to strict legal procedures." Of course, this had to conflict with the messiness of witchcraft trials. For Levack, the higher authorities gave priority to the ideal of a central regulation of justice over vaguer ideals like homogenizing the population or disciplining the lower classes (Levack 1996–98:114–15).

So much for the idea of a "civilizing offensive" by the absolutist state, aiming at "submission of souls and bodies," as a general explanation of witchcraft trials in Europe.[9] This reorientation among historians proved very helpful for understanding the recent witchcraft trials in Cameroon that Fisiy and I studied. Even though at first we supposed a concerted offensive of the state behind this remarkable reversal in jurisprudence, it soon became clear that more local factors played a crucial role (Fisiy and Geschiere 1990; Geschiere 1997:194). There were considerable discrepancies among regions within the country in judges' readiness to take on these cases.[10] But most important, and in line with Levack's analysis, the state's lawyers seemed to be insistent in sticking to the positivist spirit of their law training. For them "tangible proof" remained essential, and that was and is very hard to establish in witchcraft cases.[11] Levack's image of lower state courts and authorities struggling to adapt to ferocious pressure from the local population to do something about a proliferation of witchcraft is quite convincing for Cameroon as well.

Yet I wonder whether the pendulum in European witchcraft studies is not swinging too far—*from* the role of state-formation seen as central, *to* it being marginalized and quite limited. After all, the idea—so powerfully developed in, for instance, Christina Larner's work (1981 and 1984), following in Norman Cohn's traces (Cohn 1975)—still stands that the peasants' idea of a *maleficium* had to be complemented by notions of a Satanic sect in order to lead to large-scale persecution of witches. It is true that Cohn showed that this articulation had a long history—witchcraft becoming associated with heresy from the late fourteenth century on and subsequently with Satan himself. True also that Muchembled may have exaggerated the opposition in the court files between two discourses, one of the peasants and another one of the judges, since—as, for instance, Robisheau (2009) shows—the devil was certainly present in the peasants' imaginary as well. Still, Larner seems right in insisting that at least some involvement of ecclesiastical and worldly authorities was necessary in order to make the vital link between *maleficium* and devil (Larner 1984:46; cf. also Larner 1981). Clearly, the historians' propensity, encouraged by the very nature of their sources, to study witchcraft in a broader setting of changing relations of domination and subordination can still serve as an example to anthropologists.

But what about the other side of the coin: anthropologists' supposed advantage of witnessing witchcraft-in-action as an ongoing societal concern? In some respects, this advantage seems a mixed blessing. It may serve only to make the anthropologist more conscious of the very elusiveness of the topic. One handicap is, of course, that so much witchcraft-in-action remains invisible to the anthropologists even if they are on the spot. But at least as frustrating is that living amid the turmoil of witchcraft rumors, more or less explicit accusations, and a maze of hints that are often not even verbalized but rather expressed in oblique gestures and other forms of bodily behavior, anthropologists are constantly confronted with the inadequacy of the distinctions they have carefully constructed in order to create a modicum of clarity in this marshy field. Time and again surprising turns in everyday life explode such distinctions—a trusted *nganga* (healer) will suddenly be accused of horrible actions (remember the desperate attempts of government committees in South Africa to make rules for a reliable distinction between bona fide and mala fide healers). And often the anthropologist will find that informants staunchly contradict the distinctions they themselves proposed earlier with similar fervor.

All this can be frustrating, yet the great advantage is that it may force the researcher to take the relativity and the slipperiness of these notions most seriously. Or to put it more concretely: I am often envious but also worried by the confidence with which at least some historians posit radical distinctions, such as the one between witches and witch-finders (or "cunning people," "white witches," *désorceleurs*—see below). We shall see that in Europe as well, such apparent clarity is constantly obfuscated by the shifting character of these conceptual oppositions in daily life—again there is a direct link to our central theme, the intertwinement of witchcraft and intimacy, albeit following different trajectories.

Witchcraft, Proximity, and Kinship in Early Modern Europe

Of course there is no question of trying to offer here even a beginning of an overview of historical studies on witchcraft trials in Europe. Especially since 1980 the harvest has become extremely rich. By then there was already significant input from American historians, along with their French and British colleagues. But in more recent decades there has also been a continuous stream of historical research published in German, Italian, Dutch, and many other languages. So the aim of this chapter can be only to make a few comparative remarks on my original topic: the view of witchcraft as a hidden attack from close by.

As said, this idea has a central place in the ambitious "global" definition that the British historian Ronald Hutton historian construed on the basis of his comparison of historical studies on Europe and anthropological data on other societies. His second characteristic, maybe the most substantial one, is that a witch "works to harm neighbors or kin rather than strangers, so that she or he is a threat to other members of the community" (Hutton 2004:422). Hutton substantiates this with references to Ralph Austen's seminal statement, already quoted, that "the efficacy of witchcraft is believed to increase in direct proportion to the intimacy between witch and victim" (Austen 1993:89), and to my own treatment of witchcraft in Africa as "the dark side of kinship" (Geschiere 1997:11). Hutton adds that the emphasis on kinship applies to India and the Americas as well, but less so to Europe. There the relation with "frictions of communal living are just as strong," but rather between neighbors.[12] Apparently the theme of witchcraft-intimacy suggests not only parallels but also differences between African and European patterns. It may be helpful to explore these differences through a brief analysis of one of the richest historical ethnographies from the vast literature on Europe.

The 2009 study by the American historian Thomas Robisheaux, *The Last Witch of Langenburg*, may be the most detailed study of a witch trial we have for Europe. By complementing the relevant files with a wide range of other sources—not only debates among contemporary academics on witches and Satan or on how witchcraft should or should not be persecuted (some of whom becoming directly involved in the trial concerned), but also de-tailed study of the area's geography and analysis of a wide range of data on economic and social developments of the period—Robisheaux succeeds in giving a rich and multifacetted picture of this series of events. Moreover, his descriptions are so lively—yet without stretching the information at his disposal—that the book reads like a detective story, the somber end of which is unfortunately known already. Indeed, in his preface the author himself compares his study to a "modern-day detective story," but adds that he rather sees it as a "social drama" in the style of the anthropologist Victor Turner (Robisheaux 2009:13). The book is, indeed, a brilliant example of how historians can produce ethnography.

The basic story is simple. On February 20, 1672 (Shrove Tuesday), Eva Küstner, daughter of the miller of the village of Hürden, went to offer Shrove-tide cakes that her mother had baked to several neighbors.[13] She offered a few to a friend of hers, Anna Fessler, who had given birth to her second baby one month earlier. Eva asked Anna especially to eat one cake—"Take the pretty yellow one, it will not hurt you." That night Anna got very sick. In the morning she died, her body horribly swollen with a long black stripe from hip to breast. Immediately rumors of witchcraft started circulating throughout the region, which was still haunted by the exposure and execution of several witches a few years earlier. Since Anna Fessler's body looked so suspicious, the municipal physician of the nearby city Schwäbisch Hall was brought in; he did an autopsy and concluded that, indeed, poisoning had been the cause of her death. But he was prudent enough not to venture any guess about the source of the poison (chaps. 1–2).

From the start Eva's mother, Anna Schmieg, the miller's wife, was the main target of frenzied rumors. After all, she was the one who had baked the cakes. But on top of that she had built up a fearsome reputation for a sharp tongue and aggressive behavior—cursing people even over minor conflicts, not hesitating to come to blows with other women, and especially fierce when she felt her husband's honor was at stake. As a miller's wife she also attracted considerable envy—she did not at all fit the stereotype of the witch as an old and lonely woman. A few days later, the count's men came to arrest Anna Schmieg at the mill. A wit-ness reported that as she was taken away she said to her husband Hans, "Good night, you will never see me again in this life." But later, in front of her interrogators, she vehemently denied this, since she knew it could serve as "proof" that she could see into the future (93–94).

The first chapters of Robisheaux's book show an admirable in-depth knowledge of the everyday circumstances of all the people involved—not only of the main figures, the two Annas, but also of, for instance, the women around Anna Fessler's bed (when Eva came to offer the fateful cakes, she was still "lying in" after the childbirth) and their husbands and other neighbors, who were all heard as witnesses. Any anthropologist might envy such detailed factual knowledge, especially its depth in time: Robisheaux describes at length the details of Anna Schmieg's quite mobile life (how her father and subsequently her mother died, how she worked as a servant in the inn in a neighboring town, then met her husband end moved with him to a mill elsewhere until the count appointed him a miller in Hürden), but also the vicissitudes of her husband, how he had fallen into disgrace with the count and then was reinstalled , and so on. This fine analysis of village life and its tensions is complemented by an equally detailed (and vivid) analysis of the complex judicial apparatus that was set in laborious motion when, only two days after Anna Fessler's death, the reports—and popular rumors about evil deeds—reached von Gülchen, the chief counselor and director of the chancellery of Count Heinrich Friedrich of Langenburg.

Langenburg (Württemberg) was one of the small Lutheran principalities that in those days still made up a large part of the Holy Roman Empire. In every respect it fits with Behringer's description of the kind of "halting state formation" that in his view offered a much more propitious setting for the eruption of epidemic witchcraft trials than did powerful absolutist states (Behringer 2004). The principality consisted of only the town of Langenbach (with the count's castle) and a dozen villages. Yet despite the small spatial scope of his authority, the count had full jurisdiction, including over "high crimes" like witchcraft. Robisheaux emphasizes not only the count's "keen sense of dynastic duty and pride" but also "his faith and a sense of responsibility before God" and his "remarkable familiarity with his lands and people" (74). His main counselor, von Gülchen, is described as an equally serious and dedicated man, most conscientiously trying to find his way in the highly complicated debates on how a jurist like him should use his professional knowledge in order to protect the land against evil conspiracies while being fair to the suspects. The last aspect was all the more important since throughout the region it was by now accepted that witchcraft could not be treated as a *crimen exceptum* (extraordinary crime)—as in most of the sixteenth century, when the Satanic character of witchcraft, as a conspiracy against the sacred order as such, was still seen as warranting torture at a judge's discretion. In the course of the seventeenth century it became generally accepted that this crime should fall under *processus ordinarii* (ordinary procedures)—which meant especially that torture in order to get a confession could be applied only under special circumstances. The need to obtain the witch's confession in order to satisfy the prosecutor's conscience, but without applying unlimited torture, was to give trials like Anna Schmieg's a particular oppressive course. Robisheaux's descriptions, notably in his final chapters, on how she was "interrogated" interchangeably by the executioner's torture and the court preacher's heavy moral pressure have a nightmarish quality.

Von Gülchen's first challenge was that he needed more "proof" before he could legitimately order Anna Schmieg to be tortured. An obvious way to obtain it was to try to set her family members against each other. However, Anna's husband, Hans Schmieg, stuck bravely with his wife—which according to Robisheaux was certainly not general practice: "all too often husbands in similar circumstances distanced themselves from their wives" (92). Hans even went to the local tavern to challenge neighbors' gossip about his wife, saying he was willing "to put up all his property to show that his wife was completely innocent." But Eva, their daughter, followed a different course. During the first interrogations she merely denied that she had had anything to do with the baking of the cakes; about her mother she wanted to say only that she did not know whether she was a witch or not. But there were signs of great animosity between mother and daughter. Only later in the book does it become clear that there were very concrete reasons for this animosity. A year earlier Eva had started a daring affair with Philip Kütschner, a boy from the neighborhood. She was then only eighteen years old, but in this area young adults would normally not become engaged until the age of twenty-five or twenty-six. The affair was all the more shocking because her parents had not known anything about it. In the summer of 1671 it became clear that Eva was pregnant, which not only caused a big scandal in the village but also definitively thwarted all her parents' plans for finding her a husband who in time could take over the mill (16). This may have been one of the reasons why, after several interrogations by von Gülchen, Eva was ready to utter severe accusations against her mother, even implying that her mother planned to poison her as well. The two were made to confront each other, and despite heavy cursing by her mother, Eva maintained her statement.

This gave von Gülchen enough material to draw up a lengthy "subsumption"—a common practice among jurists at the time (233): building up a detailed interpretation of the evidence he had against Anna. He focused on proving poisoning but continued to include additional material pointing to witchcraft. Then he had the whole file submitted to the University of Nürnberg at Altdorf for expert advice. After lengthy deliberations, the professors of law and medicine concluded that poisoning with arsenic was highly probable, so they no longer needed to deal with possible evidence of witchcraft (235). However, to complete his case von Gülchen still needed Anna Schmieg's confession. In his own words, she still should *büssen* (confess her sins and do penance)—a notion that came right out of the Lutheran liturgy. She had to confess "out of concern for the salvation of her soul that her hard and obdurate heart be softened, so . . . she could be assured of the grace of God" (263). This "blending of the legal and religious purpose of a criminal trial"—justifying a heavy combination of both bodily and moral violence against the suspected witch—is a truly haunting theme in Robisheaux's analysis.

However, the need to obtain a confession created unexpected difficulties. Anna was duly shown the instruments of torture by Endris Fuchs, the executioner, but she refused to confess. She even "uttered the curse that every executioner or judge feared most, threatening to charge those people who brought her into this game before God on the Judgment Day" (267). Increasing torture was applied—first her hands tied behind her back and then pulled up so that she was lifted from the floor; then thumbscrews were applied "until the blood ran out"—but Anna refused to confess.

This put von Gülchen on the spot. Legally he could impose torture again only if new evidence was produced. He asked the Altdorf experts once more for advice, but their reaction was this time completely negative—given that there was no confession or new evidence, they concluded that Anna Schmieg had to be released from prison. This was completely unacceptable for von Gülchen—particularly since new rumors about other witches in the area were coming up, signs of unrest among the peasants. So he took a desperate step. He decided to ask for another expert opinion, this time from the university of Strassbourg, where he and other Langenburg elites had studied; it had been "a beacon for fervent Lutheran orthodoxy and piety" (275). This proved to be a master stroke. The Strassbourg jurists came to a very different conclusion from that of the Altdorfers. Citing the absence of a confession from Anna as incriminating (!), and following Jean Bodin in his vision of "a grand cosmic political and spiritual struggle,"[14] they condoned further use of torture (283).

This set the stage for the final episode. Together with Court Preacher Dietzel, von Gülchen planned a joint approach of torture and moral pressure. Anna had to confront long sermons and stern moral reproaches by

Dietzel, interchanged with increasingly heavy torture by Master Endriss, the executioner. This combination finally broke her will—or as von Gülchen would have it, it "opened her heart." Even more torture—again interspersed with "intense individualized counseling and instruction" (304)—was required to force her to confess further details, in precise agreement with the script her interrogators had in mind, and also a long list of accomplices. On November 2 she had a final confrontation with Eva, her daughter, and two days later with her husband Hans. On both occasions she managed to withdraw her denunciations against the two of them. On November 8 she was publicly executed together with another "witch," Barbara Sleicher. All the count's subjects were ordered to attend—including the children, in order to edify them. Since both witches had confessed and converted to God, they received a milder sentence—they were not burned alive, but after Master Endris had "torn their flesh by red-hot tongs" he strangled them. Only after this were their bodies burned (306–8).

Yet this was still not the end of the suffering of the Schmieg family. After Anna's execution Eva was released and cleared of all suspicion by the authorities. This was a support she direly needed since during the trials she had been in constant danger of becoming a suspect herself, partly because of her own ambiguous statements. Moreover, as a witch's daughter she would remain an obvious target for suspicion. Clearly the authorities wanted to reward her for her cooperation in exposing her mother's witchcraft. However, after her return to the mill, Eva almost immediately started to accuse her brother Michael and his new fiancée Barbara of trying to poison her. She was now boasting that she had become a witch-finder, denouncing several other people in the village. Eva's accusations had been rather vague, but Michael broke down nonetheless under repeated interrogations and confessed. In jail he was joined by his father, the miller Hans Schmieg himself, who was accused by the executioner, Endris Fuchs.

In February 1673 there was another surprising turn: in the night of the 16th both Hans and his son slipped out of their prison cells, climbed over the town wall, and disappeared. Rumors suggested that Master Endris must have helped them to escape. Indeed, the latter had become himself enmeshed in witchcraft gossip because of his accusations against Hans Schmieg (Endris had accused Schmieg of asking him for certain magical tools, but by this he implicated himself also, since there was strong suspicion that he had supplied the tools). The escape of father and son Schmieg most conveniently destroyed any possibility of their testifying against Endris. Even Eva did not succeed in liberating herself from continuous witchcraft gossip. Her marriage was fraught with distrust and hatred, even though she bore two more children. In 1975 she was forced to confess that she had had an affair with a passing soldier. Her husband divorced her, and she was banned from the village.

Robisheaux describes this sad aftermath in his penultimate chapter, which is appropriately called "Ruin." But he closes this book with a chapter titled "Stories" showing how the memory of Anna Schmieg and other executed witches from the area lived on, with surprising reversals. Around 1750, in the context of ongoing bitter fights with neighboring Catholics, one of the successors to Court Preacher Dietzel wrote a lengthy history of the region in which Anna and her companions still figure as allies of the devil, but in a quite modest role. They are now only one example—among many others, like wars, pestilence, storms, and cattle diseases—of how Satan continued to work evil in the land and how important it therefore remained to constantly reaffirm the true Lutheran faith.[15] However, after 1900 Lutheran Pietism inspired a completely different reading. A certain Agnes Günther, wife of a well-known Lutheran theologian, used Anna's story for a theater play, *On the Witch Who Was a Saint*, that became a huge success. Günther, who claimed to be led by her own "spirit guide" (a certain Gisela), painted Anna and her fellow witches rather as victims of terrible ignorance who became angels through their suffering and whose deep spirituality, unaffected by cruel persecution, would be finally redeemed in heaven. In his last lines, Robisheaux modestly locates his book in this never-ending series of stories.

An African Reading

This long summary can give only a very cursory idea of the riches of Robisheaux's ethnography and all the layers he opens up in Anna Schmieg's story. With apologies for the many simplifications in the above, I hope the summary still shows that it is worthwhile to follow this story in some detail, to see how complex the mixture of differences and parallels is with the stories and events anthropologists study in Africa. Some themes do return, yet the context is overwhelmingly different.

Before focusing on two central elements of the argumentation until now—the relation with intimacy and the ambiguity of all distinctions—I want to note a few intriguing differences of a more general scope. A first one, which really came as a surprise to me, was how all-embracing was the moral hold of ecclesiastical and worldly authorities over the peasantry in

Langenburg. A most striking example of this is what happened when Anna Schmieg's daughter Eva had to confess that she was pregnant. She and her unfortunate lover, Philip Kütschner, were locked up and had to appear before the marriage court, presided over (again) by Court Preacher Dietzel, who admonished them in a long sermon, not only for "fornication" but also for "transgressing the stern proscriptions against dancing and drinking." After two weeks they were pardoned by the count and released from prison. He decreed that they would not be expelled from his territory, and he allowed them to get married. Yet he imposed a most dramatic public humiliation for their wedding ceremony: they had to walk up to the church accompanied by a district officer, and both wearing a wreath of straw (instead of flowers) on their heads (Robisheaux 2009:218).[16] Such a heavy discipline of two young people just because of intercourse before marriage!

More directly related to the witchcraft issue is the moral offensive, frightening in its totalitarian dimensions, that was unleashed against Anna Schmieg in order to make her confess. This was essential not only to redeem her prosecutors' conscience but also because her sins had put the community as such—and even the whole cosmic order—in terrible danger. Only by purifying her soul and bringing about her reconversion to God could Satan's grip on the community be broken. This was the deeper reason that Anna had to be subjected to exceptionally "intensive individual counseling and instruction" combined with torture (304). Robisheaux's chapters 16 and 17 give a haunting description of the massive effort deemed necessary to force her to a confession.

The intensity of this moral offensive, no doubt shocking to modern Western readers, differs profoundly from popular reactions in present-day Africa as well. My informants are certainly morally shocked by new revelations about what the witches are brewing. Moreover, in Africa nonconfessing witches are generally seen as particularly dangerous since apparently they are refusing to give up their powers, not allowing the healer to "neutralize" them. Therefore they are in serious danger of being lynched. But I have not been confronted with any equivalent to the obsession in the Langenburg trial with forcing the witch to confess in order to avert cosmic dangers. In everyday life in Africa people's attitude toward witchcraft is often quite cynical: one has to accept that it exists and that people will use it in order to strengthen their position. Often people suggest that the witch who is caught—either by the authorities (see below) or by the other witches—got what she or he deserved but do not indulge in moral indignation beyond this. Even many of my Pentecostal friends in Cameroon, who are deeply involved in the upsurge of moral preoccupation with the devil as an omnipresent threat, can often be quite pragmatic about the omnipresence of witchcraft in everyday life.

Another difference from anthropological studies is how difficult it is to get the figure of the witch in focus from Robisheaux's book (and from many other studies of European witchcraft trials, in fact). Robisheaux's picture of von Gülchen, the main prosecutor, and his motives is much clearer than that of the main protagonist, Anna Schmieg. Only in the latter chapters, exploring Anna's struggle against the pressure to confess and her final "opening of the heart," gets her personality more filled out. Of course, the earlier chapters provide much detail about her life and her quarrels with her neighbors. Yet one cannot help wonder what she is up to in her aggressive moods, for instance, when she warns her neighbor that she will "poison the pasture" where his cow had been grazing in order to "make it die" (63); or, while drinking in a tavern, throwing a goat's head at someone who was slandering the honor of her husband (122).

Doing research in Africa makes one realize how complicated the balancing of signs and suggestions on occult powers is in everyday life. My assistant during my research among the Maka taught me right from the start that it can be dangerous to insist that one is "innocent," not only because it makes you temptingly easy prey for the witches but also because it is not the way to earn people's respect. When people say about someone that his or her belly is "empty"—the belly is the seat of the *djambe* (occult force)—or that one has a *djambe* "like a fish," this is not necessarily a compliment. It rather means someone is a *lem* (a weakling)—this in contrast to a *yague moud*, an ideal type that the Maka invariably describe as *un homme bien blindé*, a man who is "well armored." Such a magical aura inspires respect. In my 1997 book I made a comparison with a poker game: in everyday life it is important now and then to drop hints that you know your way in the occult world, or at least have your special protections; yet you should never be too emphatic about it, because this could make you vulnerable to accusations.[17]

Many historians of the European witchcraft trials seem to struggle with the question—often betraying true amazement—of how it was ever possible that European people were so preoccupied with witchcraft. In her challenging study *The Witch*, Diane Purkiss accuses them of "rites of distantiation":

Rather than trying to understand how witch-beliefs were structured for and by the believer, historians have often bent their energies towards explaining witch-beliefs away. Assuming witch-beliefs were an abnormality and a pathology, they sought to explain how such ideas could have arisen, rather than what those ideas were. . . . The only serious question to be asked about witchcraft, it seems, is still 'why, oh why?,' perhaps because only this question is distancing. (Purkiss 1996:61)[18]

Purkiss's somewhat ironical comment certainly does not do justice to Robisheaux's and others' recent studies. Yet it is true that historians often tend to see the witches' confessions as merely products of terrible pressures from their prosecutor. The sources historians use—all the horrors of torture and harsh interrogation—may reinforce the tendency to try to look through such dark obsessions and see the witch as an innocent victim and her confessions as mere fantasy. This of course also helps one to avoid the tricky issue of witchcraft's "reality."[19] Yet even if one wants to avoid this basic question of reality—and there are good reasons to do so—it is still hard to deny the probability that when belief in witchcraft's efficacy is widespread, at least some people will be tempted to play into it. Robisheaux is certainly conscious of this. He mentions, for instance, that Anna may have used her reputation as a "hellish woman" in order to play upon her neighbors' fears of witches. But he leaves it at that.[20]

However, in this respect—which hangs closely together with the ambiguities of the witch and her intimate powers—there is certainly not an absolute contrast to the African examples from the chapters above. For instance, the Italian historian Oscar Di Simplicio (2002 and 2009) shows that it is possible, on the basis of historical sources, to give a fuller picture of the witch in her or his dealings with neighbors.

Di Simplicio's subtle analysis of the inquisitorial archives of Siena conjures up complex images of people who are accused as witches but clearly act as healers at the same time. One of them, Maria from Roccastrada, a forty-five-year-old midwife, was arrested in 1589 as a witch, severely interrogated by the inquisitor, but released after a mild verdict. On her return to the village "she walked the main street shouting threats of retaliation: 'Those who have witnessed against me will repent. . . . There will be no more births in this village'" (Di Simplicio 2009:136). At the trial of "Big Angelica" from Radicondoli (1594), a seventy-year-old woman with a great reputation for healing "bewitched infants," another healer declared: "She threatens to stab whoever is willing to testify [against her]" (Di Simplicio 2009:135). Di Simplicio relates this to a general conviction that witches could heal what they had previously harmed (132)—which he sees as a basic trait of "a system of village witchcraft beliefs" (123). This "system" must have had its own ambigui-

ties in view of the many-faceted confusions he highlights between healing and bewitching. It is precisely by giving ample space to all these
ambiguities that he provides such a vivid picture of how persons used
these representations in everyday life.

In a somewhat different vein, Lyndall Roper shows in her challenging
study of witchcraft trials in Augsburg (Roper 1994) that a psychoanalytic
approach, inspiring a consequent focus on the body, can help also to
bring the figure of the witch more into the picture. Concentrating on the
witches' confessions, she proposes to read them neither as products of a
"collective psychosis" nor as leftovers from older pagan beliefs, since in
both views the witch becomes no more than "a conduit . . . of fantasies
outside herself" (those of her interrogators in the first case, and of past
wisdoms in the latter). She rather sets out to take the witch's fantasies
seriously and study the process of negotiation with her interrogators in
order to produce a convincing confession (230, 240). In the cases of
"lying-in maids," who were often accused to have attacked the mother-
hood of the women they worked for, Roper sees the admission of envy
as the turning point. Once the maid had confessed envy, she was ready
to see herself as a potential witch. "This was the breaking point which
then catapulted her into a range of other confessions about the Devil"
(214). In a subsequent chapter Roper relates the confessing witch's
elaborations upon the devil—in constant and oppressive interactions
with her stern interrogators—in a more strictly psychoanalytical sense
to fantasies about the father figure. Clearly it could be very tempting in
Europe as well to hint at having special powers.

This relates to a more central point in the African examples above and
the preceding argumentation: the precariousness of all conceptual distinctions—notably that between witch and healer. The very riches and sub-
tlety of the data Robisheaux has been able to accumulate and the flow of
his vivid descriptions show time and again how easily different roles could
shade into each other. For example, Eva, Anna Schmieg's daughter, turns
from a witch into a witch-finder, and then again into a witch. The distinctions between "common folk magic" (or "folk medicine") and witchcraft
are constantly shifting: Hans Schmieg's burying the head of a black cat under his mill could be seen as "just superstition," but other circumstances
turned it in the court's eyes into a possible sign of witchcraft (150). The
most ambiguous person in the story is no doubt the somber figure of Master Endris Fuchs, who was Anna Schmieg's executioner. This role, generally
seen as dangerous, seemed to qualify him at the same time not only as a
"folk healer" but also as a "seer" and "witch-finder" (154). But this was not

all: the ambiguities of his efforts at witch-finding brought him to the verge of being accused himself as a witch. Only the mysterious escape of Hans Schmieg (for which some blamed Fuchs himself—317) saved him from being persecuted.[21]

Such shifting grounds are especially problematic when the basic distinction between witch and healer is at stake. This topic seems to divide historians as much as anthropologists/Africanists (see above). Robisheaux does not dwell very long on these supposed antipodes to the witches. The only healer/witch-finder who gets more profile in his study is executioner Fuchs, just mentioned, who in the eyes of both the court and the population seem to come dangerously close to being a witch himself. It is important to emphasize such fluidities in everyday life, since other historians insist—like the Africanists quoted before—on a strict separation between witches and healers (called also "cunning folk," "white witches," *indovini, désorceleurs*). They do recognize that the authorities—in Europe as in Africa—tend to use the term *witch* for both roles. But this seems to make at least some historians all the more intent on untangling such "confusion." This applies especially to studies of the ongoing role of "cunning folk" and other kinds of "wise people" in European societies after the witchcraft persecutions had subsided. In the eighteenth and nineteenth centuries, for instance, De Blécourt and Davies emphasize that such "magical practitioners" continued to play an important role throughout Europe, but they insist also that such healers—even if they were sometimes addressed as "witches"—have to be set apart from notions about "evil-doing women."[22]

However, most historians of the times when witchcraft seemed to take on epidemic proportions in Europe are more prudent. Not only do they note that the authorities often did not make any distinction in their persecutions (ecclesiastical courts in particular attacked witch-finders and healers as aggressively as witches), but they note that in the eyes of the population as well, such distinctions tended to be quite precarious. Neighbors were quick to suspect a "wise woman" of using her powers for harm. Briggs (1996:171) notes that "witches and witch-doctors form one of the tightest of all symbiotic relationships" and dwells on "the ambiguities attaching to the position and techniques of the healers" (122). And even Keith Thomas, who was one of the first historians in the academic debate to draw attention to the role of the "cunning folk," notes a widespread belief among the people that they might work in partnership with the witches whose evil they were supposed to undo (Thomas 1973:656).[23]

Christina Larner is as outspoken on this point as on others. Her graphic comment could be a quote from one of my Maka friends from Cameroon:

Power to heal was two-edged. Power to heal could be withheld; it could be deployed in a whole ambiguous area of love potions, . . . prophesying . . . and so on. In fact very few healers confined themselves to healing. Special powers were special powers. The healer could be persuaded to become a killer . . . or even more likely could initiate curses and vengeances on her own behalf if crossed or refused payment. (Larner 1984:151)

The Dangers of Intimacy: Neighbors or Family?

The major point on which parallels between the studies on Europe and the African examples above shade into differences is the focus, central to this book, on witchcraft in relation to closeness/distance. Nearly all authors seem to agree that in Europe as well, witches are supposed to attack especially from close by. However their victims will be neighbors rather than kin.[24] But can the two be so easily opposed?

As noted above, Hutton (2004) with his ambitious "global definition" of witchcraft, is categorical on this point: in Africa, India, and America witches may often be kin, but Europe is the exception; there, witches are neighbors and the main accusations come from outside the home. A powerful case for this is made also by Robin Briggs in his overview of European witchcraft studies under the programmatic title *Witches and Neighbours* (1996). Briggs includes a whole chapter titled "Love and Hatred: Spouses and Kin," but it gives an image that is strikingly different from the notion of the house as a hotbed of accusations as in the African examples above. Briggs recognizes that "if ties of blood bind people together, it is often with a special intensity of mutual hatred" (226), and he cites cases in which internal accusations and fears do tear a family apart. Yet the chapter is mainly about whether a woman who is denounced as a witch by a neighbor would be defended by her own folk. And Briggs concludes that "family members normally rallied to defend one another in a crisis" (252). Clearly accusations and rumors come mainly from outside the home; they may even stimulate people from one home to make a common front.[25]

However, the more ethnographic a study becomes, the more difficult it seems to be to maintain such a distinction. In a very subtle analysis of the long-term transformations of a peasant community in Württemberg in its interaction with changing forms of *Herrschaft* (domination) from 1580 to 1800, David Sabean (1984) also distinguishes neighbors and kin. But he immediately complicates this distinction by adding another one, between affines and blood relatives. Through his close reading of the eager confessions of Anna Catharina Weissenbühler, a thirteen-year-old daughter of a dissolute family who works as a nanny in the home of a distant cousin (at least she sometimes referred to him as *Vetter*), Sabean conjures up a vertiginous articulation of distinct layers. Of special interest is the opposition he deduces from her ever more complicated stories between "food" and "the word." One recurrent motif is the interrupted meal; indeed, Anna Catharina's contacts with the devil made it very difficult for her to eat. Another is her inability to recite the Lord's Prayer. She explains that "the devil sits on her tongue, so that she can hardly swallow; when she should have recited something from the sermon, she was unable to speak for a while" (104).

Sabean relates the "metaphor" of food to relations within the village, and the struggles with "the word" to the crystallization of *Herrschaft* and the way villagers related to outside elites' efforts to discipline them (1984:104–5).[26] For the first aspect, he concludes that the story highlights a crucial demarcation: witchcraft is *passed on* in a consanguine line (between blood relatives), but witches are supposed to *attack* their affines or their neighbors.[27] This very fine distinction is most interesting in itself, yet it raises the question whether witchcraft discourse was ever so precise and fixed in its distinctions. Robisheaux's story of the undoing of the "last witch of Langenburg" lays out, by its very detail, a much more complicated picture. It is true that Anna Schmieg, the witch, is originally accused of attacking her neighbors and not her kin. Moreover, her husband takes a courageous stance, continuing to defend her. But as things develop, the accusations start to penetrate her own home: daughter Eva begins accusing her mother of being a witch and subsequently even pretends that Anna tried to poison her. Later on, Anna accuses her own son of being a witch, while Eva also directs her accusations against her brother and his new fiancée. In the end the family is torn apart by witchcraft accusations.

In Europe as well, then, the conceptual knot of proximity and occult aggression is too complicated to be undone by the simple opposition of "neighbors and not kin." More complex differences between what is and is not seen as "the house" may play a role.

Favret-Saada on the Bocage: *Désorceleurs* Denouncing Neighbors

Precisely on these aspects, central to this book's argument, it is interesting to compare to Jeanne Favret-Saada's seminal study of *sorcellerie* in the Bocage (rural Normandy) in the 1970s. Favret-Saada comes to quite different conclusions on two points discussed above: she emphasizes a radical distinction between *sorcier* (witch) and *désorceleur* (healer), and in her analysis it is vital that the witch is always identified as outside the house—certainly close by, but a neighbor and not a relative. Of course, Favret-Saada's work

(1977/80; 2009) has special aspects in comparison with the historical studies on Europe cited above. Not only did she work in a present-day context, but she approached the topic also as an anthropologist. This proved to be quite difficult in the beginning, since it took her considerable time to overcome strong distrust among the farmers, who hardly wanted to talk to her. But once people had more or less placed her in the shady domain of *la sorcellerie*, she could tap into a surprisingly rich circulation of rumors about desperate struggles between households, many stretching back over years. This makes her sources decidedly different from those of the historians, just as the way in which she herself became involved in these secret dealings. Yet it is of interest—all the more since in her 2009 study (unfortunately still not translated into English) she places her earlier work in historical perspective—to look at her interpretations in line with the historical studies on Europe during earlier centuries.

The very reasons for the farmers' deep distrust against the young anthropologist and her interest in the occult indicate already how different the setting was from early modern Europe, notably with respect to the locals' relations to the outside world. Favret-Saada started her work just after a series of scandals had exploded in the regional and national press. Several journalists had written sensational articles about the proliferation of amazing forms of superstition "only a few hours away from Paris." An article on the "magician of Aron" described with some irony how this expert made husbands accept that their sterile wives would pass the night with him. Another on *la Dame blonde* described how this *désorceleuse* (healer) made the mistress of a farm ride naked on her cows, straddling them back to front. The farmers deeply resented such reporting, in which they were invariably represented as backward and gullible. No wonder their comments to the ethnographer were initially very cynical ("désorceler, c'est pour l'argent. . . . pour coucher"—unbewitching is only for money and sex; Favret-Saada 1977:65). Things only changed gradually after one family that she tried to interview attributed to her the knowledge of a *désorceleur* (lit., unbewitcher). Her quizzical reply—she could try to heal "with words"—apparently did not discourage them. Her position became even clearer when an "announcer" (throughout her work Favret-Saada highlights the special role of a person who warns others that they are being bewitched) told her she was herself under heavy attack. Because of all sorts of personal mishaps, she was ready to accept the role of the *ensorcelée* (a person being bewitched). She started long-term therapy with a *désorceleuse*, Madam Flora,[28] and in the end became her assistant. This long and often painful journey resulted in a vivid study (Favret-Saada 1977) that not only surprised readers by its topic and the riches of its material but also gained general admiration because of the sharpness of her analysis and the origi-nality of her insights.[29]

As noted, Favret-Saada is formal about the distinction *sorcier-désorceleur*. For instance, she sharply disagrees with Jules Lecoeur—a nineteenth-century folklorist she quotes in general with great approval—for using the term *sorcier* for both witches and *désorceleurs* (2009:59, cf. also 69–77; and 1977:283). In her view, the two *fonctions* have to be radically separated, and the terms refer to different persons. The ways Madam Flora, Favret-Saada's own *désorceleuse*, interrogates her clients may often be of a somewhat frightening intensity, yet there is no sign that the client would have any reason to fear her special powers. However, her 1977 monograph builds up to a spectacular climax in which all the roles the author distinguished so carefully suddenly start to shift and turn into their own opposites.

> In the course of the book Favret-Saada condenses the complicated pat-terns in her very detailed case studies in graphs of increasing com-plexity that circle around three poles, the triangle of *ensorcelé, sorcier, désorceleur* (cf. chaps. 6 and 11). Yet the case she is describing toward the end, that of Jean Papin and his wife Joséphine, suddenly seems to invert the neat triangles. The case plays a central role in the study. It was Jean Papin and his wife who started suggesting to the ethnogra-pher that she might have the gifts of a *désorceleuse* herself. The Papin case—like most of Favret-Saada's cases—had a long history. Jean had had a minor accident just before his marriage; as a result he had be-come unable to consummate the marriage, and since then the farm had been plagued by all sorts of misfortune. Joséphine, and more reluctantly Jean, became engaged in a long search for the *sorcier* who was behind all of it. Only when Favret-Saada brought the Papins in contact with her own *désorceleuse* did a deeper reason emerge: before the marriage, another *désorceleur* had identified Jean as the *sorcier* who had attacked his client. This incompetent *désorceleur* had been of course dead wrong. Yet he had sent *le mal* to *le pauvre* Jean, who had never fully recovered from this.

Favret-Saada's analysis of the implications of the surprising turn of this case is quite masterful. Suddenly all three categories start to float: Jean was not only *ensorcelé* but, at least according to some, also *sorcier*. However, the most spectacular transformation is that of the *désorceleur* who because of his incompetence had attacked Jean as an evil *sorcier*. The expression *rendre le mal par le mal* (return evil for evil) that Favret-Saada quotes is strongly evocative of the way Cameroonian *nganga* constantly insist that all they do is *renvoyer le mal* (send back the evil—cf. chap. 3 above). And it seems to have the same implications here. For the *ensorcelé* the *désorceleur* is often his last hope and therefore his hero. But for the neighbor whom the *désorceleur* identifies as the *sorcier* who attacked his client (often the victim's best friend) and who is suddenly sharply isolated, all this means an evil and direct attack on his integrity. For him the *désorceleur* visiting his former friend is an evil witch.[30] Favret-Saada even suggests that the leitmotif through the *désorceleur*'s long therapy is to make the *ensorcelé* willing to "return the evil"—often a difficult step since thus he becomes like the *sorcier* himself (1999:47, 81). The circularities that seem to haunt discourses on witchcraft in Africa reemerge here despite all the apparent clarity of the distinctions in European visions.

Precisely because Favret-Saada's ethnography is so vivid and rich, it is worthwhile to follow into more detail the other distinction on which she insists: the *sorcier* is the neighbor outside the house and not the relative inside. Favret-Saada emphasizes that people will look for the witch close by, just as in the European studies of earlier days. After all, bewitching is supposed to require regular contact, especially physical contact. But the *désorceleurs* always discourage people from looking among their close kin and rather divert attention to one of the neighbors. Initially victims often suspect, for instance, their own brothers—and in view of unequal sharing of inheritances there is ample reason for this—but the *désorceleur* always redirects their attention to people close by, yet not kin. On this point as well Favret-Saada is formal: the people identified as witches are neighbors, maybe even one's best friend, but never kin.

Indeed, the complex therapy the *désorceleurs* are prescribing—not just the ritual of protection that is the climax of the therapy but also a series of prescriptions that have to be followed to the letter day by day—expresses a fervent effort to close the house against outsiders. The whole farm has to be fenced, and all entry points have to be protected with bags holding special powders. Moreover, avoidance has to be maintained in all aspects of everyday life: one has to avoid all contact with the *sorcier*, never visit his house, refuse to shake hands with him, never look into his eyes; if he addresses you, just repeat the last word; if he enters your compound despite all this, quickly throw blessed salt against his ass (*il faut lui saler le cul*). The *désorceleur*'s main ritual only crowns this long-term operation of closure: after all these therapeutic preparations, the healer will stage the big act, often a real struggle ("ugh, this one is really powerful") for breaking the spell. This ritual can take different forms, but if things go well, it will bring the witch running to the place in great agony: cooking an ox heart and piercing it with pins will make him feel as if he were being stabbed all over; roasting salt in a baking pan so that it jumps and cracks will make him dance and jerk (Favret-Saada 2009:34, 46; see also 1977:250–97). This is a sure sign that the *désorceleur* has succeeded in gaining the upper hand—that he managed indeed *à rendre le mal par le mal* (to return evil for evil). From now on the *ensorcelés* will eagerly look for any sign of decay in the neighboring farm, for all their own complaints—fatigue and illness, loss of livestock, cows that give no milk, fields that do not produce—should now haunt the neighbors.

For Favret-Saada, *sorcellerie* in the French countryside does not originate from jealousy within the family or from within the house; rather, it is a struggle of house against house. Therefore, therapy against it is a drastic closure of the house against outsiders, not a reconciling of the people within the house as in the preceding chapters on Africa.

Especially in her 2009 book Favret-Saada places her insights in a longer historical perspective by comparing with a very detailed folklore study, *Esquisses du Bocage normand* by Jules Lecoeur, already mentioned, from 1883–87 (Favret-Saada 2009:55–76). Of special interest for our topic is that Lecoeur's descriptions of popular ideas on occult attacks, from the time that has been called *l'apogée de la civilisation paysanne* (the heyday of peasant culture) in France, differ in crucial respects from the patterns Favret-Saada was confronted with in the 1970s. She relates this difference to the further crystallization of the small *exploitation agricole familiale* (family farm) as the dominant socioeconomic form in the area in the twentieth century. In many respects the imaginary on the dangers of *sorcellerie* as she studied them in the 1970s corresponded to a closure of the house as the unit of production, management, and consumption. This socioeconomic closure seems to be completely in line with the main pattern in the farmers' speculations about occult aggression.

Some examples from Lecoeur's nineteenth-century descriptions suggest that in those days tensions among kin may have been more important in witchcraft accusations.[31] But apparently things have changed since then. But also Favret-Saada's reckoning of who is kin and who is not seems to be influenced by the narrow definitions of the house that were apparently used by her informants. In some cases the perceived witch is a cousin or an affine (see, for instance Favret-Saada 1977:322), but she does not see this as an exception; apparently since they lived outside the victim's house, they do not count as kin, at least not full kin. This trend toward closing the house may be the determining context for Favret-Saada's emphasis on neighbor and not kin; it may also influence people's imaginary on *la sorcellerie* in specific ways.

There are indeed striking contrasts to the African examples and the idea of witchcraft as the dark side of kinship. But summing these up as a difference between neighborhood and family—European conceptions of the witch centering on the neighbor versus African notions centering on kin— may be a simplification. It rather seems that different conceptions of the house, and thus of kinship, are involved. Favret-Saada's insistence on the closure of the house seems to apply, though maybe less strictly, to the historical examples from sixteenth- and seventeenth-century Europe as well. In all these contexts witchcraft is certainly related to proximity and everyday contact, but it is at least to some extent located outside the house; indeed, in struggles over witchcraft houses tend to close themselves.[32] This is a very different from the image of the house in the Maka conception of the *djambe le ndjaw* (the witchcraft of the house, which was central in the preceding chapters). In the Maka example—as in many other African ones— the origin of witchcraft is, indeed, primarily looked for within the house. But a more important difference may be that in many African contexts the limits of the house are relative. The Maka term *ndjaw boud*—literary 'the men of one house," now mostly translated as "family"—can have narrower or wider dimensions depending on the context: it can refer to the people living in one compound, but it can also include related groups living close by in separate compounds, or even migrants, who are still seen as members of "the house" no matter how far away they live. From the literature on Europe—both Favret-Saada and the historical studies—a conception of the house emerges that is more fixed and limited, more or less determined by the spatial limits of the house or compound.

It might be interesting to relate this to another contrast. African witchcraft stories are about witches and their victims, but they dwell at least as much on the endless struggles among the witches themselves. Remember the "martyr stories" in which, for instance, a man dies unexpectedly and people think he has fallen victim to a treacherous witchcraft attack. But others will suggest that he himself was a witch who got the worst of one of the terrible fights among witches (maybe because he refused to sacrifice another relative). In Europe, in contrast, witchcraft stories seem to focus mostly on the witch-victim relationship and much less on treacherous struggles among the witches themselves. In the sixteenth and seventeenth centuries this may be related to the outside pressures of state and ecclesiastical courts whose interventions aimed to protect innocent victims and eradicate the witches, who were seen as allies of the devil and therefore threats to the cosmic order itself. Yet the same emphasis is to be found in Favret-Saada's stories, in a context in which the local witch-craft imaginary is much more left to its own devices. Favret-Saada herself is also quite formal on this point: a *désorceleur* will attack only *sorciers* who bewitched his or her clients, never other *désorceleurs* (1977:357). There is a huge difference here with the African *nganga*, who are believed to be con-stantly attacking and ambushing each other. In Favret-Saada's work stories about battles among the witches themselves are as absent as they are in the historians' studies.

This must have direct implications for issues of scale. As said before, in many African contexts witches are assumed to have a special hold over their own relatives and to direct their attacks mainly at them. Yet witches amongst themselves are not limited by the bounds of kinship. They can always attack each other, whether kin or nonkin: as soon as someone "goes out" (leaves his body), he becomes visible and therefore vulnerable to all other witches. This is part of what gives witchcraft in African contexts such a frighteningly wide scope. In comparison, the witchcraft imaginary in Eu-rope seems to be quite parochial. There hardly seems to be an equivalent to the other side of the representations in the African examples above: witchcraft as a discourse that may be rooted in local realities yet directly opens up to the world outside.[33] In Africa, this outlook to the external world seems to be given with the basic image of witchcraft: witches be-traying their own relatives to their companions from outside during the witches' sabbath—remember the image above of witchcraft as a treacher-ous opening in the closure of the family, draining the community of its life force. It is precisely the ambiguous role of these notions on the interface of inside-outside—the intimacy of the family and the unfamiliar world outside—that gives them so much resilience in modern contexts. It allows witchcraft to "globalize" without losing its local moorings. In Europe the resilience of local ideas in wider social settings seems to be less marked.[34] Of course, here as well witchcraft was supposed to attain global dimen-sions, but in a more abstract sense: in the sixteenth and seventeenth cen-turies it came to be seen as a conspiracy of Satan against the cosmic order as such. But the practical relevance of these local notions for understand-ing new forms of enrichment and the increase of scale of social relations remained more limited.

Closing or Stretching "the House"

All this seems to give the conceptual knot of witchcraft in its articulations with distance and closeness quite different implications in Europe and in Africa. At first sight the scope of witchcraft seems to be greater in the European conceptions—it requires closeness, yet it is not located inside the house but rather covers the whole neighborhood. In many African contexts it is located *within* the house. Yet the confusing thing is that almost everywhere in Africa the house has—or maybe it is safer to say *had*—an open character, in line with the great elasticity of kinship relations. Remember the stories above of transcontinental migrants from Africa who still feel threatened by the witchcraft of people at home—apparently they have not yet achieved enough distance to be impervious to "the witchcraft of the house." Kinship in these contexts seems to attain truly global dimensions. In the early 1970s my Maka informants would already tell me mockingly, "Oui, oui, la famille africaine est très, très grande" (yes, the African family is very big), when I tried to make sense of the very complicated equations they used in order to capture a certain relationship in kinship terms. Since then with growing mobility, now even transcontinental, this stretching of kinship has assumed unprecedented forms.

Is it possible to link this to different notions of kinship and different conceptions of intimacy: a European one bent on closing the house and an African one favoring its opening? Or, more broadly, a trend toward a shrinking of kinship and an ever-growing emphasis on the nuclear family in Europe, versus the almost limitless elasticity of kinship, highlighted above, in Africa? Such contrasts open up vast perspectives. It is, for instance, tempting to relate differences in the development of kinship relations to Jack Goody's elaborations, quoted in the prologue, upon the much discussed contrast between "wealth-in-people" and "wealth-in-things."[35] The first pattern would be characteristic of Africa, where land remained an open resource, so that control over people was the determining factor in the reproduction of power and inequality. The second would be rather characteristic of Eurasia, where it was possible to gain control over people and their labor through the accumulation of "things," notably land (landowners could make the landless dependent upon them because of their accumulation of land).

The interest in the context of the present book is that Goody relates these differences to variations in arrangements of kinship and marriage (dowry in Eurasia, which encouraged a hierarchization of society; bride price and polygyny in Africa, with opposite effects—see also n12 in the prologue). The reckoning of kinship would be more inclusive in many parts of Africa, reflecting the urgent need to attract as many people as possible to the local unit; such a setting seems to promote an open, inclusive conception of the house. In the European context kinship would rather tend toward closure of the group in order to protect its heritage, thus institutionalizing more or less fixed forms of inequality—a configuration that encourages a closure of the house, as the seat of control over scarce resources that have to be protected against outsiders . Such differences may be further reinforced by the emergence—or nonemergence—of alternative forms of social security, making people less dependent on the family. An important difference in this context might be that to many throughout Africa the family still seems the main basis for security, precisely because of its all-inclusive tendencies. It may therefore be of interest to explore to what extent Goody's vast contrasts are relevant for recent developments— notably the constant increase of scale for many African societies of kinship relations, which now acquire a global span, giving the flow-back of remittances and development projects to the village of origin a special urgency. The globalization of concomitant notions of witchcraft might be placed against this vast historical background.

Yet there are good reasons to be careful with such daring generalizations, since, as said, there are no doubt important internal variations. Social ones: richer European families—and notably the aristocracy—certainly set great store on maintaining wider kinship networks (but in these cases as well, this implied at the same time a drastic closure of the group). Also regional variations: as we saw, the studies by Joseph Tonda (2002 and 2005) and others on Congo suggest a dramatic undermining of the family there, most strongly exemplified by the fact that people no longer have to be buried in the village of birth. Moreover, it remains to be seen to what extent the Pentecostals' attack on the family as the seat of the devil will bring, in at least some parts of Africa, a further crystallization of the nuclear family to the detriment of broader networks.

Nevertheless, despite the need for prudence, there is a clear advantage to following the differences highlighted above—different patterns in people's ways of articulating intimacy and witchcraft—and relating them to long-term variations in the ways societies produce and reproduce themselves (to borrow Goody's terms again): it can help in surpassing simplistic culturalist explanations. It might be tempting—especially to anthropologists—to try to relate the impressive elasticity of the house or the family in many African contexts, and the concomitant preoccupation with witchcraft from inside, to a particular essence of African kinship, as a sort of cultural given. But in the end such explanations become redundant and quickly dated in view of the equally impressive dynamics in people's ways of "working" with kinship and its dangerous implications—producing constantly new forms, often of a hybrid character in articulation with new possibilities coming in from outside. Studying such contrasts historically—along the lines Goody proposed already some time ago—as resulting from different articulations between the organization of kinship and inheritance, on the one hand, and changing material circumstances, on the other, might be more rewarding.

The long-term and quite variable processes of how kinship formations became involved in wider economic circuits are at least equally important. A concept Jean-François Bayart emphasized throughout his work could be useful here: his emphasis on *stratégies d'extraversion* (strategies of extraversion) as particularly present in forms of accumulation in Africa.[36] Again, the centrality of such strategies is related to local circumstances—limited possibilities for enforcing surplus production at a larger scale, which often made control over trade (or warfare) more profitable. But even more important might be the way Africa came to be included in the world economy. The present dependence of African elites on development cooperation can be seen as a new version of this old tendency toward *extraversion*. I will return below to such vast insights—both Goody's production and reproduction and Bayart's *stratégies d'extraversion*—and their implication for understanding different ways of articulating witchcraft and intimacy.

As noted, there is good reason to be prudent with generalizations, especially on a continental scale. Africa and Europe certainly cannot be compared as homogeneous blocks—there are too many internal variations. Yet it seems safe to conclude from the comparisons in this chapter that historical differences in perceptions of intimacy and distance—in defining "the house" and the span of kinship—have been vital for the reproduction of ideas on witchcraft and their inherent dynamics. From the literature on Africa and Europe certain tendencies emerge from the reckoning of kinship that seem to relate, on the one hand, to very real differences in material contexts and, on the other, to varying conceptions of the link between intimacy and danger. Or to put it more directly: the remarkable mobility of witchcraft in African conceptions—its capacity to relate vast global processes of change so directly to local realities—appears to be linked to special conceptions of kinship and "the house."

5

COMPARATIVE PERSPECTIVES II

Candomblé de Bahia—Between Witchcraft and Religion

IN THE CONTEXT OF THIS BOOK it may be self-evident to compare with Europe in view of the many references in Africanist literature on the witchcraft conundrum to the European witch hunts of early modern times. But a comparison with the trajectory of Candomblé in Northeast Brazil and its impressive rise from disrespectable origins to a respected "African" religion is at least as challenging, for various reasons. First of all, there is the direct historical link with Africa, strongly emphasized on both sides of the Atlantic. But the ideas and practices that Candomblé priests celebrate as "African" followed a markedly different course at the other side of the ocean. There sorcery/witchcraft likewise was (and is) linked to intimacy, but Candomblé seems to have developed its own ways of establishing trust so as to overcome these dark suspicions.

Still far into the past century Candomblé was equated by many—not only Portuguese colonialists but also liberal elites and many commoners— with *feitiçaria* (sorcery), considered pernicious.[1] However, over the past fifty years, the major Candomblé temples with their powerful priestesses have become national symbols of trustworthiness. To put it more polemically: what was seen as "witchcraft," a sort of antireligion, in Africa turned into a religion respected by at least a vocal portion of the Brazilian public.[2] A leading question for this chapter, then, is how in the Bahian context trust could be built not by radically opposing the hidden forces (as the Pentecostals do in Africa by the equation with the devil) but rather by building upon them. How could representations that used to be so strongly associated with *feitiçaria* become the basis for the prestige of Candomblé temples with their splendid rituals that seemed to offer only protection and spiritual peace? A related question is whether the ambiguity of these forces, so strongly apparent in African contexts, could be as completely vanquished in the Brazilian context as many Candomblé studies suggest. Lately this has become a raging issue, since the Candomblé temples have come under vigorous attack from Pentecostal preachers who do not hesitate to associate them again—and in no uncertain terms—with *feitiçaria*.

Another difference from Africa may be important in this context. As numerous authors attest, the fear of hidden attacks may be as strong in Brazil as in many African countries. Yet, there are hardly any parallels with the epidemic outbreaks of witch hunts that haunt the history of Africa— both colonial and postcolonial—and that of Europe. In Brazil the emphasis seems to be much more on healing and offering protection than on detecting and punishing culprits. Of course, these contrasts are not as sharp as they may appear in this summary. Still, they warrant asking how different trends can be related to specific patterns in the intertwinement of intimacy, occult aggression, and trust. In Brazil as in Africa, people see a close link between hidden aggression and intimacy, but this nexus—and more generally the body of ideas supposedly borrowed from Africa—acquired new implications in the very different historical configuration that developed there.

Candomblé: Commonalities with and Differences from Africa

In summer 2008, after ten days of intensive teaching at a most inspiring summer school at the Federal University of Bahia,[3] I had the opportunity to make a brief trip into the Sertão, north of Salvador, and carry out a series of interviews with local healers and shrine priests. This was possible only because Luis Nicolau Parés (professor at the Federal University of Bahia and author of a series of seminal texts on the history of Candomblé) agreed to accompany me.[4] We were keen to visit the zone since we both had just read a challenging PhD dissertation by Brian Brazeal (University of Chicago, 2007) on the impact in this zone of Candomblé—especially of the temples in the small city of Cachoeira, which is, next to Salvador, the main historical center of this Afro-Brazilian cult. The Sertão, the dry zone in the Northeast of Brazil, is often sharply contrasted to the more fertile lands around Salvador da Bahia, historically the area of large-scale plantations (mainly sugar) with concentrations of slaves. In the Sertão everything is dryer, poorer, and harsher. In his dissertation Brazeal sketches a kind of religious frontier between the two areas, highlighting how the Cachoeira temples seek to recruit clients among the poor *sertajenos* (people from the Sertão). However, they have difficulty controlling their adherents in this outlying zone where their representatives are confronted with less prestigious local forms of healing.

Our interviews went quite well. Nicolau Parés introduced me as a colleague who worked with healers in Africa. This immediately attracted interest—for Africanists Brazil, and certainly the Northeast, is a paradise since it is one of the few areas in the world where people will not commiserate when you say your work is on Africa; on the contrary, direct knowledge of this continent commands respect, even in isolated villages of the Sertão. However, despite the cordial reception, the interviews were quite confusing—for me at least—since I repeatedly thought I recognized things, only to discover that everything was quite different. Similar to the contexts in which I did research in Africa was the omnipresent fear of occult aggression. People would speak of *feitiçaria* as a danger that was lurking everywhere in society.[5] As in the African examples above, this form of occult aggression seemed to come mainly from close by.[6] Yet there were differences as well. The family seemed to be relegated to the background by frequent use of kinship terms (*mother, daughter,* less often *father, son*) in religious contexts: in the Candomblé temples but also by healers (*curandeiros*) more generally. This may reflect the role of these shrines as a sort of replacement for the family after the disruption wrought by slavery (see below).

Familiar for me was the kind of balancing act that these healers had to manage.[7] A recurrent theme in the interviews was the difference between *linha branca* (white) and *linha preta* (black).[8] Of course, most healers would emphasize that they always stayed on the "white" side; the "black" side seemed to be only for their colleagues.[9] But people from the same neighborhood would be more explicit: all these healers dabbled in the black side as well. In many respects this reminded of the *nganga* and their difficult balancing between good and evil ways of using their special powers. It was all the more surprising—and this was the first major difference I stumbled upon—that the stories were mainly about protecting and healing people, and much less than in the African contexts I know about exposing witches or other secret evildoers and punishing them. We did not get any stories reminiscent of stern *nganga* setting out to "purify" a neighborhood by their "science," denouncing people as evil witches, and dragging them to the *gendarmes* as in some of the Cameroonian examples above. People seemed to expect protection and healing from the *curandeiros*; identifying witches seemed to be less important. The healers themselves would say that if they did not succeed in lifting the evil, they could always send people to the prestigious Candomblé shrines in Cachoeira. The powerful "gods" of the *mães* and *pais di santo* (priestesses and priests) would deal with such evil in their own way. In the midst of an omnipresent threat of hidden aggression, Candomblé seemed to constitute a beacon of trustworthiness—at least to some.

The other surprise was how close this Candomblé—which I knew from a very rich literature as a proud African-Brazilian religion—was associated with *feitiçaria* in people's stories about everyday events. This turned out to have a long history. In the colonial records any suggestion of an African ritual or celebration was associated with evil and the work of the devil (de Mello e Souza [1986] 2003, chap. 1). This did not change much after 1889, when liberal elites put an end to the monarchy and instituted a republic (slavery had been abolished only one year earlier—one of the last decrees of a fading royalty). For the liberals, the multiplication of African cult houses—frequented not only by people born in Africa but also, more shockingly, by (ex-)slaves born in Brazil and even by whites—was a painful sign of the country's backwardness, and maybe even the cause of its stagnation. Only very gradually—from the 1930s on—did Candomblé's spectacular emergence as a "true religion" come about, within a very specific configuration of changing ideas on race and national identity (Parés 2004, 2007, and 2011; Matory 2005; van de Port 2011).

However, despite their growing prestige, the temples remain haunted by constant references to malevolent sorcery. In the literature, this is a subtext often hidden under the author's fascination with the rich imaginary and ritual proudly exhibited by the temples, but cropping up at the most unexpected moments—for instance, in rivalry between *terreiros* or even inside these temples. This hidden aspect is mostly just mentioned as an unfortunate exception, without further elaboration—and this obvious embarrassment seems to turn it into a guilty secret.[10] More recently, this darker side has been denounced via virulent attacks from the Pentecostal churches that have had spectacular success throughout Brazil. As said, Pentecostal ministers do not hesitate to attack Candomblé priests as allies of the devil who are profoundly enmeshed in malevolent sorcery (for a telling example, Birman 2011:228n9; see also Maggie 2011:160; Sansi 2011:36). According to many observers Candomblé, despite its continuing or even increasing prestige among the elites, is losing support among the popular masses under the Pentecostal onslaught. Even in Bahia, commoners flock to the ever bigger Pentecostal churches, where Candomblé priests are denounced as dangerous sorcerers—an attack that, at least to some, is convincing since it confirms rumors that have always circulated in society.

This rapid summary is clearly in need of nuancing, which I will try to do below. Still, it already raises intriguing questions. Why does Bahian people's preoccupation with hidden threats as an omnipresent danger—more or less parallel to present-day obsessions in many African contexts—not lead to the kinds of concerted actions against "the witches" that regularly create havoc in Africa? Is this related to the rise of Candomblé as a religion? But then how—or to what extent—does this new religion avoid being sucked into the vicious circles of sorcery/witchcraft discourse like so many of its African counterparts? How do the priests, and even more the priestesses, succeed in being accepted by many as beacons of trust, overcoming the ambiguities that continue to plague African healers?

History: From Witchcraft to Religion—The Struggle for Purity

The classical anthropological studies of Candomblé—published around the middle of the twentieth century—which contributed so much to its recognition as a highly moral religion, were from the start marked by melancholia. All of them mourned Candomblé's apparent loss of an earlier purity. The *mães de santo* of the prominent Nagô temples (Nagô or Ketu is the local term referring to the present-day Yoruba from southwest Nigeria) were depicted as being in a constant fight to retain the African heritage brought by the slaves. But to the classical authors this appeared to be a losing battle. Roger Bastide, for instance, in his huge work *Les réligions afro-brésiliennes* (1960), which he presented as a contribution to "a sociology of the interpenetration of civilizations," sees decay setting in on all sides. The centers of the Northeast, *dahoméen or yourouba*, may still maintain their coherence as "a means of social control, an instrument of solidarity and communion" (408, 418). But according to Bastide, elsewhere only the trickster god *Eschou* remains of the African pantheon, and he is being turned into a power for evil sorcery. *Désorganisation* is setting in, reducing the *mémoire collective* of an African religion to the individualized *macumbeiro* (sorcerer) of the big cities like Rio or Sao Paolo, "isolated, sinister and feared as a *redoutable sorcier* [frightening sorcerer]" (416).

Taking a much lighter tone, in her well-known *City of Women* (1947) American anthropologist Ruth Landes sketched a similar vista of decay that threatened to undermine the purity of the African heritage. In the typical style of Franz Boas, the great ancestor of American anthropology, she was sent to Brazil in the 1930s with a very open-ended task: "to make a study of Negro life there." Especially typical of this anthropological school was the idea of studying something quite different from—or even opposite to—American society: "We had heard that the large Negro population [in Brazil] lived with ease and freedom among the general population, and we wanted to know the details. We wanted to know also how that interracial situation differed from our own in the United States" (Landes 1947:1).[11]

Landes tried to show that an important reason for this greater ease and freedom was to be found in the wisdom and the energy with which the great *mães de santo* (priestesses) defended the African heritage of their temples, and the disciplined freedom Candomblé brought to women in general—of course, all this in distinct contrast to her own American society. Landes was a shrewd observer, and she seemed to have had a sharper eye for ambiguities and irony than Bastide. She was, for instance, quite conscious of the ambiguities of Eliseo Martiniano do Bonfim, one of her main informants—already quite old when she met him, and a towering figure in the affirmation of Candomblé's African roots. At the end of the nineteenth century he had traveled to Africa for an extended period and had extensive training with religious experts in Yorubaland; he had used all this knowledge in a most dynamic way to try to purify Candomblé of non-African elements. Landes knew that the hardships of life forced even this proud man to dabble in sorcery activities of a dubious nature (1947:22, 208–9). Yet she insisted in seeing these aspects as a degeneration of an original African purity. In her view other elements—like the central role in some temples of male priests who allowed themselves to be "mounted" (possessed) by the gods (Landes termed them "passive homosexuals"); the undisciplined performance of *caboclo* spirits, supposedly from a native (that is, Amerindian) background; and certainly malevolent sorcery in general—likewise manifested degeneration. All these elements were disturbances of an older "African heritage." The irony is that these elements kept cropping up in her stories, often at inconvenient moments.

> Indeed, such "disturbances" confounded Landes's very first visit to a Candomblé temple (typically, she chose the Casa Branca do Engenho Velho, the Nagô/Yoruba temple that is supposed to be the oldest in Salvador). First the dancing of the women was somewhat rudely interrupted by a man who was clearly possessed by a *caboclo* spirit and insisted on dancing among them despite all efforts to block his access to the dance floor. (In the end the *mãe de santo* allowed him to dance, but next day a note was attached to a big tree at the temple's entrance announcing that men were not allowed to dance in this temple—probably a useless warning since *caboclos* tend to return time and again to these temples, welcome or not.) Even more ironic was that while walking down a steep slope, Landes twisted her ankle so sharply that all the care of the priestesses was in vain—which led them to declare that she had been the object of a very vicious sorcery attack right in the heart of the temple (Landes 1947:44).

What makes Landes's book still so appealing more than sixty years after publication is that she does not try to hide such events even though they seem to be at odds with the general thrust of her argument. Yet she insisted on seeing them as an unfortunate counterpoint that did not belong in "true" Candomblé as practiced by the powerful "mothers" of the pure Nagô (Yoruba) *terreiros*.[12]

Interestingly, historians have taken exactly the opposite view: a fascination with mixing rather than a celebration of purity. Laura de Mello e Souza's very rich study ([1986] 2003) of popular religion in the sixteenth, seventeenth, and eighteenth centuries paints a broad picture of how Candomblé-like *terreiros* emerged gradually from the *batuques*—drum sessions with ritual dances—that black slaves held more or less in secret whenever they got the chance. De Mello e Souza's sources (mostly colonial archives) from the seventeenth and eighteenth centuries introduced a new term, *calundus* (next to the older term *batuques*), which apparently indicated that the drum sessions were accompanied by spirit possession and healing; in this sense the *calundus* can be seen as preliminaries to the Candomblé *terreiro*. But her main aim is to show that early on such African elements were already mixed with European and other elements. Her analysis is in terms of syncretism and not of purity. She shows that for the colonials—and especially for Jesuits and the Inquisition—the threat of syncretism in the colony was equivalent to the fear of heresy in the metropolis. This meant that any trace of African influence was automatically equated with the work of the devil, and therefore also with witchcraft/sorcery. But the colonial authorities were not the only ones who saw things this way. De Mello e Souza often cites complaints by commoners who denounce black and mulatto *curandeiros* as sorcerers (xv, 121, 129).

One of the most vivid cases she discusses is the tragic affair of Luisa Pinto, a freedwoman from Minas Gerais, "publicly reputed to be a sorceress," who was brought before the Inquisition in Lisbon in 1742.[13] The denunciations against her described a ritual that greatly resembled those of present-day Candomblé. For her *calundu*, she would stand

> on a little altar with a canopy, a scimitar in her hand, a wide ribbon tied around her head, with the ends of the ribbon toward the back, garbed in the manner of an angel, and two Negro women, Angolan as well, would sing while a Negro man would play *atabaque*, which is a small drum, and they say that the Negro women and Negro man are slaves of the aforesaid, and that they play and sing for a length of one or two hours, [and] she would appear to be out of her mind, saying things that no one understood, and people she cured would lie down on the ground; she would move

over them diverse times, and it was on these occasions that she received winds of divination. (Souza [1986] 2003:170; cf. also p. 233)

Despite Luisa's courageous and quite perspicacious denials—she insisted that she did not know the devil, and she emphasized the Catholic elements in her practices—the inquisitor found sure signs of a diabolic pact in her special abilities. She was subjected to full torture, after which she confessed.

João José Reis's work on the nineteenth century and Luis Nicolau Parés's history of the Jeje nation, one of the oldest Candomblé associations, sketch the difficult transition from such *calundus* centered on the performance of one *curandeiro* (healer) to more organized and permanent Candomblé-style *terreiros* (Reis 1993; Parés [2007] 2011). But both authors emphasize that this was certainly not a unilinear, clearly outlined process—rather a hesitant accumulation of changes, full of reversals and digressions. An important transition was the multiplication of deities around one shrine. While in earlier decades healers would claim a special relation with one spirit, the Candomblé temples emerging very gradually in the nineteenth century would claim special relations with a whole pantheon. Different "nations" grouped themselves around different sets of deities—Angolan *inquices*, Jeje *voduns*, and, most prestigious of all Nagô (Yoruba) *orixás*—but most of these gods were considered to have equivalents among the deities of other nations.[14] These sets of deities played a crucial role in initiation rites, another key aspect of Candomblé. Priests could establish and maintain a *terreiro* only by regularly initiating *barcos* (boats—a heavy metaphor in a slave society!) of novices. These were mostly women who came to the priests in order to be healed from all sorts of afflictions. The priest would identify which deity was troubling the client. During a Candomblé session the client would become possessed—"mounted"—by this god. A long initiation had to follow during which the novice would learn to live with "her" god, and this would lead to a lifelong attachment to the temple and the priest(ess) that was almost impossible to break. It was these long-term initiations that turned the shrines into permanent institutions—temples, or "convents" to follow Bastide's terminology—built on a piece of land (*terreiro*) owned by the leading priest or priestess that could be inherited by his or her successors.[15]

In many respects these centers, mostly well hidden in the bush, constituted a refuge for slaves—hiding fugitives, offering at least a temporary respite from the harshness of slavery. But in other respects the *terreiros* perpetuated at least some aspects of slave society. The initiations were very demanding: novices were locked up for months in a room, often under very harsh conditions; the full initiation process could last for several years, during which the novices were more or less at the mercy of the priest(ess); and as a result of all this, they incurred lifelong obligations. Indeed, Reis speaks of "despotic priests," and he reports on an 1876 case of an "African priest" who wants to sell someone else's slave who "is now under his spell" (2011:65, 67; see also van de Port 2011:139, 200). He shows also that most priests who succeeded in founding a temple were freed slaves; probably many of them had been able to buy their freedom with the money they had accumulated by working as a *curandeiro*.[16]

Of particular importance to the topic of this book is that the temple—*terreiro*, literally "locality"—became an alternative to the house or the family for slaves who had lost their social identity due to the horrors of the Middle Passage. Kinship terminology was (and is) used as a matter of self-evidence both inside the *terreiro* and in relations between *terreiros*.[17] The novices became "daughters"—less often "sons"—of the *mãe* or *pai de santo* (mother- or father-priest). Similarly, the religious ancestry of one's initiator became crucial to legitimize one's status as a true priest. Thus Casa Branca do Engenho Velho (also called Ilê Iyá Nassô), now generally recognized as the oldest Candomblé house—it is supposed to have been founded in 1830—acted as the mother house to two other high-profile temples in Salvador, Gantois and Opô Afonjá, since the founders of the latter two had been initiated in Casa Branca (Butler 2001:142; Matory 2005:180). Such relations of religious kinship created lines of descent between different houses, but they also determined in principle the succession within each house. In such contexts kinship expressed religious affiliation rather than links of birth and upbringing.[18] However, in practice the rules were often far from clear. Nicolau Parés (Parés [2007] 2011:chap. 6:5, 8, 11) emphasizes that biological kinship remained very important inside the temples, which led to accusations of nepotism, internal contests over succession, followers switching to other temples, and so on.

Historians show that the highly institutionalized present-day Candomblé temple must be seen as an institute that emerged gradually and not without struggle from a chaotic field marked by dazzling forms of syncretism. This makes the present-day obsession with purity and authenticity that prevails especially among the leading Nagô (Yoruba) temples all the more intriguing. How could the appeal to the purity of an African heritage acquire such force, and why were relative outsiders—not only foreign anthropologists like Bastide or Landes (and many others) but also Brazilian academics like Nina Rodrigues and Arthur Ramos—so captivated by this vision? In retrospect it is clear that this issue of purity was crucial for Candomblé's transformation into a respected religion, the topic of this chapter. Lorand Matory's seminal study *Black Atlantic Religion* (2005) raises this question most poignantly and gives it an extra dimension. Matory emphasizes that this celebration of African purity not only is at odds with the historical data but is also a striking exception in the Brazilian context, where especially since the 1930s—under the impact of Gilberto Freyre and others—"mixing" was elevated as the hallmark of Brazilian national character. In sharp contrast to this, but more or less since the same time (the 1930s), the great *mães de santo* who became the venerated mothers of Candomblé—*mãe* Aninha and later *mãe* Stella of Opô Afonjá, and *mãe* Meninha of Gantois—made it an article of faith that there was no place in "real" Candomblé for foreign incursions; even the impact of European or colonial elements was categorically denied.[19]

Matory quotes with some approval a group of more recent "anti-essentialist" authors who place doubt on the celebration of Nagô (Yoruba) purity.[20] According to them the supremacy of the Nagô nation is to be seen not as an outcome of African history (with the Yoruba having a special role, as the official hagiography of the Nagô temples suggests) but rather as the product of "arbitrary, local invention by whites . . . Brazilian, French and American academics. . . . since the 1930s." In this vision, "the prestige attached to the claim of 'Nagô purity' is a mere artifact of Euro-Brazilian scholars' consent to protect from the police only those houses that embraced the *scholars'* definition of Africanness, which included a disavowal of 'black magic'" (Matory 2005:45, see also 157).

Matory shares this vision to a certain extent, but not its implied emphasis on white agency. For him, black agency remains crucial in the emancipation of Candomblé and its appeal to a Nagô purity.[21] He tries to show that in many respects it was the *mães de santo* (and to a lesser extent the *pais*) who led the academics rather than the other way round. But even more important for him is the continuing interaction—even throughout the period of slave trade, and all the more afterward—across the Atlantic between Salvador, on the one hand, and, on the other, the West African coast: at first especially with Ouidah, the main port for the slave-trading kingdom of Dahomey (now in Benin), and later with the Yoruba area in present-day southwest Nigeria, with Lagos as its emerging center.

For Matory as well, Eliseo Martiniano do Bonfim—the same one who made such a deep impression on Ruth Landes—played a key role in the emergence of the Nagô nation as the leading one in Salvador's Candomblé. As mentioned above, Martiniano had traveled to Lagos in 1875, stayed there for eleven years, and received extensive religious training (Matory 2005:46; see also Landes 1947:22). But Matory emphasizes that Martiniano was certainly not the first African-Brazilian to return to Africa. Already during the high era of the slave trade, quite a few Africans—freedpersons, but also slaves sent by their masters—repeated the notorious Middle Passage in reverse. This is confirmed by a 2007 study by Lisa Castillo and Luis Nicolau Parés, who unearthed a rich collection of documents supporting the oral tradition that already in the first half of the nineteenth century Iyá Nassô, supposedly the founder-priestess of the Casa Branca do Engenho Velho temple (also called Ilê Iyá Nassô and, as said, reputed to be the oldest Candomblé house) went with her "daughter" Marcelina and "granddaughter" Maria-Magdalena to the "Yoruba" city of Ketu, and later returned to Bahia (see also Butler 2001).[22] Castillo and Nicolau Parés identify Iyá Nassô (a Yoruba title) as a certain Francisca da Silva, a freedwoman, who first owned Marcelina as her slave, then initiated her into her temple (thus becoming her mother in a religious sense) and subsequently freed her. Marcelina left Ketu after just two years to return to Salvador (probably in 1839); her daughter Maria-Magdalena followed several years later. Castillo and Nicolau Parés show how frequent such to-and-fro trips became during the nineteenth century.

These stories with mythical appeal fit into a larger context of ongoing exchange between Brazil and the West African coast. Indeed, since the 1800s *brasileiros*, with Francisco Felix de Souza as their well-known leader, were a major presence in Ouidah, more or less autonomous from the successive Dahomey kings but always closely collaborating with them.[23] Trade in African goods—kola nuts, special kinds of soap, and religious items—remained very important. Matory (2005:121) makes a direct link with the role of *mãe* Aninha as the founder of the prominent Opô Afonjá temple and a staunch advocate for a return to African purity. Supposedly it was through her involvement in trade with Africa in the early decades of the twentieth century that she accumulated the money necessary for buying the land for her temple. She came to be Martiniano's inseparable companion, and their collaboration, especially during the 1930s, was, according to Matory, crucial in founding the claim to Nagô/Yoruba purity as the dominant trend in Candomblé—subsequently accepted by the "white outsiders" who became so fascinated with this "African religion." The obsessive emphasis on purity served not only to valorize the religious expertise Martiniano and other returnees brought back from their visits to Africa but also to confirm the value of the African products sold by several priestesses.

Many recent authors (Matory 2005, but also Parés [2007] 2011; Reis 1993, 2001, and 2011) emphasize, moreover, certain demographic shifts in the slave trade. Until the beginning of the nineteenth century most slaves arriving in Brazil came from the coast of West-Central Africa. These are supposed to have brought the "Angolan" *inquices* still celebrated in *terreiros* of the Angolan nation (compare *nkisi*, a term for fetishes in widespread use in the Congo area up to the present day). These "Angolan" temples may still be more numerous than those of the Nagô (Yoruba) nation, yet the proud *mães de santo* of the main Nagô temples look down on their cult as wild and impure. In the nineteenth century Salvador received increasing numbers of slaves from the Mina coast (at the time the current name for the West African coast stretching from Accra in present-day Ghana to Lagos in present-day Nigeria). Especially after 1830, with the final collapse of the famous Old Oyo empire in southwest Nigeria—due to attacks from Islamized groups around Ilorin, a tail end of the *djihad* that pervaded the whole Sudan area—slaves from groups that would later be labeled Yoruba became ever more numerous.[24] This shift set the background for the rapid rise of the Nagô nation to dominance in Salvador's Candomblé.[25]

However, for Matory, historical events with a very different background were equally important—notably the rise of Lagos as a new intellectual center. In 1861 the British established a protectorate over Lagos, in their continuing struggle to put an end to the slave trade (then still going on, in part by the *brasileiros* mentioned above). This allowed them to repatriate slaves coming from that region whom they had intercepted on the ocean, liberated, and first settled in Freetown in Sierra Leone. Many of these liberated slaves came from present-day southwest Nigeria and were now returned to the Yoruba region in Lagos's hinterland. In the meantime, however, they had attended the mission school in Freetown, and thus Lagos became the intellectual center of an emerging Yoruba identity—the impact of which was strong since these new intellectuals' literacy proved to be a powerful tool in spreading the new ideas. After the 1880s, however, this "Lagos renaissance" was nipped in the bud when Britain occupied the whole of present-day Nigeria and started to lay foundations for a real colony. In the new colonial setting there was no longer scope for African intellectuals of independent mind like the Lagosians. Many of them reacted by vigorously attacking the racism of British colonial rule. Returnees from Brazil became closely involved with the ups and downs of the "Lagos renaissance." For Matory the continuing interaction with this group was crucial in what people in Salvador call the *aNagônizaçao* (Nagônization) of Salvador Candomblé—Matory speaks also of the "Nagô juggernaut"—beginning in the first decades of the twentieth century.

In his fine-grained analysis of the rise of the Jeje Candomblé, Luis Nicolau Parés similarly emphasizes the continuing interaction between West Africa and Bahia, but he focuses on the more western parts of the Mina coast (present-day Benin/Dahomey and Togo) in order to highlight the special role the Jeje nation played in the emergence of Candomblé. As said, the Jeje call the gods, who "mount" the priests, the priestesses, and the initiated, *voduns*—a term still in use in southern Ghana, Togo, and Benin. Nowadays, though, the few remaining Jeje temples also use—at least outside the temples—the Yoruba term *orixás* as more or less an equivalent, a sign that they seem to have become increasingly subsumed under the dominant Nagô regime. However, even though the Jeje nation seems destined to disappear, Nicolau Parés suggests in a very subtle analysis that the Jeje nation and its borrowings from Dahomey must have played a crucial role in the transition from *calundu* to Candomblé. Against Bastide and Verger, Nicolau Parés emphasizes that the multiplication of gods in one temple—many *orixás*, *voduns*, or *inquices* manifesting themselves during one session—was not a novelty emerging only in Brazil. There are clear signs that a similar transition took place quite early—possibly in Abomey, capital of the kingdom of Dahomey, and in the port city of Ouidah.[26] Also the emphasis on initiation as crucial to a temple's continuity—priests legitimizing themselves only through initiating consecutive *barcos* (boats) of novices—corresponds to institutions developed early on, especially along that part of the coast. The special merit of Nicolau Parés's analysis of the interstitial role of the Jeje temples, now overshadowed by the prestigious Nagô *terreiros*, is that he shows that these older temples built not on a static African "tradition" but on the dynamics of cults on the Mina coast that were themselves products of constant changes.

The particularities of the continuing interaction between the West African coast and Bahia set the stage for an emerging celebration of Yoruba purity that became crucial to the emancipation of Candomblé as a religion. It is clear that this growing emphasis on African—read Nagô/Yoruba—purity as a hallmark of a true "religion" was historically circumscribed by a set of specific factors and linkages. Yet its effects were most real: this vision was very effective in helping the leading Nagô temples in particular to shed associations seen as disreputable. We shall see that in this context special conceptions of the link between intimacy and occult power emerged, centered on the temples that could profile themselves as beacons of trust. Apparently even in these "houses" intimacy still turns out to be highly ambiguous in practice. Yet the history of Candomblé, tortuous as it may have been, shows also that it is possible to build quite effective forms of trust not by denying the invisible forces but, in contrast, by embracing them.

National Identity and Regional Politics
Another quite different set of factors was at least as important for Candomblé's rise as an ever more respected "religion": this was the crystallization

of a specific politico-cultural context at the national and the regional levels. Especially after the 1930s, a series of developments increasingly favored
the prominent *mães de santo*. Yet, again, this was certainly not a unilinear
development. On the contrary, there were constant ambiguities and surprising turns. Well into the 1970s, Candomblé temples were raided by the
police. However, already decades earlier there were persistent rumors that
mãe Aninha of Opô Afonjá had such good relations with dictator-president
Getúlio Vargas that she could intervene with him on behalf of opponents
persecuted by the police. Moreover, the constant difficulties with the police triggered the founding in 1937 of the Union of the Afro-Brazilian Sects
of Bahia—in 1946 transformed into Federation of the Afro-Brazilian Cult—
which tried to establish its own control over the temples. The union/fed-
eration pretended (and still does) that this control would enable it to separate the bona fide temples from shadier elements—thus posing as some
sort of guarantee vis-à-vis the police and the authorities of Candomblé's
trustworthiness.[27]

In a vivid and challenging study, *Ecstatic Encounters*—with the programmatic subtitle *Bahian Candomblé and the Quest for the Really Real*—Mattijs van
de Port (2011) shows how complex these developments were, full of internal contradictions and reversals, but despite all these twists confirming
time and again the sacredness and the aura of power of Candomblé as
a religion. The aim of his book is certainly not to write a history of Candomblé. Van de Port rather stresses, in good Lacanian style, that he is interested in Candomblé because it is such a powerful and at the same time
enigmatic expression of "The Real." Profusely quoting Lacanian thinkers
such as Žižek, Eagleton, and many others, he is clearly fascinated by Candomblé's potential, throughout all the deep changes of the last hundred
years, to defy "symbolic closure"—that is, to repeatedly escape any clear
classification or definite characterization, retaining its aura of secret power
and thus appearing to be beyond history. But even though (or maybe because?) his main interest seems to be in the movement's apparent capacity
to surpass history, van de Port offers a vivid account of the contradictory
changes that marked Candomblé's historical rise to respect and general
recognition.

His book starts from a reorientation in Brazil's national consciousness
in the 1920s that was to be crucial for Candomblé. A first sign was the rise
of the *modernistas*, a group of avant-garde artists, mainly from São Paulo,
who advocated a determined breach with the country's established liberal
elites and their celebration of Europe as the example for the Brazilian nation. For the *Modernistas* Brazil´s "primitive" side, so abhorred by the liberals, was a source of strength and should be celebrated as the hallmark of

an original Brazilian identity. They were strongly influenced by European surrealists and their veneration of the primitive. However, for these Brazilian artists the primitive was not something far away that had to be recovered but an ongoing reality that was available on the spot for the young nation to re-create itself. Initially they looked for this creative primitive not so much in black culture as in the country's Amerindian heritage.[28] Distant Bahia and its black heritage entered the national awareness somewhat later, especially through the novels of Jorge Amado, which quickly became enormously popular throughout the country (and beyond). The attraction of Amado's novels was his vivid and very carnal imagery of "the street." Candomblé's mysteries—both its violence and its healing—played a crucial role in this imagery as the center of a Bahian (= black) culture.

Amado was part of the "regionalist" movement, whose other kingpin, Gilberto Freyre—mentioned above and also a Northeasterner—started the cult of Brazil as a *mestiço* nation: its racial hybridity had to be seen not a weakness but as a source of pride. Such ideas were appropriated—and adapted for its own purposes—by the populist and increasingly authoritarian Vargas regime (roughly 1930–54)[29] in its attacks on the old liberal elites—depicted as "backward elites" who were blocking the ascent of the Brazilian people. For these politicians Candomblé could play a most welcome role as one of the repositories of the power of the people. No wonder *mãe* Aninha could develop such a special relation with President Vargas. Yet such a political use required a certain disciplining of Candomblé "to clean it of its dangerous dimension, its unsettling, disruptive and fear-inducing power" (van de Port 2011:125). The Union of Afro-Brazilian Sects, founded as mentioned in 1937, was to provide for this.

At the provincial level, Juracy Magalhaes—in the 1930s Vargas's "inventor" for Bahia—and Antonio Carlos Magelhaes (not related), the area's main political boss from the 1960s until after 2000, played crucial roles, both in making Candomblé the epitome for Bahia, and in cleaning up its appearances.[30] The temples' role as assets for encouraging tourism further encouraged such cleansing operations. Van de Port (2011:135) quotes a tourist guide from as early as 1958 reassuring a wary traveler: "In orthodox Candomblé, it can't be stressed enough, one only finds the practicing of religion. The place called 'terreiro' is a place of worship and that is all there is to it. There is no witchcraft being practiced here, nor *curanderismo* in the sense of a contravention of the law . . ."

However, such "aestheticizing" of Candomblé—reducing it to a kind of "public folklore"—was frequently crossed by other interventions. In the 1960s, for instance, a series of films by Trigueirinho Neto, Glauber Rocha, and others aimed to break through these tame images of the cult, opposing it to bourgeois values and highlighting the harsh realities it had to address (van de Port 2011:141). In the 1970s the Bahian based Tropicália movement, headed by such celebrities as Caetano Veloso, Maria Bethânia, and Gilberto Gil—all famous singers from the region—brought Candomblé the support of national idols. Around the same time the temples became sites of transnational attraction for new forms of religiosity—van de Port (2011:141) refers to "the dawning of the age of Aquarius"—and also ecological movements; several priestesses started to emphasize Candomblé's deep respect for trees and sacred groves. From the 1990s on, the budding gay movement used the contested but very visible role of homosexual priests in the temple as an opening for annexing Candomblé as a religion of gays. And even the black movement—after long hesitation toward a religion that seemed to dampen political protest—came to celebrate it as an icon for the black struggle (van de Port 2011:148, 152). Emancipated as a true "religion," Candomblé had become a "symbol bank" from which any group could draw.

The originality of van de Port's analysis is to insist that despite all this investment in it by a wide array of interests and groups—his chapters 3 and 4 give a vivid overview of this kaleidoscopic turmoil—Candomblé never was annexed by any of these groups. On the contrary, despite its leaders' willingness to respond to all the overtures from politicians, leading artists, ecologists, gays, the black movement, and many others, the religion remained an emanation of wild powers that no one could control or even fathom.

> Time and again, Candomblé imagery has managed to resist the over-kill. . . . In spirit possession, Candomblé stages a body that, in the eye of the outside observer, seems to be totally outside control, subject to unknown forces. The sheer carnality of Candomblé practices, their being rooted in the drives and forces of the body, charges the images derived from these practices with an ill-concealed eroticism, or better still, with *jouissance*, the amoral dimension of all human existence that escapes all cultural signification. (van de Port 2011:155, with reference to Barthes)

In this view, Candomblé continues to defy any attempt at "symbolic closure" or any form of domestication that threatens to rob it of its power. Yet in his later chapters van de Port notes new elements that might imply a certain containment. Like Matory, he is questioning the increasing emphasis on African purity that led an authority like *mãe* Stella to explicitly reject any forms of syncretism—though unbridled practices of syncretism can be seen as the very source of Candomblé's power.[31] The celebration of total hierarchy to protect this purity—as the same *mãe* Stella put it: "hierarchy is all; beginning, middle, and end" (van de Port 2011:245)—also seems hard to reconcile with Candomblé as *jouissance*. Van de Port dwells also on the increasingly high profile of national celebrities in temple sessions—hugging the priestess while others have to prostrate themselves—which seems to increase the dangers of a fairly one-sided dependency on these elites for maintenance of the temples and the expensive rituals. The concomitant and sharply increasing interest among Candomblé priestesses in gaining access to new media, especially TV—after a long period of avoiding any form of publicity and a tendency to harbor secrets—has important effects: "televisual looks" increasingly influence the formatting of the cult in its rites and other practices. All this suggests an increasingly "white" Candomblé (van de Port 2011:209, 222, 244, 270n77). But in the end van de Port is convinced that due to its reliance on spirit possession, Candomblé will continue to escape any form of closure. For our topic a question that is obvious—certainly as seen from Africa—is what this tendency toward increasing institutionalization as a religion implies for Candomblé's darker side, the association with occult powers and hidden aggression. Another question, maybe even more important, is whether this ongoing refusal of "symbolic closure" can help to explain Candomblé's particular ways of establishing very real forms of trust despite inherent danger.

Feitiçaria versus Purity

According to Matory, the increasing emphasis on African purity started with Elisio Martiniano do Bonfim and mãe Aninha in the 1930s. Van de Port emphasizes *mãe* Stella's stringent condemnation of syncretism in 1984 as a turning point in this respect. But whatever the differences, it is clear that this whole idea of African purity had powerful effects on the rich and multifarious literature on Candomblé. In many studies, the darker side of its representations and practices is relegated to the background or even completely denied. This makes it particularly interesting to follow how these aspects nonetheless turn up in the classical studies of the 1930s and 1940s and continue to manifest themselves in everyday practice.

In this respect Landes's 1947 book is again of special interest. In contrast to other contemporary authors, she does pay attention to the more frightening aspects of the temples. For instance, she was clearly intrigued by a *mãe de santo* called Sabina who is described as quite flashy, sporting an unusual "modern" profile. However, Sabina turned out to be quite controversial as a "mother" of a temple since she had not been properly initiated. She explained to Landes that this was not necessary in the *caboclo* tradition to which she belonged—she claimed "to be made by the spirit of an Indian . . . who came to her in dreams" (159). And, indeed, she had a considerable following of people who were convinced of her powers.

When Landes went to visit her, Sabina gave her—quite unexpectedly and without being asked to do so—a brief display of these powers: "the Indian" suddenly possessed her while she was talking to Landes, and he made his "horse" (that is Sabina, the priestess) speak in threatening ways. However, his orders were suspiciously blunt: Landes had to pay a significant sum of money and submit to an intense initiation, or else . . . (188–91). That night, back in her hotel, Landes had a terrible nightmare of a "huge attacking head of a fierce cat whose eyes burned and bore down upon me; and in the split second before my awakening the cat head broke into a sardonic grin" (191). The message of Landes's section on Sabina is clear: this *mãe de santo* was prepared to use her powers for personal gain and even evil. So apparently Candomblé could be linked to malevolent sorcery. However, Landes is quick to point out that Sabina was not a real "mother"; she approvingly quotes a disdainful comment of her very good friend *mãe* Meninha of the famous Gantois temple: "*That* one grew up wild! No hand of mother or saint made *her*!" (158). Landes agreed with her good friend Édison Carneiro (another disciple of Nina Rodriguez who accompanied Landes on many visits) that this whole *caboclo* tradition was a "breakaway" from the Yoruba "orthodoxy" at the root of Candomblé (158). Clearly, in Landes's view, malign sorcery showed its ugly face only in aberrations from this "African" religion. No wonder that studies from such a perspective have little interest in the more hidden ways in which Candomblé temples in everyday life become involved in people's preoccupations about occult dangers.

In the second half of the twentieth century this perspective was made ever more explicit by the leading *mães de santo*. Typical is the categorical positioning since the 1980s of *mãe* Stella, the powerful mother of the Opô Afonjá temple, not only against any form of syncretism in Candomblé but also against "immediatism." Her disapproval of "immediatism" is a direct attack on *caboclo* worship where priests boast of the immediate results of their work. For *mãe* Stella this is "an impious practice for the pursuit of immediate material benefits in lieu of long-term piety" (Matory 2005:255, 337n28). However, such a determined appeal to absolute purity as the hallmark of the Nagô tradition is constantly contradicted in practice since *cab-*

oclo spirits continue to invade even the rituals of highly respectable Nagô temples. Remember Landes's experience at the Casa Branca temple, where during her very first attendance at a Candomblé session a man possessed by a *caboclo* spirit insisted in dancing among the frightened women—a type of emergency that keeps occurring in Nagô temples. Moreover, in present-day Salvador there continue to be strong rumors of dignitaries at the leading temples who meddle in all sorts of ways with *curandeiro* (healer) practices. A somewhat paradoxical consequence of leading Candomblé priests' formal insistence on an "African" purity that denies such practices—a current vision in much of the literature—is that it becomes difficult to understand what exactly these temples can then offer to the common people. Why do people need the priestesses at all, if they refuse to support their everyday struggles against hidden attacks?

A few more recent studies try to highlight the more hidden side. In a seminal but unfortunately still unpublished paper, "Candomblé, Accusations of Sorcery and Struggles for Power," Luis Nicolau Parés (Parés 2007) emphasizes the need for more attention to the magical services that are so important for understanding the involvement of many Candomblé temples with people's everyday problems. In his monograph on the Jeje nation (Parés [2007] 2011), he refers to recurring rumors about the sorcery powers of great priests and priestesses deployed in struggles within and between *terreiros*. For the republican period (roughly since 1890), Yvonne Maggie (1992) made a challenging study of the authorities' efforts to distinguish between the true *pais de santo* and charlatans—that is, sorcerers. She most explicitly distances herself from the celebration of Nagô/Yoruba purity by ethnographers like Ramos, Carneiro, and Bastide, arguing that their focus on public rituals in honor of the *orixás* made them neglect "the more private treatment of sorcery and witchcraft" (Maggie 2011:149).[32] Van de Port (2011:101, 107, 185) emphasizes people's fear, especially among the poor, of becoming involved with the temples. Many of his friends associated Candomblé with "black magic" and "bewitching." Some made an opposition between "beautiful Candomblé" and "scary *macumba*" (sorcery), but it was always a relative distinction—in practice many seemed to closely associate Candomblé with *macumba*. People complained about the very heavy obligations incurred toward the *santos* once these had claimed them. "'Awesome' would be a term more congenial to their understanding of the cult. Their Candomblé was a repository of powerful dangerous forces; and you would only seek access to that repository when one or another life crisis forced you to do so" (van de Port 2011:108).[33]

Matory, too, dwells on people's fears of Candomblé. He mentions, for instance, that "real" men will flee the sacred dancing space at the first sign of an oncoming possession for fear of being "mounted" by a deity; this would reduce them to an *adé* (homosexual bottom). A difficult moment in Matory's life story of his special friend *pai* Francisco comes when the latter as a young man enters a temple out of sheer curiosity to have a look at the ritual, and is suddenly "mounted." He falls to the ground, and following established practice the priest straddles his supine body in order to "harvest" (*recolher*) him. Only through a great effort by his grandmother does her dear grandson not disappear into the temple (Matory 2005:214, 236). Such fears seem to be quite general. Poorer people in particular are afraid of being "caught." After all, once one is "mounted," one has to be initiated in order to learn and live with the deity, and this implies lifelong obligations.

Van de Port quotes a saying: "Few go out of love, the great majority out of pain" (109).[34] This contrasts to a "Bahian proverb" quoted by Emmanuelle Kadya Tall (2009:142): "One goes to Candomblé because of bad luck or illnesses, but one stays there out of love." Or compare the famous singer Maria Bethânia's ecstatic comment on her relation with *mãe* Meninha of the Gantois temple: "She is the light. Pure gold. She is the sweet embrace, the ever-listening ear. . . . She only showed me beauty, delicacy and tenderness. . . . God means no harm; the *santo*, if a *santo*, doesn't do wrong. This creates an intimacy, a trust, and a relaxation that is wonderful" (quoted by van de Port 2011:143). There were insistent rumors that Bethânia, as a celebrity, was obliged to undergo only a very brief and spurious initiation; she was spared all the disciplining hardships that "normal" novices have to undergo over a long period.[35] Clearly to be directly received by one of the venerated priestesses of the leading Nagô temples, your social status makes a world of difference.

Certain variations and shifts in the economic supports of the temples may be important in this respect. Interestingly, Reis (2001 and 2011) notes, in the nineteenth century, men and women had different options for establishing a full-fledged *terreiro*. Within the slavery society, working as a *curandeiro* (healer) was practically the only way for men to accumulate enough funds to buy land, a prerequisite for creating a *terreiro*. Women could profit from more varied options: trade in food crops or prepared food, trade in cloth or other primary necessities. According to Matory, similar differences still play a role. He points out that ever since Candomblé became respectable (roughly since the middle of the last century), almost all state subventions and other forms of outside sponsorships went to the prominent *mães de santo* and their temples. The elites have become increasingly convinced that "real" Candomblé implies a matriarchate. Male priests, having much less access to such support, must rely on revenues from commerce—which in practice often means services as *curandeiros*—to finance the temple's expensive rituals (Matory 2005:230). People in Salvador say nowadays that the main Candomblé temples depend completely on the sponsorship of rich initiates from Rio or São Paulo whose initiation may have been short, yet long enough to make them feel obliged to continue supporting the temple. *Mãe* Stella's Opô Afonjá temple is sometimes cited as a striking example since—at least according to some—the running of its everyday affairs is strongly influenced by whites from São Paulo. Some observers also see this strong presence of non-Bahians from the South as the reason for the recent comeback of Angolan temples where *caboclos* and Exú (formally a Nagô deity, but well-known for his ambiguity and his dangerous twists) take center stage. Purists may see these temples as corrupted versions of Candomblé, but they seem to remain in much closer contact with the commoners' everyday needs of protection, healing, and other forms of (magical) support.

This fluctuating nature of Candomblé, between religion and *macumba*, is addressed in a challenging way by Brian Brazeal in his 2007 dissertation on Candomblé temples in Cachoeira and their activities in the Sertão, the dry region in the northeast of Bahia. Cachoeira is a small city to the north of Salvador that has seen better days. Historically it was a major hub in the economy of the Reconcavo (the part of Bahia where large-scale plantations with slave labor had developed). It still is a second center of Candomblé next to Salvador. Brazeal's work in this smaller city is of interest, as he is able to point out a contrast: the great Nagô houses in Salvador are in a quite exceptional position due to their success in attracting state subventions and sponsorship from rich clients from the South. A leitmotif in his study is that this was much less available to most other houses, and certainly not to the temples in outlying Cachoeira. This explains their sometimes desperate search for new clients in order to pay for all the expensive initiation ceremonies and other celebrations. Hence Brazeal concludes that the view of Landes, Ramos, and others of "sorcery, associated with homosexuality, greed, charlatanism [as a] betrayal of Brazil's African heritage" can hardly apply to most of the temples. That view may hold for the temples these ethnographers frequented, which gradually succeeded in assuring themselves of other sources of support. But Brazeal concludes that for the poorer temples (that is, the large majority), such a "denial of the performance of magic for profit cannot possibly be true" (Brazeal 2007:299).

Brazeal refers especially to the *curandeiro* activities of many *ogãs*, male helpers of the priests who are not initiated themselves but perform all sorts of tasks—drumming, slaughtering sacrificial animals—in every temple. He emphasizes that the wealthy white *ogãs* who played prominent Maecenas-type roles in the temples visited by Landes, Ramos, and others are a relative rarity.[36] Most *ogãs* use their association with the temple in more practical ways: "Their unique relationships with the *orixàs* allow them to work *ebós* [powerful medicine] for both healing and witchcraft in ways forbidden to their *vodunsi* colleagues [initiated priestesses]" (300). Brazeal notes also that the white *ogãs*, as relative outsiders, "are often held in scorn by those *ogãs* who work the spirits themselves. The former are called *ogãs de sala* or *ogãs* of the outer room" (300). The implication is that they are largely ignorant of what goes on inside the temple. "Their immaculate white clothes are rarely, if ever, stained with the blood of the sacrifice" (300). Brazeal pleads for more attention "to the processes by which the majority of the temples of Afro-Brazilian religions fund their devotions," since this can give a clearer idea of "why so many people seek out their services" and offer insight into "the lives of thousands upon thousands of religious adepts whose practice has been ignored in the main body of literature on Bahian Candomblé" (302). Maybe Brazeal is overly harsh toward Candomblé studies (especially the more recent ones), but his perspective brings us much closer to the ambiguities of healing and danger in the cases from Africa quoted in earlier chapters—notably to the vision of the *nganga* (healer) as a source of protection but also of terrible danger.

Yet, important as it may be to redress the picture of Candomblé piety and purity by paying attention to its ambiguities, the main interest of its tortuous history is that despite all this the temples succeeded in building up shelters of effective trust. The strength of, for instance, Inger Sjøslev's ethnography (2006 and 1999) is that she shows the everydayness of such trust. Sjørslev was initiated in a similar temple as Brazeal—one of Cachoeira's smaller temples, one that constantly struggled to make ends meet. So in her writings there is little scope for extolling the splendor of her temple's festivities. Neither does she deny the tensions and the compromises under pressure of the hardships of life. But she shows also what the temple rituals and the *mãe di santo* mean for the everyday life of her initiated sisters—a fixed orientation point and a quiet commitment to making things work. In Brazeal's ethnography there is, despite all the emphasis on the dark side and the struggles of the temples, a similar counterpoint: his trust in his own temple and its priestesses is beyond doubt. The same delicate balance comes to the fore in his fascinating chapters on what could be called "the frontier" of Candomblé.

Candomblé on the Frontier: Everyday Struggles against Evil

An interesting context for trying to answer questions about how the Candomblé imaginary intervenes in everyday struggles against evil is provided by the second part of Brazeal's doctoral study (2007), in which he follows the outreach of Cachoeira temples into the poor Sertão area. Indeed, it may be precisely because this author worked on the margins of Candomblé that his interpretations highlight aspects that have remained understudied in the mainstream literature on the new religion.[37] Brazeal describes how he accompanied helpers from the temples in Cachoeira on trips to small and little accessible towns in the Sertão to offer their services (chaps. 8–12). Thus he became involved in the complex and often confused ritual exchanges between these temples and local healers. Some local healers claim links with a Cachoeira temple; others profile themselves as Umbanda rather than Candomblé. Among the population at large the Cachoeira temples clearly have great prestige as sources of special religious authority. Yet at the same time the *sertanejos* (people from the Sertão) see the city as a source of danger; its telling nickname is *cidade da macumba* (city of witchcraft; 175). Brazeal describes in fine detail how his Cachoeira companions use their links with the temples to outdo local healers, admonishing the latter to stay in the right path. There proves to be a delicate and always threatened balance between good and evil. In order to combat evil one has to work especially with Exú, the tricky Nagô deity, or with one of his *escravos* (lit. slaves). However, it remains vital to continue to celebrate the *orixás*—preferably in collaboration with a temple in Cachoeira. If one neglects the *orixás*, there is a danger that Exú in one of his more negative manifestations will take over and the healer himself will become a dangerous sorcerer.

A telling example of such delicate balancing is furnished by a case study of a visit during which Brazeal himself became involved in a confrontation between healers. He had traveled with one of them, Valdeci—a "helper" (that is, not a *vodunsi* medium herself) from the temple where he lived in Cachoeira—to her area of origin in the Sertão. There they joined a *festa* of an Umbanda priestess together with Dilma, a healer who boasted an impressive pedigree through her initiation by a prestigious *mãe de santo* of a Ketu temple in Cachoeira. After her initiation Dilma had returned to the Sertão to practice as a healer in alliance with local *mães* and *pais de santo*, but these collaborations invariably ended "with acrimony and the exchange of maleficent *ebós* [medicine]" (201).

The *festa* Brazeal attended with her had a bad ending also, due to Dilma's outrageous behavior. She became possessed (or was it simply drunk?) at the wrong moments and intoned songs that were out of place, shaming both the drummers, who could not follow her, and the priestess who hosted them all. Valdeci's stern efforts to discipline Dilma were in vain, and the three of them had to leave in shame. Even the next day, Dilma continued her efforts to humiliate and outdo Valdeci by appearing in the attire a novice wears during her initiation—apparently in order to remind Valdeci that she herself had not been initiated. However, Valdeci was not at all impressed by Dilma's threatening behavior. She explained to Brazeal that all this was a sure sign that Dilma had allowed Exú to take over: she had neglected the *orixás* (in fact she had not visited her Cachoeira temple for ten years), and this meant she herself was becoming part of the evil she was supposed to combat. Brazeal concludes his rich case study by emphasizing that such confusions can explain why Cachoeira has become, as stated, the *cidade da macumba* (city of witchcraft) for the people from the Sertão. The often desperate efforts of religious experts from Cachoeira to recruit clients in the Sertão make it increasingly difficult to distinguish charlatans from priests.

A similar pattern emerges from a different case study. In chapter 10 Brazeal offers a series of portraits of priests and *curandeiros* from Jacobina, about two hundred kilometers toward the interior from Salvador de Bahia. The place's nickname is "the city of gold," because of several gold rushes in the past. Among the Jacobina healers, Brazeal draws an interesting contrast between Joel Sebastião Xavier and a certain Moisés. Joel apparently played the role of a nestor in the town. Not only had he created an "Angolan" *terreiro* in Jacobina—being initiated himself into this "nation"—but he was also the local delegate of the Federation of Afro-Brazilian Cult (FEBDACAP), mentioned before: the association founded in 1937 to control Candomblé and Umbanda temples throughout the region. During Brazeal's fieldwork in the area between 2003 and 2005, Joel's role as delegate and his performance as *pai de santo* within his own *terreiro* differed sharply from the performance of his first *filho de santo* (initiate), Moisés. In contrast to most initiates, Moisés boasted openly about his success in sorcery. He was regularly possessed by various Exús, and he was happy to cater to all sorts of requests, including "the more earthly ones," from his clients. He was reputed to have great control over the darker powers of Candomblé.[38] When Luis Nicolau Parés and I visited the town in 2008, relations between Joel and his pupil had apparently deteriorated rapidly. Joel was still proud to show us his *terreiro*. But he was not doing very well. His plans for enlarging the temple had still not been realized. Other people did not see him as one of the main healers in the town. In contrast, Moisés's reputation as a powerful practitioner had increased markedly. However, Joel warned us not to visit him because he was going from bad to worse. In recent years Moisés had spent considerable time in São Paulo, and there he had become deeply involved in all sorts of Umbanda practices, attracting richer clients and making considerable money. Since his return he was mostly being mounted by Zé Pelintra and Maria Padilha, both quite disreputable emanations of Exú—the first one drinks and swears excessively, the second one exhibits whorish behavior. To us, Joel emphasized that Exú himself was a most respected god of the *orixá* pantheon but did have these unfortunately rowdy emanations.

Of course, we nonetheless did our best to contact Moisés, but he made it quite clear that he wanted to meet us only if we were prospective clients. In Joel's view, Moisés's greed had made him stray from the proper path of a Candomblé initiate. Joel was especially worried that Moisés seemed to eschew further contact with him, his own *pai de santo*. This put Moisés in serious danger of being taken over by Exú and turned into an evil sorcerer.

In these stories, it is easy to see the same circularity of witchcraft that stood out in cases from my earlier chapters on Africa. The explanation by Valdeci, Brazeal's friend from the Nagô temple in Cachoeira, that in order to combat evil one has to work with evil (Brazeal 2007:184) recalls the African *nganga* who insist that all they do is to "return the evil" to the one who has unleashed it. Yet, as noted in chapter 3, the one who is thus attacked will see the *nganga* himself or herself as a dangerous witch. However, Brazeal's account also highlights a crucial difference—namely, that for Valdeci the *orixás* offer a possible way out (remember what was said before about the delicate balance in Candomblé between danger and trust). The existence of the Candomblé temples allows healers to work with Exú and still not be captured by one of his more pernicious emanations. As long as they maintain their relations with the temple *orixás*, these will keep them from succumbing to evil. Paradoxically, even though Cachoeira is seen as the "city of witchcraft," the city's temples with their *orixás* can become beacons of trust through their control of these dangerous forces.

Another noteworthy difference is that even in these stories, evidencing as they do the ambivalences of the rapport between healer and client, the figure of the witch—or rather of "the witches" working as a coven—is scarcely present. Even in de Mello e Souza's rich array of stories from earlier centuries there is little reference to persons leaving their bodies at night and flying off to meet companions and hatch evil plots against their own people—a recurrent image in discourses on occult powers from Africa (and elsewhere). In the Brazilian stories occult aggression likewise comes from close by, but the figure of evil is rather a *curandeiro* (healer); this person may work at the request of someone in the victim's close environment, yet the locus of evil power is in the person of the expert.[39] Of course this is not a radical contrast. In more modern contexts in Africa—in cities and in transnational connections—the figure of the witch similarly seems to recede behind people's fears of the specialist (the *nganga*, the *marabout*) who uses secrets in an evil way. Yet even in the Ghanaian and Nigerian videos that are deeply pervaded by the Pentecostal worldview, evil comes from covens of greedy persons who transform themselves in weird ways and meet in secret places. Of course, for the Pentecostals these are only avatars of the devil. But in Africa, the incarnations of this imported figure still seem to be deeply marked by the familiar village imaginary of witches' covens and their nocturnal meetings as a shadow world complementing the everyday. Even in the most chaotic urban contexts in Africa, "the" village remains a point of reference, and with this its flipside of nightly conspiracies (see Geschiere forthcoming). In Brazil, as a colony of settlement deeply marked by slavery, there is no clear equivalent to this role of "the" village as a place of origin. Again, the conclusion might be that Brazil's slavery past deeply marks people's conception of the occult. Paradoxically it also seems to have set the conditions for the evolution of what used to be considered dangerous sorcery into a respected religion and a celebration of purity. In many respects, the temple seems to have replaced the family as a haven of intimacy, reflected in the use of kinship terms for internal relations. What does this imply for the imagining of occult dangers?

Candomblé: The Occult as a Basis for Trust?

The leitmotif of this book, the close link between occult aggression and intimacy, certainly returns in the Candomblé context in Brazil. Yet here intimacy took on new forms, and with it the challenge of how to establish trust nonetheless. As a reaction to the horrors and the disruption of slavery, the family was reinvented on the basis of religious affiliation to the emerging Candomblé temples.[40] The long-term and highly demanding initiation rites in particular created a novel kind of intimacy, emphasized by the consistent use of kinship terms in the new *terreiros*. Here as well, this proved a fertile environment for rumors about hidden aggression.[41] Thus, occult powers—as the flipside of religious kinship—became located inside a temple. But the status of these temples as clearly delineated and more or less permanent institutions may have facilitated the inclusion of representations of dangerous forces in a broader religious discourse that facilitated establishing trust.

The more recent literature I have cited shows that this flourishing of Candomblé temples as havens of trust, apparently overcoming the ambiguity of occult forces, was not a self-evident consequence of the borrowing of certain conceptions from the African coast. It rather should be seen as a precarious result of a particular conjuncture of historical trends. The recognition of Candomblé as a respected religion was conditioned by an abrupt but widespread shift in the search for a new Brazilian identity in the 1930s, celebrating *mestiçagem* as the hallmark of a new Brazil. Equally crucial, but in a longer time perspective, were continuing exchanges with the West African coast—even during the high period of slavery and rapidly increasing afterward—which kept Afro-Brazilians in close contact with developments in that region. The spectacular rise of the illustrious Nagô Candomblé temples and their struggle to preserve purity relegated *curandeiro* practices, increasingly seen as undesirable, to the background; yet these continued to manifest themselves in the very heart of these temples.

Despite all the ambiguities highlighted above, the rise of these temples consolidated a new view of the relation between witchcraft and religion. What used to be classified by authorities and commoners as dangerous sorcery was increasingly reevaluated as a religion. The sacred character of the *mães* and *pais de santo* with their *orixás* as allies created a basis of trust that people could appeal to in order to keep occult dangers in check, at least to a certain extent. Of course, the contrast with Africa should not be exaggerated. Notably the *voodoo* cults on the West African Mina coast (between Accra and Lagos) developed many of the same traits—no wonder, given the continued contacts with developments in Brazil. These cults also institutionalized long-term initiations—often inside an enclosed space—which were seen as crucial to both novices' well-being and priests' authority (Lovell 2002:67–78). And, most important, as Nicolau Parés emphasizes (Parés [2007] 2011:chap. 7), there as well a transition took place in the eighteenth century: temples were no longer built for one fetish but to celebrate a whole pantheon. But there are also significant differences in accent. In the cults along the Mina coast the ambivalence between serving the gods and serving witchcraft remains much more visible—certainly not hidden under a discourse on purity, as in the case of Candomblé. Nadia Lovell (2002) and Judy Rosenthal (1998), who worked on two different cults in South Togo, discuss several cases where a *voodoo* priest is not sure whether to treat his patient as a victim of a witchcraft attack or as one who suffers the revenge of a god.[42] Priests can also be easily accused of dabbling in witchcraft themselves (see Rosenthal 1998:52, 232; Lovell 2002:103, 105).

A point of convergence is the clear way these African *voodoo* cults express elements of the slave trade. In the Gorovodu order among the Ewe of South Togo, studied by Judy Rosenthal, the spirits that possess the mediums are supposed to be slaves from the North (in former days sold by the locals to transatlantic slave-dealers).[43] This parallels the reminiscences of slavery in Candomblé ritual, highlighted above: priests in the nineteenth century claiming initiates as their slaves, or the practice, continuing today, that a priest stands over a dancer toppled by a god to "harvest" him or her as a novice.[44] Moreover, the transition already mentioned toward temples with a multiple pantheon must have been possible only through the emergence of cosmopolitan societies created by the slave trade at both sides of the Atlantic. We saw that for Nicolau Parés the transition was not a Brazilian novelty, marking the passage from simple *calundu* shrines to more complex Candomblé temples, as Bastide and others supposed. Nicolau Parés rather shows that it was already prepared in Dahomey; thus it must be seen as a reflection of a new kind of cosmopolitanism along the West African coast produced by the slave trade. After all, in the African context, the cult's transformation from honoring one fetish to celebrating a multiple pantheon must have been quite a novelty. This brings us back to Matory's view of the new religion as emerging from ongoing interaction between the two sides of the black Atlantic, to be seen as one whole.

This interaction could be understood as taking place at the interface of different time frames—different *durées*.[45] Indeed, the different trajectories of the witchcraft-religion divide in Africa and Brazil seem to be marked by the distinct timing of similar transitions. The shift that marked Brazilian national consciousness in the 1930s—from the republicans' hope to follow in Europe's traces (inspiring determined efforts to "whiten" the nation) to a celebration of *mestiçagem*—had parallels in Africa, but much later. After independence—for most African states around 1960s—a belief in modernization inspired both the new African elites and the expatriate development exports to promote rapid westernization. In those days more or less obligatory bows to "African traditions" had little concrete import. Only toward 1980 did a reevaluation of African "traditions" acquire more impact. Then the proliferation of "traditional healers," prophets, and African churches received more recognition from the authorities. In the 1980s, for instance, Ghana's impetuous president, Jerry Rawlings, made a substantial effort to promote an African religion—Afrikania—that would give local traditions of healing (with Ewe healers well represented) more impact in a modern context. However, this experiment at emancipating African healers and prophets in counterpoint to mission churches came too late for gaining momentum equal to that of Candomblé half a century earlier in Brazil. Marleen de Witte, in her seminal PhD thesis (2008), shows how the Afrikania movement was squashed by the emerging Pentecostal "juggernaut"—to borrow Matory's terminology—that in Ghana was also acquiring momentum in the 1980s.

However, more recent developments seem to display new convergences: in Brazil as well, religious movements like Candomblé now seem destined to lose out—at least as far as the favors of the wider population are concerned—to powerful Pentecostal movements. Yet again, the difference seems to be that the Candomblé temples had the time to build a firmly protected niche before this new storm rose up. So for Brazil, the outcome of the struggle between Pentecostalism and Candomblé seems to be still far from decided.

✳

An intriguing question remains: to what extent can Candomblé's role as a recognized religion and its apparent ability to contain people's fear of sorcery—at least to a certain extent—serve as an example for the African predicament? The question may appear somewhat "innocent"—to borrow an expression from African witchcraft discourse that is certainly not that positive (in fact the term often means just stupid). Yet there is good reason for it. The emergence of Candomblé and, to a lesser extent, Umbanda as orders with their own coherence can explain why, despite omnipresent rumors about malevolent sorcery attacks, Brazil was spared the epidemic witch hunts that have been haunting so many regions in Africa.

> The healers that Nicolau Parés and I interviewed in 2008 around Jacobina and in Cachoeira gave different answers when I asked them why curing seemed to be more important to them than punishing the witch. Why didn't they try to identify the witches so that they could attack them and neutralize their powers, as many healers in Africa do? One said that of course she could "see" who had done the harm, but that she would never tell the victim what she had seen. Another said that it was no longer necessary to attack the culprit once the victim was under her (the healer's) protection. Several healers took it for granted that "the spirits" would take care of this part of the matter; their own role was only to heal the victim and leave the rest to the spirits. Yet when we were leaving, one very old healer in Cachoeira asked me whether I needed any special protection. If so, I should come back; he could handle anyone who attacked me.

The references to the spirits in Brazilian and African discourses seem to express different visions. In Africa, at least in the parts where I worked, a core image is the healers who, due to their second sight, can "see" the witches, attack them, and force them to lift their spell. The Brazilian appeal to "the spirits" seems to pass over an important part of this imaginary:

it is no longer so important to identify the witch, let alone to punish him or her—the spirits will take care of this.

Are these Brazilian examples relevant for present-day stalemates in Africa? Of course, Candomblé emerged from a unique historical configuration. The horrible disruption wrought by slavery, destroying the coherence of kinship communities, set the conditions for the precarious emergence of new, more open religious institutions: the temples, where the link between intimacy, danger, and trust could be worked out in new ways. Most important was that the further growth of these temples was favored by a national context that created scope for definitions of national identity in which appeals to African purity could flourish. It is not probable that a similar historical configuration will repeat itself elsewhere—especially given the global and apparently unstoppable rise of Pentecostalism, which has little patience with any appeal to African purity and imposes a view in which the distinction between good and evil is sharp and overrides all other concerns.

Still, the rise of Candomblé and its role in surpassing dyadic oppositions—like the one between witchcraft and religion—is of great interest as a countercase to growing popular diffidence and lack of trust in African contexts. It shows how a new basis of trust could be institutionalized so as to calm old fears aggravated by new changes. But it shows also that such institutionalization is possible only due to outside supports—in the Candomblé case, the vital support of the authorities and wealthy clients from the southern parts of the country. A crucial question is whether in the face of growing dependencies, Candomblé will succeed in retaining what van de Port (2011:14) calls its "inarticulability"—its resolute resistance to being defined—which may be the true source of its wild power. Maybe it has been, paradoxically, its indomitable character that enabled it to effectively build havens of trust.

Interlude

FURTHER COMPARISONS: MELANESIA AND JAVA
Ontological Differences or Aphasia before "the Uncanny"?

IN THIS SHORT INTERLUDE I want to comment briefly on other tempting comparisons. The choice to consider Melanesia and Java, after Brazil and Europe, may give the impression of a somewhat random approach to comparison (à la Frazer?). Yet there are particular reasons that make these cases of special interest to compare with the earlier chapters on Africa. Since Max Marwick, the grand old man of witchcraft studies in Africa, Melanesia has been known as a sort of "counter-case" where the link of occult aggression with proximity is flipped. In his 1964 paper Marwick proposed a rather stark opposition between, on the one hand, witchcraft in Africa as an inside job and, on the other, sorcery in Oceania as coming from outside. This has set the terms for comparisons ever since, but there are strong indications that this radical opposition is misleading. The comparison with Melanesia might rather bring out further complications of the inside-outside separation in relation to witchcraft. However, the very starkness of the opposition had wider implications: it seems to be related to Melanesian anthropology becoming a hotbed for ideas about ontological differences that would set the area apart from elsewhere. And since, as said, the notion of ontology is making a comeback in anthropology in general, it might be worthwhile to reflect on its usefulness for the anthropological study of witchcraft in changing settings.

The challenge of recent witchcraft studies on Java is quite different. The sudden eruption of bloody witch hunts in the eastern part of the island at the same time as the fall of President Suharto (1998) attracted much attention. Developments here, horrible as they were, followed patterns that were not dissimilar to events in Africa. They inspired James Siegel to launch a seminal attempt to surpass current anthropological approaches in order to give full scope to the horror of such events. He warns that anthropologists' focus on sociopolitical or cultural backgrounds may work to circumvent the horror of such experiences. Instead he proposes to stay close to what people experience by focusing on their struggle for "naming the witch" in order to get over an unsettling confrontation with "the uncanny." Since he develops this approach in close debate with other approaches to witchcraft, including from recent Africanist literature, it is particularly interesting to see how his explorations relate to this book's argumentation. The question for this interlude is to what extent such interpretations—in terms of "ontological" differences or an omnipresent "uncanny" that can manifest itself at any time—offer helpful starting points for this book's concluding chapter.

Africa and Melanesia: Different Ontologies?

Comparing Melanesia to Africa has quite a history in anthropology for various aspects, including occult forms of aggression. Max Marwick used his presidential address at a conference in Canberra in 1964[1] to make a sharp contrast in this respect when he focused on "one of the differences that seem to exist between Oceania and the rest of the world, but particularly Africa, in reports on the social directions being taken by witchcraft and sorcery. In Africa these belief systems seem to reflect tensions within a community, whereas in Oceania they more commonly express tensions between communities" (Marwick [1964] 1970:281). In his lecture Marwick emphasized that his knowledge of Oceanian ethnography was still very limited. Yet this modesty did not hinder him from suggesting a radical difference: in Africa the central figure in "these belief systems" is the witch, who is mostly an insider; in Oceania it is the sorcerer, who is mostly an outsider (290–91). Marwick's text was marked by the preference for clear conceptual distinctions that, as said, was characteristic of the classical witchcraft studies in anthropology: he laboriously opposed, for instance, "destructive magic put to legitimate use" to acts of sorcery as "illegitimate applications"—distinctions that later in the text he had to relativize (283). His text also betrayed some impatience with the lack of proper case studies in the literature on Oceania—apparently the author saw African anthropology as more advanced in this respect.

No wonder that a reply came from the Oceanists' side, even though this took some time. It came especially from people working on Melanesia, generally seen as a hotbed of rumors on witchcraft and sorcery within wider Oceania. In her conclusion to the 1987 collection *Sorcerer and Witch in Melanesia*, which she edited, Michele Stephen opposed in no uncertain terms the impact of "Africanists' guidelines" that would distort the interpretation of occult aggression in Melanesian studies (351). Yet she almost surpassed Marwick in a mania for imposing clear distinctions—albeit different ones. In her view, one of the unfortunate effects of the impact of

African models was a neglect of the witchcraft-sorcery distinction, which she saw as basic for understanding the Melanesian data. In this part of the world the sorcerer would be always social while the witch would be "less than human" and utterly asocial (264, 275–57). When the data forced Stephen to accept intermediate types, she blamed these on the effects of "social change" (278, 284). Remarkable is also the dazzling proliferation of groups dealt with in her conclusion, each having its own "belief system." Any idea that representations of the occult do travel, are borrowed, and thus are hybridized seems to be lacking—Stephen mentions such possibilities only for situations of, again, "social change," which she saw apparently as a sort of abnormal interval.[2] Thus, her long article (more than fifty pages) creates the impression of a courageous but quite desperate effort to fit extremely volatile data into a clear classification system.

On one point, however, Stephen opted for a more open approach. Marwick's rigid opposition between inside and outside was for her untenable and in dire need of being differentiated. A recurrent element in her overview was that in many Melanesian societies the sorcerer as the outside enemy can kill only with the help of an inside ally who provides the leavings of the victim—without such intimate leavings no sorcery attack can succeed (254).[3] The emphasis in Melanesian patterns may vary, but Stephen's rich overview showed that the inside-outside interface is as crucial in people's imaginations of how occult aggression works in Melanesia as it is in Africa. Further, the sheer swarm of all the different Melanesian groups dealt with by Stephen indicated the spuriousness of trying to oppose the region to Africa as more or less homogeneous blocks.

Within the rich literature on sorcery/witchcraft in Melanesia, many contributions can be mentioned that took a more dynamic approach that can do better justice to the constant flux surrounding these notions. Already in 1981, in her overview of a special issue of *Social Analysis* (on "sorcery and social change in Melanesia"), Shirley Lindenbaum concluded:

> The sorcery syndromes of Papua New Guinea are the complex ideologies of particular kinds of moral economy, neither old nor entirely new. We are left with the conclusion that there is no such thing as traditional sorcery. Sorcery is the ideology of a transitional moment, rather than an old "tradition." (Lindenbaum 1981:127)[4]

For this author, people's preoccupation with witchcraft/sorcery in Melanesia, as in Africa or Europe, was related to "contradictory claims of kin-based communities and the newer world of trade and business" (Lindenbaum 1981:120).

A more recent study, Andrew Lattas's fascinating *Dreams, Madness, and Fairy Tales in New Britain* (2010) similarly focuses on the dynamics of such representations under the impact of global change. His vivid ethnography evokes contrasts with Africa but on quite different points from a simple internal-external opposition à la Marwick.

A spectacular element in the wild turmoil of stories that make this book so lively is the special role of whites in "the underground." Lattas shows that an obsessive theme in New Britain people's understanding of the modern world is their "sense of capture, containment and befoolment by Europeans and educated Melanesians" (xx). Yet people are convinced that in the "underground" there is an alternative world, much "truer" than the one created by the invasion of the whites, where modern consumption goods are also accumulated: these are waiting to be returned to the Melanesians as their rightful owners. Visionary "shamans" are supposed to be in constant touch with the ancestors in the underground through their telephones and television. Most important is that these ancestors are whites. However, they are very different from whites in the daily world. Rather than exploiting Melanesians, they give them free access to all the wonders of the modern world—not only the new forms of telecommunication but also cars, planes and spectacular boats. Censure, the "shaman" of a successful cargo cult in the 1970s who subsequently lost most of his followers, convinced them that a big stone gave access to the wondrous world of their own whites. The stone would burst open, revealing a big highway and a fancy car that would take him and his flock to the underground to visit the ancestors. The stories portray an obsession with travel: people cover enormous distances—to Australia, America, and Japan—in huge boats or planes. But Lattas adds that in this global travel, people are "guided through the modern world by kinship ties" (60). At their global destinations, people often meet whites who turn out to be their own ancestors and who reveal them the truth about all the riches waiting for them—thus dispelling the lies told by missionaries, government officials, and the new Melanesian elites. The equation of ancestors with whites is a key trope in a vision that Lattas summarizes as "a Melanesian modernity."

This imaginary certainly has parallels with African conceptions of a world of spirits where riches—especially new commodities—are accumulated and the real decisions are being made. Whites are also present in this hidden world in Africa, but a crucial difference is that they are certainly not seen as well-meaning ancestors. On the contrary, as noted above, in many parts of Africa—especially along the West African coast—whites are still believed to play a key role in a most nefarious form of witchcraft connected to the new riches, transforming people into zombies and "selling" them for profit. Many authors see here a clear reflection of the trauma of the slave trade (cf. chap. 2 above and Austen 1993; de Rosny 1981). On this point, the differences between Melanesians' and Africans' views on how modern changes are marked by occult forces seem to relate directly to the variable ways in which local societies became embedded in wider colonial and capitalist frameworks.

Such historical variations may also explain differences in recent developments. For instance, the New Tribes Mission from California, which descended upon New Britain—the Melanesian island where Lattas did research—seems to have been able to impose a strict divide, still in the mid1980s. Apparently this rich mission—its missionaries lived in air-conditioned houses and had their own air transport facilities—was still all-white. Their control over the locals was so strict that the latter dared to tell their stories about the underground and white ancestors to Lattas only in secret. In this respect it might be interesting to compare Lattas's stories about a proliferation of "shamans" and prophets with anthropologist Tonda's study, cited earlier, of a similar growth of healers and prophets in Congo. Again, this comparison highlights historical differences rather than inherent cultural contrasts. In Tonda's books (2002 and 2005) all sorts of in-between experts are present. Religious leaders may insist that they differ from "traditional healers," but in practice one role seems to shade into the other. In Congo, the impact of Pentecostalism did not lead to a neat dichotomy such as that found in New Britain between the New Tribes Mission and rebellious experts who adhered to ancestral truths. Tonda found it was impossible to study *tradipracticiens* in isolation from local Pentecostalist leaders; their interaction shaped their performance.[5] Lattas also highlights hybridization in many forms—local experts having their own "telephones" and so on—but this seems to take place in separate spheres. In Africa, even the new Pentecostal movements have become rapidly and thoroughly appropriated by African preachers, who are taking over the leading positions from white missionaries, initiating their own churches, and shaping their cults and other practices according to their own ideas. This is a far cry from the almost totalitarian control that the missionaries from the New Tribes Mission—apparently still mainly whites—were exercising over their "believers."

Historicizing present-day variations by relating them to different trajectories in contacts of these societies with outsiders sits uneasily with ideas à la Marwick of a radical cultural contrast between Africa and Melanesia as some sort of given, outside history. I still remember my dismay in 2002 after I presented a paper on the dynamics of witchcraft among the Maka (Cameroon) to the Africa seminar at the University of Chicago, when Marshall Sahlins summarized it as illustrating the "ontological differences between African and Melanesian cosmology" (oral communication). Indeed, the notion of ontological differences seems to fare particularly well in Melanesian studies.[6] Thus, despite all his emphasis on the hybrid character of the New Britain stories about the "underground" as produced in specific encounters between the islanders and Western invaders, Lattas sees no problems in referring to a "cultural ontology of selfhood" that is apparently specific to Melanesia (Lattas 2010:49; cf. also p. L).

As noted in this book's prologue, ontology seems to be making a comeback in anthropology in general. This is most promising if the inspiration comes from innovative and challenging versions of this notion as in the work of Deleuze and Latour, who both emphasize ontology's multiplicities and contingencies.[7] However, many anthropologists still seem to be plagued by a persistent tendency to use the notion in a more closed sense to evoke supposedly radical contrasts—"ontological differences"—between cultures and even regions (for instance, between Melanesia and Africa, or, even more currently, these two in opposition to Europe). Then there is indeed a clear tension with the historicizing approach I am taking here, since such culturalist versions of the ontology notion unavoidably evoke a vision of essential cultural differences as given, more or less outside history, that can be surpassed only with great difficulty.[8] The examples above suggest that it is more productive to understand cultural variations against a background of different trajectories through which local societies became embedded in wider frameworks of power and exchange. In most African contexts the colonial dichotomy was always highly porous, undermined from the start by constant pressures from Africans invading the new centers of power. In Melanesia, by contrast, prophets still feel forced to construe their vision of modernity in a separate "underground"—no wonder, since until recently white civil servants could imprison people for illicit burying practices, while the white missionaries of the New Tribes Mission still seem to inspire a holy fear in their flock for being caught out with their own visions. Such obedience is reminiscent of the early phases of missionization in Africa. But there things have changed deeply since then.

Attention to cultural differences is of course most welcome. Yet explaining these as ontological differences—when a notion like ontology is employed in a culturalist sense, assuming essential differences of being between different groups—is problematic in present-day contexts. We live in a paradoxical world that is both deeply affected by creative hybridization and haunted by determined efforts to re-create an impossible cultural purity. A few examples can show how dangerous such a culturalist preoccupation with purity and radical contrasts can become in present-day contexts. The developments in Ivory Coast over the last fifteen years highlight the chaos wreaked by a search for cultural purity. In the 1990s President Bedié stimulated a cell of intellectuals, among them the country's leading anthropologists, to produce an ideological construction around *Ivoirité* and *ivoiriens de souche* (lit. Ivorians of the trunk) as a radically different way of being, with a specific ontology; his successor Gbagbo, himself a highly qualified historian, used this ahistorical construct to violently exclude Northerners from the nation (see Banégas 2006; Marshall 2006). In a similar vein, albeit in a very different setting, the successes of the New Right in several European countries can be cited as worrying examples of how an essentialist notion of "culture"—as a clearly circumscribed way of being and in ontological contrast to other "invading" cultures—can be used to justify harsh forms of exclusion in "modern" democracies as well.[9] Anthropologists may want to take a stand against this trend, and in particular against the problematic ways our notion of culture is employed by such restorative movements. It is highly questionable whether ontology—at least as it is used within anthropology now—is a useful concept for resisting such hijackings of our notion of culture.[10]

※

The comparison with Melanesia highlights how important it is to go beyond a simple opposition between sorcery from outside versus witchcraft from inside. What is at stake is rather to follow different ways of relating witchcraft notions to the inside-outside threshold. Such comparisons can show the more general danger of framing radical cultural contrasts in terms of ontology. Assuming ontological differences can easily lead to a fetishization of difference and a neglect of the continuous borrowing and hybridization that shape cultural responses to similar issues. The usefulness of comparisons like the one above may be to show that a common theme—people's imagined link between occult aggression and forms of intimacy—can be elaborated in highly different ways in time and space. But for understanding such different elaborations it might be more helpful to follow the specific trajectories of important historical changes in each case, rather than taking the easy way out of assuming "ontological" cultural differences. James Siegel's effort to understand the full horror of witchcraft panics in terms of "the uncanny" exemplifies a more sensitive approach.

Java: "Post-Suharto Witches" and the Uncanny

In 1998 after Indonesian president Suharto left office—forced by a long series of marches and demonstrations—there was a sudden eruption of witch hunts and lynchings on the island of Java, especially in Banyuwangi on the eastern tip. Within three months, about 120 people were killed as "sorcerers." In the chaos following Suharto's departure, the police seemed unable to stop the killings. But only a few months later, and with a considerable show of force, hundreds of killers were arrested and brought to trial. Somewhat later—probably still in 1998[11]—anthropologist James Siegel went to the area and carried out a long series of interviews with the killers and the descendants of the victims. His reporting on these interviews conveys the full horror of what happened—often very brutal slaughtering of "sorcerers" by mobs who suddenly invaded their houses; it also testifies to the anthropologist's struggle to understand the blandness with which people said they had to kill, else "it would have killed us" (2006: 113). It is especially Siegel's effort to understand the depth of this lethal combination of fear and rage that makes his search for a more sensitive anthropological approach to such events so challenging.

> The events themselves, murderous as they were, conform to many aspects of the examples above. Proximity played a crucial role in the suspicions and assassinations: victims, sorcerers, and killers were each other's neighbors or even relatives. Yet it is striking that anthropologists who worked in the area came up with quite different interpretations—so it may be worthwhile to compare Siegel's to those of others. Campbell and Conner (2000), leaning heavily on interpretations from postcolonial Africa, explain the unprecedented scale of local violence against sorcerers as "an expression of the tensions and contradictions of globalization."[12] However, for Nicholas Herriman, who worked in these villages in 2001 and 2002, neither the killings nor the scale of them was new—according to him there was a long history of sorcery/witchcraft killings in the area and there had been regular peaks ("outbreaks") throughout the postcolonial period. Herriman has a very clear-cut explanation for the 1998 outbreak: the villagers assumed that due to the sudden fall of Suharto the local state authorities would no longer intervene and punish witch-killings.[13]

On both points Herriman's interpretations are completely opposed to Siegel's. The latter emphasizes that the killings, certainly on this scale, were a new phenomenon: in the past "only individual witches were attacked. . . . [but] now the threat of the sorcerer is general. . . . Thus the need for a collective action" (Siegel 2006:129–30). For this author the wave of witch-killings signaled a terrible anxiety among the people, and the most direct reason would have been the sudden collapse of the state. Siegel emphasizes that despite sometimes brutal exercise of power at the local level, this state had provided a certain familiarity through the long links of patronage that came together in the figure of Suharto. Thus the collapse of the state center created deep uncertainty, making people insecure about their own identity in the changing order of things—they seemed at the mercy of undefined power. Amid this confusion, "naming the witch" seemed to offer at least some sort of foothold, affirming one's own identity as "not-witch" (160, 189). Clearly, although at least two observers were on the spot soon after the events, very different interpretations are possible.

Yet whatever these differences in interpretation of the local events, Siegel's appeal to study such witchcraft frenzies as struggles with a sensation of "the uncanny"—as a latent and unpredictable presence in all societies and cultures—stands out as a seminal challenge for anthropology in general. It was the very terror of people's stories about the killings in Banyuwangi that made it urgent for him to gain a more sensitive understanding of their deep anxieties and ruthless cruelty in the face of "witchcraft."

Siegel starts his argumentation by opposing the anthropological tendency to analyze witchcraft in terms of social context to approaches by historians and others focusing on episodes of utter violence that are understood as exceptional breaches of the normal order (1).[14] He notes that a weakness of the anthropological approach is that it risks normalizing witchcraft as a given within the social order, thus neglecting the havoc that these imaginaries can create and the sudden outbreaks of rage, fear, and violence. For Siegel, a striking example of this trend toward "institutionalizing witchcraft" is Evans-Pritchard's classical study *Witchcraft, Oracles and Magic among the Azande* (1937). In this South Sudan society witchcraft seemed to be under control—it was an explanation of misfortune that was not allowed to surpass certain limits; in this sense it was institutionalized. Clearly Siegel has some doubts about "this cheerful understanding of the witch" that for him follows "from the anthropological tendency to avoid thinking about both the violence of witchcraft and the fear it inspires" (9—see also 106).

Siegel agrees that this violence inheres in the social—in this sense anthropologists are right—but the horror he was confronted with in his interviews in Bunyawangi shows him that we have to go beyond this: "the question of destructive violence and its provenance" must have a place in an anthropological approach (2). This inspires him to a daring step: he brings in Immanuel Kant and his notion of *das Erhabene* (the sublime): "From the view of its practice, belief in witches can be seen as a form of the sublime" (23). He is especially interested in Kant's emphasis that a person's confrontations with the sublime and the subsequent struggle to define the limits of one's "powers of cognition" are vital to the crystallization of self-consciousness. Kant's classical example of the experience of the sublime was the reaction people may have to nature and the sensation it can give of awe and lack of words to express it. As Siegel explains:

> Faced with such, we feel overcome. Our mental powers fail us. But we recuperate ourselves because even if we cannot define whatever it is that is in front of us, in taking in its objectivity we realize that we do have powers of cognition: we understand the objectivity of something that before did not exist for us. To recognize the limitations of our powers of cognition is thus to confirm that we really do have certain capacities" (Siegel 2006:23–24).

Thus we come out strengthened from such an experience of the sublime; our powers of cognition help us also realize their limits; an experience that seems to be borderless is contained and ordered.[15]

Siegel recognizes similar patterns in people's reactions in Bunyawangi (or in Africa). In his view, these examples show that a confrontation with the sublime can have other possible outcomes than affirming our powers of cognition through the realization of their limits. For Kant, the sublime seemed to be mainly something known in retrospect, as a more or less contained experience: "After the event we see what we went through using our powers of memory and analysis. But suppose that we had not recovered such abilities. We would then suspect, rather than know, that something was affecting us. Would the result not be fear? And would we not call that fear the fear of the uncanny?" (Siegel 2006:24). This quite abrupt transition from the sublime to the uncanny—from Kant to Freud—is crucial for Siegel's analysis. When people are not capable of bringing closure to the experience of the awesome, the sublime turns into the uncanny. To Siegel, this is the explanation why people are often at a loss for words in the face of witchcraft: they are at the limits of their "powers of cognition," but they cannot accept such limits (as in Kant's vision of a confrontation with the sublime) since the danger remains too close. In our explorations of witchcraft until now there was little place for Kant and the sublime (on the contrary and for clear reasons: the topic hardly allows for this). But with the transition to Freud and the uncanny we are on familiar ground. And Siegel does show that this passage from the sublime to the uncanny opens up fascinating perspectives.

Siegel develops this idea of a loss of words in the face of witchcraft in dialogue with Lévi-Strauss's famous essay *Le sorcier et sa magie* (1949), notably the section on the trial of a young man accused of witchcraft among the Zuni. Siegel does not agree with Lévi-Strauss's analysis of this case on certain points (see below), but he is very much taken by the latter's central idea: the boy finally confesses to being a witch because the "Warriors," through their stern cross-examining, push him to say what they suspect but cannot formulate themselves. This is the novel insight through which Lévi-Strauss tries to explain this enigmatic affair, and Siegel summarizes it approvingly: "Their [the Zuni Warriors'] suspicion marks their lack of symbolic capacity. The boy taking his clue from it, makes up for their inability to formulate. He makes up a story, the central figure of which is himself, and it is accepted" (Siegel 2006:213).[16] Clearly, for Siegel here is a moment of recognition where Lévi-Strauss's analysis joins his understanding of his disconcerting interviews in Bunyawangi. There as well, a sense of a confrontation with something awesome prevailed, but also a dire lack of a name to give it.[17] In the Zuni case, the boy's confession of being a "witch" came as a kind of liberation: the term *witch* solved a situation of aphasia and helped to contain an unspeakable experience. Siegel's informants in Bunyawangi betrayed a similar embarrassment, a similar searching for words; labeling some people in their midst as witches helped them to contain uncanny dangers. Hence Siegel's title *Naming the Witch*—he sees the very act of choosing this term as the outcome of a difficult struggle.[18]

The next step in his analysis is to trace what in this particular situation triggered this uncanny sensation (remember that in his view the outbreak of witch-killings was a moment without precedent in this area, and in Java in general). The answer was already mentioned above: the sudden collapse of the Suharto regime created a panicky feeling of loss. Harsh as the state could be, it gave at least some sort of protection, guaranteeing people that they had a recognizable identity under the "New Order." However, in Siegel's view specific historical circumstances like the sudden end of the New Order can never offer a final explanation.[19] The question remains why some people experienced this as a moment of uncanny danger and others apparently did not (or did less so).[20] It is the always present possibility of sensing the uncanny that makes people desperately look for a term—a form of cognition—to contain it. In such situations terms like *witch* seem to become inescapably relevant.

Yet to Siegel there is an inherent problem with a term like *witch*. It is a term "that is incapable of doing more than designating that something is at work which is not understood, which is identified only to the extent that it remains not only unknown, but also continues to have unpredictable consequences" (Siegel 2006:25; see also 219, 227). Maybe we could call "witch" a leaking category. It appears to give an interpretation, but it never gives closure—that is, it never produces the kind of power of cognition Kant is referring to. Its problem is that it always evokes the unknown.[21] This is why in the end Siegel disagrees with Lévi-Strauss's analysis of the Zuni case. According to Lévi-Strauss, the boy's confession of being a witch resolved the problem, the elders set him free, and he was accepted into the community again. However, Siegel notes a curious distortion here, since Lévi-Strauss somewhat surprisingly omits the intervention of Mrs. Stevenson, who was present as the representative of the Bureau of American Ethnology, and on whose report his analysis is based. Her intervention was quite decisive. Stevenson refused to accept the elders' verdict that the boy was guilty and had to be executed. She intervened most forcefully, claiming to have neutralized his powers. Apparently only her direct threat of alerting the government to another witch-killing saved the boy's life. Lévi-Strauss concluded—in Siegel's words—that the witch was "integrated. . . . because he unifies a voice which had been dispersed among contending individuals."[22] But for Siegel the very fact that in the Zuni case the witch was obviously not integrated shows that the term did not unify. The boy spoke "from elsewhere, in the voice of a nameless other" (Siegel 2006:216).[23] In this case, as so often, "naming the witch" did not restore order: the term's "failure to normalize" would have produced murder had it not been for the presence of Mrs. Stevenson (224). Without her intervention, the boy would have been executed just like the Banyuwangi witches.

The above is a much too short and therefore simplified[24] summary of a very sophisticated and original effort to renew the anthropological approach to witchcraft. It is not only the seminal ways in which Siegel relates the topic to high-flying philosophical explorations—Kant, Derrida, and many others—but also a certain playfulness with unexpected escapades that makes Siegel's book an adventure to read. The main value is, as said, the determined attempt not to let the horror of the events be covered up by academic interpretations.

※

What is the relevance of Siegel's challenging explorations to the analysis developed in this book? His equation of witchcraft with the uncanny, in particular, corresponds directly with my emphasis on the link with intimacy. For him—as for Freud—it is crucial that the uncanny is closely linked to the familiar: what is so frightening is the familiar turned weird.[25] Yet there are also clear differences with the interpretations above. An important one is that Siegel focuses on a sudden witch panic that takes unprecedented forms; this is what, at least in his analysis, is vital for understanding the events in Banyuwangi. This raises the question to what extent his approach in terms of experiences of the uncanny is applicable to situations where witchcraft is quite frightening yet part of the normal course of things (remember the Duala proverb "You have to learn to live with your witch"). Siegel leaves open the possibility that in certain contexts the "witch"-label does produce some sort of closure, although even in the Azande case he thinks this will always be highly precarious because of the "inability to appropriate the strange power of the witch" (Siegel 2006:219, cf. 221). And he is probably right that the differences between unprecedented witchcraft crazes and situations where the witch is part and parcel of everyday life are not that great. Even in contexts like present-day Africa where witchcraft is a familiar reality, people are most preoccupied with new forms of witchcraft that would break out of the existing frameworks—witchcraft "running wild." So there seems to be a constant tendency to defamiliarize it, completely in line with Siegel's emphasis on the impossibility of taming the uncanny.

A more striking difference is with Siegel's emphasis on a lack of words before the uncanny. For him it is a lack of powers of cognition that turns the sublime into the uncanny; "naming the witch" seems to offer a solution, but it is a precarious one that does not really bring closure to the uncanny experience. Indeed, a lack of closure is obvious in all the examples above, but it is hard to speak of a lack of words in relation to them. On the contrary, there is a ferocious production of words: people seem to have no difficulty in "naming witches"; there is rather an overproduction of witches, who are seen everywhere.

Siegel (2006:21–26) refers at some length to my "uncanny experience" that was the starting point of my 1997 book *The Modernity of Witchcraft*. It begins by describing how, at the beginning of my fieldwork in Cameroon, my car broke down at night in the middle of the forest and my assistant started referring to all the witches swarming around without our being able to see them, as we were "innocents." But in my experience, this was not a situation of lack of words. On the contrary, it triggered endless stories from my assistant and others on the *djambe* or *sorcellerie* that allowed for all sorts of interpretations. Elsewhere I have tried to show that it is precisely this "overproduction of meaning" that makes these representations so utterly indiscriminate in their effects.[26] People never seem to tire of pursuing different interpretations of what a *djindjamb* (witch) is able to do (remember in chap. 1 all the different interpretations of the death of Eba, who was a "martyr" according to some since he had refused to give up another relative to the witches). In line with Siegel's interpretation, there is certainly no end, no closure, to people's imagination of the *djindjamb* (witch); but for the Maka there is never a lack of words.[27] Similarly, the confessions that nowadays are so strongly encouraged by Pentecostal ministers throughout Africa come out in torrents of words—people never seem to run short of words for dwelling again and again on ever newer and more amazing details of the ways of witchcraft (see also Meyer 1999; de Boeck 2005; de Witte 2008; Marshall 2009). Or compare the terrible pressure to confess placed on "the last witch of Langenburg" in southwest Germany in 1672. This was certainly a painful process, but again we find no trace of any "speechlessness"—on the contrary, there was a proliferation of rumors about parallel cases and the various ways that witches were courting the devil. The main issue seemed to be how the confessors could make the main suspect, Anna Schmieg, utter the crucial word *Hexe* (witch). The word itself certainly did not have to be searched for—in fact, it was overly available—but *she* had to say it. The problem was certainly not that she chose words that surprised her interrogators, and therefore there is no trace here of what is crucial to Lévi-Strauss's reinterpretation of Mrs. Stevenson's report on the Zuni case. As said, for Lévi-Strauss it is vital that the boy expressed things that his interrogators suspected but did not dare to put into words—a striking interpretation, in view of the almost universal idea that elders are those best able to navigate the occult world (or at least have to pretend that this is the case). In Langenbach there was no such uncertainty among Anna's interrogators. On the contrary, her torture stopped only after her confession reiterated in exact words what they wanted to hear. Then it did effect some sort of closure—at least in the eyes of the interrogators— by breaking the hold the devil still had over the community. Similarly in the Candombé examples: no difficulties in "naming the witch"—on the contrary, a proliferation of rumors that made the term overly available.

The differences—between the searching for words emphasized by Lévi-Strauss and by Siegel, on the one hand, and the avalanche of words and images in the other cases—are certainly noteworthy. Yet they may not be radical. Isn't it possible to assume that an overabundance of words has effects similar to a lack of them? In both cases it is very difficult to reach a well-delimited clarity. Maybe putting speechlessness and overproduction of words in the same basket spoils the effect of relating witchcraft to Kant's sublime, since this is associated with a lack of words. But an overproduction of words raises similar problems: in both cases problems of closure arise that for Siegel mark the transition from the sublime to the uncanny. Whether there is a search for words or an abundance of them, the result might be the same: the impossibility of putting the experience of the uncanny to rest.

The broader value of bringing in the uncanny—the impact the notion may have in helping us to break out of what I called "the witchcraft conundrum"—is beautifully worded by Siegel:

> If witchcraft were merely a conception, enlightenment might remove it from history once and for all as mere superstition. Superstition is excessive credulity, in the West usually thought to be the result of cultural lag. It is thus unjustified belief; what reason cannot establish has to be left unexplained. But witchcraft does not go away, no matter how convincing the explanations are of its lack of basis. It might be better not to understand witchcraft as ignorance to be banished through explanation, but as based on a credulity which forces itself on people in certain situations. Witchcraft would then not be founded on ideas or stereotypes of witches but on the uncanny which appears without regularity. (Siegel 2006:222)

Behind witchcraft emerges the uncanny as a more general category that is of any time and place. "Naming the witch" is an often unsatisfactory way of trying to master a sensation of the uncanny, because "witch" as a concept always opens up to the unknown. It is also impossible to predict when the uncanny will manifest itself. But it is possible to try to follow how people attempt to use their powers of cognition to gain a certain control over experiences of the uncanny—or to analyze when such control fails, and how this may lead to violence. Siegel's challenging interpretations seem to bring us back to the issue of trust, which might be a different formulation of the questions he is raising. The possibilities or impossibilities of bringing closure to an experience of the uncanny through cognition might be vital for the establishment (or nonestablishment) of trust in situations of inherent danger. Focusing on trust can help us to translate different ways of dealing with the uncanny into more concrete propositions for research. The uncanny—the horrible realization that the familiar can turn against us—may be unpredictable, and as Siegel emphasizes, it can always rear up.

Yet in the everyday, life often goes on—so there often seems to be at least a possibility of containing the experience to a certain degree, through some form of cognition. Thus it may be worthwhile to return to the question of how people try to establish trust despite uncertainty. This might at least help us to discover certain patterns and regularities in people's dealings with the uncanny.

6

BACK TO TRUST

New Distances, New Challenges

THERE ARE MANY MORE challenging windows for comparison, from the innocuous Wicca movement in the West to vodou in Haiti, often unjustly associated with only its terrorizing excrescences,[1] or the exuberant sorcery cult of Sunyam in Sri Lanka.[2] Enough to fill another book. However, by now it may be time to return to the points of departure in the prologue to this book—notably to the central question of how, despite all the dangers emanating from intimacy, it is still possible to establish trust in the people with whom one has to live. This was also the point reached in the interlude, following James Siegel's sensitive explorations of witchcraft as an unspeakable experience of the uncanny. His warning that the uncanny can manifest itself at any moment—since it is as omnipresent as it is unpredictable—seems to make establishing trust a painful undertaking. In this concluding chapter I want to focus especially on recent changes—the opening up of new spaces through new media and new politico-religious frameworks—and the challenges they pose for reconciling intimacy, danger, and trust. This focus on changes can highlight factors that might be crucial more generally to the affirming (or the refusal) of trust as a suspension of doubt in the face of intimate danger. I start again from examples from my fieldwork in Cameroon, but these will be discussed in a broader, comparative perspective, in relation to examples from other parts of Africa and elsewhere.

At the back of all this is, of course, the more specific question to what extent it is possible to infer special circumstances that can explain why this struggle over trust despite intimate danger is particularly intense in many parts of present-day Africa. The link between intimacy and unsettling danger, so forcefully condensed in the notion of the uncanny, may be general, but it is hard to deny that people in Africa nowadays feel particularly harassed by such dangers. To repeat the complaint of many of my Cameroonian friends, quoted in the prologue: why is it that modernity in Africa seems to come with an intensification of witchcraft, rather than making it wither away? One of the main recent changes in many parts of the continent is that witchcraft has come out in the open. Of course, it is very hard to prove that it is on the increase, even if people are convinced of this. Any form of quantification is always tricky in this marshy field. But it is clear that in recent decades witchcraft has taken center stage in public debate. In the first decades after independence (around 1960) many people were reluctant to talk openly about it—this meant, as said, denying that Africa was modernizing—but now witchcraft has become a hot topic in newspapers, on TV and radio, and in public debate, whether in political discussions, religious settings, or the rumor machine of *radio trottoir*. Modern mass media—notably the booming video-film industry—play a crucial role in this. Indeed, the secret conspiracies of "the witches" have become a favorite topic on the screen and in other media. No wonder modernity in Africa seems to reinforce witchcraft rather than weakening it. Moreover, this publicizing of witchcraft on the screen is only one aspect of its becoming ever more visible in everyday life. Huge religious gatherings in Pentecostal churches and others often roar and shake with witchcraft confessions and harangues against it.[3]

This bringing out into the open of ideas and practices that were (and are) rooted in intimate spheres raises intriguing questions. What are the implications for changing conceptions of intimacy, and hence of witchcraft? And, even more important, how does it affect people's struggles to establish trust nonetheless? By focusing on such shifts in establishing trust, despite all the dangers of intimacy, it will be possible to compare with older ways of maintaining relations, and hopefully also to isolate specific factors that make the struggle for trust so harsh in Africa. One of the suggestions of this chapter will be that new interventions—like the Pentecostal ones—are marked by a radical approach, aiming for a complete eradication of witchcraft; but that in practice this strategy actually tends to confirm witchcraft as omnipresent. In this respect there is a marked difference with local ways of dealing with it, in terms of the Duala proverb quoted earlier: "You have to learn to live with your witch." Another issue is whether recent shifts in establishing trust can be related to the special role that kinship relations continue to play in many parts of this continent? It is striking in these contexts that global changes—politico-economic ones, but also others—impinge on local realities with remarkable immediacy. This seems to be reflected in new ways of dealing with the threat of witchcraft—for instance in the Pentecostal insistence on equating witchcraft and family pressure with the devil. The paradox is that these new solutions bring an increase of scale: witchcraft is now seen as part of a cosmic battle between God and the devil, yet people continue to locate the latter in the microcontext of village and family.

Witchcraft on Screen: Changing Parameters of Intimacy and Trust

The large 2005 Yaoundé conference Justice et Sorcellerie, organized by Eric de Rosny, was full of surprises—those *moments d'énonciation* (provocative situations) that for Andrea Ceriana Mayneri (2010) occur when local and academic discourses meet.[4] As noted, the conference's topic had attracted a big crowd. The first day so many people showed up that the session had to be shifted to a basketball court, over which a huge tent was erected so as to properly seat all the invitees and also the much more numerous attendants who had come on their own initiative—a clear sign of how hot an issue what the law could do (or could not do) against witchcraft had become throughout society. De Rosny had succeeded in bringing together not only academics and his own group of *nganga* (*tradipracticiens*, as he preferred to call them), but also people from the Ministry of Justice—judges, prosecutors—and lawyers. For me it was fascinating to hear judges and *nganga* debate the reality of witchcraft and the problems of establishing "tangible proof" in this marshy terrain.[5]

A *moment d'énonciation* that I found particularly intriguing came on the second day, during the showing of a short film, *Un oeil dans les ténèbres* by Cyrille Bitting.[6] By then the audience was somewhat less numerous, so that we could adjourn to the teaching amphitheater where the meeting had been originally scheduled. Still, a few hundred people were present and the room was packed. The film in itself was not that surprising. It gave a vivid report, with subsequent comments from a few experts, of an event that is not uncommon in village life: a confessing child witch who denounces a number of adults as accomplices. During a short discussion after the showing of the movie, the filmmaker explained that he had happened to pass through the village of Puma, which has a small administrative post, along the old road from Douala to Yaoundé. There he noticed some unrest around the local post of the *gendarmerie*. He had stopped, and at his request he had been allowed to film what was happening.

> The plot of the film was quite simple. A man brought a young girl (probably twelve years old) to the *gendarmes*. They were followed by a small but very excited crowd of people from the same neighborhood. The man explained that the girl had made terrible confessions. When interrogated, she started to repeat them in front of the gendarmes. Her story

was that at night she would go out with her witchcraft coven. A few nights earlier they had asked her to deliver the brother of her paternal grandfather. However, the old man was the last of her close relatives who was still alive. Therefore she had decided to refuse (remember the trope in many witchcraft stories of the witch as a martyr who refuses to betray yet another relative and therefore has to face the wild crowd of witches all alone). But instead of giving up herself to the witches, she had decided to confess to the authorities.

The gendarmes' *commandant de brigade*, looking somewhat bewildered, further interrogated the girl, asking her to explain what exactly they were doing at night. After this, the girl was not to be stopped. She started to detail how they would take a plane together, how they would bind their victims like goats and slaughter them in order to eat them— the victims' blood became the oil in which they were to be cooked, bamboo splinters served as knives to cut them up, and so on and so on. She enumerated all the villagers who were with her in the witch gang. A few of these had been dragged along to the gendarmes' office and were interrogated on the spot. They all strenuously denied any involvement. An elderly woman challenged the girl to show the baskets in which they supposedly transported the victims, and the knives used to kill them, but the girl tossed her head and offered further details about the old baskets they would find on the rubbish dump that were suddenly mended when they picked them up and served as cooking pots, about bamboo splinters that magically turned into very sharp knives, and so on. An accused old man insisted that he did not even know the girl. In response she started to laugh wildly and said: "I am *une grande femme* [an adult woman] in that world, I am his wife. He is the pilot of our plane. Last night I was sitting next to him—his left hand was on the wheel, but he kept his right hand on my breasts." The man's desperate retort—"Breasts? She has none"—was lost amid the exclamations of the bystanders.

In the film a few experts were subsequently confronted with these scenes. A psychiatrist declared that he was quite convinced by the girl's declarations since, upon being asked to repeat things, she would come up with the same story and the same details. A Catholic priest was equally convinced: the film showed clearly that *la sorcellerie* was very much a reality; what was clearly needed was a determined offensive to eradicate it once and for all.

I was not shocked by the images of the girl and her wild confessions, nor by the growing bewilderment on the faces of the accused when they began to realize that their denials were of little avail against the torrent of words and details that came from the girl's mouth. As noted earlier, in 1971, almost immediately after I had settled in a Maka village in the eastern part of the country, it was shaken by what people saw as a new epidemic of child witchcraft, the *gbati*, that had spread from the north and that empowered children to kill their own father and mother (or other relatives). I had also seen *gbati*-children, interrogated by the *nganga* (healer), confess with great alacrity whole series of murders and attacks.[7] Instead, what came as a shock to me while watching the film at the conference was my sudden realization that I was about the only person in the whole hall who was not intuitively on the side of the girl. A large part of the audience consisted of students at the Catholic University. Others were civil servants from various institutions. Yet it was quite clear that the whole room was behind the girl: her ever wilder declarations were applauded, while the furious denials of the accused were booed.

This uniform reaction was very different from the many witchcraft "palavers" (informal local courts) I had attended in the villages. Such palavers never evoke a similar uniformity in people's reactions. On the contrary, they are always full of contestation and often end in violent altercations. In most cases, the accused are strongly supported by their own people. As one young man said after a particularly tense witchcraft palaver: "In the olden days we used to split the village over such palavers, but now the state forbids this." In general, people will not accept at face value the statements by the supposed victims or their witnesses. There is often a lot of skepticism: details are checked and inconsistencies are pointed out.[8] Further, and even more important, in the local setting witchcraft accusations are always tricky and dangerous, since they all too often work out as a boomerang, flying back to the person who started the witchcraft rumor. As a Maka saying has it: "People who always talk witchcraft are like the owl. At night they are the first to go out." Or as an elder explained to me: "An accusation is like a *corossol* [a thorny fruit, *Annona muricata*]—no one wants to catch it, you try to quickly send it on to someone else." Among villagers, it is very difficult not to become involved yourself once you start accusing others.

This is, of course, completely different when witchcraft is being shown on film. For the audience at the conference there was no risk at all of becoming personally involved. Witchcraft on the screen confirms the reality of these horrible accusations and confessions, but at a safe distance: it becomes a more abstracted reality, very shocking and dangerous in general terms, but not as uncomfortably close as when one is drawn into a village palaver where such frightening events are discussed.[9] The showing of this movie to such a large audience at a conference was still a fairly exceptional occasion in Cameroon. There are several movies in the budding Cameroonian film industry that similarly address witchcraft,[10] but these films are rarely shown in the country itself, and certainly not to large audiences. However, especially in the densely populated western and southwestern parts of the country, where English and Pidgin are quite widespread, another kind of movie has become very popular since the late 1990s: commercial Ghanaian and Nigerian video-films (see below). They are regularly shown on Anglophone programs of Cameroon TV, and they are available for sale everywhere. Especially in Anglophone households it is not uncommon to have these video-films playing constantly on the TV screen, one after the other, during visits and other occasions. These films—most of them heavily influenced by the Pentecostal message—are of interest here since a central theme is witchcraft as a work of the devil and how it is vanquished by a courageous Pentecostal priest (see Meyer 2013). Like the short film showed at the Yaoundé conference, these films permit the audience to feel involved in the horrors of witchcraft—in the Pentecostal view directly linked to the devil and therefore all too real—but from a safe distance.

Pentecostalism, the Devil, and the Scaling Up of Witchcraft

The wave of Pentecostalism spreading through Africa—mainly the non-Islamized parts, but even entering some Islamized areas—is playing a key role in bringing witchcraft into the public sphere. It brings also a view of witchcraft reproduced on a larger canvas, as being central in a battle of cosmic dimensions between good and evil. The great innovation that Pentecostalism brought to Africa was, indeed, the equation of witchcraft to the devil. Of course, this was not completely new. In the nineteenth century at least some Christian missionaries tended to make a similar equation (see Meyer 1992 and 1999). Yet in general missionaries—like the new colonial authorities—tended to deny the reality of witchcraft, seeing it as an imaginary offense. They directed their attacks against witch doctors, accusing them of fraud and of falsely accusing and mistreating persons. People often interpreted this as an unfortunate tendency of the new authorities to protect the witches. In contrast, Pentecostals in Africa have one thing in common, despite all their differences: the insistence that witchcraft is the work of the devil and therefore all too real (see Meyer 1999; Marshall 2009). This implies also that witchcraft becomes part of a broader worldview, a crucial issue in a cosmic battle between God and Satan. However, in this worldwide vision the family and the link with intimacy come in through the backdoor.[11] A fixed corollary of the Pentecostal view on witchcraft, as exemplified by the Ghanaian and Nigerian videos, is the idea that the devil works through tradition—in concrete terms, through the family and the village. The devil may be a truly global figure, but Pentecostals in Africa focus on the village-family complex as the locus where all the dangers of tradition are being reproduced.[12] Of course, in other parts of the world as well, figures like the devil are chosen icons for the projection of local specificities. Yet while, for instance, in European witchcraft discourse the devil had marks that were very much his own (goat's legs, horns, etc.), his avatars in the representations of Pentecostals in Africa are often a victim's relatives. This ambiguity—reintroducing the local in the very heart of what seems to be global—may be crucial for understanding the specific implications of modernity for the continuing conundrum of witchcraft, intimacy, and trust in African settings.

The Ghanaian and Nigerian video-video-films—increasingly popular also in other parts of Africa—not only play a crucial role in the new mediation of witchcraft but also bring across most vividly this ambiguity of a cosmic battle fought out inside the microcosm of the family. In a forthcoming book on the Ghanaian video film industry, Birgit Meyer (2013) offers a rich analysis of the Pentecostal impact on this new medium. From the mid-1980s on, video technology became a welcome boon for producing movies. On the African continent, Ghanaian producers and directors were particularly quick to realize the possibilities of the new medium. Already in 1985 William Akuffo and Richard Quartey produced a blockbuster, *Zinabu*, about a beautiful woman seducing eager young men with her beauty and riches (the film was clearly inspired by the Mammywata figure, notorious throughout West and Central Africa). However, the very success of the first video-films (and those from Nigeria) led the Rawlings government of Ghana to ban such films altogether. Yet in 1987 the ban was lifted again, and the subsequent years brought a true flowering of the Ghanaian video industry with an ever-increasing production of movies. After 2000, the Ghanaian industry started to face stiff competition from Nigerian videos. With their much more sensational plots and gruesome special effects, the latter seemed to conquer the market, even inside Ghana. However, toward 2007 at least some Ghanaian producers managed to reestablish themselves, with help from the newer VHS technology that enabled people to play the videos at home and thus favored private sales.

Witchcraft—and especially its link to modern riches—seems to have been a central theme in the budding Ghanaian video industry right from the start. In the course of time other hot themes—porn, mental illness, the global fraud of 419s—emerged, yet witchcraft kept coming back. From the beginning it was also closely linked to Pentecostal ideas, but there were and are some variations in this respect. In the first Zinabu film, for instance, there is no special role for Pentecostals, but in the sequel they are very present.[13] Akuffo, the maker of another early blockbuster, *Diabolo*—on a man turning himself to a snake that slips into a sleeping girl's vagina, after which she starts to vomit money—insisted less on Pentecostal inspiration. He claimed his example in conceiving the Diabiolo figure was rather the movie *A Werewolf in London* (Meyer 2013:chap. 4). Yet he gave his lead figure the name Diabolo, knowing very well that people would make the association with the devil and Pentecostal ideas. Not all filmmakers manifest themselves as staunch Pentecostalists. In 2005, in a filmed series of interviews with Tobias Wendl, pioneer Richard Quartey emphasized his Pentecostal convictions, but other leading filmmakers (not only Akuffo but also, for instance, Socrates Safo) took their distance from the belief in spirits, witches, and so on. Akuffo even confessed that he would love to make a film about another topic and hoped that in the future the public would be "prepared" for this.[14] Meyer (2013:chap. 1) notes that Safo did experiment with other topics—for instance, a film to celebrate high moments from precolonial history—but had to accept that people had little interest in them. In the interviews with Wendl, all filmmakers agree that they have to make "films believed by the people" and must follow them "if this is what people are believing"—and "this" is apparently the Pentecostal struggle against witchcraft; no wonder it became a major theme in the films. The striking dominance that Pentecostal ideas soon acquired in the up-and-coming video-film industry in Ghana seems to reflect what Meyer calls "the pentecostalization of the public sphere" in Ghana (Meyer 2013, introduction). A fascinating theme in her forthcoming book and her earlier studies is how rapid and all-embracing this pentecostalization has become, not only in the videos but in all walks of life (see also Meyer 1999, 2000, and 2004).[15]

The Pentecostal tenor of almost all these video-films centers, of course, on the struggle against Satan—many films feature long, long scenes of painful exorcism—but this is almost always related to a theme of the betrayal from within: the figure of a next of kin as the witch. Apparently, the horror of Satan striking from close by conveys a tension to the plot that is most appealing to both spectators and filmmakers. Take the plot of *Expectations*, a video-film directed by Ezekiel Dugbartey Nanor toward the end of the 1990s.

The film could also have been called "The Temptations of Gifty," since it is about the many sufferings endured by a beautiful young woman with that name before she can give birth to her son with her husband Nana. In the beginning, their marriage seems to be blessed. Their friend, a Pentecostal pastor, tells them about a prophecy that they will produce a son who will succeed to Nana's chieftaincy. This is soon confirmed by a message from the kingmakers in the rural town. However, we have seen already in a few earlier scenes that the witches in their nightly conspiracy have decided to stop this—Gifty's son will remain unborn. Indeed, several years later Gifty has still not given birth. One day when Nana is away, his mother tells Gifty that because she is barren she must make room for another wife who can produce an heir. Gifty flees in tears to the village, to her loving mother, tomboy sister, and drunken uncle. All Nana's subsequent efforts to fetch her back are sabotaged by either the witches or his mother. Another woman, Lucy, mysteriously appears in his office and succeeds in ingratiating herself with his mother. Finally Nana marries her, and she duly produces an heir. Gifty languishes in her family's home and suffers from hard work on their farm.

When the pastor and his wife return after a long absence, they are shocked to be introduced to Lucy, Nana's new wife, and tell Nana in no uncertain terms that the prophecy has to be respected: Gifty has to come back to the house, and he must produce an heir with her. Nana accepts and an uneasy truce follows—Gifty living in the guestroom and Nana sleeping with her more and more often. When—after much praying and strong support from the pastor—she becomes pregnant, jealous Lucy decides to stop it. She visits a fetish priest, who "treats" a chicken and a yam, then has them cooked by the maid and offered to Gifty. However, Lucy's little son slips in and eats something from the plate. Gifty has prayed before eating—so we see a cross descending over her plate and dispersing the poison—but Lucy has not taught her son to pray (she sometimes claims to be a Muslim). So the son dies. Nana is beside himself, accuses Gifty of having poisoned his son, and has her condemned by the court. In prison, Gifty is harassed by three cellmates, who make a caricature of her praying and mock her for being pregnant.

However, precisely when the witches in their meeting decide to put an end to her life (to make certain she cannot give birth), the prayers of the pastor have effect, and the witches are punished with horrible swellings on their cheeks. As expected, Lucy proves to be one of them. But the great surprise is that the witch who started it all turns out to be Gifty's own sister, the tomboy Dufie. Always jealous of Gifty and her beauty, she had decided long ago to "deliver" her to the witches. The village, the very place where Gifty had sought refuge when she was in trouble, turns out to be the source of all her misery!

Similar themes emerge in *Abrò ne Bayie* by C. Emeka Uba (Don), pro-duced in 2007.

> In this film it is no secret at all who is the witch. On the contrary, the film starts with Dufie (who later turns out to be the mother of the household) being admonished by the witches that she must deliver her son. Dufie begs for a little delay—she pleads that her son is a "prayer warrior," so delivering him to the witches is very difficult. But she is told that she has to deliver quickly now ("if you fail . . . we will deal with you according to our rules"—that is, she will have to surrender herself). The next morning, Dufie's husband wonders how she got her head bruised.
>
> But then son Vincent comes to introduce his new fiancée, Rosemary—not only a beautiful girl but also an example to everyone in the church. Dufie does everything she can to stop the marriage—poisoning her son's food, attacking the girl "magically," and so on. Soon Rosemary cannot take it anymore and asks for a reprieve. The witches send their dwarf, now changed into a big man, to seduce her—in which he succeeds remarkably quickly, because Rosemary has been feeling neglected. They send also the gorgeous Natascha to seduce Vincent. He proposes. The main pastor of the church tries to stop it, since he is suspicious. But Dufie and Natascha succeed in denouncing him as a rapist. The marriage of Vincent and Natascha is duly performed, and then celebrated at the witches' sabbath. Soon Vincent falls ill, and the doctors are unable to cure him. Finally one of them tells the worried father to look outside the hospital.
>
> The father and "desperate" Natascha drag the young man from one healer to another. Finally they find a pastor who takes the matter in hand. He is at first hesitant to make direct accusations ("we don't as-cribe witchcraft to anyone in this place"), but he adds that "only a close association can get you harmed," and then with no further hesitation names Dufie and Natascha as the witches. A terrible battle ensues as the queen of the witches rushes in to support Dufie and Natascha, but finally the pastor prevails. Dufie is annihilated, Vincent wakes up again, and even Natascha is saved through a long nocturnal ritual. From now on, she will be with the church.

It is striking that the witches in these films and their nocturnal sesssions are reminiscent of folkloric images from Europe—long nails, matted hair, distorted noses, even pointed black hats. However, such resemblances cease to be surprising when, for instance, in Wendl's filmed interviews cited before we see filmmaker Richard Quartey Sato take Hope Robbins's *The Encyclopedia of Witchcraft and Demonology* from his bookshelf.[16] It is equally striking that these two movies are not very friendly to women (to say the least). Gifty's tomboy sister may arouse some sympathy—but perhaps only among Western spectators?—with her attacks on her drunken uncle and her cynical comments about what marriage does to women. Yet in the end she proves to be the meanest witch of all. Rosemary, in the last movie summarized above, who at first seems to be an exemplary Pentecostal girl, allows herself to be seduced all too easily by a no-good as soon as she feels neglected by Vincent. Even the mothers have their nasty sides. That applies, of course, particularly to Dufie, the mother in the second movie, who might be described as an arch-witch. But even Nana's mother (in the first film)—though she is definitely not a witch—creates havoc in his life with her constant worry about an heir.

However, it would be too easy to take this negative image as a self-evident consequence of a male perspective (the large majority of the film-makers—producers, scriptwriters, and cameramen included—are male).[17] After all, they consciously cater to the taste of their public and, as said, want to make films "believed by the people." They know very well that their audience consists in large part of women, notably Pentecostal women (Meyer 2013:chap. 3). Therefore, in most of these movies the parade of evil women (greedy, lascivious, and potential witches) is balanced by one or two women who do conform to the Pentecostal ideal: modest and above all firm in their faith. Consider Gifty's steadfast belief; in *Abrò ne Bayie* such a counterweight is harder to find, but probably Natascha, at first an evil witch but later deeply faithful, satisfies the audience's need for an edifying model.

The main warning that both films convey most powerfully is that Satan's danger comes from close by—from inside the family or the village. This is what makes the battle unending. At the end of the second part of *Abrò ne Bayie*, we are transported to "several years later" and Dufie, the evil mother, suddenly emerges from a dust road, beautifully dressed and wearing a flamboyant red hat. She disappears but then reemerges in Natascha's house, warning Natascha that she has to return to the witches. In church a female believer tells Vincent that his wife Natascha is a witch. However, there are signs that this woman might be herself part of an evil plot. Viewers are encouraged to get the next installment in the series if they want to know how all this will end. The message is clear: precisely because Satan lodges inside the family—even inside Vincent's new church "family"—it is almost impossible to eradicate him definitively.

Child Witches in Kinshasa: Transformations of Witchcraft and Kinship

A similar complex intertwinement—Pentecostalism's scaling up of witch-craft by mediating it through the devil, yet at the same time confirming its roots in the microrealities of the family and home—emerges from a quite different setting: the proliferation of accused child witches in Kinshasa and more recently also in Lagos, pushed out by their own families and having to fend for themselves in the streets. In his challenging study of this development in Kinshasa, Belgian anthropologist Filip de Boeck (2005) analyzes it as a reversal of basic links in the kinship order and of the principles of gift giving and reciprocity in general. He highlights the central role in all this of the new Pentecostal churches and other apocalyptic movements that pullulate in Kinshasa, maybe even more than elsewhere in Africa.[18]

De Boeck (2005:190) emphasizes rightly that in itself the attribution of dangerous witchcraft powers to children is nothing new. Remember the alacrity with which the child witch in the film shown at the Yaoundé conference launched her confessions. This pattern goes back to time immemorial.[19] Yet the sheer dimensions of the problem de Boeck describes for Kinshasa since the 1990s are baffling. In 2000 the NGO Save the Children estimated that two thousand children were affected by such accusations in Kinshasa, but already in 2003 it increased its estimate to twenty thousand (BBC report, January 17, 2003). And since then the number seems to have only increased. There is a recurrent pattern in these horror stories. Parents are alerted by a series of misfortunes. Certain signs point to one of the children as the cause of the trouble. They take the child to a priest (Pentecostal or of another spiritual movement), who "sees" that the child is indeed a witch. The family will refuse to take the child home, since she or he is now feared as a source of further mishaps. The child's only alternative is then to go and live on the street. Sometimes the priest will keep the child and make it undergo a long and hard period of seclusion during which powers are neutralized. But even after this, families will be reluctant to take the child back. Often he or she still ends up on the street.

However, de Boeck also emphasizes that many of the children he talked to see the street as a welcome escape from pressures at home. Like the child witch in the film quoted before, they enjoy talking about their special powers.[20] To quote one of de Boeck's cases:

My name is Mamuya. I am 14 years old. I became a witch because of a boyfriend of mine, Komazulu. One day he gave me a mango. During the following night he came to visit me in my parents' house and threatened that he would kill me if I didn't offer him human meat in return for the mango he had given me earlier. From that moment I became his nocturnal companion and entered his group of witches. I didn't tell my mother. In our group we are three. At night we fly with our airplane, which we make from the bark of a mango tree, to the houses of our victims. When we fly out at night I transform myself into a cockroach. Komazulu is the pilot of our airplane. He is the one who kills. He gives me some meat and some blood, and then I eat and drink. . . . Komazulu is a colonel in the "second world," and he has offered me the grade of captain if I sacrifice a person. That is why I killed my baby brother. . . . With our group we have already killed eight persons. Our victims haven't done any harm to us. (from de Boeck's interview of the girl in the Church of the Holy Spirit, Selembao, Kinshasa, Sept. 1999—in the rest of the interview the girl tells how the prayers of the church's priests have made her "come out of the world of the shadows"; de Boeck 2005:192; see also de Boeck 2004)

The similarities with the examples above from Cameroon are striking. Recall how the girl in the film at the Yaoundé conference provided details about the airplane of her witch group and how she boasted of her position next to the pilot, apparently the leader of the group. Like the child witches in the Maka villages with their *gbati*, Mamuya enjoys talking about eating meat. The story of how her friend Komazulu gave her a mango and came back to ask for human meat in order to pay her "debt" echoes the plot of the *famla* stories, summarized in chapter 2 above, that create such distress in Cameroon: a young man comes to the city, a stranger offers him a beer, he accepts and suddenly realizes that he is included in a *famla* coven; he has incurred a debt that can be acquitted only by the "selling" of one of his close relatives. For de Boeck such stories confirm people's feelings that witchcraft is no longer tied to kinship: like the *famla* boy, the Congolese girl is recruited to the witchcraft coven by a gift from an outsider. Yet, as in the *famla* case, it is in the intimacy of the home that she finds the first victim she must kill. As in other Congo cases, subsequent victims come from farther away—so the link with kinship becomes more tenuous. But the story also suggests that it is difficult to break it completely.[21]

De Boeck criticizes the tendency in many press reports to blame the proliferation of child witches on initiatives by pastors, Pentecostals and others. This is the viewpoint of most of the NGOs involved, who believe that it is often the *pasteurs* who recognize the child as a witch and then admonish the parents to bring him or her to them for healing. According to de Boeck the pattern is more complex: the role of the pastors is rather to confirm and legitimate accusations that have already emerged within the family.

Thus their intervention is, in his view, not without positive aspects. Many NGOs tend to treat the problem of street children as purely a humanitarian issue, without any attention to the deeper cultural implications of the witchcraft accusations. The pastors try to address precisely these cultural aspects—notably the family context—by organizing within their church a "witch-finding" moment that would bring a solution to the issue along familial lines. Yet de Boeck also shows that the pastors' interventions play a crucial role in the reaffirmation of child witchcraft as an acute danger within the home—thus helping to make the witch appear to be "omnipresent in the social field." For him as well, "the space of the churches is one of the most prominent sites in which the coincidence of the figure of the witch and the child is produced" (2005:195); and he agrees that pastors' involvement in these affairs has taken on unprecedented proportions.

De Boeck's texts (2004 and 2005) give a detailed analysis of the treatment the children undergo in the various churches. Apparently a more or less formalized model for such therapies has already been developed (which is no surprise if one considers the numbers involved: some churches take in up to a hundred children a week!). During a long period of seclusion varying from a few weeks to even several months, the children have to fast and are subjected to all sorts of ritual purifications. Laxatives and emetics are employed to cleanse the children's bodies of the flesh of the victims they have eaten.[22] This is combined with strenuous interrogations by the pastor or his helpers, sometimes in the presence of their parents; however, often the latter are too frightened to be confronted with the child. During these sessions "there slowly emerges a narrative of disruption and descent into evil which will also help to structure the 'outing ritual' of confession in the public space of the church later on" (de Boeck 2005:196).

An important consequence of this intensive seclusion period is that at the "outing ritual," the public confession in front of the church community, the children's narratives mostly correspond to a standard pattern. This public ceremony is followed by a series of more private exorcism sessions, called *délivrance* (deliverance), usually carried out by female church members known as *intercesseuses* (intercessors). The child is placed in the middle of a circle and the women make him or her the focus of intensive prayer, punctuated by laying on of hands, trances, speaking in tongues, singing of songs, and exhortations by the leading *intercesseuse*, all this to underline that a crucial passage—a deep purification—is taking place. The church people will normally try to involve the child's mother or other family members in the session in the hope of "facilitating a reintegration of the cleansed child-witch into the family." But often the family members are, again, too afraid to even attend the session, let alone take the child back (de Boeck 2005:196).

For de Boeck this proliferation of child witches, as an issue that dominates life in the city, is a marker of deep transformations in the very heart of the kinship structure. It marks the implosion of the current gerontocratic model, in which the elders' authority affirms the coherence of the family. In its place he sees a new model emerging marked by deep generational strife and a loss of control over younger family members. In line with this view, he highlights the unprecedented emergence of children as crucial actors in urban society more broadly. The rumors about child witches often shade into the aggressions of child soldiers—an omnipresent source of fear in Congo—who can act as adults because of the force of their weapons. They are also reminiscent of the impact of the young kids who have had success in "hunting diamonds" near the Angolan border and derive unprecedented power from their new wealth. In de Boeck's view, child witches reflect a very real shift in relations of authority and dependency between the generations. An important corollary of these profound changes in the working of family relations is the idea—mentioned above as emerging in many parts of Africa—that witchcraft has lost its moorings in kinship. De Boeck quotes a complaint that has now become standard among Luunda villagers that the "witchcraft of the elders" is being replaced by *ulaj wa chisakasak*—that is, "'chaotic witchcraft' that can come from all directions, and no longer exclusively from your immediate kingroup" (de Boeck 2005:202).

Above, I noted that the idea of witchcraft no longer being rooted in kinship has to be relativized: in many contexts, in Cameroon and elsewhere in the continent, it is rather the tenacity of this nexus that is striking. It is certainly true that there as well witchcraft is not only linked to kinship. Even in the old stories, deals for acquiring special powers—which often required sacrificing people—could be concluded outside of kinship; but in the end there was always a link with kinship.[23] Similarly, in modern times, even when rumors about the occult place it far outside the sphere of kinship and family—as in the stories about the *feymen*, the global tricksters with their amazing wealth and "magical money"—kinship seems to come in through the backdoor if one follows the cases in their dénouement (see chap. 2 above). And, as emphasized above, even in Congo's distressing cases of child witches, as described by de Boeck, kinship still hovers in the background.[24]

Nevertheless, the Congolese examples also highlight a major shift. De Boeck notes a shrinking of the family in Kinshasa (2005:208). In everyday life it is the relations with mother and grandmothers that still count for children; their relations with their father and his family tend to become ever more tenuous. In line with the emergence of women as independent actors—as elsewhere in post–Structural Adjustment Africa, they seem to do a lot better in the informal sector—men's role in the family seems to become less and less important. Of course, even in the new context, increasingly centered on intergenerational confrontations, intimate relations remain a hotbed of witchcraft suspicions. But a crucial difference with deep implications is that, as noted above, the notion of an obligation to bury the dead in the village of origin seems to be absent in Kinshasa, as in Brazzaville.[25] There is a striking contrast with the deep preoccupation among urbanites in many other parts of Africa to continue to take their dead back to the village in order to bury them there. In earlier chapters, this obligation was taken as a powerful factor for understanding the impressive elasticity of African patterns of kinship—now even bridging transcontinental distances and retaining a hold over migrants oversea.

Apparently we have to take into account quite different trajectories in this respect. The Congolese examples seem to point in a different direction from the examples above from Cameroon (as well as from Ivory Coast, Ghana, Nigeria, Kenya, and even Cape Town). In the latter cases there seems to be a constant stretching of kinship relations so as to bridge ever deeper inequalities and ever greater distances. Of course "kinship" takes on new practices and meanings in such wider settings. Yet there is a consistent effort to retain some family coherence. The funeral at home (again a novel institution, product of new forms of migration) serves as an anchor of belonging. This stretching of kinship sets the parameters for a constant increase of scale of witchcraft rumors. In Congo, in contrast, at least in the big cities, there seems to be rather a tendency toward a shrinking of the family, relative neglect of kin relations with people who have moved elsewhere and of the village as a source of belonging. Again, this does not mean that intimacy does not remain a fertile soil for witchcraft fears—as is clearly illustrated by people's obsession with child witches inside the home—but apparently the contours of intimacy are here shaped by a different trajectory.

In other respects there are clear parallels with the examples from Ghana or Cameroun. Typically the churches' exorcisms of child witches in Kinshasa are shown on TV (de Boeck 2005:201). Thus, the Pentecostal therapies of child witches contribute to giving witchcraft new visibility in public spaces. Moreover, these therapies produce a similar increase of scale of people's vision of witchcraft, as was noted above. As even children are turned into soldiers of the devil, they also seem to be involved in a global

struggle between God and his evil counterpart. Yet these young emanations of the devil remain, again, rooted in the local realities of family, house,
and children. There is the same ambiguity here making trust—victory over
the dangers of intimacy—a precarious affair that has to be constantly reaffirmed.[26] This ambiguity of the Kinshasa child witches between the global
and the local, as in the plots of the Ghanaian video-films, contrasts sharply
with the witch hunts in early modern Europe. There the equation with
the devil was equally important in making witchcraft a central issue in a
cosmic battle, but in Europe the devil became so central that the occult
forces seemed to lose their local bearings (see chap. 4 above). I will return
to this since, as said, it might be that this continuing direct articulation
with kinship and the house despite all changes is crucial for understanding
the particular resilience of witchcraft ideas in African settings.

Satan and the Spirits in Islamic Africa

Similar trends can be observed in other parts of Africa that, until now at
least, have remained mainly outside the scope of Pentecostal outreach.
Several authors have already pointed to the parallels between the Pentecostal impact and the effects of new Islamic movements in Islamized
parts of the continent.[27] Such parallels are certainly relevant for the impact on local ideas about occult forces. Adeline Masquelier's 2009 study
of an Islamic movement in Niger is of special interest here because of her
focus on the effects of Muslim revivalism at the everyday level—as seen
"from below." Masquelier notes that "Islam and Muslim religious practices
rarely feature in anthropological discussions of the occult in postcolonial
Africa," and she sees her study as contributing to "an emerging anthropology of Islam in Africa that takes as its analytical object the relation between magic, power and modernity" (2009:154; see also Masquelier 2008).
Indeed, her book highlights most interesting parallels with the scaling-up
effects of Pentecostal interventions in the realm of the occult. Another
major contribution of Masquelier's study is that she shows most convincingly how the simplistic opposition between Sufi and reformist Islam has
to be superseded.[28]

A central protagonist in her 2009 book is Mahamane Awal, more widely
known as Malam (teacher) Awal, whose rapid rise and equally rapid
decline in the rural town of Dogondoutchi (where Masquelier has done
fieldwork since 1988) graphically illustrate the "heterogeneous" nature
of the Islamic landscape in the Sahel—the intertwinement of Sufi and
reformist positions. Awal arrived in 1997 in the town, which for some

time already had been marked by a deepening rift between reformists—mainly followers of the Izala movement that originated in northern Nigeria—and more "traditionalist" clerics, who imposed on their followers the rituals *and* the expenses that characterize Sufi Islam. Awal, already known for his extremely eloquent attacks on the Izala reformist movement, was invited to come to Dogondoutchi by the traditionalist faction of the town. On the very day of his arrival he delivered a fierce sermon against Izala, to the satisfaction of the traditionalist clerics. However, they quickly found out that they too had reasons for worry, for Awal proved to launch his attacks—and his rhetorical fervor—in all directions. He soon started to denounce these traditionalist clerics for their greed in imposing unnecessary burdens on the believers.

Masquelier (2009:5) explains his rapidly growing popularity partly by his eloquence—his sermons stood out for their vivacity and directness, laced with entertaining stories and offering straightforward advice on everyday difficulties. But she relates it also to his taking a kind of third position, liberating people on the one hand from the extreme austerity of Izala—with Awal, they would at least be permitted to continue Sufi rituals that were dear to them—and, on the other, from the heavy payments to Sufi clerics: if they joined Awal's new brotherhood, the Awaliyya, they could still perform these rituals but hardly had to pay anything for them. This did not mean that Awal preached an easy Islam. On the contrary, his demands on women in particular were heavy and severe. In his sermons he addressed them as the weak spot that contaminated the purity of the town's Islam (which would also be the cause of the dramatically increasing poverty of the majority of the population—especially after the imposition of drastic structural adjustment measures in the middle of the 1990s). Awal insisted that women had to live in seclusion if financially possible and must cover their shame with veils and long dresses—central points in the reformist creed of Izala. Yet they also had to join in Sufi rituals, singing and even performing dances. Clearly this preacher saw no problem in mixing reformist and Sufi elements, and it was as clear that this mixture was quite attractive to the population.

A point that gave his popularity a special boost was his particular way of dealing with occult forces, who in this area usually manifest themselves as roaming spirits that can harm the living. Masquelier notes, as a general trend, that Islam makes people disregard these spirits, which are increasingly seen as relics of a heathen past. Yet these spirits are still around, and they remain multifarious, as is clear from Awal's story. His ultimate victory was in a confrontation with a *doguwa*, a special kind of spirit, mostly associated with a particular mark in the landscape: a tree, a boulder. Thus the *doguwa* laid out "a spiritual geography in which the first settlers had anchored their history" (Masquelier 2009:157). In exchange for protecting this geography, they had to be constantly reconciled with gifts and sacrifices. However, the increasing neglect of the spirits due to progressive Islamization had embittered many of them. The problem is that for true believers any contact with these spirits, indeed any sign of belief in their force, is anathema. Such neglect led the spirits to launch increasingly dangerous attacks on people and their possessions. The area of Dogondoutchi had the reputation, enhanced by generations of French colonial *administrateurs*, of being a hot spot for these spirits. Under the burden of the increasing economic crisis in the 1990s many came to believed that the spirits had become particularly active and restive. This enhanced all the more the importance of Malam Awal's courage in confronting a notoriously vengeful one.

In 1997, the success of his preaching in Dogondoutchi encouraged this *malam* to build the center for his *zawiya* (brotherhood) there. Thus the town, until then something of a backwater, would become a new Islamic center of regional and potentially global radiation. Someone offered him a vacant plot of land for the construction of his Friday mosque and adjoining quarters. However, as soon as people started to work for him on this construction they were attacked by particularly aggressive ants. Apparently only then Awal found out what local people had known all along: the place was inhabited by a particularly aggressive *doguwa* whose nasty attacks had chased away already a whole series of previous settlers. This was why the plot had remained empty for quite some time (one wonders if this was also why it had been offered to Awal). As *doguwa* spirits do, this one could transform herself into aggressive animals: a swarm of angry bees or, as in this case, biting ants. Nevertheless, on being told all this, Awal was undeterred. He went to the land and addressed the ants (according to his believers only he could see the *doguwa* responsible for the attack, but even this did not frighten him off). He told them to go away and that he would be "their new neighbor." After this the ants indeed left, and the building could continue without further problems.

It is noteworthy in this story that Awal recognized that he had addressed the *doguwa*. In an interview with Masquelier he confirmed that he "knew how to talk to spirits, a power he claimed to have received from God" (Masquelier 2009:150). Muslims, certainly *malamija* (teachers), are required to avoid any contacts with the spirits. Any attempt to deal—or even communicate—with them can be explained as putting into doubt's God's omnipotence. Yet, just like Pentecostals, most Islamic teachers equate these spirits with Satan, which means here as well a form of mediation that permits recognition of the reality of their powers. But Awal went further, apparently recognizing how important it was to give a clear space in his preaching to local ideas about the spirits. Masquelier (2005:154) notes that the story of the building of the mosque and Awal's successful expulsion of the spirit had a double charge. In order to prove the superiority of his powers, he allowed the *doguwa* a special place in his Muslim imaginary. Indeed, its reality made his victory all the more spectacular. This "re-membering" of the spirits became a key element in the story of Awal's holiness.

Just like the Pentecostal interventions, responses like Awal's result in a scaling up of the local imaginary. The power of the spirits is mediated by seeing them as emanations of Satan himself. Thus the local spirits are included in a broader image of a cosmic battle between evil and good, God and the devil. This mediation through Satan brings an increase of scale, in the most literal sense. Significantly, Masquelier (2009:156) notes that the *bori*—a Hausa term for spirits in general—have now become a kind of generalized antipode to the true religion, and that thus the notion is applied in an ever wider sense: "ever more spirits are incorporated into the *bori* pantheon." However, this increase of scale—the spirits now involved in a cosmic battle that seems to surpass local confines—continues to be expressed in local terms. Malam Awal's main victory was over a spirit whose particularities are rooted in the local context. Again, it is striking how directly new messages—effecting a mediation of local forms of evil through the more general figure of the devil—appeal to local realities, confirming the power of these evil spirits. Masquelier also shows that the new forms of trust built on this mediation of local evil through the devil remain highly shaky, even if trust is now built on an appeal to a wider order: the credibility Malam Awal earned with his followers dissipated as quickly as he built it up.[29] The by now familiar ambiguity of a widening vision that remains nonetheless rooted in local realities is apparent here as well.[30]

Mediation, Increase of Scale, and the Struggle over Trust: African Specificities

Clearly, increasingly complex mediations of witchcraft—through its recent equation with the devil and, more practically, through its being performed on the screen—give it a new place in public space. It is being imagined on a larger scale, not as a local struggle but as part of wider battle between good and evil. This allows for new modes of distancing. Yet we have seen that such distancing remains particularly difficult in African contexts—

think of Pentecostals' continuing search for the devil inside the family, or Malam Awal's struggle with Satan, who manifested himself as a local spirit. Can such ambiguities of a global that is still seen as entrenched in the local help us understand why in many parts of the African continent people remain preoccupied with modernity's being so closely linked to witchcraft? To what extent does the shift highlighted above—a perceived increase of scale of evil conspiracies that remain nonetheless rooted in local realities—bring new possibilities for establishing trust vis-à-vis forms of evil that still seem to be so uncomfortably close? And how do these new openings relate to older efforts to establish trust?

From the explorations in the preceding chapters and notably from the comparisons, all sorts of analytical concepts have emerged that can serve for tackling such questions. As emphasized already repeatedly, the relevance of ontology notions—still current in Pacific studies and apparently making a comeback in anthropology in general—is doubtful when they remain marked by the culturalist proclivity that haunted anthropology for so long. Such notions are particularly inadequate in a constantly moving configuration such as witchcraft, intimacy, and trust. As said, the continuous shifts in people's views of occult forces and new distances and the rapidity with which elements from elsewhere are hybridized with local ideas undermine any assumption of radical cultural contrasts: consider the rapid emergence of a more or less institutionalized therapy for child witches (whose proliferation is in itself a new phenomenon) in Kinshasa's churches, or the equally rapid globalization in the post–cold war context of notions of *famla*, the Cameroonian version of a new witchcraft of wealth—*nouveaux riches* witches supposedly "selling" their zombie victims now on a truly global scale.

Freud's notion of the uncanny—*das Heimliche* that at any moment can turn into something all the more *unheimlich* since it is so close by—raises intriguing questions in these widening contexts as well. How is this uneasy *heimlich/unheimlich* nexus affected by the further mediation of witchcraft and its publicizing? What are the effects of such an increase of scale in both witchcraft notions and social relations on the balancing of distance and proximity, mobility and intimacy, in people's conceptions of occult forces? Simmel's notion of a suspension of doubt as a vital—but difficult to grasp—element for the establishment of trust also suggests questions in these new settings: for instance, questions regarding the changing relationship between more public and more private ways of containing uncertainty, and their effectiveness for establishing at least some sort of trust in everyday life. In more concrete terms: if witchcraft goes public, as has been happening over recent decades in Africa (due to the Pentecostal impact and other influences), does this facilitate or rather impede the affirmation of trust?

It is worthy of note that the further mediation of witchcraft—bringing an increase of scale through new media, accompanied by new ways of distancing oneself—seems to go together with efforts to completely eradicate *das Unheimliche* in order to establish an absolute form of trust that leaves no room for doubt, let alone a "suspension of doubt." In sixteenth- and seventeenth-century Europe, for instance, the mediation of local beliefs through attributing witchcraft to the devil inspired many people—both authorities and commoners—to launch a total offensive against it. This abrupt drive for a total eradication of witchcraft cannot be detached from its gradual equation with the work of the devil during the preceding centuries. The emphasis of Robert Muchembled (1978) on a "civilizing offensive from above" as a major force in the witch hunts may be right in a general sense, despite all the subsequent criticism on this point (see chap. 4 above). His one-sided attention to the role of religious and political authorities as main initiators of this offensive may have led him to neglect the possibly even stronger pressure "from below" for draconic measures against the witches. Still, it is clear that the widespread horror about the supposed proliferation of witchcraft was strongly reinforced by its identification as the work of the devil, and that this idea was imposed by initiatives from above. In Africa, the equation with the devil had similar effects. The Pentecostals see their struggle against witchcraft as an ultimate struggle to break the devil's hold over people. And the Islamic *malamai* (teachers) in Masquelier's book similarly battled for an ultimate defeat of the spirits, seen as emanations of Satan. Yet in all those contexts the completeness of the offensive and the claim to establish total trust had the opposite effect of confirming the very reality of the dark forces. This paradoxical result—the fact that both the Pentecostals and the *malamai* (and to a certain extent even the clerics and judges in early modern Europe) seemed to need witchcraft as a counterpoint—raises doubts about the effectiveness of such total offensives in practice.

I encountered the same absolute stance at the end of the Yaoundé conference Justice et Sorcellerie (2005) mentioned before, when I was suddenly attacked by a Cameroonian priest (a well-trained Jesuit) for doubting the reality of what he called *l'école de la sorcellerie* (the school of witchcraft). For him the solution was clear: this school had to be found and destroyed. That would bring an end to witchcraft itself.

Throughout the conference the issue of the "reality" of witchcraft had kept coming up, often at unexpected moments and in quite uncomfortable ways. It was raised in no uncertain terms after the very first lecture of the conference, presented by a French colleague, Alban Bensa (EHESS, Paris), whose main fieldwork is in New Caledonia. The organizers had invited him to open the conference in order to make it clear that Cameroon (or Africa) was not exceptional in its preoccupation with a proliferation of witchcraft. Bensa offered an engaging presentation that indeed helped to place the conference theme in a more general perspective. However the very first question to him, from a young man at the back of the hall, took him by surprise: did he believe in the reality of witchcraft? Bensa replied, in good Parisian *intello* style, with a brief "Eh bien, non—je n'y crois pas" (Well, no—I do not believe in it), implying that the question was completely irrelevant to him and its answer obvious. The reaction among the audience was quite different: If he did not believe in it, how could he understand what was at stake? How could he as an outsider ever arrive at a deeper understanding of what was at stake in witchcraft affairs?

This question about "belief" is, of course, a modern one. In the village it would be a nonsensical question since it implies a possibility of choice—as if one could choose to believe or not. Even the staunchest Presbyterian *catéchiste* takes it for granted that occult forces are real (all the more reason to condemn them utterly). In a scientific environment—after all, the conference took place on the university campus—such a question becomes relevant, but in this case as some sort of a catch question: it clearly served, as so often in people's dealings with white anthropologists and other scientists, to marginalize them: they might pretend to understand witchcraft, but their categorical disbelief made any "real" understanding impossible.

My presentation was on the second day of the Yaoundé conference—so I had time to prepare an answer to the tricky question of "belief." The question duly came, and I took the line anthropologists generally take since the impact of Foucauldian notions in our discipline. I emphasized that discourses create their own reality and that this applied particularly to a powerful discourse like witchcraft; that even natural scientists had learned to accept that there are different "realities"; and that therefore witchcraft could have its own claim to truth alongside scientific analysis. This answer seemed to pass muster, and an animated discussion followed on other aspects of my talk.

However, I was not to be let off the hook so easily. When, after the conference, we had a short discussion with the organizers about the success of the meeting, I unexpectedly landed in a confrontation about "reality'" similar to that of my colleague Bensa. A Cameroonian Jesuit,

Father Martin Birba, who as a staff member of the Catholic University had chaired one of the last sessions with great rhetorical force, started to elaborate on his idea of an *école de la sorcellerie*, which he had mentioned in his interventions during the conference. For him, this school was crucial to both the continuing reproduction of witchcraft and its possible eradication. During an informal discussion after the conference was over, he insisted again and again that there was only one way to put an end to *la sorcellerie*: we had to find this *école* and destroy it. Only then would all these manifestations of evil be ended.

I was intrigued by his notion of an *école de la sorcellerie*. Again, it is a kind of modernizing expression: for many Cameroonians the school is still the epitome of modernity. Apparently in Birba's view, even *la sorcellerie* was included in the modern world; even this secret knowledge was reproduced in a modern way. So I tried to challenge him on this notion: Did he really think that such a school could be found? Where was it located? But he sensed my doubts and turned on me with clear irritation. He was not at all convinced by my emphasis on words: witchcraft was not real because people spoke so much about it—that was *not* what was at stake. My approach risked concealing the very reality of witchcraft. He followed this up with a long story of how some people had confessed to have attended this school of witchcraft. He was certain: this school was out there in the bush, and we had to find and destroy it. My line about witchcraft as a discursive practice was for him completely beside the point. The aim had to be a complete eradication of this evil, and finding the school was the obvious way to achieve this.

Again, one might wonder whether such a frontal attack, striving to establish final trust beyond any doubt, can be effective: Father Birba's goal of a total eradication of witchcraft required the conceptual construct of an *école* that was its center and could be destroyed. But he was at a loss to explain how to find this mystical school. During the subsequent discussion the main organizer of the conference, Père Eric de Rosny—the Jesuit priest, already mentioned, who had been initiated as a *nganga* (traditional healer) and combined the two roles with great perspicacity—expressed some doubts about this idea of a school of witchcraft. He suggested that secrets are rather passed on in the niches of everyday life, in the kitchen, during moments of rest after work, or at other moments of conviviality. [31] The difference between this more mundane view and Father Birba's vision of an *école de la sorcellerie* has important implications. If witchcraft is passed on in everyday situations—kitchen, work, drinking—then a complete eradication is hardly possible since these representation and practices are too firmly anchored in the intimacies of everyday life.

The frontal attack aiming for a complete eradication of witchcraft—as implied in the Pentecostal equation with the devil or in Father Birba's plea for the complete destruction of *l'école de la sorcellerie*—differs radically from solutions of the witchcraft/intimacy/trust conundrum that have been worked out in everyday life in many African contexts, and that can best be summarized by the Duala proverb I have quoted often: "You have to learn to live with your witch." This local wisdom seems to come much closer to Siegel's vision of the uncanny that is always lurking and never can be definitively eradicated, or to Freud's ideas of *das Heimliche* that can always suddenly turn into *das Unheimliche*. It might be worthwhile to further explore what kinds of practicalities follow from such an attitude. Maybe the Duala proverb does not offer a definitive solution, but the radical approaches proposed by present-day Pentecostalism in Africa with its crusades, or by the determined offensive of ecclesiastical and local state tribunals in early modern Europe, have proved to be downright counterproductive—affirming the idea of witchcraft as an omnipresent danger rather than weakening it.

From the African examples above of how people try to live with this danger, various "tactics" emerged.[32] One was an effort to establish distance: leaving for the city or even transcontinental migration, trying as much as possible to avoid occasions for renewed immersion in the village. We saw that such efforts seemed to be rendered useless time and again by the increasing mobility attributed to these forces, and thus the increasing scope of the "witchcraft of the house." In the 1970s the distance of the city from the village still seemed to constitute some protection, but by the 1990s little was left of this; in the 1980s witchcraft was still supposed "not to cross the water," but in subsequent decades migrants in Europe and elsewhere have felt ever more threatened by the dangers from home.

Another tactic was to try to forestall jealousy and its dangers by carefully striving for a "just redistribution" of the fruits of one's success among relatives. The cases above suggested that this as well becomes ever more difficult with the rapidly increasing inequalities between successful "sons of the village" in the city or elsewhere and their "brothers" at home. Remember the cases above showing how hard it became to maintain this idea of a just redistribution when new assets—degrees completed at the university, a huge ranch—were at stake. Again, no wonder then that people complain of witchcraft being strengthened rather than weakened by the impact of modernity.

In the prologue to this book I suggested that this linking of modernity to witchcraft seems to be crucial to the continuing intensity of people's preoccupation with occult threats in many parts of Africa. The question was also to what extent this might be related to specific aspects of the impact of modern developments in African contexts—notably to the immediacy with which these developments are articulated with the private sphere of the family and the house. Indeed, the pattern analyzed above for changing imaginaries of the occult—witchcraft being subjected to an increase of scale yet remaining rooted in the local—is a recurrent one, also in other aspects of African societies and their recent history. The uncertainties of the world market, the brutalities of state formation and the development industry, but also education, modern health care, and new religious movements may all bring a clear increase of scale in people's perceptions and their social relations—in Africa as elsewhere. Yet what might be special to this continent is the directness with which such new frameworks and openings are grafted onto the local realities of family and kin, with intermediate institutions playing at most a marginal role. Since colonial times African producers have been singularly lacking in protection against the vagaries of the world market; government interventions have affected family organizations in most direct ways—often leading to completely unexpected results, yet most real in their effects.[33]

Such immediacy is reflected in the examples above of recent forms of "mediation" of witchcraft. As said, the equation of witchcraft with the devil by Pentecostals and others in Africa can be seen—just as in early modern Europe—as a new increase of scale of these local notions, making them part of a global struggle between good and evil. In both Europe and Africa this inspired (and still inspires) a determined offensive to eradicate these devilish forces. In both contexts such an offensive confirmed and still confirms the very reality of the threats it is attacking. But a difference is that in Africa the devil is "privatized" by being located in the very heart of the family. The private contours of this evil make it part and parcel of everyday life, and therefore extremely difficult to eradicate. The European judges felt obliged to force the accused to confess their pact with the devil. For instance, the terrible moral pressure on the "last witch of Langenburg" in the late seventeenth century in Württemberg was seen as necessary in the context of a cosmic battle—it was crucial for breaking Satan's hold over the community (see Robisheaux 2009 and chap. 4 above). The denunciations of witchcraft in Africa by the Pentecostals have different implications: they may bring a similar increase of scale by relating it directly to the devil, but, as said, they mostly continue somewhat paradoxically to locate this evil in the microworld of family and village—thus reaffirming basic tenets of people's ideas about witchcraft. It is precisely this linking that makes it so difficult to break out of it (see also Meyer 1999).

There is a basic ambiguity in the Pentecostal pairing of a struggle for a radical victory over witchcraft as a work of the devil and the affirmation of the roots of this particular evil within people's very intimacy. This makes Pentecostal "crusades" a shaky basis for establishing new and total forms of trust, precisely because the preachers confirm that *das Unheimliche* (witchcraft) is part and parcel of das *Heimliche* (family). One can wonder about the viability of a project aiming to surpass the hold of the family on religious grounds alone. After all, the broader socioeconomic situation of enduring crisis and poverty seems to be little conducive to the emergence of other forms of social security. When such forms are still lacking, religious efforts to supplant the family may remain partial at most. Then the insistence that the familial context is the seat of witchcraft can only reinforce witchcraft as an omnipresent threat.

The Brazilian Candomblé example is also marked by a certain increase of scale, but following a different trajectory and with different implications for trust. Profiting from a broader configuration that was quite favorable—at least until in Brazil too the upsurge of Pentecostalism became a powerful counterforce—it did not work toward a radical eradication of occult powers but rather used them to construe a certain basis for trust. The spirits, whose African origin was strongly emphasized, became embedded in a broader trans-Atlantic configuration. They were no longer tied to familial contexts—which had evaporated in the horrors of the Middle Passage—but became located in temples and there transformed into gods. Their dangerous potentialities remained present, but mostly only implicitly. Favored by a shifting national context in the course of the last century, the temples developed a cult with a more or less stable local basis that could offer protection to ever broader constituencies. The link between intimacy and danger remained—remember the rumors about the potential dangers of being drawn into the intimate sphere of the *terreiros*—but the cults provided the full scope of the protective potentialities of these occult forces.

Of course, in this respect as well there is not an absolute contrast with developments at the other side of the Atlantic. As noted (chap. 5), especially along the West African coast, in the context of increasing cosmopolitanism created by the slave trade and all the uprooting it brought, similar cults developed around *voduns* and other deities. However, the broader politico-historical constellation has been different there. In Africa, these cults remained marginalized under colonial rule until 1960, and this marginalization was often perpetuated and strengthened by the modernizing tide of the first decades of subsequent postcolonial rule. When the cults could finally profit from a reevaluation of African "traditions"—as in the Afrikania movement in Ghana, since the 1980s supported by President Rawlings as a "traditional African religion" (see chap. 5 above and de Witte 2008)—they were almost immediately overtaken by the powerful Pentecostal surge. The Candomblé temples in Brazil are now confronted by a similar Pentecostal tide—and as in Africa, the Brazilian preachers have no patience with Candomblé's claims to be a religion; for them it is just "witchcraft," as in the African context. But due to the much better consolidated position of Candomblé temples, especially the more renowned ones, these are in a stronger position to confront the Pentecostal onslaught than was a movement like Afrikania. Over time, the articulation of different *durées*—to borrow one of the favorite themes of Jean-François Bayart (2004)—followed different courses, and this directly affects present-day relations.

In Africa, by contrast, the family has remained at the very heart of recent changes—and not only in the field of religion and spiritual struggles against evil. As noted, the immediate articulation of global changes with the microsphere of family and village applied to other fields as well throughout the colonial and postcolonial periods. Indeed, it still does. The same pattern emerges, for instance, from the recent effects of political and economic liberalization in the post–cold war context. To cite a telling example: in many African contexts decentralization—one of the shibboleths of the neoliberal development policy brought a return of "the" local community, since neoliberals (somewhat surprisingly) combined a strong belief in "the market" with an equally strong defense of a communitarian approach; hence their tendency to try to resurrect "tradition," "customary" chiefs, and other forms of association that they apparently assume to have a timeless existence. Similarly, democratization made local belonging and "the" village crucial in national politics, even if for many politicians the village had become an almost virtual reality (see further Geschiere 2009b and the literature quoted there). The impressive elasticity of African kinship in the new contexts—spanning even transcontinental distances without apparently losing its coherence—plays into such immediate articulations of global changes and the domestic sphere of the family.[34]

Again, it might be tempting to see this continuing centrality of kinship as a typically African trait—more or less given with "African culture." Yet such an approach would neglect the considerable variations in this respect, and also the impressive dynamics of kinship as a principle of organization—remember the examples throughout this book of how the link between witchcraft and the intimacy of the family kept changing drastically and rapidly. So, to conclude, I want to return to the merits of more historical approaches, like Goody's ambitious panorama sketching how material circumstances prevailing on the African continent helped develop certain patterns in the production and reproduction of social forms.[35] Goody's emphasis on the special traits that kinship developed in a context of "wealth-in-people" (rather than "'wealth-in-things," as in most parts of Eurasia) is still relevant for understanding the dynamics of African kinship in new global contexts.[36] Of course this is a very broad vision that has to be filled in by following the historical trajectories that are specific for each context. Yet it allows us to perceive crucial points of tension in changing settings and to position these against a broader background. For instance, it is quite clear that the inclusive tendencies of African kinship conceptions—fitting in a context of open resources where, indeed, the control over people was the main source of wealth—are countered by more recent tendencies toward a closure of the family now that "things" (land and other assets) have become of permanent value in the family's heritage in many parts of the African continent (see Geschiere 2009b; Berry 1985). It is precisely this tension between inclusive tendencies that still mark kinship reckoning and a practice of increasing closure of the family that makes the link between witchcraft and the intimacy of "the house" so threatening. Remember what was said above about the kinship relations that seemed to be strained to a breaking point by ever deeper inequalities yet still retained their coherence.

The direct articulation of modernity with the sphere of the family that is so striking in many African contexts seems to be equally related to certain historical specificities in the way local societies became embedded in broader configurations of exchange and domination. A historical approach that helps to address such specificities is Jean-François Bayart's elaborations, mentioned earlier, upon the centrality of *stratégies d'extraversion* in the contacts of African societies with the outside world. Such an emphasis on "extraversion" applied to the precolonial elites throughout Africa, who tended to build their power on their control over external relations (rather than through exploitation of the producers inside their realm). But it applies equally—albeit in a different form—to the postcolonial elites of the times of development: they are still mainly outward-looking in the sense that external relations remain vital for the reproduction of their power base.[37] Clearly, *extraversion* has a long history in Africa. Yet in everyday life this outward orientation—which recently took on new force with many young people's determined choice to "go global"—is most directly related to microrealities of home and the family. The centrality of *stratégies d'extraversion* in African formations confirms again the openness of the private sphere to outside influences. To put it differently, mobility and the urge to "go out" have always been basic in African social formations.[38] This is reflected in the ease with which witchcraft conceptions—which were always about unexpected forms of mobility—are grafted onto the constant increase of scale of social relations, expressing a fascination with new opportunities outside. Yet this drive toward mobility is directly articulated with the intimate sphere: even the Cameroonian "bushfallers" of recent years (see chap. 3 above and Alpes 2011) organize their adventurous transcontinental migration projects with their family, and if they succeed in making it to *bush* (Europe, the Gulf) they remain directly beholden to the family at home in all sorts of ways. Again it is striking how closely intertwined the global and the local are, with intermediate levels playing at most a tenuous role.

The specific traits of such an immediate articulation of global developments—new forms of mobility and new opportunities—with intimate realities may suggest a broader historical explanation of why in many parts of Africa people seem to remain so obsessed with witchcraft as an omnipresent danger, even as a corollary of modernity itself. Yet such specificities do not preclude the possibility that in such preoccupations "witchcraft" stands for issues that haunt societies everywhere in the world. For instance, the present-day obsession in many Western countries with child abuse in intimate contexts offers parallel examples of the uncanny that may be uncomfortably close to many (cf. Jean Comaroff 1997; LaFontaine 1998). African elaborations of the uncanny, even though they are shaped by a specific historical context, are certainly not a sign of the continent's radical "othcrncss"—on the contrary, they open a window that can help us better understand the ambiguities of intimacy in general.

Une didactique contre la sorcellerie?

In 1972, after my first long-term fieldwork in the Maka area, I received a visit in my home in Amsterdam from three Dutch priests who had worked all their lives in that part of Cameroon. I thought at first it was just a *visite de politesse*—which it was to a certain extent. But they also came with a mission. They had understood that in my fieldwork I had stumbled upon the omnipresence of the notion of *djambe* (witchcraft), and they wanted my help in developing *une didactique contre la sorcellerie* (a pedagogy against witchcraft). They felt this was one of the most urgent things needed in their work. Could I as an anthropologist not help them with this? We had a long and very interesting discussion that was continued on later occasions. Yet I still feel that I failed them miserably because of my inability to come up with concrete suggestions.

In my 1997 book on the topic, I expressed the hope that if we contextualize the moments when acute fears of witchcraft arise—leading to suspicion, distrust, and even outright accusations and conflicts—the hold of these ideas over people's minds might at least be relativized. And indeed, such contextualizing is a recurrent theme in that book. So I was quite happy that several people—including intellectuals in the city but also people in villages—were keen to get a copy of the earlier French version of the book; some even started to read it. However, I soon noticed that their interest was mainly inspired by a hope of finding new secrets in the book. Indeed, most abandoned their reading when it became clear that little was to be found in that vein. My plea for exploring contexts in order to relativize hardly seemed to come across.

Maybe the very idea of *une didactique conte la sorcellerie* asks too much—at least if by this is meant a complete victory over witchcraft ideas. One of the main points coming out of the comparisons above might be that efforts at a complete eradication of these beliefs has never succeeded—indeed, they often had the opposing effect of confirming the reality of such threats. The Pentecostals in Africa with their fierce crusades against witchcraft in the name of God, who will overpower the devil, only succeed in reinforcing popular beliefs and anxieties. And even the much more ferocious witch hunts in early modern Europe did not bring a definitive victory. The beliefs lingered on (see Ladurie 1973; de Blécourt 1990). They were only gradually marginalized as scientific discourse acquired increasing power in the functioning of society.[39] But the ideas are still there and come up in new forms and at unexpected moments (cf. Jean Comaroff 1997; LaFontaine 1998). Probably Siegel is right that they express confrontations with an uncanny that will always continue to manifest itself at unexpected places and moments.[40] So a radical break resulting in definitive trust—realizing an intimacy without danger and an ontological trust without any need for suspension of doubt—may be too much to ask for.

Still, it is difficult to deny the relevance of the idea of a *didactique contre la sorcellerie* when one is continually confronted with people's terrible dismay over dark threats, or with the havoc that witchcraft suspicions create in social relations. Is a more humble approach not possible, outlining at least tentative possibilities for strengthening trust in practice, despite such intimate dangers? Again, Freud's vision of *das Heimliche* turning into something terribly *unheimlich*—especially threatening since it is so close—remains a promising guide. Yet in relation to the examples above this idea seems also to teach a certain modesty.[41] One cannot live without *das (Un)Heimliche*—so a definitive eradication is impossible; one can only try to limit its potentiality to turn into a fearsome danger. Thus we are back at the by now well-known refrain of "learning to live with one's sorcerer."

Yet we saw also that living with the family and its danger becomes ever more difficult. New inequalities make the ideal of "just redistribution" ever more contested, and trying to create distance is of no avail since the "witchcraft of the house" is supposed to graft itself onto the increase of scale of social relations. However, the close link of kinship and witchcraft allows for all sorts of possibilities—nothing is fixed in this relation. De Certeau's visionary lines on *l'étrange* hiding in the niches of hegemonic structures and working changes from within (de Certeau 1970:7—and see chap. 3 above) might give some hope here. Small shifts inside the organization of kinship can have important consequences. Remember the examples above of how in some contexts obligations within the family can be reconciled to new circumstances, shielding people at least to a certain extent from both witchcraft accusations and attacks.[42]

The argument in this book also suggests another more general reflection. Can the cogency that witchcraft fears acquire in certain times and places be relativized by the realization that these representations are one possible expression of the more general truth that intimacy is basically ambiguous—offering support but also summoning up deep dangers? Such a recognition can at least help to deconstruct the aura of exceptionality with which witchcraft discourse is surrounded.

> The contrast between the two cases at the end of chapter 3 (on trust) may be relevant here. In the case of Franklin, who despite an inborn propensity to share and redistribute suddenly became enmeshed in an apparently unstoppable turmoil of witchcraft rumors when two of his sons finished their academic studies, a certain threshold seemed to have been passed. In his large family there always was inside jealousy, but this tended to be denied and concealed behind an ostentatious show of solidarity. This made the sudden avalanche of harsh witchcraft accusations all the more disruptive. In the case of Benoit—the successful international development expert who had the courage to return home and start a big farm—this threshold has not been crossed (at least not yet). But there is a quiet recognition of inside jealousy as a potential danger, so that evoking a baroque imaginary of witchcraft horrors might be less necessary.

The question might not be whether inside jealousy will rear its head, since it is always around. The challenge is rather to understand why it is so easily connected to the weird imagery of *djambe, evu,* and such. A factor encouraging such a connection is no doubt the availability of such ideas. The new mediatization of witchcraft—its forceful publicizing in many parts of Africa in recent decades—certainly plays a role in this. In earlier decades occult forces were never discussed so openly. Yet other recent changes may have more beneficial effects. Not only the Pentecostal attacks on the family but also a more general relativizing of kinship as the principal basis of solidarity might diminish the cogency of witchcraft notions. Is it possible to generalize this and conclude that when the family becomes less vital for social survival, it may be easier to accept as a fact of life that inside jealousy can be terribly dangerous? Or to put it more directly: if people become more ready to accept inside jealousy—even within the house and the family—as a fact of life, will it then be less necessary to evoke the imaginary of witchcraft with all its horrors?

Accepting that intimacy is inherently dangerous as a general truth, not as something that has to be denied, can help to direct people's fears toward a source that is omnipresent indeed—after all, social relations are basic to all human endeavor—and also most visible in the everyday world. Then such fears can be addressed in more pragmatic ways.[43] Only my readers—and especially African readers who live with the horror of witchcraft as an everyday reality—can judge whether recognizing the ambiguities of intimacy as a basic strand in witchcraft conceptions and the horrors they evoke can help to relativize their hold over people's minds.

Notes

Prologue

1. Freud [1919] 2003; Simmel [1902–3] 1950:402; see also Mary Douglas on "witchcraft nestling in the crevices of structure" (in the chapter "Internal Lines" of *Purity and Danger*, Douglas 1966:136—many thanks to Nils Bubandt for referring me to this passage); Michel de Certeau on "l'étrange. . . . [qui] mène une existence d'en dessous, une résistance interne, jamais réduite" (de Certeau 1970:7: the uncanny leading an existence from below, an internal resistance, never weakening—my translation); Stoler 2005, notably chap. 1, on the intimate as the locus of deep tensions in imperial settings; Siegel 2006 on familiar relations suddenly taking on an uncanny appearance; and Thiranagama 2010 and 2011 on the close link between intimacy, fear, and betrayal under LTTE (Tamil Tigers) rule and its obsession with the presence of traitors inside.

2. See Lévi-Strauss 1987:62; see also Siegel 2006:44.

3. Joseph Tonda (2005) uses the term *magma* to characterize in a most evocative way the osmosis of widely different elements (traditional, missionary, colonial, etc.) in one constantly expanding mass from which the frightening figure of *Le Souverain moderne*, the "Leviathan" of postcolonial Africa, emerges (apparently his image refers to magma in its steaming fluid state, not yet in its rock-hard state when cooled off).

4. Cf. historian Wolfgang Behringer, who notes with an impressive richness of detail in his ambitious "global history" of witchcraft (2004) how common these elements are throughout history and space.

5. Easy contrasts like the one Marwick tentatively made in 1964 between African witches as insiders and Oceanic sorcerers as outsiders do not hold upon closer analysis. The same is true for the contrast between witches in Africa as often relatives versus European witches as neighbors (and not kin). See chapter 4 and interlude, below.

6. Of course *witchcraft* is not the only term people use to refer to this all-pervasive force that seems to absorb all distinctions. *Magic* is another current notion. Cf. also Bernault 2009 on the currency—up till today—of the notion of *fétichisme* rather than *sorcellerie* in Gabon and other parts of francophone Africa; see further chapter 1 below, n13.

7. The Maka term for "house", *ndjaw*—as in the expression *djambe le ndjaw* (the house as the cradle of witchcraft)—returns also in the common notion *ndjaw boud*, the "people of the house." But these people may live dispersed over a considerable distance. The Maka notion of *ndjaw*, "house," as a localized space shades easily into that of a group linked by kinship (sometimes clearly fictional) spread over different localities.

8. The quotation is from a reader's report. It may be unusual to quote readers' reports, but I cannot express more elegantly and succinctly what I want to say.

9. This penchant in development discourse has only been reinforced in recent times by the "neoliberal" approach's betting on "community." Indeed, one of the paradoxes of the neoliberal turn for Africa is that it combines renewed emphasis on the market as the solution to all problems with an unfailing belief in "the" community, "tradition," and the family. Vivid examples are to be found in Juan Obarrio's thesis (2007) on the emergence of what he calls the "Structural Adjustment state" in Mozambique. He describes how, for instance, during a meeting a senior American UNDP official angrily replied to the doubts of a few social scientists about the ease with which he took "the" local community as the starting point for projects: "These communities know who they are and know also their boundaries perfectly well." Obarrio quotes also a British consultant for USAID who insisted that communities "will be like corporations, unified single legal subjects under the new land law" (Obarrio 2007:105). Cf. also Buur and Kyed 2007 regarding the unexpected comeback of traditional chiefs in neoliberal Mozambique.

10. Oral communication in the seminar Culture and Development, Leiden University, 1990; see also Mbembe 2010a and 2010b.

11. This renewed interest seems to be encouraged by Gilles Deleuze's and Bruno Latour's explorations of the ontology notion. Seminal as these may be, there appears to occur some shift when anthropologists relate to them, since in our discipline *ontology* refers all too easily to a vision of radical cultural contrasts that, moreover, often degrades into a conceptual opposition between the West and "the rest." If ontology is about multiplicity and about proliferating *rhizomes*, the concept can be most inspiring. But continuing to work from assumptions of "ontological" cultural contrasts between societies or cultures is most unproductive in the present-day world, so deeply marked by creative hybridization and cultural mixing (see further the interlude below, nn7, 8, 10).

12. Goody set out to show that this opposition between extensive and intensive agriculture (hoe vs. plow) related to the contrast between bridewealth in Africa (paid by the family of the man to the family of the bride) versus dowry (the bride takes part of the family heritage into her marriage) in Eurasia, and also to a series of other oppositions: for example, open access to land for Africa that made direct control over people vital for any form of accumulation, while in Eurasia landlords could control labor due to their hold over scarce land and technology. In the first setting inheritance was of little value (no permanent cultivation of land) and polygyny was an important way of accumulating labor; in the second setting control over inheritance was crucial and hence there was stringent surveillance

of daughters and their marriages to maintain control over "things." Of course this brief sketch is much too simplistic. Yet Goody's explorations do suggest divergent trajectories in societies' reproduction of social relations—divergences that are of direct consequence for people's ways of demarcating kinship and the house. For further elaboration, see chapters 4 and 6 below. There I elaborate also on the relevance of Jean-François Bayart's notion of *stratégies d'extraversion* as special to the organization of production and reproduction of African societies, as well as to the crystallization of corresponding *imaginaires*; see also Jane Guyer's seminal explorations of the implications of the centrality of "wealth-in-people"—that is, on the specifics of the convertibility of people/things—in African societies (1993 and 2004). The question will be to what extent these historical specificities can help to outline particular trends in the development of notions of "the house" and the dangers of its intimacy in present-day African contexts.

13. See chapter 1 for further discussion of these criticisms.

14. See n12 above on the wider frameworks suggested by Goody, Bayart, and Guyer.

Chapter 1

1. Andrea Ceriana Mayneri (2010) would qualify this as *un moment d'énonciation* or a "provocative situation." One of the fertile insights developed in his work is that popular and scientific discourses on occult forces take shape in contexts where they are constantly provoking each other. This mutual provocation marks both of them in complex ways (see also Ceriana Mayneri 2012 and n20 below).

2. See Geschiere 2009a; Ndjio 2012; Awondo and others 2012. The connection of witchcraft with same-sex relations is present in many parts of Africa, but it seems to emerge with particular force in Equatorial Africa, for instance in the context of recent witch hunts against presumed homosexuals (see Brocqua 2012; Awondo 2012 on Cameroon; Aterianus-Owanga 2012 on Gabon). In these contexts the pronounced link with witchcraft seems to go together with a particular image of same-sex relations and the homosexual: the "phallocrate" who uses anal penetration as an expression of ultimate dominance and subjection (see Mbembe 2006; see also Awondo and others 2012)

3. Especially since the 1990s (for Ghana already earlier—see Meyer 1999), this apparent omnipresence of witchcraft was reinforced by the rapid spread of Pentecostalism that equated witchcraft with the work of the devil, who is seen as lurking everywhere (but to some Pentecostals the devil seems to disappear ever more behind witchcraft, as a more familiar threat). Many have noted that precisely by combating witchcraft Pentecostalism reinforces people's belief in its reality (see, for instance, Meyer 1998a and 1999; Marshall 2009; Fancello 2011).

4. See the references in n14 below.

5. The whole conundrum around the witchcraft notion seems to be a good example of Michael Taussig's insistence on the power of "epistemological murk": such notions become powerful precisely because they defy any attempt at clarification (Taussig 1987). Witchcraft might be a stark example of how the confusions in popular parlor and academic debate can be mutually reinforcing.

6. Cf., for instance, the emphasis on same-sex intercourse as a recurrent theme in the Maka stories about the *shumbu*: these nightly encounters are marked not only by cannibalism but also by sexual debauchery. In the night world everything is turned upside down; this is why same-sex intercourse prevails, though according to most Maka it is unheard of in everyday life (which remains to be seen). In the *shumbu* men do "it" with men, and "even" women with women. In Cameroon, as elsewhere in Equatorial Africa (see n3 above), this equation of homosexuality with witchcraft—in the past mostly mentioned only briefly by most researchers—has taken on new vigor with the ferocious witch hunts against supposed homosexuals, staged by the state and the Catholic Church but also by some parts of the population. One reason that homosexuality has quite suddenly become a burning issue all over the African continent might be the Internet propagation a hitherto unknown gay-lesbian consciousness, not as a hidden practice but as a specific identity. But a backlash against international human rights missions proclaiming that homosexuality should no longer be a criminal offense also plays an important role. "Who are these people that they come here to impose the depravities of the West on Africa?" a Cameroonian prosecutor fumed at me during a private dinner; that afternoon he had received a Canadian human rights mission (see Geschiere 2009a).

7. *Nganga* is a common Bantu term in use throughout the large part of Africa where Bantu languages are spoken (roughly south of the Douala–Mombasa line). It recurs in many different forms (for instance, *inyanga* in several languages in South Africa). The "real" Maka word is *nkong* (clearly related to the general Bantu root as well), but Maka people often use the term *nganga*. I prefer to use this term here since it facilitates comparisons with ideas and practices elsewhere in Africa.

8. Compare, for instance, Séraphin 2000, on the centrality of *la sorcellerie* and *l'invisible* in everyday life in the city of Douala, for many Cameroonians a focus of modernity in the country.

9. After his PhD, Fisiy was soon recruited by the World Bank, where his career was meteoric (at the moment he is director of its Social Development Department). If academia had been able to retain him, this book would have been written by the two of us together.

10. The term *djambe* was completely new to Fisiy, since he comes from the Northwest, where very different terms—albeit with similar content—are used; these, in turn, were new to me.

11. A concomitant argument against refusing to use current terms like *sorcellerie* and *witchcraft* is that it means ignoring what such translations of local notions into a different language do. However, as Birgit Meyer has insisted ever since her early work on "translation" (cf. Meyer 1999, her by now classical study *Translating the Devil*, on Pentecostals' use of the notion of Satan), we have to take the "politics of use" of such translations most seriously. The question regarding the (in)correctness of translation might not be the crucial one. If people adopt terms as current equivalents, it is vital to try to follow what shifts in meaning and use are involved.

Academics have no choice but to relate to the current uses of the terms they are confronted with (see also Meyer 2002).

12. See M. Crick 1979 and Geschiere 1997, chap. 1 and afterword. Cf. also specifically on Cameroon, Abega, and Abe 2006:34: "The term *witchcraft* does not refer to anything in the local languages of Cameroon. It is difficult to find an equivalent, a term to translate it. One might think of a transferred category, a thing conceived of by an outside observer, the European, seeing a somewhat bizarre phenomenon, the contours of which he cannot perceive very well, but which resembles nonetheless something familiar to him" (my translation).

13. Of course, much more can be said about the specific implications and history of the terms *witchcraft* and *sorcellerie*. In her 2009 article Florence Bernault compares *sorcellerie* with other notions, notably *fétichisme*, which according to her was dominant in colonial texts on the occult in Equatorial Africa (I am not sure that this is true for Cameroon). She notes, with clear irony, as an "advantage" of the *fétichisme* notion that its racist tenor was blatantly clear. This may be one of the reasons that it was superseded in academic studies by *sorcellerie*. But this notion is even more dangerous in her view, since it has similar implications that remain more implicit. Hence Bernault's critique that in more recent studies of witchcraft and modernity, anthropologists seem to take the term for granted, overlooking its historical associations; the term would suggest people's inability to separate politics and the religious and thus affirm the image of Africa as the opposite of the ideal of secular power. More attention to the historicity of all these notions is certainly important (see Ceriana Mayneri 2010 and 2012). Yet this will not help anthropologists to break away from the current use of words in the societies studied. In Cameroon *sorcellerie* is much more current than *fétichisme*; the same applies to *witchcraft* elsewhere in Africa (and in other parts of the world). This greater generality affords considerable comparative advantages. Most of these terms were indeed deeply marked by an academic context where secularization seemed to be a universal trend. Yet even in academia such trends may be reversed (cf. the "return of religion" in studies of Europe) so that terms can acquire new connotations. Deconstructing and historicizing a term like *sorcellerie* is certainly an important approach for relativizing the idea of Africa's exceptionality. Another might be to show the generality of the issues involved in the broader comparative approach that I want to try out in this book. For such an approach it is a clear advantage that terms like *sorcellerie* and *witchcraft* are current in other parts of the world, both for undermining the image of Africa as radically different and for superseding unsolvable terminological dilemmas (see Geschiere 1997).

14. Cf. for Africa, Ashforth 2005; Auslander 1993; Bastian 1993; Bellagamba 2008; Beneduce 2010 and 2012; Bernault 2005; Bernault and Tonda 2000; Bond and Ciekawy 2001; Ceriana Mayneri 2010; Ciekawy 1998; Cinnamon 2012; Comaroff and Comaroff 1993, 1999, and 2004; Crais 2002; de Boeck 2005 and 2009; Luongo 2011; Martinelli and Bouju 2012; Moore and Sanders 2001; Niehaus 2001 and 2012; Offiong 1991; T. Sanders 2003; J. H. Smith 2008; Stroeken 2010; van Binsbergen

2001; West 2005 and 2007; Yengo 2008a; and many others. For Melanesia, Lattas 2010; for Polynesia, Besnier 2009; for East Indonesia, Bubandt 2013; for Latin America, Whitehead and Wright 2004. For Africa, see also related studies on spirit possession (for instance Behrend 1999) and healing (Devisch and Brodeur 1999).

15. The first who did so was Rutherford (1999); see also Englund and Leach 2000; more recently, for instance, Henry and Tall (2008) and Stroeken (2010) adopted this paradigm notion for completely dismissing criticisms.

16. Moreover, the return of topics like witchcraft and sorcery does not seem to be limited to Africa. Cf., for instance, Kapferer 2002:1–2; he notes it with some surprise since it goes (in his view) against anthropologists' fear of what he calls "voyeuristic exoticism," yet he is very much in favor of this return, since for him "magic, sorcery and witchcraft are at the epistemological centre of anthropology."

17. The exception being C. Henry and E. K. Tall, who in their introduction to a special issue of *Cahiers d'Etudes Africaines* on *Territoires sorciers* (2008) honor me as the prime suspect: my book (Geschiere 1997) "could pass as important" ("a pu passer pour important") since, inspired by Jean-Francois Bayart, I analyze witchcraft as a "popular mode of political action." Apparently it has escaped these authors that in this book I tried to show that witchcraft can be a weapon of both the poor and the rich and powerful, serving for both leveling *and* accumulation; moreover, they ignore that I analyze this ambivalence not only as a by-product of modernity but as a tension that runs through stories going back to precolonial times. In a similar vein, Koen Stroeken (2010:19) quotes Fisiy and me on "witchcraft as a fixed corollary of modernity"; for him this seems to imply that we propose to study the resilience of these notions as *only* a reflection of modern inequalities/uncertainties without taking into account how they were produced by a long "tradition." Maybe he passed over the long sections of my 1997 book on the role of *djambe* (witchcraft) and *miedou* (medicine) in stories about precolonial warlords. A more important difference concerns his use of the term *system* ("system of ritual traditions, practices of healing and diagnosis"—Stroeken 2010:20), while throughout my book I sought to highlight the inconsistencies and lack of closure that have marked these ideas for as long as we can go back. But a very interesting difference like this disappears behind the erection of a "witchcraft and modernity paradigm" as a closed model. Cf. also Palmie 2002:338n2, where he warns me regarding "an overextension of an ethnographic concept (problematic as it is to begin with) as the descriptor of an allegedly 'global(izing)' condition." The concept Palmie refers to here seems to be witchcraft, which for me would summarize a globalizing condition. All this on the basis of my simple observation that certain aspects of witchcraft discourse make it a tempting way for people to address the riddles of modern developments (see Geschiere 1997 and 2011). Overextensions seem to be everywhere in this debate!

18. See, for instance, Comaroff and Comaroff 2004.

19. Ceriana Mayneri 2010:156. Cf. also the challenging ways in which Ceriana Mayneri distinguishes varying popular interpretations of the supposed proliferation of occult aggression. He concludes that the Banda in the Central African Republic are

preoccupied with the loss (*dépossession*) of ancestral wisdom rather than with a lack of modern things (as, for instance, among the Maka and other Cameroonian groups). To the Banda the apparent omnipresence of witchcraft in the present day follows less from the glaring inequalities in people's access to modernity than from the egoism of their ancestors who refused to pass on the traditional secrets that could have controlled witchcraft today. His fine-tuned historical analysis—aiming to detect how exactly, in misunderstandings between missionaries, administrators, and interpreters, the term *sorcellerie* was grafted onto local notions—shows most convincingly how to avoid treating witchcraft as either a "traditional relic" or just a by-product of modernity. His emphasis on differing trends in popular preoccupations with witchcraft in present-day contexts and his close attention to the historicity of terms, both local ones and those used by academics, indicate promising new directions for the study of witchcraft building on the changes in the 1990's (see also n13 above on Bernault and n20 below). From a different viewpoint, Bubandt (2013) develops an equally challenging alternative by reflecting on witchcraft among the Buli (Eastern Indonesia) as parallel to the "aporia" Derrida (and Aristotle) saw as basic to Western thinking. Bubandt's emphasis that witchcraft for the Buli is not a belief but rather an unresolvable doubt (how to know the "unknowable"?) makes him reverse the link between witchcraft and modernity: for the Buli witchcraft is not a discourse for understanding modernity (how would this be possible in view of its basic uncertainty?); they rather wrestle with the disappointment that modernity did not bring an end to witchcraft.

20. It is especially in connection to the choice of terms in our publications that I share Bernault's and Ceriana Mayneri's warnings that anthropologists of the new wave of witchcraft studies should have paid more attention to "their own role in the construction of ethnographical knowledge" (Ceriana Mayneri 2010:120; see also Bernault 2009). However, I feel also that recent authors tend to overestimate the weight of the anthropological intervention, certainly while in the field. I admire Ceriana Mayneri's analysis of how local and scientific discourse on the occult are constantly provoking each other (his analysis of being involved as anthropologist in a "provocative situation"—a notion he develops after Heike Behrend's 1999 book *Alice Lakwena and the Holy Spirits*, notably her seminal introductory chapter, "The Troubles of an Anthropologist," on what it means to work in a confrontational situation as was created by Lakwena and her Holy Spirit Movement in northern Uganda). But in my experience the anthropologist studying witchcraft is caught in the middle of such provocations, unable to side completely with either the scientific or the local discourse (see Geschiere 1998). The scientific discourse acted, indeed, as a sort of counterpoint against which also my Maka informants developed their formulations about the witches having their own *science*. But it was propagated by their contacts with modern medicine, schools, and churches. In the field, the uninitiated anthropologist is seen as utterly naive in the domain of the occult (people always reminded me that I had at most "a fish in my belly"). Once initiated, the anthropologist is considered to be at risk of becoming an easy

prey of other witches. However, in publications the anthropologist's position may be less humble, and the choice of terms in his or her publications certainly makes a difference. In general I think Ceriana Mayneri's analysis of the "provocative situation" that complicates studying witchcraft is most challenging. But it would be helpful to be more specific about the carriers of the discourses that provoke each other in specific situations; and also to take into account that anthropologists play an uncertain role in the spreading of scientific discourse, being caught between many parties, some of which have much more powerful voices. This is why I very much like Bellagamba's plea for addressing this provocative situation not in term of "I" but rather in terms of "we"—that is, referring to the broader field in which the researcher performs as well as the variety of subjects who have something to say about African witchcraft (oral communication; see also Bellagamba 2008:179).

21. The most famous but also the most criticized one was of course Evans-Pritchard's opposition of witchcraft and sorcery, which made it into almost all introductions to anthropology (Evans-Pritchard 1937—but for an early criticism see Turner 1964). Now the general idea seems to be that the distinction does not hold for most societies (see for example Besnier 2010:210 on Polynesia). But see also Kapferer's 2002 effort to save the distinction between witchcraft and sorcery by relating it in a much more flexible way to Douglas's opposition between grid and group (Kapferer 2002:13). Compare also John Middleton's effort to oppose a beneficial power within the Lugbara discourse on the occult, used by elders to maintain their authority, to an evil force used by witches. Only toward the end of Middleton's article does it become clear that the terminological distinction is quite fluid; apparently whether an old man's force is seen as positive power or negative witchcraft depends on context (see Middleton 1963). Stroeken (2010:23, 83) has made another valiant and most sophisticated attempt to impose radical discontinuities (notably between 'magic" and "witchcraft") in this marshy field. For him, such distinctions still dominate rural life among the Sukuma (Tanzania); they would be eroded only "in town" (but is it possible to distinguish the rural and the urban so clearly?). In the areas where I worked, the murkiness of discourses on the occult—undermining each and every conceptual distinction and allowing for constantly shifting interpretations—was evident in village life and stories about olden days as much as in relations in urban settings. Over and against anthropologists' academic inclination to create clarity through neat distinctions, it is crucial to take this subversive tendency of witchcraft discourses most seriously. It seems to make any effort to impose unequivocal definitions impossible and also counterproductive, because precisely the diffuseness of the central notions seems to be the secret of their resilience.

22. Cf. also the title of this collection, edited by Kapferer: *Beyond Rationalism* (2002).

23. Cf. van de Port 2011 and his powerful analysis of a similar paradox around Candomblé (Bahia); also see chapter 5 below.

24. Of course the relation between witchcraft/magic and science is much more com-

plex than that. Compare several contributions in Meyer and Pels's 2003 collection *Magic and Modernity* which emphasize the intertwinement of magic and science in European history and its consequences for our conceptual apparatus. Compare also the current trend among many *nganga* (healers) in various parts of Africa to emphasize the scientific character of their knowledge (Geschiere 1997). However, in practice such pretensions often collide with the equally strong insistence of these healers that their scientific knowledge is secret and should not be exposed. This is also why claims to see witchcraft as "just another form of knowledge" (as, for instance, in the interpretations of the Cameroonian anthropologist cum *nganga* Edjenguèlè Mbonji—oral communication; see Mbonji 2000) might be difficult to reconcile with a practice in which hiding knowledge is a prerequisite for retaining its power. For a sensitive analysis of such attempts to articulate local forms of healing with science, cf. Beneduce's text (2010) on the "professionalization" of healers in Cameroon. Beneduce shows notably how the *nganga* land in a fix when they give in to official pressures toward "professionalization" because this requires leaving some of their expertise behind and making other parts of their secret expertise visible.

25. To quote an anonymous reader's report from University of Chicago Press: the solution might be to follow the *figure* of the witch, in all its varying manifestations, rather than try to capture the *idea* of the witch.

26. For a very sophisticated example of a more general use of the notion of sorcery, see Harry West's challenging *Ethnography as Sorcery* (2007). Written as a sequel to his highly subtle monograph on N. Mozambique (West 2005), this book works toward a broader notion of sorcery. From a seminal series of ethnographic examples, West's conclusion gradually emerges that ethnography can be seen as an equivalent to witchcraft/sorcery in the sense that both are basically an effort to construe a coherent kind of knowledge out of highly fragmented scraps of information. Therefore the ethnographer (at least the successful one) may be easily equated with a sorcerer/healer by his or her informants. Hence the striking title of the book. West's view is certainly challenging, and his subtle argument is highly perceptive and rooted in great ethnographic riches. Yet I wonder whether he is not diluting witchcraft discourse too much. For my informants witchcraft was and is definitely a special kind of construction, marked by all sorts of specific notions and practices that clearly distinguish it from, for instance, what an ethnographer does (especially an "innocent" one—that is, someone who is not initiated). The question is whether it is not necessary to look for more specific marks of witchcraft discourse, despite all intriguing parallels with ethnography—often quite flattering to the anthropologist—or with other forms of knowledge (see the debate in *African Studies Review* 51, no. 3 (2008): 135–49). For my informants the very idea that I might have similar abilities as a *nganga* (healer) would be quite ridiculous: how could I pretend to see what the witches were plotting since I did not even have the "second pair of eyes"? A notion like *djambe*/witchcraft may be fluid and polyinterpretable, yet there is a certain core that makes at least some

interpretations impossible (see also n20 above on the tendency among anthropologists who focus on their own role in studying witchcraft to overrate their impact in the field).

27. See Ellis and Ter Haar 2004 and 2009; also Ter Haar 2008. Cf. also Birgit Meyer's nuanced answer to Ranger and also Ellis and Ter Haar. In line with the analysis below, Meyer emphasizes that "attention paid to modernity and globalization does not necessarily imply a disregard for local specificities, but may, on the contrary, entice a historical and ethnographic study of how the aggregation of the occult [as in popular visions of witchcraft as an all-pervading force—PG] occurs in particular settings. . . . Such phenomena require more than unmasking them as inauthentic." She warns, moreover, pace Ellis and Ter Haar, that viewing, for instance, ritual murder as "part of African religion still affirms a problematic exoticizing view" (Meyer 2009:413–14).

28. Cf. Ranger's firm conclusion, with reference to his own pioneering work on the role of spirit mediums who offered vital support to the guerrillas in the Zimbabwe liberation war in the 1970s: "Despite this new work on 'magic' and 'the occult' I shall continue to use 'religion' and 'witchcraft' as distinct and opposed terms" (Ranger 2006:361).

29. See, for instance, Spierenburg 2003. Ranger himself notes how precarious the distinction can be. He quotes, for instance, Benjamin Ray, *African Religions: Symbol, Ritual and Community* (Prentice Hall, 2000), on the Manianga notion of witchcraft: "The same power (*kindoki*) may also be used for good. Those who use it to protect the community are respected and not called witches, those who use it to harm people are feared and hated" (in Ranger 2006:354). Apparently both for Ranger and for Ray, such distinctions are unequivocal. Striking is the absence of any idea that if it is the same force permitting good *and* bad use, different interpretations may be possible. What is seen as good use by one person may be a clear sign of evil witchcraft to another; what counts as constructive at one moment can be reconstructed later on to have been horribly evil. Even classic monographs on witchcraft from British anthropology are full of such contests over interpretation (cf. V. Turner 1954; J. Middleton 1960), showing the precariousness of distinctions in this field.

30. Cf. Mary 2009:140: "In Africa, as elsewhere, the missionary process of diabolizing witchcraft aims to put an end to the ambiguities of pagan figures and their powers of fascination"—my translation. In a different but related view, James Siegel (2003 and 2006) characterizes witchcraft as a discourse that makes impossible linkages between phenomena that in principle should never be related to one another; this is why it is so shocking and so dangerous.

31. Cf. the fierce attack by Jeff Peires (2004) on Clifton Crais's interpretation of the killing of Hamilton Hope, a colonial official, in the Eastern Cape in 1880. Crais (2002) tried to show that the murder had to be explained as a "ritual murder" following "indigenous grammars of knowledge" and local ideas about power—which he subsumed under a broad category of a "moral economy of magic." Peires is certainly right that there are distinctions to be made within the wide

category of "magic" as used by Crais. But how can he be sure that evil witchcraft and instrumental magic (supposedly less evil, and for Peires not to be confused with the former) remained so clearly separated? The clearness of Peires's distinctions may underestimate the fluidity that the notions involved often have. The strength of Crais's approach is that he shows quite vividly how in this central event different conceptions of power and weakness shaded into one another.

32. See above (prologue, p. xix) on intimacy, kinship, and proximity as overlapping notions.

33. This trope of the witch-as-a-martyr is certainly not special to the Maka. See below (chap. 2) on parallel stories elsewhere. See also Roitman 2003 on the general and challenging idea of "debt as productive," creating new forms of accumulation. Roitman applies this view especially in a political-economic sense to explore emerging forms of exchange and redistribution ("reciprocal distrust") in more or less hidden economic circuits that have proliferated in Africa since structural adjustment; but there is a clear convergence here with popular ideas about the proliferation of witchcraft in which the idea of debt is also central (see also Geschiere 2000).

34. Cf. Malinowski 1935, Evans-Pritchard 1937, Marwick 1965; even Meyer Fortes in his *Kinship and the Social Order* (1970:237–38) couples a heavy accent on kinship as "the axiom of amity" to the warning that "witchcraft and sorcery" may hide inside "the nuclear units of kinship structure." For a powerful recent formulation of this link, cf. also Mary 2009:55: "Thus, according to the *nganga* themselves, it is in the very heart of the African 'deep I' [*le moi profond africain*] that the witch other lives [or writhes] who devours you from the inside and feeds the chain of dependencies in which you are caught" (my translation). See also Lallemand 1988 for a pioneering study of witchcraft as inherent part of the conception of the family (168, 174) in Central Togo—expressed in a "horrible phantasmagoria of familiars devouring each other" (my translation).

35. Cf. also Turner 2010:123, who compares the association of witchcraft and kinship with the obsession among Hutu and Tutsi from Burundi with "traitors inside." He relates also to Veena Das's study of the explosion of violence against the Sikhs in India after the murder of Indira Gandhi in 1984. Das's informants (both Hindu and Sikh) made a contrast between "true kinship," based on loyalty and trust, and "false kinship through which previous intimacies between communities are disavowed" (Das 1998:111). However, there is a difference here that may be meaningful: for my Maka informants witchcraft was certainly not a sign that kinship was "false"; on the contrary, it was a potential inherent to any form of kinship.

36. Cf., for instance, Ralph Austen's emphasis that "witchcraft efficacy is held to be a direct function of the intimacy between witch and victim" (Austen 1993:90). It may not be by accident that this aspect is so heavily emphasized in one of the first contributions to address the link between witchcraft and globalization. It was just when witchcraft studies in Africa began to address the role of this imaginary in wider contexts than the village that the continuing element of intimacy became particularly notable. Earlier, on the other side of the Atlantic, Bonno

Thoden van Velzen and Ineke van Wetering had applied such a broader view in inspiring ways (Thoden van Velzen and van Wetering 1988 and 1989—see also 2004). In their studies of Maroon societies in Surinam, dramatic shifts in prophetic cults and the struggle against witchcraft are analyzed in challenging ways as inherently related to broader politico-economic changes.

37. Cf. also the film *Le cercle des Pouvoirs* by Daniel Kamwa, set as well in Douala and inspired by similar ideas—notably the betrayal of intimates as the crucial condition for getting access to the new magic of wealth (see also Alexei Tcheuyap's sharp analysis of this film—Tcheuyap 2009).

38. Cf. also Isak Niehaus's insightful work (2001) on accusations of witchcraft and the complex articulation between, on the one hand, tensions within the family/neighborhood and, on the other, a long history of migrant labor in the South African Lowveld. Niehaus shows in a more recent publication (2012) that accusations now concern direct kin more often than in the past. See also chapter 2 below. Bernault 2006 offers a challenging extension of the witchcraft/intimacy theme by developing the idea that under colonial rule there emerged "destructive understandings" (rather than distance and opposition) between colonials and locals—the first even becoming "intimate partners in the remaking of local cosmologies." Compare also Redding 1996 on perceptions of "government witchcraft" and "tax receipts becoming a fetish" that triggered the Mpondo revolt in Transkei (South Africa) around 1960.

39. Cf. also Behringer 2006 and Hutton 2004. A problem of the latter's "global definition" of witchcraft is that this historian seems to have little sensitivity to the volatile character these notions take on in practice; most of the criteria he mentions in his definition are so fixed and concrete that they seem to freeze the central notion (see chap. 4 n12 below). However, in his list of criteria the link with intimacy stands out, since it is the only criterion that seems elastic enough to return in highly different situations and variable forms.

40. These criticisms are diametrically opposed to at least some of the attacks, noted before (n17), on the "witchcraft and modernity paradigm" as neglecting the long history of witchcraft discourse.

41. The title—based on a common Pentecostal slogan—of one of Meyer's influential articles (1998) on the upsurge of Pentecostalism in Ghana.

42. Recently Joël Robbins (2007), starting from Melanesian examples, launched a similar attack on anthropologists who in his view always tend to fall back on the continuity of local elements (thus, ignoring the novelty of emergent arrangements). Of course, one can wonder whether it is not too easy to stereotype in this way a whole discipline—which is moreover in constant movement (see, for instance, H. Moore 2011). Robbins focuses especially on studies from religious anthropology; wouldn't the perspective be somewhat different if he had paid more attention to, for instance, economic anthropology, where a central theme has always been the transition from premarket to market societies, seen as leading to severe discontinuities? Still, critiques like these can be refreshing for anthropologists (all the more so in view of the renewed interest in the discipline in a notion

like ontology, which can so easily bring back culturalist trends that appeared to be definitively surpassed—see the prologue as well as the comparative interlude below).

43. That there is in fact some reason for concern about anthropologists' penchant for assuming continuity in this field may be clear from a quote from Lévi-Strauss (1958), who characterizes witchcraft as "being sterile and therefore incapable of progress" and concludes: "For centuries and no doubt millennia . . . the same beliefs and the same techniques are continued or reproduce themselves, often in the smallest detail" (my translation). This is quoted via Favret-Saada 2009:52, who adds a most effective critique of this ahistorical perspective.

44. See also André Mary's seminal book *Visionnaires et prophètes de l'Afrique contemporaine* (2009).

45. Cf. also Tonda 2002:237 on "the reproduction of witchcraft beyond what is think-able and possible in the clan and lineage context" and "the recomposition of witchcraft . . . that goes beyond the anthropological limits of what is thinkable and possible" (my translation). Cf. also Bernault 2005 and 2009. I will come back to Tonda's notion of *déparentalisation*—implying that witchcraft ideas develop now in a context that is completely outside the limits of lineage and kinship—and my doubts about its general applicability. Regional differences—specific aspects of everyday life in the larger Congolese cities—may play a role here (see below in this section and also chap. 6). In other parts of the continent it is rather the resilience and continuing stretching of kinship relations that remains striking.

46. In other parts of Africa the encounter with Islam had brought an idea of religion earlier (but then, Tonda focuses especially on West Equatorial Africa—although wisely avoiding any strict geographical delimitations for his explorations).

47. Cf. Tonda 2005:264, where he quotes with approval the Comaroffs' idea of "a long conversation." The notion of "articulation" comes of course from the old Marxist debate on an "articulation of modes of production," which was marred by the heaviness of the mode of production concept but did show the possibilities of the articulation notion for historically following uncertainties and variety in the grafting of capitalism onto preexisting forms of production and exploitation (see notably Rey 1973).

48. Cf. also Pederson 2011.

49. Cf. Behringer 2004, who in his "global history of witchcraft" documents such commonalities with an impressive richness of detail. This historian is also dissatis-fied with anthropology but for completely different reasons. Like other histori-ans (Hutton 2004; Di Simplicio 2002), he is rather impatient with anthropologists' squeamishness about using more general concepts like witchcraft. This would have been an important reason that comparison with historians' studies never took off. One can sympathize with their impatience when reading the concluding contribution by a very young Thomas Beidelman to Mary Douglas's well-known collection *Witchcraft Confessions and Accusations* (1970). This collection was the result of a conference whose explicit aim was to compare historians' and anthropolo-gists' studies of witchcraft. Yet anthropologist Beidelman opens his concluding

contribution by categorically stating that "witchcraft and sorcery . . . differ radically from society to society" and also expresses severe skepticism about comparative work that requires imposing "a nominal category" (351). No wonder that during this conference the comparison between historians and anthropologists hardly worked (cf. also the ironical comments with which Douglas opens her introduction—xiii). Noteworthy for its absence from Beidelman's statement is any awareness that these ideas travel—certainly in a globalizing world—and that they are not just waiting for the anthropologist to be neatly categorized. Today the attention among anthropologists to the openness of these notions, their constant dynamics, and the ease with which they incorporate elements from outside may give new scope for a dialogue with historians (see also chap. 4, below).

50. See also Copet-Rougier 1986 on the Mkako of Eastern Cameroon.

51. Cf. the seminal account by Eric de Rosny, a French Jesuit who was initiated as a *nganga* in Douala in the 1960s. The climax in his initiation was when his master demanded him "a hairless animal" (= a human being). However, in view of his special position, de Rosny was allowed to offer a goat—hence the title of his beautiful book *Les Yeux de ma chèvre* (1981—English translation, *Healers in the Night*, 2004).

52. Miriam Goheen drew my attention to this saying that was very current in Anglophone Cameroon in the 1980s—see Goheen 1996.

53. Cf. Julien Bonhomme's study (2009) of the recent excitement about "penis-snatchers" (a stranger shakes hand with you and your penis is gone) that spread like wildfire throughout West Africa. Bonhomme makes a radical distinction between "traditional" *sorcellerie* related to kinship and new forms *d'une insécurité interactionnelle* characteristic of the anonymity of the modern city. The emphasis on strangers seems to take this danger far afield from any imaginary centered on closeness (see also Mandel 2008). Yet even here it remains important to look for unexpected links with the witchcraft from "inside the house'" that also constantly emerges in the anonymity of the city; but this may require a more in-depth following of cases of supposed "penis-snatching" and their mixture of familiarity and strangeness in everyday contexts. Cf. the outcome of Ndjio's cases above. Cf. also Beneduce 2012 for a striking example of how the witchcraft from within a family in Mali abruptly emerged from a magic plan to smuggle blood to China in order to guarantee access to riches in this faraway country. See also Lallemand's subtle case study (1988) of a highly complex outbreak of accusations of "soul-eating" inside a family compound in Central Togo. At first the accusations point to a relative outsider (a woman who has worked for some time in Ghana)—which makes people wonder how she could choose victims from outside her own family. But then things realign with people's expectations: it turns out that she had an ally—a fellow witch—inside the family.

54. The notion of the village's becoming a "virtual reality" for Africans comes from Wim van Binsbergen (2001). I have some hesitation about this notion, since for many urban elites in Africa it remains self-evident that they have to be buried in the village; this eventually turns the village into a very concrete reality (see

Geschiere 2005 and forthcoming). Yet the growing distance from the village certainly may give it virtual aspects.

55. Regional differences may play an important role in this context. For instance, it is striking that—as Tonda shows in rich detail (2005:223)—in Brazzaville, Kinshasa, and other Congolese cities there is hardly any question of taking deceased urbanites back to their home village to be buried there. This is very different from other parts of the continent, where the funeral at home—that is, in the village—is still a high point in the reaffirmation of belonging and the coherence of the family; it is also a moment deeply feared by many urbanites, since their obligatory attendance at funerals in the village offers the villagers opportunities to get even with their "brothers in town"' who have neglected their duty to redistribute (see further Geschiere 2009b, chap. 5). The general practice of burying in the city itself in the two Congos, where funerals are increasingly monopolized by unruly youths, may be a sign of a much further weakening of urban-rural ties: a true *déparentélisation*? (See also de Boeck 2006 and his 2010 film on funerals in Kinshasa, *Cemetery State*; see also Noret and Petit 2011 on Lubumbashi.)

56. See below, and also Taliani 2012 on Nigerians and Cameroonians in Turino, and Sabar 2010 on Ghanaians in Tel Aviv. See also Yengo 2008a on the continuing link between *sorcellerie* and *parenté* in Brazzaville. Especially interesting in the analysis of this last author is the way he emphasizes the constant dynamic of this link, both *sorcellerie* and *parenté* taking on constantly new forms. In my earlier book (1997)—which for Yengo (2008a:300) seems to be just an example of myopic "modernism"—I had tried to grasp these dynamics by emphasizing how the constant stretching of kinship contributed to the general idea of witchcraft's being out of bounds.

57. Cf. what was said in the prologue about intimacy as not marked by a substantial core but by "a refusal of generality"—that is, by marking a domain as special; this can be done in all sorts of ways.

58. Jankowiak 2008. The only exception among the ten contributions is Daniel Smith's perceptive analysis (2008) of the intertwinement of different "arenas of intimacy" among the Igbo in southeastern Nigeria. Smith shows how intimacy among (male) friends affects the intimacy of men with their (female) lovers and their wives (the latter two spheres are also in constant interaction). The great merit of his analysis is that he thus shows that intimacy is never taken for granted but is continuously reshaped and under constant pressure. See also Povinelli 2006, who likewise tends to associate intimacy with love, sex, and the conjugal family (at least in the modern liberal version of "the intimate event"). Yet she also shows via highly sophisticated argumentation what deep ramifications can be deduced from this: the liberal view of the intimate (love) is central to the disciplining of the subject; it is a fallacy to try, as many people tend to do, to set the intimate as an area of relative freedom over and against society's constraints; the intimate is instead closely interwoven with the constraints of what Povinelli calls the "genealogical society" (see notably 3, 13, 182, 210). Apparently, even when intimacy is equated with love, this can still imply a more negative view of it.

59. The blandness with which here the famous sociologist follows publications by American psychotherapists—for instance, a certain Jody Hayes, who insists in his book *Smart Love* (1990) on the link between intimacy and autonomy—is a bit worrying. Consider Hayes's use of simplistic dyadic oppositions like "addictive" vs. "intimate": "pressuring for sex" vs. "freedom of choice"; "lack of trust" vs. "appropriate trust"; "fusion" vs. "loving detachment." Thus, any notion of intimacy's ambiguities is effectively covered up by a kind of feel-good creed (Hayes, 1990, *Smart Love* [London: Arrow], 31, quoted in Giddens 1992:95). Compare also American psychoanalysts Bersani and Philips's heavy criticism of what they call "the pathological optimism of proponents of ego psychology," which they see as based on a complete distortion of Freudian ideas (Bersani and Philips 2008:74). Even in the modern West, which seems to be Giddens's only orientation point, people may be quite reluctant to become involved in any form of intimacy because it is seen as entailing a growing dependency (and thus threatening one's autonomy). In this sense there is not so much distance from the African view of intimacy as potentially dangerous because it entails vulnerability. More attention to the ambiguities of modernity might have helped Giddens to do more justice to the flip side of intimate relations.

60. For a completely different take on "intimacy," see Richard Sennett's 1974 classic book *The Fall of Public Man*. For Sennett, the public space that was expanding during the nineteenth century has been more recently invaded by considerations that fit with more intimate spheres of life (for example, the personal appeal of a certain politician). People tend to judge relations in the public sphere ever more on the basis of intimate experiences. This leads to a loss of public know-how, earlier forms of sociability in the public sphere being ever more undermined by what Sennett calls "the tyranny of intimacy." Again, a striking contrast to Giddens's celebration of intimacy as a sort of pinnacle of modernity.

61. Herzfeld's cultural intimacy became the theme of an AAA panel that led to the publication of an interesting collection (Shryock's *Off Stage, On Display*, 2004). Yet the focus of this collection was certainly not a deeper exploration of the tendency to equate intimacy with trust and solidarity. Rather, several contributions and the introduction were oriented toward the ethical predicament of anthropologists when the intimacy they have built up with the people among whom they do fieldwork comes under siege as they have to perform in public—that is, when "their" region becomes a hotspot in global events and their expertise is sought by the media. This is certainly a difficult predicament. Yet one can regret that, apparently, for anthropologists the notion of intimacy seems to refer first of all to their own intimate experiences in the field. There is a danger that anthropologists' reflexivity on their own role in the field—in itself most welcome, but lately ever expanding—tends to turn the ideal of a dialogue with informants (à la Clifford 1988) into an interest in the self that acquires narcissistic overtones (see Geschiere 2010). But see also Herzfeld's 2012 comment (in his afterword to a *JRAI* special issue on "hospitality") that "intimacy always carries the possibility of

danger" (many thanks to Apostolos Andrikopoulos for drawing my attention to this passage).

62. Many thanks to Susan van Zyl, Laia de Soto, and Roberto Beneduce for counseling me on Freud with so much patience and wisdom. The work by Bonno Thoden van Velzen on anthropology and psychoanalysis has also been a source of inspiration for me (see Thoden van Velzen 1997).

63. Dutch is of interest here since it knows similar terms but splits up the double meaning of *heimlich*. This term can be translated in Dutch as *huiselijk* (from *huis*, home) in its more positive sense (homely) but also as *heimelijk* in its more negative sense (secretive). Worth noting is, however, that the Dutch *heimelijk* relates to *heim*, an old-fashioned word for "home." So despite the split between *huiselijk* and *heimelijk*, there is some trace here of the double meaning of home (*huis/heim*), more or less parallel to the tendency of the German *heimlich* to shift to its very opposite, *unheimlich*.

64. Cf. also Georg Simmel's short essay on *der Fremde* (the stranger). His insistence that the stranger "is an element of the group itself" but also "the inner enemy" applies to the witch in respects that Simmel himself may not have foreseen (see Simmel [1902–3] 1950:402).

65. Indeed, it has become impossible to give even a provisional survey of the vast recent literature on trust. But see Ystanes 2012 for a seminal overview of important contributions.

66. Cf. Max Gluckman's famous passage on witchcraft beliefs being even more effective than Anglican anthems in restoring social order (Gluckman 1955:94).

67. Quoted by Sahlins [1965] 1974:196, who unfortunately does not give a reference for this quotation.

68. *Essai sur le don: Forme et raison de l'échange dans les sociétés archaiques* ([1923–24] 1950).

69. I did not find the word *réciprocité* at all in Mauss's original text, nor *réciproquer*; *réciproque* is there only a few times. In the earlier 1954 translation, *rendre le don* was translated as "to repay the gift"—still incorrect but less distorting than "reciprocate." Such distorted borrowings make it all the more interesting to follow up in detail the genealogy of the notion of reciprocity in anthropology and the implications this notion acquired. Many thanks to Juan Obarrio, Rafael Sanchez, and Patricia Spyer for reintroducing me to Mauss.

70. For the Maori notion *hau*—which has some sort of primal status in Mauss's *Essai sur le don*—Mauss even signals a link between gift giving and witchcraft. See Mauss [1923–24] 1950:155–60, 254; cf. also his digression (255) on the double meaning of the word *Gift* in German: "gift" but also "poison" (with parallels in other Germanic languages).

71. In Sahlins's new book on kinship (2013) he calls it "mutuality of being" (rather than "reciprocity"), still with very positive overtones; thus he disregards how close a notion like "intersubjective participation" comes to witchcraft talk. "Mutuality of being" can have positive implications but also dangerous ones.

72. At the very end of Mauss's text (279) there is an example (King Arthur and his

Round Table) that approaches Sahlins's image of "generalized reciprocity" in small-scale communities. Yet even here trust is clearly balanced in Mauss's view by hidden competition.

73. Tim Ingold (1986:232), for instance, insists that even in "hunter-gatherer societies" negative reciprocity exists at the very core of the system in the form of "demand sharing." Given this, Ingold proposes a concentric-circles model that looks the same as Sahlins's but has a crucial twist: in the inner circle (relatives) there are now two signs: + for sharing but also – for demands. With "demands" we are close to jealousy and thus to witchcraft. See also Gregory 1994:925. Note the contrast with the romantic tenor of Sahlins's image of reciprocity within hunter-gatherer communities (see appendix A in Sahlins 1974:231).

74. And not only anthropologists; compare Charles Tilley's *Trust and Rule* (2005)—see chapter 3 below.

75. For instance, Giddens completely ignored such battles inside the intimate sphere of life when he proclaimed that only in "late modern societies" is there a need for "active trust"—a deliberate "leap of faith"; this in contrast to "traditional and early modern societies," where trust would be based only on a "passive acceptance of circumstances" (Giddens cited by Möllering 2001:411). On the contrary, it seems that especially in face-to-face communities, in view of the omnipresent threat from within (witchcraft), trust can only be blind. Simmel's "almost religious, further element" as crucial for trust (see below) seems to take precedence over "passive acceptance."

76. Many thanks to Mattijs van de Port for drawing my attention to this article.

77. It is on this point that I completely agree with Bubandt's approach, quoted before, to witchcraft as "aporia" à la Derrida—that is, as doubt rather than as belief (see Bubandt 2013 on Buli, an island in Eastern Indonesia). Bubandt's attack on witchcraft studies for trying to understand people's references to witchcraft as efforts toward clarification is certainly relevant (how can witchcraft ever explain or even clarify things? its basic trait is uncertainty). I wonder though whether his strong emphasis on aporia as uncertainty does not hide that unclarity can engender very effective power—in this sense witchcraft seems to me to be more than just uncertainty and doubt. But he is certainly right that such doubt is never completely overcome. Or, in the terms used above, trust is never a given; it is always precarious and situational.

Chapter 2

1. Throughout this area, the present-day *chefs coutumiers* are to a large extent colonial creations—despite their emphatic pretense of being "traditional" (see Geschiere 1993).

2. The Maka area was very important for the Germans, because it was seen as one of the richest areas in Africa for harvesting wild rubber. After 1890 the sudden demand for rubber for bicycle and car tires created a true boom—which ended as abruptly as it began after 1912, when Malaysian rubber plantations began to produce rubber of a much better quality.

3. The new Cameroonian elites were seen by the villagers (and most emphatically by themselves) as *Blancs* (later on *nouveaux Blancs*, but in the 1970s just *Blancs*).

4. The villagers kept telling me that anybody arrested by the *gendarmes*, no matter what the complaint was, would first receive an *avertissement* (warning) of twenty-five lashes when he was dragged into their *bureau*, before anything was discussed.

5. See Hyden 1980 for a similar image of the state "floating like a balloon" over the "economy of affection" (= the village society) of "the uncaptured peasantry" of Africa. See also my criticism (Geschiere 1984) of this idea of an "uncaptured peasantry"—at the time very popular among Africanists—precisely because Hyden seems to overlook how deeply state formation and market economy had shaped this "economy of affection," especially in its apparently "traditional" aspects.

6. Following good anthropological usage, all names of villages and persons in cases from my anthropological fieldwork in the Maka area are pseudonyms; however, I make an exception for public figures with great reputation (historical figures, prominent healers, or politicians with national allure).

7. I discussed this case in Geschiere 1997. I only briefly mention it here since it played a key role in linking my research on politics to witchcraft.

8. In the 1970s the Mercedes was still the status symbol of the new politico-administrative elite (with reference to the German past that played an important but complicated role in the country's struggle for independence). However, in the 1990s the Mercedes was more and more replaced by the Pajero as the status vehicle.

9. In Cameroon—notably in the former French part—the development of "independent churches," cults, prophetic movements, and such remained quite limited until the end of the 1980s—certainly in comparison to neighboring countries like Gabon, Congo-Brazzaville, and Nigeria (and in other parts of Africa); see chapter 3n41 below.

10. De Rosny (1981) shows that the discourse around *ekong*—the gruesome stories about people feeling that they are captured, hands bound behind their backs, and not able to see the face of their captors, who march them off to unknown places—reflects old traumas of the slave trade. Sometimes the zombies in these stories are transported in lorries—this might refer to the horrors of forced labor in colonial days (see also Geschiere 1997). See also Tonda 2005:79, quoting a *mémoire de maîtrise de sociologie* by Alexandre Ngoua (*La sorcellerie du Kong à Bitam: Une manifestation symbolique de l'économie capitaliste* [Libreville: Department of Sociology, 2004]), which mentions—most interestingly—the use of a mirror in order to "sell" a parent through this *kong*. Unfortunately I could not get access to this *mémoire*, but I will return to the role of mirrors in witchcraft imaginary in the area.

11. Cf. Rosalind Shaw's challenging interpretation of how the articulation of the new transatlantic slave trade with local inequalities in Sierra Leone not only produced witchcraft and but was also produced by it (2002, chap. 7). The novelty of her interpretation is that she turns around current analyses. She shows that witch-

craft very quickly became crucial for producing slaves to be sold (many of them were poorer people accused of witchcraft). Thus she sees witchcraft not only as an expression of inequalities—the current view—but also as a major factor in producing inequality. Cf. also Austen 1993 for a somewhat similar perspective.

12. In 1914, at the outbreak of the First World War, the British and French invaded the German colony of Kamerun and arranged for a division of the territory. The present-day Southwest and Northwest Provinces—smaller in size but more densely populated—came under British rule; the rest was claimed by the French.

13. In many respects the northwestern Grassfields (which is Anglophone) form one ecological and cultural area with the present-day West Province (the land of the aforementioned Bamileke in the Francophone part of the country): equally mountainous yet densely populated, and an area from which many migrants come.

14. *Nyongo* is the local name for *ekong*, *kong*, or *famla*—all different names for the new form of witchcraft that enabled witches to transform their victims into zombies and to grow rich on their labor in the invisible world.

15. Cf. the evocative title of the recent book by Jean-Pierre Warnier on these chiefs: *The Pot King* (2009).

16. In his 1986 book, President Biya (himself a Bulu and therefore a representative of the chiefless forest societies) explicitly stated that customary chiefs could form a hindrance to development—a statement that met with general indignation in the western provinces and in the North, where people still held to their chiefs. But after 1990 the regime suddenly became very active in filling empty chief positions and trying to woo sitting *chefs coutumiers* (see Geschiere 1993).

17. Such questions should certainly not relativize the major theoretical impact the notion had in the broader context of "postcolonial studies." Still, it might be important to note that the generalizing characterization of present-day societies as "postcolonial" can have the danger of covering major differences and transitions—for instance, the still quite enigmatic but certainly incisive changes after the end of the cold war (see Bayart 2010a).

18. The authoritarianism of the Cameroonian regime under Ahidjo and the early years of Biya was extremely strict. Ambitious politicians were constantly reminded that they owed their appointment only to the party summit and not to their popularity with the people. Any effort to create a popular following—for instance, in one's own region—was immediately denounced by one's rivals; then one risked being accused of *subversion* and of trying to disturb the unity of all Cameroonians behind the president. *Subversion* was a very heavy word in those days. For this many people ended up in Tcholliré or another of Ahidjo's notorious concentration camps (see Geschiere 1982:288 and Bayart 1989; also Hibou's challenging analysis of the general contours of authoritarianism—Hibou 2011).

19. In 1992 this still had had only limited success, and blatant rigging was necessary to bring Biya the victory. Most observers agreed that in reality the main opposition candidate, John Fru Ndi for the SDF, had won. But in subsequent elections such rigging was not necessary anymore. Two elections later (2006) Biya obtained

a landslide victory against the same Fru Ndi. The politics of belonging had done its work, and the opposition was completely divided by the regime's clever use of elite associations, "traditional chiefs," and autochthony movements against "strangers." In 2011 Biya was reelected for the third time (the government had pushed through a change of the Constitution to make this possible) with an even greater victory over the same opponent.

20. This law was pushed through by the World Bank (together with the World Wildlife Fund) and imposed stringent decentralization; it also promoted the creation of community forests, which immediately triggered fierce struggles over who did and who did not belong to the village communities in the forest (see Geschiere 2009b:chap. 3).

21. For Piot, structural adjustment and the concomitant shrinking of public services meant that "the presence . . . of the state was experienced in the everyday lives of its citizens as an absence" (1910:38)—an intriguing phrase that might apply to Cameroon in some ways. There people are certainly more conscious of the limits of the state than they were in the days of one-party rule (cf. Karsenty 1999 on the struggles over the forest and the demise of the authoritarian state). Yet the harsh interventions of the *gendarmes* still make the state highly present—maybe even more than before, since the interventions have become so unpredictable. It is clear in any case that the Maka elites realize that the presence of the state has become different now.

22. Compare the Opération nationale d'identification launched by Laurent Gbagbo immediately after he became president of Ivory Coast. The basic idea was that for the new national census everyone had to return to the village "of origin." People who could not claim a village of origin would automatically lose their citizenship. As Séry Wayoro, *directeur d' identification* of the operation, explained: "Whoever claims to be Ivorian must have a village. Someone who has done everything to forget the name of his village or who is incapable of showing he belongs to a village is a person without bearings and is so dangerous that we must ask him where he comes from" (quoted in Marshall 2006:28).

23. Cf. Joseph Tonda's emphasis that after the colonial encounter a completely new *sorcellerie* emerges in Gabon and Congo, liberated from the lineage frameworks (Tonda 2002 and 2005, and see chap. 1 above).

24. See Malaquais 2001a and b; Ndjio 2006. There are many explanations of the term *feyman*, which is apparently as enigmatic as the people denoted by it. The most likely one may be that of Dominique Malaquais (2001b), who explains it as a composite of *man* and the French *faire* (in the local sense of *faire quelqu'un*, "doing someone in").

25. According to recent rumors, he died in a Yemenite prison. Yet people are not sure of this; some expect him to reemerge anytime. After all, he is "the king of all *feymen.*"

26. See Malaquais's evocative descriptions of *feymen*'s often quaint architectural experiments (2001a and b).

27. Cf. the titles of Jean-Louis Dongmo's book *Le dynamisme bamileke* (1981) and one by

Jean-Pierre Warnier, *L'esprit d'enterprise au Cameroun* (1993), both on the emergence of this "Bamileke bourgeoisie."

28. Lately people in Cameroon talk a lot less about *feymen*. It seems that their heyday has passed, maybe because they were caught in an impossible dilemma—either to allow themselves to be co-opted by the regime and the village or to go completely global in a time that frontiers are closing.

29. I only heard about the notion when in 2006 my former PhD student Jill Alpes came back from a short trip to Cameroon and proposed focusing on it for her PhD research. In November 2011 she defended the thesis—"Bushfalling: How Young Cameroonians Dare to Migrate"—which contains an interesting analysis of people's perspectives on the notion, supported by strong case studies of (mostly failed) projects of "bushfallers"; see also Francis Nyamnjoh 2011. The ongoing obsession of young people with bushfalling—which in practice means getting out through quite desperate ploys—contrasts markedly with the official figures of economic growth for Cameroon (6% and more) over the last few years.

30. Alpes (2011:5) mentions, for instance, that when her research assistant was offered a scholarship to Europe it took some persuasion to convince her that this was a much better way to go abroad than leaving like a "real bushfaller."

31. Or sea, or even ocean. Apparently this was also a way of reassuring anthropologists from abroad that they would come to no harm (oral communication from Miriam Goheen—see also Goheen 1996).

32. European police seem to be less ready to accept that—apart from *vodun*—an important reason the girls do not want to be sent back is that returning from overseas without having succeeded is often deeply shameful.

33. See Van Dijk, Rasing, Tellegen, and Van Binsbergen 2003:18; see also van Dijk 2001.

34. Sabar adds that since 2003 the African community in Tel Aviv has disintegrated due to "stepped-up deportations of undocumented migrant labourers" (Sabar 2010:114, 131).

35. In this case Pentecostalism hardly seemed to offer any effective protection against pressure from the family. In many settings Pentecostal preachers emphatically try to liberate the believers from family pressures, often equating the village with the devil. In general Pentecostalism is now one of the most powerful alternatives in Africa to localist discourse on belonging in terms of autochthony or ethnicity. It aims to offer a supralocal belonging: the community of all true believers, which has a global span (and indeed offers concrete support to transcontinental migrants—see chapter 3 below; also Meyer 1999; van Dijk 2002 and 2005). Clearly in the Tel Aviv example the church's pastor hardly succeeded in countering the family pressure from home. It would be of urgent interest to know more about the role of neo-orthodox religions in the life of transcontinental migrants and their struggle with impatient threats by the family at home.

36. Sabar 2010:122. Yet another informant added a warning to the Israelis: "Everywhere you go people will talk about the witches who entered the country. . . . Once we used to trust your rabbis because they were guarding its territory. This is their duty. . . . Every local spirit has to guard its territory. When they did it we

were also protected. . . . Now with the war in Iraq and all the problems in the government and Wall Street falling down, then they are not protecting us enough . . . then the witches enter. . . . Maybe they [the rabbis] have other problems now . . . but they should know this is dangerous not only for us but also for you" (Sabar 2010:128). The Pentecostal pastor (also Ghanaian) confirmed those fears and asked the community to pray with him: "Let us cast away the demons, the evil spirits. . . . Help us God in our fight against jealousy and evil. . . . Sometimes our own people at home don't understand us . . . when we can't send money home they are angry. Our sister Brigitte is suffering. . . . They have sent on her the bad witches." (Sabar 2010:123). Cf. also van Dijk 2002 and 2004 on similar struggles of Ghanaian immigrants in the Netherlands with witchcraft threats from the family back home.

37. Here Sabar's analysis (like mine) differs sharply from Tonda's interpretation, already mentioned, that at least for Congo the colonial encounter brought a sharp discontinuity by creating *des lieux non-lignagers* so that *la sorcellerie* was liberated from the lineage frameworks (Tonda 2002 and 2005). As said, the ongoing hold of the family/witchcraft complex even over migrants overseas actually underlines the extreme resilience of these links. Of course, kinship takes on new forms when covering new distances; it often seems to be stretched to a breaking point. Yet it seems also to maintain a powerful grip even on people far away. However, as said before, there may be important regional differences in this respect (see nn45 and 55 in chap. 1).

38. Sabar (2010:120) concludes that migration brings an "extension of . . . the contradictions of the African family today"—a formulation that cogently sums up my analysis above. Her informants remained deeply attached to the family at home, yet at the same time they were deeply afraid of them.

39. *L'oeil dans les ténèbres* by Cyrille Bitting, Multi Media Center, Yaoundé, undated.

40. Cf. also Richard Werbner's beautiful biography of a Zimbabwean family (1999). Here as well, the family was beset by internal witchcraft suspicions; but before the civil war elders knew how to control these to a certain extent; with the crisis of war, such control broke down and suspicions seemed to have free rein. Cf. also Ciekawy 2001; Offiong 1991.

41. Cf. also Rosalind Shaw's seminal analysis of the key role witchcraft played in articulating the emerging trade in slaves to local inequalities: "The ties that connect victims to witches, then, as well as witches to other witches are those of kinship: witches both consume their kin and reproduce themselves through their kin" (2002:214).

42. Cf. also the (auto)biographies collected by Bogumil Jewsiewicki (1993) from different parts of Congo/Zaire, with elements of similar stories.

43. Cf Meyer 1995; see also Tonda 2005; de Boeck 2009.

Chapter 3

1. For a graphic elaboration of this term, see Comaroff and Comaroff 2000.

2. See Möllering 2001 and Ystanes 2012 for an analytical overview of studies on trust.

3. For good examples of this see Fukuyama 1995 and Gambetta 1988.

4. A striking example is offered by Francis Fukuyama's second book *Trust: The Social Virtues and the Creation of Prosperity* (1995). In his preface the author states that after the success of his *The End of History and the Last Man* (1992) it was only logical that the sequel should be about economics; and apparently it was equally logical that its focus should be then on trust—for this is, as the blurb text explains, "what we need to know in order to win the coming struggle about world dominance." Fukuyama's approach in this book, heralded by none less than Amitzai Etzioni as "a whole new way of doing economics," brings him uncomfortably close to culture which, as he recognizes on p. 34, "is not rational choice." He recognizes also that economists tend to be at a loss when they have to deal with culture ("in the view of many economists, culture becomes a grab bag or residual category used to explain whatever cannot be accounted for by general theories of human behavior," 34). However, in his ambitious contrast between societies with "low" and "high trust" he similarly uses culture (or "habit") as a sort of black box, hardly analyzing the cultural differences that for him seem to explain everything. As a consequence, his oppositions become apodictic and have, certainly in retrospect, surprisingly little predictive value. "High trust" societies, which are supposed to do better since "familistic" enterprises have been integrated into wider networks of trust (corporations), include not only Germany but also Japan (which already by the time of the book's publication had entered a long-term slump from which it has still not recovered). "Low trust" societies, supposedly doing worse since they are centered on familistic forms of enterprise, include not only France but also Korea and even China—again in stark contrast to what happened subsequently! Fukuyama sternly admonishes the United States to follow the first set of examples, all the more so since he feels his country is sliding dangerously toward the second set. Both French and US citizens might be quite surprised! See in contrast Englund 2007a for a subtle example of how the notion of trust can be given meaning ethnographically.

5. Cf. Simmel [1900] 1989:216: "Only in the case of credit, of the trust in somebody, a further moment is added that is difficult to describe, but in its purest form embodied in religious faith"; he compares this to the current saying "dass man an jemanden glaubt'" (that one "believes in someone"); and he concludes that such trust is to a high degree "a simple inductive conclusion," but that it contains on top of this "jenes sozial-psychologischen, dem religiösen verwandten 'Glaubens'" (this social-psychological "faith" that is related to the religious)—my translations.

6. In such a vision trust is never an all-or-nothing phenomenon, since it has to be constantly confirmed and reproduced; one could say it is always historical or even "microhistorical" (with many thanks to Cecilia McCallum, UFBA, Salvador de Bahia, for this comment). There is a striking contrast here with the common trend in studies by economists or sociologists who aim to sketch broad panoramas and therefore tend to speak of situations as marked by trust or no-trust—as if it would ever be possible to see trust as a given, as some sort of ontological certainty (cf., for instance, Fukuyama 1995).

7. For a similar tendency, see, for instance, Fukuyama's book quoted before (1995). For him also it seems to be evident that trust starts with "familistic" forms of enterprise (even though a failure to surpass this framework makes the society as a whole marked by "low trust"—see 28 and passim).

8. Very helpful—particularly in such intimate situations—is Tilly's starting point that trust is about taking risks: the willingness to "set valued resources . . . at risk to the malfeasance. . . . of others" (2005:12). But even for this historicizing author, rational choice—the "good reasons"—seems to take priority: trust is especially about compensation; expanding one's network of trust requires a clear prospect of compensation for the extra risks taken. It remains to be seen whether such an emphasis on expected compensation is helpful for understanding the desperate struggle to maintain trust despite the omnipresent threat of aggression within more intimate spheres of life.

9. Hyden 1980. In line with the emphasis above on the close link between witchcraft and intimacy, the term *economy of affection* seems to be singularly inapt to address the precariously balanced relations at the local level.

10. *Poto-poto* is the local name (derived from French *poteau*—pole) for constructions having walls consisting of poles tied together with branches and then filled with mud (with roofs mostly made from the leafy branches of the raffia palm). Nowadays it is seen as poor people's housing. Richer villagers live in houses with roofs made of corrugated iron plates and walls of pressed-mud bricks covered with cement.

11. This is why witches who refuse to confess are seen as the really dangerous ones. Their refusal shows that they want to hold on to their dangerous powers. Only if a witch confesses can the *nganga* neutralize his or her dangerous powers. In practice this means that a person accused of witchcraft is under enormous pressure: a refusal to confess can trigger harsh sanctions.

12. See also de Rosny 1981.

13. Yet I am certainly not the first to point to this circularity. Even an anthropologist like S. F. Nadel (1935:436), whom one can hardly suspect of being sensationalist, stated categorically, "In order to . . . fight witchcraft one must possess witchcraft oneself." Cf. also Beneduce 2010:119 for a haunting description of such ambiguity by a Baka (Pygmy) healer from South Cameroon, who spoke about his sensations when walking in the forest and how the constant possibility—for you *and* for the people you encounter—of becoming invisible means that it is no longer clear "who is prey and who is predator."

14. See for spectacular examples of such ambiguity in Taussig 1987 on Colombia and Favret-Saada 1977 [1980] on present-day Europe (for the latter, also see chap. 4 below).

15. A similar ambiguity emerges when Adam Ashforth is quoting a *sangoma*, for whom he clearly had great respect. The old man told him that someone asked him to use his powers to kill another man. "Of course" the healer refused to do this. Yet the prospective client clearly had his own ideas of what *sangoma* do and do not (Ashforth 2000).

16. See also chap.1, above, on recent debates on the difficult distinction between religion and witchcraft.

17. In 2011, while on a visit in France, Eric died quite unexpectedly. His passing away is a great loss to his many friends in Cameroon and all over the world. He leaves impressive work—both his beautiful books and his untiring efforts in exploring new routes for spiritual healing.

18. De Rosny also advocates using the term *tradipracticien* (as some sort of synonym to *contre-sorcier*).

19. Cf. a recurrent formula in André Mary's book *Visionnaires et prophètes en Afrique contemporaine* (2009): "repondre le mal par le mal"—answer evil with evil; see for instance p. 15.

20. Cf. also Bernault 2009:756–57 on the difficulties of separating *nganga* from *ndoki* (witch) in Equatorial Africa.

21. As noted, the abrupt spread of such a new form is nothing exceptional. In Cameroon, as elsewhere, the world of witchcraft seems to be marked by constant innovations—"fashions"—that spread like an epidemic and subsequently become part of the usual witchcraft lore. There is a clear logic to this. The witchcraft world is supposed to be marked by constant battles and rivalry. Being able to use a new weapon has the advantage of surprise—thus one may be able to overcome the opponent's defenses (see further Geschiere 1997).

22. The boys' readiness to utter such half-confessions may not be surprising in view of the cure against the *gbati*. Most *nganga* would prescribe that the boys be fed huge quantities of greasy food (meat with a lot of palm oil) until they vomited. The *nganga* would then find the *gbati* in their vomit. Most of the boys concerned in our village were quite neglected kids (some were orphans halfheartedly adopted by other family members). But even in more prosperous families young boys get only the leftovers from their parents' meal—very little meat or oil.

23. This *nganga* also made the boys overeat and then vomit. From their puke he produced, as proof that he had exorcised the *gbati*, little black cords with knots—each knot would stand for a person on their death list.

24. Again a very ambiguous signal. *Mongoliens* (French for Down syndrome—Maka: *kiasle*, dwarf) are associated with huge snakes that live deep in the forest and are very dangerous; yet they can also protect against witchcraft.

25. Professor Ralushai's committee had to look into the causes of the dramatic witch hunts, mentioned above, by self-styled "ANC comrades" in the northern part of the country around 1990.

26. See Taussig 1993:85 and the way he uses Simmel's notion of a "public secret." The *nganga* are a striking example of this idea that secret knowledge can be effective only if it is at least made public that there is a secret. Too much publicity will hurt the power of the secret, but no publicity at all makes it redundant (see also Meyer and Pels 2003).

27. Of course Mendouga legitimated her mirror by linking it to her professor. One day he had shown her the narrow bottle and the sticks. Then he made her fall in a deep sleep. When she woke up, she found that the sticks were already in the

bottle. How her professor had done it she did not know, but the whole thing showed his phenomenal power.

28. The term *was* (go out) refers to witches' leaving their body at night and joining the *shumbu*, the witches' meeting.

29. Many male *nganga* make it a point of honor to cross-dress—possibly to show that they are above even this distinction that is basic for normal people.

30. The tie was a special sign. In the village hardly anybody wears one—only the *vende kirke* (elders of the Presbyterian church) might put on a tie when going to church.

31. Cf. Mary 2009:55: "Les nganga sont les premiers à encourager les soupçons (avec d'autres: prophètes et pasteurs)"—*nganga* are the first to encourage suspicions (with others: prophets, pastors).

32. Indeed, many *nanga* will say that one of the reasons they joined the new Association of Traditional Healers—a fairly shadowy association that has existed since the mid-1990s with some informal support from the government—is that it helps to exclude aggressive Nigerian healers who are invading the country.

33. Cf. the case of "Mme. Jeanne" above (chapter 2), who returned to her father's village and started to accuse one of its *évolués* of having the *kong*.

34. Cf. Gemmeke 2008 on the mobility of *marabouts* in Dakar between city and countryside. In their determined efforts to distinguish between charlatans and real healers, people see a rural background as sign of trustworthiness, especially for female *marabouts*. They are seen as closer to nature, and that is considered important for dealing with women's needs (finding a spouse, keeping a marriage, and above all assuring fertility). Yet these rural roots are out of sight for the clients; this reinforces uncertainty.

35. De Rosny (1981:196; 1992:95) also notes with some worry this emergence of younger and more aggressive healers (see also Yombi 1984). Still, in general de Rosny's view of the *nganga* is much more positive than mine. The difference might be that in his study of healers he concentrates on generally respected ones. My approach started rather with potential clients, who are the targets of the aggressive pressures of many healers of doubtful renown. Moreover, it seems that increasing possibilities of working together with state authorities have reinforced this trend. See further Geschiere 1997, notably chap. 6 nn28–29.

36. Cf. the fate of the Malinese *marabout* Mamadou Cissé, who first served Mobutu in Congo, then Kerekou in Benin (and later many others), but ended up in prison in Benin in 1991—precisely because his "secret" role in aiding all these power holders had become common knowledge (see Bayart 1989:251).

37. Compare, for instance, Burnham and Christensen 1983 on Karnu among the Gbaya. Cf. also Titi Nwel 1986 on Thong Likeng and his church Liyomba among the Ngumba. There is a clear contrast in this respect not only with Cameroon's neighboring countries (Nigeria, Gabon, Congo-Brazzaville, and Central African Republic) but also with, for instance, Ivory Coast and Benin. In all these countries, as elsewhere in Africa, there was a proliferation of religious movements splitting off from official mission churches—"independent" churches, sects, and

"prophets"—already during the colonial period. I have never come across a defin-itive explanation for why such movements remained quite limited in Cameroon. Some of my informants in Cameroon blamed it on the state's severe measures to discourage any launch of an independent religious movement. This certainly happened under the postcolonial state, which under President Ahidjo was in-tent on nipping in the bud any association emerging outside the one-party. But people agree that the colonial state - certainly in French Cameroon—was equally bent on suppressing independent religious movements. A special reason for this would have been that Cameroon was a mandated territory; the French authori-ties deeply mistrusted American Presbyterian missionaries, who had planted their mission in Cameroon already at the time of the German conquest but could not be expelled because of this mandate status. De Rosny (2004:121 and personal communication) saw a link with specific aspects of the German missions—nota-bly their success in training local catechists who became true popular leaders—and the heritage they left; during the French period several missionaries and bishops in Cameroon still came from the Alsace, where German influence was strong. De Rosny emphasized also that in Cameroon the idea of independence was not taken up by prophets but rather by politicians with strong popular ap-peal (especially Ruben Um Nyobe, the UPC leader who developed a personal charisma that made him into a sort of prophet, but a secular one). In an equally interesting personal communication, Tonda has related the difference to the ma-jor role that the tradition of old kingdoms (Congo, Teke, and others) played in the exuberance of messianic movements in the Congos. Whatever the explanation is for the relative scarcity of such movements in (post)colonial Cameroon, the 1989 lifting of the official ban on freedom of association was a true watershed in the country's religious history as well. Nowadays in Cameroon as well there is a great proliferation of all shades of prophets, religious leaders, and religious healers (see Séraphin 2004).

38. Father de Rosny (personal communication, 2010) felt that academics' intense in-terest in Pentecostalism as a new phenomenon takes insufficient account of the fact that in recent years in Cameroon the main growth has been in the older churches, Catholic, Presbyterian, and Baptists, rather than in new Pentecostal congregations. Akoko 2007 has a very interesting chapter (chap. 5) on what he calls "the Pentecostalization" of the Presbyterian Church in Cameroon. By in-cluding much Pentecostal-style worship in their services, the Presbyterians—like other older churches—try to stop people from crossing over to the Pentecostals. Maybe this phenomenon helps to explain the fairly limited growth of Pentecos-talism in Cameroon.

39. Cf. the therapies of the *nganga* in Douala in their struggle against the *ekong* that de Rosny describes so vividly in his *Les yeux de ma chèvre* (1981). Their laborious journey through the night to faraway Mt. Kupe to retrieve the zombies of the *ekong* victims aims to restore harmony in the family, rather than denounce and punish the culprits.

40. See Meyer 1999, van Dijk 2002, and de Witte 2008 on Ghana; Marshall 2009 on Ni-

geria; Tonda 2002 and 2005 on Congo-Brazzaville; Akoko 2007 on Cameroon. For detailed bibliographies of the by now vast literature on Pentecostalism in Africa, see Marshall 2009 and de Witte 2008.

41. Of course there are obvious parallels here with the approach of the first missionaries in Africa, who often tried to detach the first converts from their families. However, as soon as the missions became more established, they tried to include whole families in their conversion projects. For instance, the *sixas* in South Cameroon—boarding schools at mission stations where young women were trained to become Christian housewives—indicated a determined effort to change the family from the inside (see Mongo Beti 1956; Vincent 1976; Guyer 1984:44). But this increasing involvement of the churches with the family made them defenseless against the creeping impact of witchcraft closely linked to this familial sphere. The Pentecostal message seems to manifest an effort to take distance once more.

42. I should add that most of these friends are quite well-to-do. It might be easier for people from less prosperous families to try to take their distance. Cf., for instance, Marloes Janson's book (now in press) on the dramatic impact of the Tabligi Jamat mission from India in Gambia. Janson points out its numerous parallels with the Pentecostal message. Tabligi converts, mostly young men and women, seem to be even more radical in breaking with their families. They come, indeed, mostly from poorer families. For them, moreover, sticking to the Tabligi rules has definite economic advantages; for instance, they can marry without paying bridewealth, which liberates the young from the control of the elders.

43. Cf. the endless stream of accusations against American gospel preachers and their equally endless confessions and repentance.

44. This Afrikania movement was strongly supported by Rawlings when he was the country's president, but de Witte emphasizes that more recently it seems to have lost all official support, so it is more or less at the mercy of Pentecostal attacks.

45. Tonda presents his view as a direct criticism of Meyer's earlier work on Pentecostalism in Ghana (Meyer 1999). According to him, her work is inspired by the idea of a "Great Divide" between Pentecostalism and witchcraft, so Meyer would see "African culture"—or *l'esprit sorcellaire*, or whatever label is used for local forms— as the ultimate cause of the crisis in Africa. In contrast, Tonda insists that *le travail de Dieu* is deeply implicated in the osmosis that produced *le Souverain moderne*. I doubt that Meyer will recognize herself in this extrapolation of her interpretations—she has always been very conscious of the danger of culturalism and strongly opposed to any assumption of a continuity of "African culture." Regional differences may also play a role here. Especially in Ghana, people go to great lengths to distinguish religion from witchcraft—which certainly does not exclude a close intertwining between the two, but then it must be at a more hidden level (as Meyer amply shows in her work). In Congo, in contrast, the syncretism may be more manifest.

46. Again, Tonda 2005 provides particularly spectacular examples of this for Congo and Gabon. But see also de Boeck 2004 for Kinshasa, Warnier 1993 for Cameroon,

D. J. Smith 2007 for Nigeria. Cf. also the debate in Pentecostal circles on the conditions under which luxury goods can be stripped of their dangers (Meyer 1999; van Dijk 2005; Tonda 2005).

47. But compare Geschiere 1997 on the double charge of witchcraft notions that often combine a leveling tenor (weapon of the poor against the rich) with accumulative implications (witchcraft as a support that brings riches and power).

48. Cf. the parallel discussed above (chap. 2) between the problems of elite associations in Northern Togo (as discussed in Piot 2010) and among the Maka. In both cases, the post–cold war crisis and the changing role of the state in the 1990s brought increasing elite involvement with the village of origin. Yet in both cases this also brought intensified preoccupation among the elites with witchcraft as the main stumbling block for developing the village.

49. Cf. Douglas's trenchant characteristic of witchcraft accusations as "a clumsy and double-edged weapon" (Douglas 1963:126).

50. Cf. the pioneering studies by Bonno Thoden van Velzen and Wilhelmina van Wetering, who already in the 1980s underlined such progressive implications for prophetic cults in a Maroon society in Surinam: "[These] collective fantasies are more than harmless 'thought experiments' about modern conditions. They enhance the readiness of disciples to try new courses of action" (Thoden van Velzen and van Wetering 1988:401; cf. also 1989 and 2004).

51. As said, this ideology is about the formal equality of all adult men and accompanies severe inequalities of gender and generation.

52. This is a major theme in the vast literature on the Grassfields. See, for instance, Warnier 2009 and Rowlands 1985.

53. Cf. below on the fixed adage in rumors about the new witchcraft of wealth: these people had to "sell their own parents" in order to get rich.

54. Warnier 1993:74–76, also 235. Alain Henry compares the preference for an outsider as bookkeeper to the role of the lawyer in mafia cells—always a nonrelative, but precisely because of this more trustworthy (personal communication; cf. also Henry 1991 and Henry, Tchente, and Guillerme-Dieumegard 1991). Warnier (personal communication) suggests equally interesting parallels with the role of eunuchs in highly confidential posts in many empires and kingdom; he mentions also French kings' practice in early modern times of putting a cardinal in a central minister's position—for instance Richelieu under Louis XIII and Mazarin during the regency of Louis XIV—with the aim of relieving the pressures of kinship and aristocracy on the king. All these examples show a recurring pattern—a pronounced preference for nonkin in key positions of confidence—illustrating the severe limits on trust when kin are involved.

55. Of course, these various forms of creating trust feature different claims to truth: the pretense of modern *nganga* to be scientific, or the Pentecostal conviction that the devil really exists and that it is his evil that turns people into witches, requires a particular form of belief, different from, for instance, the conviction that relatives have a hold over each other in the *djambe*. Yet the effects are the same: a basic uncertainty regarding whether behind the trustworthy appearance

of your companions—relatives, fellow believers in the church, or even the *nganga* themselves—a vengeful witch might hide. The strength of Simmel's stress on the "further element" in trust—which necessitates a leap that suspends doubt—is precisely that it can help us to understand the articulation of variable forms of trust.

56. See also de Certeau 1980:238–39; Hibou 2011, especially 149–53.

Chapter 4

1. These were the papers for a conference that was to commemorate the thirty-year anniversary of Evans-Prichard's *Witchcraft, Oracles and Magic among the Azande* (1967); apart from papers by anthropologists working on Africa, the collection includes a few contributions by historians (Norman Cohn and Peter Brown on medieval Europe; Keith Thomas and Alan Macfarlane with papers on early modern Europe). Douglas's introduction gives the impression that this attempt at a rapprochement of the two disciplines had not been that successful.

2. See further Geschiere 1997:215–23. The very fact that even a sharp and widely read historian/sociologist like Christine Larner in the early 1980s still thought that for comparing witchcraft notions she could just juxtapose "primitive-tribal" to her other two poles, early modern and present-day Europe, shows indirectly anthropologists' utter neglect in those days of the modern dynamics of witchcraft ideas in Africa and elsewhere (Larner 1984:81). Apparently Larner had no idea that in Africa (and other continents) witchcraft ideas were alive and kicking not just in "primitive-tribal settings" (whatever these might be) but also in rapidly changing contexts. Small wonder, since in those days anthropologists themselves still showed little interest in this.

3. Cf. Midelfort 1972:5; Monter 1976:11; and especially J. H. M. Salmon's 1989 article with the somewhat menacing title "History without Anthropology: A New Witchcraft Synthesis." Clearly these historians did not realize that anthropologists collected the data for their witchcraft studies in Africa in colonial and postcolonial settings that were at least as complex as the societies of early modern Europe (see n1 above).

4. The quotation is from a recommendation on the cover of Behringer's book by Erik Midelfort, who apparently dropped his reservations about global comparison on the topic of witchcraft.

5. Behringer settles on a very open definition: "In this book *witchcraft* is used as a generic term for all kinds of evil magic and sorcery, as perceived by contemporaries" (2004:4); however, even this general delimitation may be too narrow since, as we have seen, notions of witchcraft can relativize people's distinctions between good and evil. One of Behringer's justifications for this broad approach is his concern about ongoing witch hunts. He chides anthropologists for being more interested in philosophical or moral aspects of witchcraft than in denouncing witch hunts that are still taking place. "As a consequence we know more about historical European witch-hunts than about contemporary ones in Africa or in other parts of the world" (216, 228).

6. But compare the recent return of the notion of ontology in anthropology—and with it the culturalist overtones that anthropologists so readily find in it (see further this book's prologue and comparative interlude).

7. See Muchembled 1978a:225–27; 1978b:30. Cf. also for similar statements—though in less inflated language—Larner 1981 and 1984, who on the basis of an in-depth study of witchcraft trials in Scotland and comparisons with continental Europe proposes to explain the outbreak of witchcraft trials in sixteenth- and seventeenth-century Europe as determined by the new role of Christianity—related to the development of printing and the breakup of the universal church—as a "political ideology" for the nation-state that struggled to establish itself; in this context witchcraft, like heresy and apostasy, became a "political crime" (Larner 1984:128). See other references to similar views in Geschiere 1997:187–94.

8. Behringer mentions Calvinist areas—like Wallis or Nassau—and Lutheran ones, like Mecklenburg, as parallel examples of failing state formation (Behringer 2004:123, 125).

9. The quotes are from Muchembled 1978a:225–27.

10. In Cameroon it was mainly in the East Province, with its national reputation for being infested with witchcraft—which even seemed to personally frighten officials who were transferred there—that judges were willing to condemn witches on a larger scale.

11. See de Rosny 2005 for the papers from the large Justice et Sorcellerie conference mentioned earlier that Eric de Rosny organized in 2005 at the Catholic University of Central Africa in Yaoundé. And see chapter 6, below, on the insistence of judicial people (lawyers, judges, state's attorneys) present at the conference on the need to stick to the positivist spirit of the law: no conviction without *preuves tangibles* (concrete evidence) of aggression.

12. Hutton's four other characteristics seem to be quite general: use of nonphysical means to cause misfortune or harm to other humans; general social disapproval, usually of a very strong kind; witches are expected to work within a tradition; witches can be resisted by their fellow humans by various means. The next-to-last of these, tradition, risks summoning up the image of a timeless fount of knowledge, even though Hutton adds that techniques can be introduced from outside a given society. Here again the assumption of clearly bounded societies may lead to a neglect of the fluid nature of these notions and the ease with which they spread in new circumstances and transgress boundaries. Introduction from outside might be at least as important as reproduction of a local tradition; in fact the two are often impossible to separate.

13. Shrove Tuesday is the day before Ash Wednesday (the end of the carnival).

14. Jean Bodin was a major political theorist in the sixteenth century, famous for his "modern" ideas on royal sovereignty, yet also a convinced defender of the need to persecute witches as supporters of Satan. Robisheaux summarizes this view in quite poetical language: "Like strands of a finely woven tapestry, the cosmic and the political were woven together. . . . The earthly kingdom, like a finely polished mirror, reflected back and took part in the great cosmic struggle of good against

evil, light against darkness, God against Satan"(2009:283). He adds that the Strassbourg decision in the Schmieg case was based on a view that at that time was already becoming dated. In contrast, the Altdorfers with their insistence on the separation of religion from politics had not even deigned to look at von Glücken's laboriously accumulated evidence on Schmieg's supposed pact with the devil. For the Altdorfers the reference point was no longer God's kingdom but the political realities after the Peace of Westphalia (1648) and the obvious need to overcome internecine religious wars (Robisheaux 2009:284).

15. Here Robisheaux makes a major leap in time, leaving a gap that could be filled in. In Birgit Meyer's book on the impact of Pietist missionaries in Ghana (their emphasis on the devil and how this prepared the way for the recent explosion of Pentecostalism in that country), she includes a fascinating chapter on Pietist religion in Württemberg and its views on witchcraft and exorcism in the nineteenth century. Especially the section on Pastor Blumhardt and his successful, yet contested, exorcism of the devil in the 1840s can be read as a sequel to Anna Schmieg's tragic story (see Meyer 1999:46–53).

16. Cf. also the high average marriage age (2009:216 and my note 14 above).

17. Similar ambiguity is vividly illustrated by a short scene from Philippe Laburthe's magnum opus on the Beti, the western neighbors of the Maka who now dominate in the state. This author recounts with some irony how he was faced with an unsolvable dilemma in the field. One day when he and his assistant were interviewing some elders who asked them both to submit to an oracle: "Why do you ask all these questions? You might be witches." They were told to choose between horns, and felt very relieved when it turned out that the horns they chose proved their bellies were empty. However, the elders were not so happy: "But if you have nothing, if your belly is empty, what can you understand? We cannot tell you anything, you are like children" (Laburthe 1977:1027).

18. Traces of such "rites of distantiation" can, for instance, be detected in Robin Briggs's rich overview of European witchcraft studies (Briggs 1996). This study can be read as a determined stance against Muchembled's and others' explanation, cited above, of the upsurge of witchcraft trials in the sixteenth and seventeenth centuries as triggered by the interventions of ecclesiastical and worldly elite. Briggs insists on the rapid spread of skepticism among elites, their determined efforts to take distance from local ideas about witchcraft, and so on. Starting from an opposition—for him apparently evident—between "belief" and "reality," and from the conviction that witches did not exist (1996;6), Briggs seems more interested in reducing local beliefs to social factors than in following how they were expressed in everyday life.

19. On the issue of "reality" and the quite impossible dilemmas this creates for the anthropologist, see Geschiere 2000.

20. Robisheaux refers here *inter alia* to Larner 1981:89–102 on Scotland, who suggests that women might use their reputation for witchcraft to frighten off their enemies. Yet this point seems to be little developed in the abundant studies of the European witchcraft trials.

21. Robisheaux's emphasis on the executioner/ torturer becoming the accused witch's "most intimate companion" (2009:154) is paralleled by Lyndal Roper in her study of witchcraft trials in Augsburg: "Particularly in witch-trials, torture and the long period of time it took for a conviction to be secured gave the executioner a unique knowledge of an individual's capacity to withstand pain. . . . In a society where nakedness was rare, he knew her body better than anyone else. He washed and shaved the witch, searching all the surfaces of her body for the telltale diabolic marks—sometimes hidden 'in her shame,' her genitals. . . . In consequence a bond of intense personal dependence on the part of the witch on her persecutor might be established." Roper sees an "unmistakable sado-masochistic logic" in the interactions between the witch and her persecutors—the former offering scraps of information, then withdrawing them, thus challenging the latter to apply more torture, and so on (1994:205–6).

22. De Blécourt 1990; de Blécourt and Davies 2004:2, 12; Davies 1999. See also Favret-Saada 1977 and 2009, similarly emphasizing the contrast between *sorciers* and *désorceleurs* for the present-day French countryside.

23. See also Sanders 1995:79: "In England, cunning folk who became unpopular with their neighbours might be accused of witchcraft." Confer also Roper 1994:180. Di Simplicio 2009 suggests that midwives and other healers were more in danger of being perceived as malefic witches than others. Behringer 2004 also pays attention to the slipperiness of the distinction between witch and witch-finder in Europe. But his strong insistence that witchcraft is always evil (45–46) makes it difficult for him to take into account that similar powers could be used to heal.

24. Behringer also emphasizes the idea of the witch as an insider: "the enemy within, or the internal outsider, appears to have been perceived as much more dangerous than real outsiders"—yet states that for Europe "it would be an exaggeration to suggest that 'witchcraft can be characterized as the dark side of kinship,' as suggested by anthropologists" (2004:114).

25. Cf. also Favret-Saada's insistence on this point (1977, chap. 7, and 2009—see also next section below).

26. One can wonder whether the use of the metaphor notion (of which Sabean seems to be quite fond) is very helpful here. See West 2007 for a caution that the academic use of this notion tends to neglect the urgent reality the images concerned have for the people involved.

27. One of Sabean's arguments is that social distinctions among blood relatives might become clearly marked (due to unequal partitioning of the inheritance), while the neighbors and affines involved in witchcraft rumors tend to be equals and therefore potential rivals (1984:169–70). It is striking that those historians who pay closer attention to the contents of witches' confessions distance themselves emphatically from the stereotype of the witches as poor, old women. Cf. Sabean 1984:109: "It is not that weak marginal people are the witches but only that in a contest in which magic plays a role, the powerful win." For him witchcraft accusations always involve a contest of power—rumors about the weak will easily lead to open accusations, while similar rumors about the powerful will remain

implicit. Cf. also Roper 1994:126 on Anton Fugger from Augsburg, "the great-est merchant capitalist of the day," who in 1564 was accused by a certain Anna Megerler, healer but on trial for witchcraft, of having "employed her to give him occult knowledge which he used in his business." In this case the denunciation of a rich person did become public, but it served to hush up the trial against Megerler herself (she was spared torture since the authorities feared that this might lead to "complications"). Clearly it is not only in Africa that spectacular new forms of wealth come to be associated with the use of occult force.

28. A typical difference from historical studies is that as an anthropologist Favret-Saada only uses pseudonyms.

29. Themes central to Favret-Saada's 1977 study—how to include the anthropolo-gist's own presence in the ethnography, the impact of her questioning, the ways in which she induced informants to make implicit ideas explicit, and so on—were taken up by "postmodern" anthropology in the United States (James Clifford, George Marcus, and others) only in the late 1980s, apparently without familiarity with Favret-Saada's seminal work. Her *Les mots, la morts et les sorts* is still a pioneering example of ethnography as an ongoing "dialogue"—a notion later on propounded by Clifford (1988) and other "postmoderns" in anthropology.

30. Favret-Saada 2009:48. Even her own *désorceleur*, the dynamic Madam Flora, was referred to as a *sorcière* by others who wanted to warn Favret-Saada.

31. For instance, there is an intriguing contrast with how Lecoeur described the cul-minating ritual in the *désorceleur*'s therapy in the nineteenth century. He men-tions also the cooking and piercing of an oxen heart, but in those days only the *désorceleur* and the bewitched person would lock themselves up in the house—the rest of the family had to wait outside (as possible suspects?). See Favret-Saada 2009:63.

32. Cf. Robisheaux's example from Langenburg. The household of Anna Schmieg was quite small, at least compared to African examples. It included only Hans, Anna, their son and daughter, and to a certain extent the son-in-law and daughter-in-law (at least as long as they lived with the miller). No family living elsewhere seems to have been included in the affair. The emphasis is on the physical delimi-tations of the house and not on the wider social network of kinship relations.

33. In Robisheaux's case study there are some vague hints that in Europe gender dif-ferences played a role in this respect: women like Anna Schmieg were believed to keep their secret activities hidden "by working within the village," while her hus-band, Hans Schmieg, was rather accused of using dangerous magical substances in order to attract riches on a wider scale—more or less along the lines of the new witchcraft of the wealth along the West African coast (Robisheaux 2009:260).

34. Again, this is certainly not a complete contrast. Cf., for instance, Roper's refer-ence, quoted above, to popular perceptions that Anton Fugger, "the greatest merchant capitalist of the day," used occult knowledge to run his massive trad-ing empire (Roper 1994:126), and other hints in the European studies to equate new wealth with dealings with the occult. Still, this aspect seems to be relegated to the background. Favret-Saada's data, for example, contrast sharply with the

frenzied fantasies of witchcraft on a global scale that circulate in everyday life in present-day Africa.

35. Another approach might be to try to link such differences to a more rapid process of individualization in Europe (cf. Alan McFarlane's well-known study *The Origins of Western Individualism* [1978]). I must confess, however, that I am extremely skeptical of any attempt to contrast Europe and Africa in terms of individualism versus communitarianism. In a book that celebrates the remarkable coherence of a chiefdom in the Grassfields of northwestern Cameroon, Jean-Pierre Warnier (2009) takes his distance from such oppositions in no uncertain terms. The strong emphasis on community in this society by both authorities and their people does not exclude "a solid individualism. . . . Individualism is of all times and all societies" (Warnier 2009:119–20, my translation). I could not agree more. It may be important in this context to underline that all over the world discourse on witches has a strong individualizing tenor. Another universal?

36. For Bayart "the exteriority on which the dominant class rests its power" is a recurrent relation that is central in African social formations from pre- to postcolonial times (Bayart [1989] 1993:28). Cf. also: "The leading actors in sub-Saharan societies have tended to compensate for their difficulties in the autonomisation of their power and in intensifying the exploitation of their dependants by deliberate recourse to the strategies of extraversion, mobilising resources derived from their (possibly unequal) relationship with the external environment" (Bayart [1989] 1993:21–22). This central importance of *stratégies d'extraversion* in African settings—Bayart speaks also of *tactiques d'extraversion* (in de Certeau's sense of tactics as nesting within current forms of dominance)—is related to specific material circumstances prevailing in the continent; but it is also a recurrent nexus in contacts with the outside world: "The dominant groups who hold power in black Africa continue to live chiefly of the income they derive from their position as intermediaries *vis-à-vis* the international system" (Bayart [1989] 1993:250). African elites certainly have no monopoly on such *extériorité* (compare Bayart 1996), but it seems to be particularly central to patterns of organization in sub-Saharan Africa because it remains so basic to any form of accumulation. In a broader perspective this emphasis on *stratégies/tactiques d'extraversion* might be, again, relevant for understanding the open tenor of African conceptions of the house and kinship (see also chap. 6, n37).

Chapter 5

1. See also Beatriz Góis Dantas's pioneering study on how "'pure Nagô' is transformed from sorcery into a 'true religion'" (Dantas [1988] 2009:8; "pure Nagô" stands for the most respectable Candomblé temples).

2. Of course, the same applies to a certain degree to other "African" cults at the other side of the Atlantic, like Santería (Regla de Ocha) in Cuba (see, for instance, Palmié 2002) or Vodou in Haiti (see Corten 2001). Yet I find Candomblé the more challenging comparison—not only for reasons of scale (according to P. Manning [1990], of all the slaves deported from the west coast of Africa to the New World,

44 percent were taken to Brazil; and Candomblé as an African religion has increasingly pervaded the larger part of this huge country), but more importantly for issues of content: the rise of Candomblé as a respected religion, celebrated as part of the national heritage of Brazil, has been particularly impressive; it seems to be more generally considered a religion than are its Haitian and Cuban equivalents. This makes the contrast with "witchcraft" in Africa all the more striking.

3. Organized by Livio Sansone, who acted as my mentor—together with Jocélio Teles dos Santos and Luis Nicolau Parés—also during previous visits to Brazil.

4. See, *inter alia*, Parés [2007] 2011; 2007; 2010.

5. The term *feitiçaria* might be best translated as "sorcery" (emphasis on working with things); people hardly used the term *bruxaria*, a term closer to "witchcraft."

6. Cf. Maggie 2011:147 about people "living in fear of the mystical attacks of family, colleagues and neighbours." Cf. also Souza [1986] 2003:121; Parés and Sansi 2011:25; Parés 2007.

7. The local term for healer is *curandeiro*, but I soon found out that it was better not to use this term because; apparently it has some negative overtones (associations with black magic). All the people we interviewed refused to be called like this Instead they said they were healing and protecting by praying to God or through their contacts with Candomblé or Umbanda spirits.

8 Also *linha das esquerdas*, the left-hand line (Brazeal 2007:183).

9. Several did add that, of course, they were also able to work along the "black line" if necessary—for instance, to combat serious evil.

10. However, see Matory 2005:45; van de Port 2011:101–10, 185; Parés [2007] 2011.

11. Cf. the way Margaret Mead, Landes's fellow student at Columbia, recounts how Boas directed his students to locations where he thought his ideas could be best tested (Mead managed to get his permission to go to Samoa only after she convinced him that there she could best study the topic Boas had in mind for her: adolescence—see Mead 1972:136–43).

12. Landes, like Bastide, was influenced by Nina Rodriguez and especially Arthur Ramos, Brazilian academics who had pioneering roles in the reevaluation of Candomblé as an African religion that had to be helped in conserving the purity of its heritage. As said, this view implied that many aspects were seen as less desirable and could be written off as deviations from this African heritage—and therefore as signs of degeneration. See especially Dantas's [1988] 2009 pathbreaking study for an insightful analysis of the long struggle to separate "religion" from sorcery/witchcraft in Candomblé's history since the beginning of the twentieth century. Dantas highlights the role of intellectuals (first especially psychiatrists, later anthropologists) in trying to impose a clear-cut distinction between, on the one hand, *caboclo* spirits, associated with sorcery/witchcraft, and, on the other, "pure Nagô" as religion. She shows how necessary this opposition to *caboclo* witchcraft was to the emancipation of Nagô Candomblé as a religion; but she also shows that this was a leaky opposition, as traces of *caboclo* sorcery emerge frequently in the heart of "true Nagô" (see Dantas [1988] 2009:100, 114, 125). Cf. also Matory 2005:265: "In the 1930s, ethnographers reproduced and amplified a novel Bahian

discourse scandalously conjoining male priests, homosexuality, mixed race, *cabo-clo* worship, the Angola nation, newness or lack of tradition, and 'black magic'— all in a fictive antitype to . . . 'purely' African religion." See also Matory 1988; Parés 2004; [2007] 2011, chap. 6; van de Port 2011:186, 217.

13. The case was discussed earlier by Bastide (1960:133-3–4). See Mott 1994 for a more extensive analysis.

14. For a very subtle analysis of the emergence of such "nations" in Candomblé, see the second chapter of Parés's book on the Jeje nation ([2007] 2011). Originally these nations seemed to have grouped slaves who had a common origin, or at least had been bought at the same African port. But gradually they became more mixed in character, religious identification becoming the main criterion for belonging.

15. Nicolau Parés (Parés [2007] 2011:chap. 3) characterizes this transition also as a shift from individual *curandeiros*, who would travel around and were often associated with sorcery, to the institution of shrines around an altar at a fixed place and the staging of more or less collective public rituals.

16. Reis 2011:164. In his 1993 book on the Malê (Muslim) slave revolt of 1835, this author refers to Candomblé as a possible catalyst for slave revolts (see notably chap. 5). In his 2001 and 2011 articles on Candomblé he pays more attention to the ways in which relations between Candomblé priests and followers were deeply marked by the general context of slave society. See also Dantas [1988] 2009:43.

17. Nicolau Parés (Parés 2004:10) links the "disintegration of kinship" to "religious activities allowing for the reshaping of new communal identities." Cf. also Reis 1993:185 on the destruction of the kinship networks by the slave trade, which led Africans in Bahia to use kinship terms in a wider sense—in ethnic frameworks or religious associations like the Candomblé temples.

18. Typical is also the idea that the wild *caboclo* spirits, seen as wayward, prone to mischief, and foreign to the pure African heritage, are supposed to lack such "kin-ship" affiliations (Matory 2005:30; Teles dos Santos 1992).

19. Van de Port (2011:186) sees *mãe* Stella's 1984 declaration that there should be no room for syncretism in Candomblé as a milestone in this increasing quest for purity.

20. As said, Dantas's book ([1988] 2009) was really pathbreaking in this direction. Matory also mentions Luiz Mott, "The Churchifying of Candomblé: Priests, An-thropologists, and the Canonization of the African Religious Memory in Brazil," paper presented at the 17th International Congress of Latin American Studies Association, Los Angeles, 1992; Peter Fry's *Para inglês ver* (Rio de Janeiro: Zahar, 1982); and Alejandro Frigeiro's "The Search for Africa," MA thesis, University of California, Los Angeles, 1983.

21. For a more long-term view, see Parés 2004.

22. The documents Castillo and Nicolau Parés found bear out that this return voyage took place in 1837 (probably the women felt pressured by the backlash against Africans after the large Malê uprising of 1835 by African [freed] slaves).

23. See again Castillo and Parés 2007. Reis (1993) shows that after the 1835 rebellion,

deportation to Africa became one form of punishment for freedmen who were suspected of having been involved in one way or another—several hundreds of them would have been thus deported. He shows that this was seen by most of them as a severe (and unjust) ordeal. The return of the Casa Branca priestesses to Africa may have been, therefore, a sad occasion. And it is rather their subsequent return to Salvador that was exceptional (Reis 1993:220).

24. This complex configuration—Old Oyo attacked by Islamized groups from the north and subsequently plundered by the kings of Dahomey, who could acquire the means to expand their empire by ever larger sales of captives to European (and Brazilian) factories on the coast—can explain why Muslim slaves as well arrived in Salvador. As "Hausa," they were to play a central role in the slave rebellions throughout the nineteenth century (Reis 1993). Butler (2001:151) even mentions the emergence toward the end of the nineteenth century of Islamic Candomblé houses—a remarkable sign of the range of syncretism possible in the area, which, however, did not last. Reis (1993:124) rather emphasizes the purity of Islam in Salvador at the time of the Malê revolt (1835). Yet he remarks as well that many Candomblé houses integrated some Islamic elements in their rituals.

25. The terms *Nagô* and *Ketu* are, like the term *Yoruba*, historically circumscribed. Somewhat confusing is that the last term emerged more recently. It was only in the second half of the nineteenth century that Yoruba (probably after Yarriba, the Hausa name for the Old Oyo Kingdom) became the ethnic label for the population of southwest Nigeria (see below on the "Lagos renaissance" and the role of freed slaves—who were liberated by the British actions against slave ships, trained in mission schools in Freetown, Sierra Leone, and then sent back to the region of origin—in the spread of a new Yoruba identity; see also Peel 1969 and 2000). Prior to this, the term *Nagô* (after ANagô, the name Fon-speaking groups to the west used for people from present-day Yorubaland) became current in Bahia. Later, slaves coming from this area were also called Ketu, the name of a kingdom in the extreme west of present-day Yorubaland, close to the border with the Dahomey kingdom.

26. According to Nicolau Parés (Parés [2007] 2011:264–68, a similar transition followed only later in the cult of *orixás* in Yorubaland—for that area only after the Candomblé complex had crystallized in Brazil. It might be of interest to follow the history of these traits. Both innovations—assembling a plurality of *voduns* (gods) in one temple and instituting a longer-term initiation—may have been possible only through the society's growing cosmopolitanism. In Dahomey, and notably in Ouidah, the major port, such a cosmopolitanization took place during the eighteenth century under the impact of the slave trade. Ouidah's rapid rise as a major port in this trade made it one of the most cosmopolitan towns on the West African coast—which set the terms for the innovations that were to become hallmarks of Candomblé. Again we see that in this respect as well, at least some of the rituals of Candomblé could be seen as a product of the slave trade, even though this cult developed subsequently in Brazil into slavery's counterpoint.

27. There are striking parallels with much more recent attempts in several coun-

tries in Africa to create official organizations of "traditional healers" that would be able to impose similar distinctions—recruiting only "bona fide healers" with whom official health-care programs could collaborate. See chap. 3 above and also Geschiere 2006, where I try to show the precariousness of such projects since the very ambiguity of healers' secret powers defies all neat distinctions—certainly between good and evil.

28. Cf. their obsession with "cannibalism"—often mentioned as a marker of Amazonian culture—as a way to digest the foreign and appropriate its strength without giving up one's own identity (see van de Port 2011:113).

29. Getúlio Vargas ruled over Brazil as president from 1930 till 1945, and again from 1950 to 1954.

30. Popular rumors indicate that at least in the eyes of the people the collaboration was reciprocal, certainly in the case of "ACM" (Antonio Carlos Magelhaes). The latter would owe much of his political success to the support of Candomblé's occult forces. When in 1998 his son died in a car accident, many saw this as a sign that the dark forces were returning home. Nicolau Parés (Parés 2007) refers to popular rumors that the accident was the result of a *troca de cabeça* (exchange of heads)—"meaning that through a ritual of substitution, the father would have transferred the evil load or destiny to his son" (see also van de Port 2005). There is a strong resemblance here with the general concern in Congo/Zaire in the early 1990s when President Mobutu lost two sons in rapid succession; this was seen as a sign that Mobutu had abused the dark forces to such an extent that they were now coming to haunt his own family (see my chap. 1 for the syndrome of the witch as martyr that recurs in many African contexts). The popular rumors that ACM had become a victim of his own dabbling in the occult can be seen as another example of the "untamability" of Candomblé, emphasized by van de Port.

31. Nicolau Parés (Parés 2004:33) links the purity creed to pressures from the black movement, rapidly growing in importance over the past several decades, behind this increasing emphasis on African purity. He places *mãe* Stella's stern rejection of syncretism in the broader context of an antisyncretism movement in Afro-American religions, both in the United States and in Brazil (see also Sansone 2003). In Bahia, this also fits in a more practical sense within the broader political configuration—notably with the new possibilities of having "pure" temples recognized as monuments. Moreover, this 1984 declaration was a joint statement by several priestesses of the main Nago temples, intent on laying out their claims vis-à-vis the authorities. The prestige *mãe* Stella has acquired over recent decades is reflected in the fact that this declaration is mainly attributed to her.

32. Such insights make it all the more regrettable for non-Lusophones that so little of her work has been translated in other languages.

33. There is a clear correspondence here with the ways in which people in African settings talk about the healer (*nganga, sangoma*) as a dangerous person—see chap. 3 above.

34. Luis Nicolau Parés (oral communication) quotes a similar saying: "Who is inside does not dare to go out, who is outside does not want to go in."

35. Van de Port 2011:245; recall also the long and forceful initiation that is seen as a hallmark in the emergence of Candomblé.

36. See also Dantas [1988] 2009:145, 171n15, on the crucial role of middle-class *ogãs* (often not initiated) in the richer temples.

37. Cf. the argument of Veena Das and Deborah Poole in their introduction to *Anthropology in the Margin of the State* (2004) that it is precisely at its margins that the state shows its more hidden mechanisms.

38. A good part of Brazeal's powerful documentary film (2004) shows Moisés indeed playing this role with a certain abandon.

39. Cf. Luis Nicolau Parés's contrast between "the sorcerer" as the central figure in the Brazilian imaginary, as opposed to "the witch" in African representations (Parés 2007).

40. Probably the *irmandades* (*broederschappen*) played a crucial role in the emergence of new associations around religious shrines (many thanks to Mattijs van de Port for this comment; see also de Mello e Souza [1986] 2003).

41. See Parés [2007] 2011 and 2007; see also Brazeal 2007, chaps. 8–9; and Dantas [1988] 2009:49. The balance between support and danger within the *terreiros* is a very sensitive and complex issue. It is quite clear that the "house"—like any locus of intimacy—can be both a haven of refuge and a site of fierce rivalry and conflict. A special factor in this context is that every initiate builds her or his own "shrine" (*assento*) inside the temple, where it is guarded by the priest(ess). This can create a sense of deep security, but also an equally deep dependency. In case of conflict, the very first thing an initiate must do is to try to take the *assento* out of the temple (Parés, oral communication).

42. Parés (oral communication) emphasizes that in this respect as well there is no radical contrast: Candomblé priests may hesitate as well between attributing complaints to attacks by witches and seeing them as manifestations of a god.

43. Interestingly, Rosenthal's informants used to emphasize the beauty of these people from the North; even in the present they would point out to her people from the North (mainly Kabre) and marvel about how beautiful they were (Rosenthal 1998: 23, 44).

44. See also Parés's seminal study (2010) on memories of slavery in both Benin Vodun and Bahian Candomblé; and compare Castillo and Parés's 2010 study of the famous return to Africa of Iyá Nassô, Marcelina, and Maria Magdalena to Africa—see n22 above—in which slavery and religious kinship are closely interwoven; apparently, for instance, Marcelina became quite rich on her return to Salvador through investment—buying *and* selling—in slaves (especially women, who were also initiated in her temple).

45. See Bayart 2004:30 and his emphasis on the mixing of different *durées* (see also chaps.1 above and 6 below).

Interlude

1. This "presidential address" was for section F of the Australian and New Zealand Association for the Advancement of Science; it was reworked into an article,

"Witchcraft as a Social Strain-Gauge" (1970), that became a classic in anthropological witchcraft studies.

2. Yet already in the 1920s the literature on the well-known "cargo cults" in the area had emphasized the centrality of the trope of traveling in these representations (see F. E. Williams [1923] 1976 on "the Valaila madness," and for a more recent overview Lattas 2010).

3. Anthony Forge had already developed this model for Melanesia in his contribution to Mary Douglas's well-known 1970 collection *Witchcraft Confessions and Accusations*.

4. It is also striking that Lindenbaum concluded, in stark contrast to Stephen, that it is of no use for the Melanesian data to try to construe a clear distinction between "witch" and "sorcerer" (127n1).

5. Cf. also de Witte 2008 and Meyer forthcoming on Ghana.

6. Cf. Marilyn Strathern's well-known opposition between "individual" and "dividual conceptions of personhood" in, respectively, the West and Melanesia (Strathern 1988).

7. For an inspired use of such ontology notions, see Mol 2002 and 2012; see also Marrero-Guillamón i.p. for a seminal example of how these ideas can be applied in ethnography.

8. An interesting example of how easily notions of ontology acquire a culturalist tenor in anthropology is offered by the challenging and highly sophisticated reflections of Brazilian anthropologist Eduardo Viveiros de Castro (lately attracting much attention in British anthropology and also in France). De Castro is strongly influenced by Deleuze and also Latour. In his *Métaphysiques cannibales* (2009), he makes an urgent plea for the need to "denaturalize the ontology that shapes Western academia"; anthropology in particular should be much more open, including in its theorizing, to "native thinking." This is an important and welcome project (although less new than the author seems to think). However, it is quite surprising how quickly it boils down in his book to outlining a dyadic contrast between an "Amazonian ontology" and academic thinking (*deux schèmes ontologiques "croisés"*; 2009:49) in which (of course) the first seems to be in every respect the opposite of the latter. This is surprising since apparently the author does not see any tension with Deleuze's plea for ontology as multiple, contingent, and never ending (yet cf. also de Castro's notion of "perspectivist ontologies," which seems to allow much more space for such multiplicity). It is also surprising since in earlier publications (see 1996) de Castro himself emphasizes the historicity of Amazonian societies, including in the pre-Columbus era. Little of such historicity or multiplicity seems to be left in his 2009 sketch of *la métaphysique de la prédation* that apparently marks all Amazonian societies (he does allow for clear correspondences in this respect between Amazonian and Melanesian ontologies—but both, of course, in direct opposition to the West). In other publications (2003 and 2010) as well, de Castro's plea for ontology as the concept that will mark the future of anthropology relates (again, apparently without the author seeing any problem), on the one hand, to the emphasis on multiplicity of the notion and, on the other, to the by now somewhat tired dyadic oppositions that have

marked anthropological studies since the beginning of the discipline (like gift-based societies versus commodity-based societies—for De Castro, the problem of academia would be that it is still inspired by commodity-based metaphors and therefore has great problem understanding gift-based societies). Such simplistic oppositions seem to become ever less valuable in a world that is marked by creative hybridization of very different elements, leading to constantly new and unexpected experiments. De Castro's views of native thinking, conceived of as the very counterpoint to academic thinking, seems to lead him quite far from Foucault's challenging view of a critical ontology as "the historical analysis of the limits that are imposed on us and an experiment with the possibility of going beyond them" (Foucault 1985:50; Mol 2002:183; see also Venkatesan 2010 for a summary of the discussions of the Group for Debates in Anthropology Theory at the University of Manchester on a motion with the telling title "Ontology Is Just Another Word for Culture").

9. See Geschiere 2009b:chap. 5. A good example of the problematic implications in such contexts of an essentialist notion of culture, derived from anthropology, is the way the well-known Dutch philosopher and Heidegger expert Herman Philips opposed "the culture of tribal Islamic societies from Arab countries"—from which migrants to the Netherlands come, and which he equates also with a "shame-culture"—to Dutch secular culture (see, for instance NRC/*Handelsblad*, Sept. 27, 2003, 7; see also Geschiere 2009b:252n46). The same Philips was often quoted by the Dutch-Somali politician Hirsi Ali—now in the USA—as her most important mentor for teaching "how to think." Such examples should inspire some prudence among anthropologists about embracing the notion of ontology since in our discipline it so easily seems to acquire culturalist overtones.

10. Of course, the renaissance of the ontology notion followed varying trends in the social sciences. Among Cambridge anthropologists the notion has inspired very interesting reflections on (and experiments with) liberating anthropologists of their own "ontonorms" during fieldwork and while writing ethnography (see, for instance, Pedersen 2012). Such an epistemological use of the notion can be most stimulating, even though it remains a bit worrying that in this line of thought as well the notion seems to lead easily to dyadic oppositions along the line of "the West versus the rest" (or "their"—that is, the informants'—views versus the academic gaze). For someone like Annemarie Mol, who has a STS (Science and Technology Studies) background, the concept helps rather to get away from epistemological concerns. She proposes to use the ontology notion "in a playful and anti-philosophical way" in order to "open up to enquiry the 'reality' sciences seek to represent; in this line of work ontology has become unstable" (Mol 2012:2; see also Mol 2002 and Yates-Doerr and Mol 2012). The great advantage of such an approach is that ontology becomes multiple by definition. But the contrasts between Mol's work and the way the concept is used in much recent anthropological work also show how strong the tendency in anthropology is to relate ontology to essence; then we land unavoidably in the kind of dyadic contrasts that we have struggled so hard to get away from in recent decades.

11. I could not find any specification of when exactly Siegel did research in the area

(neither in his 2001 article on the events nor in his longer 2006 book). But it is quite clear that he did very intensive interviews within the villagers (this in contrast to Campbell and Conner [2000], who state that their article on the 1998 events is based on newspaper reports).

12. Campbell and Connor 2000:88; cf. also 62: "We argue that sorcery, rather than a resurgence of aberrant traditionalism in a time of political crisis, is intrinsic to the processes of modernity . . ."

13. Herriman 2007 and 2009. In view of the drastic contrast with Siegel's interpretations of the same events in the Banyuwangi area, it might be good to stress that Herriman's analysis—which is certainly based on very thorough research in the villages concerned—also raises some questions. The very clarity of his delimitations is surprising. In his view in each village there is a limited number of specific people who are generally recognized as "sorcerers" (is it ever possible to have such clarity in view of the category's fluid and always contested character?). Since in his view people have been denouncing sorcerers for a long time already, it is also striking that there are so few institutionalized procedures for dealing with this: victims of sorcery can only rarely be cured, and sorcerers cannot be neutralized, so the only solution is to kill the latter. Again, it is surprising that there is not more debate on how to deal with such fuzzy threats. See also Bertrand 2002 for a quite different interpretation of the role of sorcery in Javanese politics.

14. Cf. the contrast along similar lines that Douglas made in her 1970 introduction to a collection of papers of a conference where anthropologists and historians met to evaluate the thirtieth anniversary of the publication of Evans-Pritchard's classic *Witchcraft, Oracles and Magic among the Azande* (see chap. 3 above). Siegel also addresses more recent anthropological studies—especially the recent flood of studies on witchcraft in Africa, referred to in chap. 1 above—whose authors are more alert to the violence of witchcraft than the classical studies on which Douglas based her work. However, Siegel feels that the focus on contextualizing of these more recent studies still risks a certain neglect of the terror and the violence these obsessions can create.

15. For an interesting recent critique of the Kantian notion of the sublime, see Meyer 2010, who emphasizes the active role of the spectator; in her vision the sublime is social as well—it does not just appear but is evoked and therefore "formatted."

16. See also Siegel 2006:21. Siegel agrees also in general with "Lévi-Strauss' assumption . . . that witchcraft beliefs are not ideas. They are vague assumptions impossible to articulate under ordinary circumstances" (Siegel 2006:29). Cf. also Lévi-Strauss on the Zuni case: "Grâce à lui [the accused boy who confessed], la sorcellerie, et les idées qui s'y rattachent, échappent à leur mode pénible d'existence dans la conscience, comme ensemble diffus de sentiments et de représentations mal formulés, pour s'incarner en être d'expérience. L'accusé, préservé comme témoin, apporte au groupe une satisfaction de vérité, infiniment plus dense et plus riche que la satisfaction de justice qu'eût procurée son execution" (Lévi-Strauss [1949] 1958:191; Thanks to [the confessing boy], witchcraft and the ideas associated with it escape from their precarious existence in people's consciousness, as

a diffuse complex of badly formulated feelings and representations, and become incarnated into a state of experience. The accused, employed as witness, offers the group a satisfaction of truth, endlessly stronger and richer than the satisfaction of justice that his execution would have offered—my translation). As I will argue in more detail below, such formulations seem to be miles away from my experiences in the Maka area. There, just as in the other examples quoted above, ideas about witchcraft may have a certain fluidity, but they are certainly not *mal formulés*—on the contrary, elders in particular, who play similar roles as the Zuni interrogators, turn out to have a rich array of images at their disposal, and they are very conscious of having such knowledge. It might be good to remember that Lévi-Strauss is not basing his statements on an experience of everyday life in the society in question, but on a reanalysis of a 1905 text by another anthropologist, Matilda Coxe Stevenson.

17. There are clear parallels here with van de Port's analysis of the Candomblé temples in Salvador de Bahia escaping "symbolic closure" time and again (see chap. 5 above and van de Port 2011).

18. See Ashforth 2005 for a parallel interpretation of people's obsession with witchcraft in postapartheid South Africa as inspired by deep "spiritual insecurity."

19. Clearly in Siegel's approach an explanation such as the one forwarded by the anthropologist Herriman, quoted above (the witch craze started because killers thought they had a free hand after the sudden collapse of the Suharto regime), is much too direct and too simple.

20. Cf. Siegel 2006:131: "Witchcraft here was not a metaphor for something that we as analysts could name but they, the witch hunters, could not. Something amorphous and unnamable was at work. Up to this point, one can only say this: at a certain moment there was a menace felt whose origin was unknown and which was general. It surpassed the usual understandings."

21. Siegel mentions also that *witch* seems to be used as a "copula"—a key word restoring connections that seemed to be broken; yet it is an unsatisfactory copula since it connects anything with anything (Siegel 2006:205, 227–28).

22. "L'adolescent [the confessing witch] est parvenu à se transformer, de menace pour la sécurité physique de son groupe, en garant de sa cohérence mentale" (Lévi-Strauss [1949] 1958:191; The adolescent has succeeded in transforming himself from a physical threat to his group into a guarantee of its mental coherence—my translation).

23. Elsewhere Siegel (2006:218) suggests that his confession clearly referred to another kind of power introduced by the whites.

24. All the more so since I have left out Derrida, who is, of course, constantly present in Siegel's book, explicitly or between the lines (for this, see Bubandt 2013). I focused on Siegel's move from Kant to Freud since this relates especially well to the argumentation in the present book.

25. Cf. Siegel 2006:188: "The uncanny emerged, as it does, from the familiar." He refers here also to Freud as "the most important explicator of the uncanny" in terms of "the return of the oppressed" (222) and cites the example of Freud's hav-

ing a strong sense of antipathy against a stranger who enters his train compartment, until he realizes that he sees his own reflection in the swinging door. Indeed, the Bunyawangi lynchings were a shocking example of the familiar turned weird: most of the victims were very well known to the killers. One of the enigmas Siegel is wrestling with is how people could once again live together despite such horrible memories

26. See Geschiere 1997. See also Lévi-Strauss [1949[] 1958): "Nous dirons que la pensée normale souffre toujours d'un déficit de signifié, tandis que la pensée dite pathologique (au moins dans certaines de ses manifestations) dispose d'une pléthore de signifiant" (We would say that normal thought suffers always from a lack of *signifié*, while what can be called pathological thought [at least in some of its manifestations] has a plethora of *signifiant* at its disposal—my translation).The dichotomy *pensée normale/pathologique* is problematic, but otherwise this quote rejoins the powerful sensation of conceptual overproduction I had in my endless discussions about witchcraft with my Maka friends and others.

27. It is true that among the Maka as well sometimes people who feel themselves to be under attack of the witches may fall into a state of aphasia. But this is part of a general depression, and their silence is always largely compensated for by the vociferous comments from their relatives or neighbors proposing all sorts of scenarios that could explain the victim's plight.

Chapter 6

1. Cf. the mesmerizing novel *Saisons sauvages* by Kettley Mars (2010); see also Brown 1991 and Corten 2001.

2. See Kapferer 1997.

3. See Tonda 2002 and Mary 2009 on the proliferation of prophets and other visionaries—some touched by Pentecostalism, others differently inspired—in West and Equatorial Africa.

4. See also Patrick Yengo's review of the conference (Yengo 2008b) and the book that came out of it (de Rosny 2005).

5. One of the agreeable surprises was how strongly those in the legal profession at this conference insisted on the need to respect the positivist premises of the law: only when there were *preuves tangibles* of physical aggression was it possible to condemn someone accused of having used "witchcraft" to attack. This is the main bone of contention ever since the 1980s when state courts started to convict witches: how can the judge establish concrete proof of invisible forms of aggression? (See Fisiy and Geschiere 1990 and Geschiere 1997.) At the 2005 conference experts in the law insisted so much on the need for *preuves tangibles* that this seemed to exclude any possibility for using a *nganga*—who would claim that he has seen the accused "go out at night"—as a witness for the prosecution. Yet this is what judges regularly allow in practice. Indeed, despite all emphasis on the positivist spirit of the law (see Obarrio 2007), judges show themselves to be most interested—also during the conference—in all sorts of compromises (for instance, involving *chef coutumiers* as assessors in the deliberation over witchcraft

cases, which means of course that "customary" ways of establishing proof will be accepted). The judges' interest in such compromises—presented by some as radical solutions—signals how heavy the popular pressure is on the courts to do something about a supposed proliferation of witchcraft (see further Geschiere 2006, also for a comparison with developments in South Africa in this respect).

6. Multi Media Centre, Yaoundé, undated.

7. See chapter 3 above. This *gbati* was clearly different from the girl's witchcraft in the film, since the *gbati* is supposed to live only in the belly of boys who have not yet slept with a woman. But the girl's avid confessions were strongly reminiscent of the alacrity with which *gbati* boys made similar statements.

8. Cf. Gable 2002 on skepticism in local confrontations. Such an emphasis is particularly important for our topic. To outsiders, Africans' preoccupation with the supposed omnipresence of witchcraft can easily give the impression of utter credulousness. Everyday life may be full of frightening rumors, but these are constantly doubted, tested, and checked—it is certainly not the case that anything goes (see also Bubandt 2013 on witchcraft as "aporia" and doubt in eastern Indonesia).

9. See also Henry and Tall 2008:23 on the effect of the intensive mediatization of witchcraft in many African countries, bringing both confirmation of its reality and a "mise à distance"; see also Englund 2007; Meyer 2010 and 2012.

10. To mention a couple: *Quartier Mozart by* Jean Bekolo (1992) and *Le cercle des pouvoirs* by Daniel Kamwa (1998)—see Tcheuyap 2009.

11. Compare also André Mary, who similarly emphasizes that the Pentecostal equation of witchcraft with the devil brings *a mondialisation de la sorcellerie* (a globalization of witchcraft) without, however, breaking its close link with the family (2009:140).

12. Of course, in this respect as well there are variations within the continent (see, for instance, chapter 3 above, p. 91, on studies on Malawi that nuance this linking of the devil to village, family, and tradition).

13. Cf. Meyer 2013:chap. 4 on filmmaker Quartey's explanations: for him Rider Haggard's famous book *She* brought a revelation that helped him to conceive the dangerous Zinabu protagonist who, in the end, could be brought to heel only by a Pentecostal preacher.

14. Wendl 2005; cf. also Meyer 2013:chap. 4.

15. Meyer 2013 (introduction); see also Meyer 2000 and 2004. However, in her new book, Meyer also notes a few signs that this tide might be turning.

16. See also Meyer 1999 on the long-term influence of the Basler Mission on the imaginary of the devil and evil in general in southern Ghana.

17. Meyer (2013:chap. 1) mentions a few women among the filmmakers, but they are a small minority.

18. See also de Boeck 2004 and 2009; de Boeck and Plissart 2004; Yengo 2008a.

19. Cf. the classic case of the witches of Salem in 1692 New England (Boyer and Nissenbaum 1974); but also cf. the spectacular case in Trier (chap. 4 above) where, in the 1580s, the Jesuits from a newly established college supported by Bishop

von Binsfeld started to use young boys as spies to denounce witches. The boys were supposed to attend a nightly witch-sabbath so that they could see who else attended and then testify against these witches in front of the court. Yet in the process they themselves became difficult to distinguish from "real" witches (see also Behringer 2004:95–97).

20. I noticed the same in the Maka villages in the 1970s during the explosion of the *gbati*, the child witchcraft mentioned earlier.

21. But compare what was said above (chaps. 1 and 2) about the undermining of the lineage order that seems to be especially strong in the Congolese cities (cf. Tonda 2002 and 2005 on *déparentalisation*; see also chap.1 above, nn45, 55).

22. Undigested morsels of meat or bone (and all sorts of other things) found in their vomit or feces will be shown at their subsequent public confession in the church as proof of their nocturnal misdeeds. Again, the parallels with the treatment of the *gbati* child witches in the Maka villages in the 1970s are striking: in this case as well, the *nganga* (healer) forced them to eat heavy, oily food until they vomited; the cord he would find in their vomit was their *gbati*, which was thus neutralized (see chap. 3, n23).

23. Remember the story about Nkal Selek, the old warlord who terrorized the Maka in precolonial times. He could "buy" the precious war medicine by offering her his new patron, Evina. The very fact that he could sacrifice him meant that he had become a kind of "son" of Evina—see chapter 2.

24. Cf. Yengo 2008a, who analyzes the emergence of child witches in Congolese cities as an example of the dynamics in the link *sorcellerie-parenté*, both taking on constantly new forms, yet remaining inextricably linked.

25. Cf. the striking transformation, noted above (chaps. 1 and 3), of funerals in both Kinshasa and Brazzaville (see de Boeck 2006 and Tonda 2005) where young men, supported by girls, take over the body, chase away the deceased's parents, and stage the burial as an attack on the elders who are supposedly responsible for this untimely death.

26. Cf. Ruth Marshall's conclusion about the failure of Pentecostalism in Nigeria—despite its formidable upsurge—to constitute a truly hegemonic project (see Marshall 2009).

27. Janson i.p.; Masquelier 2009:155, 162.

28. Masquelier rightly prefers the term *reformist* to *fundamentalist* to designate Islamic groups in Africa advocating a return to the Qu'ran. In African studies *fundamentalist* is often used to make a radical contrast to the Sufi forms of Islam, marked by worship of saints and organized into "brotherhoods," that are supposed to dominate in Africa. Masquelier's aim is to show that such dichotomies tend to hide the "fluid, shifting and heterogeneous nature of Muslim discourses and practices" (2005:2).

29. Awal's decline in Dogondoutchi—by 2004 his following had already dwindled to just a few households—was not related to his emphatic dealing with the spirits. Masquelier rather underlines the usual tendencies in people's reaction to such charismatic preachers—they got tired of his endless condemnations and started

to notice that he himself did not at all live up to the moral standards he imposed so severely on others. An additional reason in this case was also Awal's attacks on dowry. Women—after initial enthusiasm—came to see his fulminating against dowry payments as a threat to one of their scarce socioeconomic assets (see Masquelier 2009: chaps. 6 and 8).

30. Masquelier's 2008 article highlights a similar intertwinement of wider conceptions with local issues in a different setting: the popular conviction that precisely the most outspoken Muslims have a *doguwa* spirit living in the house. This spirit, heavily concealed, is the obvious explanation for the fact that such devoted Muslims can become quite wealthy. Here is a clear connection to this book's theme of witchcraft/intimacy. Not only does the spirit live inside the house, but the general conviction is also that once such a spirit is lured into the house it will help to attract riches; however, it has to be fed human blood on a regular basis. In the end the spirit will eat all the relatives of its host and even the host himself. There is an obvious parallel here with the story of how the *djambe* came to the Maka. Once brought back by Woman into the village, the *djambe* had to be fed all the animals in the compound and finally Woman's own children—see Geschiere 1997; cf. also the general trope—among the Maka and elsewhere—about the witch as a martyr who may refuse to give up more relatives and then becomes himself or herself the victim of the witches—see chap. 2 above). A more general link to intimacy in Masquelier's material is that *doguwa* spirits may be tied to a certain spot, but can become associated with special lineages as well (Masquelier 2009:155–56, 164).

31. For de Rosny as well, the effectiveness of these secret forces is beyond doubt. But his project—and that of the group that he composed of experts from highly different backgrounds—seemed to aim at a containment of these forces and an appeasing of people's panic about their proliferation, rather than a complete eradication.

32. I use "tactic" here in de Certeau's sense: not as a necessarily goal-oriented action, but rather as a form of agency undermining the hegemonic system from within (in opposition to more openly confrontational "strategies")—see de Certeau 1980.

33. Cf. the Congolese vision of the colonial state as *Bula Matari* (the breaker or rocks), capable of shaking up things in unprecedented ways (see Jewsiewicki 1983; Tonda 2005).

34. Yet recall the many variations highlighted above, in this respect also inside Africa (see chap. 3 on the erosion of kinship in the Congos).

35. Goody 1976; see the prologue to this book and also Goody 1973.

36. After 1976 Goody himself hardly followed up on these inspiring openings. In his more recent publications he focuses on relations between different regions within Eurasia, trying to show that there were starts toward industrialization in several of these regions, not only in Europe. This is certainly a worthwhile undertaking. Yet it is a bit unfortunate that Africa figures only as a marginal counterexample in his recent publications (Goody 2010).

37. This is, of course, a simplifying summary of a much more complex argument (see also chap. 4 n36 above. In his earlier publications Bayart ([1989] 1993) related the centrality of such *stratégies d'extraversion* in African contexts to politico-economic limitations and opportunities that were (and are) salient in the African continent (more or less in line with Goody's interpretations, cited above). In this context Bayart emphasized that such a tendency toward extraversion might create dependency on outsiders but that it also brings a *rente* (his notion of a *rente de la dépendence* as a fixed corollary of strategies of extraversion was then especially an answer to the *dependencia* school, which in his view emphasized too one-sidedly the exploitation of the periphery by the centre—see Bayart 1989:46; see also Bayart 2000). Later on—notably in his work *L'illusion identitaire* (1996 [2002])—he generalized the notion of *extraversion*, defining it as basic to any form of culture, which is always shaped by rapport with the other (1996:80); see also Bayart 2008:47). See also Englund 2003 for a challenging application of this notion of Bayart's in the field of religion.

38. See Geschiere and Socpa's text on the centrality of changing patterns of mobility to people's conceptions of the future (in the forthcoming collection by Brian Goldstone, Juan Obarrio, and Charles Piot, *African Futures*).

39. The comparison with the present-day Pentecostal offensive in Africa suggests that precisely the elaborate intellectualist trappings theologians gave to the equation of witchcraft with the devil in Europe—relegating its local roots to the background—facilitated the marginalization of witchcraft notions when belief in the devil started to fade. In contrast, the devil seems to be made of sturdier stuff when, as in Africa, he is hiding behind the familiar faces of everyday life.

40. Siegel 2006:202; see also de Certeau 1970 and 1980 on *l'étrange*.

41. This is, as said, where my analysis parts with a Freudian approach. It might be interesting to pursue Freud's therapeutic answer to these shifts from *heimlich* to *unheimlich* in terms of dealing with repression. But then the aim seems to be again to achieve a radical breakthrough—demystifying these sources of anxiety by breaking through to the actual sources of aggression. I would suppose that *working with* these anxieties, rather than trying to demystify them, might offer a more feasible solution to the conundrum of witchcraft, intimacy, and trust; this is why the Brazilian example is so intriguing.

42. Cf. the examples quoted above (chap. 3) from Warnier's seminal book *L'esprit d'entreprise au Cameroun* (1993; The spirit of enterprise in Cameroun) of how Bamileke entrepreneurs—famous in the country for their economic success—manage to satisfy kinship norms without endangering the success of their business (preference for non-kin in key positions where trust is crucial; creation of a side business that can help to satisfy relatives who ask for jobs without affecting the core business; and so on. Cf. also Jean and John Comaroff's analysis (2004) of how a "very dangerous affair" in South Africa's Northwest Province could be handled by a court to the satisfaction of all parties involved by treating it as a breach of contract rather than in terms of occult aggression. The magistrate's pragmatic approach could defuse the witchcraft connotations of the case.

43. I wonder whether it is possible to construe parallels here with Sharika Thirana-gama's book (2011—also mentioned in the prologue above), notably with her visionary conclusion that even the horrors of the civil war in Sri Lanka (the terror the Tamil Tigers unleashed against their own followers and the havoc created by the government's army) were not only destructive in their effects; despite all disruption, they also produced new forms of self-formation and sociality (shifts in family relations and in inequalities between castes—see Thiranagama 2011:74–75). Is such a challenging conclusion possible for a book on the crystallization of new witchcraft traumas in present-day Africa? Pentecostalism certainly brings a new vision of witchcraft by equating it with the devil. But does this produce new forms of sociality? Precisely the fact that the devil/witchcraft is still located inside the family seems to curb a new project of society (cf. Marshall 2009 on the limits of Pentecostalism in Nigeria and its inability to realize a new project of society).

References

Abéga, S. C., and C. Abé. 2005. Approches anthropologiques de la sorcellerie. In *Justice et sorcellerie*, edited by E. deRosny, 33–47. Paris: Karthala; Yaoundé, Cameroon: Presses de l'Université Catholique de l'Afrique Centrale.

Akoko, Robert Mbe. 2007. *"Ask and you shall be given": Pentecostalism and the Economic Crisis in Cameroon*. Leiden: African Studies Centre.

Alpes, M. J. 2011. Bushfalling: How Young Cameroonians Dare to Migrate. PhD diss., University of Amsterdam.

Andrikopoulos, Apostolos. 2011. Trans-Atlantic Slavery and Contemporary Human Trafficking: The Role of the Market, the State and Kinship in Regulating Forced Labour. Paper. Harvard Summer School Accra / University of Amsterdam.

Appadurai, A. 1996. *Modernity at Large: Cultural Dimensions of Globalization*. Minneapolis: University of Minnesota Press.

Ashforth, A. 2000. *Madumo, a Man Bewitched*. Chicago: University of Chicago Press.

———. 2005. *Witchcraft, Violence, and Democracy in South Africa*. Chicago: University of Chicago Press.

Aterianus-Owanga, Alice. 2012. "L'émergence n'aime pas les femmes!" Hétérosexisme, rumeurs et imaginaires du pouvoir dans le rap gabonais. *Politique africaine* 126:49–68.

Auslander, M. 1993. "Open the wombs!" The Symbolic Politics of Modern Ngoni Witchfinding. In *Modernity and Its Malcontents: Ritual and Power in Postcolonial Africa*, edited by J. and J. Comaroff, 167–93. Chicago: University of Chicago Press.

Austen, R. A. 1993. "The Moral Economy of Witchcraft: An Essay in Comparative History." In *Modernity and Its Malcontents: Ritual and Power in Postcolonial Africa*, edited by J. and J. Comaroff, 89–110. Chicago: University of Chicago Press.

Awondo, Patrick. 2012. Homosexualité, sida et constructions politiques: Ethnographie des trajectoires entre le Cameroun et la France. PhD diss., École des Hautes Études and Sciences Sociales, Paris.

Awondo, Patrick, Peter Geschiere, and Graeme Reid. 2012. Homophobic Africa? Toward a More Nuanced View. *African Studies Review* 55, no. 3: 145–68.

Banégas, Richard. 2006. Côte d'Ivoire: Patriotism, Ethnonationalism and Other African Modes of Self-writing. *African Affairs* 105, no. 421: 535–52.

Bastian, Misty. 1993. "Bloodhounds who have no friends": Witchcraft and Locality in the Nigerian Popular Press. In *Modernity and Its Malcontents: Ritual and Power in Postcolonial Africa*, edited by J. and J. Comaroff, 129–67. Chicago: University of Chicago Press.

Bastide, R. 1960. *Les religions afro-brésiliennes: Contribution à une sociologie des interpénétrations de civilisations*. Paris: Presses universitaires de la France.

Bayart, J.-F. 1989. *L'État en Afrique: La politique du ventre*. Paris: Fayard. Here quoted from the English translation: 1993. *The State in Africa: The Politics of the Belly*. London: Longman.

———. 1996. *L'illusion identitaire*. Paris: Fayard. English translation: 2002. *The Illusion of Cultural Identity*. London: Hurst.

———. 2000. Africa in the World: A History of Extraversion. *African Affairs* 99:217–67.

———. 2004. *Le gouvernement du monde: Une critique politique de la globalisation*. Paris: Fayard. English translation: 2007. *Global Subjects: A Political Critique of Globalization*. Cambridge: Polity.

———. 2008. Culture et développement: Les luttes sociales font-elles la différence? *L'Economie Politique*, April 2008, 29–56.

———. 2010a. *Les études postcoloniales: Un carnaval académique*. Paris: Karthala.

———. 2010b. *L'Islam républicain: Ankara, Téheran, Dakar*. Paris: Albin Michel.

Bayart, J.-F., A. Mbembe, and C. Toulabor. 1992. *Le politique par le bas en Afrique noire: Contributions à une problématique de la démocratie*. Paris: Karthala.

Behrend, H. 1999. *Alice Lakwena and the Holy Spirit: War in Northern Uganda, 1985–97*. Oxford: Currey.

Behringer, Wolfgang. 2004. *Witches and Witch-Hunts: A Global History*. Cambridge: Polity.

Beidelman, Thomas O. 1970. Towards More Open Theoretical Interpretations. In *Witchcraft Confessions and Accusations*, edited by M. Douglas, 351–57. London: Tavistock.

Bellagamba, A. 2008. *L'Africa e la stregoneria: Saggio di antropologia storica*. Roma: Laterza & Figli.

Beneduce, R. 2010. Soigner l'incertitude au Cameroun: Le théâtre épique du nganga face aux économies du miracle. In *Le pluralisme médical en Afrique*, edited by L. Ladovic, 101–33. Yaoundé: Presses de l'Université Catholique de l'Afrique Centrale; Paris: Karthala.

———. 2012. Un imaginaire qui tue: Réflexions sur sorcellerie, violence et pouvoir (Cameroun et Mali). In *Sorcellerie et violence en Afrique*, edited by B. Martinelli and J.Bouju, 309–28. Paris: Karthala.

Berlant, Lauren. 1993. Intimacy. *Critical Inquiry* 24, no. 2: 281–88.

Bernault, Florence. 2006. Body, Power and Sacrifice in Equatorial Africa. *Journal of African History* 47:207–39.

———. 2009. De la modernité comme impuissance: Fétichisme et crise du politique en Afrique équatoriale et ailleurs. *Cahiers d'Etudes Africaines* 49, no. 3: 747–74.

Bernault, Florence, and Joseph Tonda. 2000. Dynamiques de l'invisible en Afrique. *Politique Africaine* 79:5–17, special issue, *Pouvoirs sorciers*, edited by Bernault and Tonda.

Berry, Sarah. 1985. *Fathers Work for Their Sons: Accumulation, Mobility and Class Formation in an Extended Yoruba Community*. Berkeley: University of California Press.

Bersani, Leo, and Adam Philips. 2008. *Intimacies*. Chicago: University of Chicago Press.

Bertrand, Romain. 2002. *Indonésie: La démocratie invisible—Violence, magie et politique à Java*. Paris: Karthala.

Beti, Mongo. 1956. *Le pauvre Christ de Bomba*. Paris: Robert Laffont.

Besnier, Niko. 2009. *Gossip and the Everyday Production of Politics*. Honolulu: University of Hawai Press.

Birman, Patricia. 2011. Sorcery, Territories, and Marginal Resistances in Rio de Janeiro. In *Sorcery in the Black Atlantic*, edited by L. Nicolau Parés and R. Sansi, 209–33. Chicago: University of Chicago Press.

Biya, P. 1986. *Pour le libéralisme communautaire*. Paris: Pierre-Marcel Favre.

Bockie, S. 1993. *Death and the Invisible Powers: The World of Kongo Belief*. Bloomington: Indiana University Press.

Bond, G. C., and D. M. Ciekawy. 2001. Introduction: Contested Domains in the Dialogues of "Witchcraft." In *Witchcraft Dialogues: Anthropological and Philosophical Exchanges*, edited by Bond and Ciekawy, 1–39. Athens: Ohio University Press.

Bonhomme, J. 2009. *Les voleurs de sexe: Anthropologie d'une rumeur africaine*. Paris: Seuil.

———. 2012. D'une violence l'autre: Sorcellerie, blindage et lynchage au Gabon. In *Sorcellerie et violence en Afrique*, edited by B.Martinelli and J.Bouju, 207–32. Paris: Karthala.

Boyer, Paul, and Stephen Nissenbuam. 1974. *Salem Possessed: The Social Origins of Witchcraft*. Cambridge, MA: Harvard University Press.

Brazeal, Brian. 2004. *The Cross and the Crossroads*. Documentary film. Lala and Bala Productions in association with Wunderlicious Entertainment.

———. 2007. Blood, Money and Fame: Nagô Magic in the Bahian Backlands. PhD diss., University of Chicago, Department of Anthropology.

Briggs, Robin. 1996. *Witches and Neighbours: The Social and Cultural Context of European Witchcraft*. London: HarperCollins.

Broch-Due, Vigdis, and Margit Ystaned. 2012. Introductory paper for workshop "The Entangled Tensions of Intimacy, Trust and the Social," Bergen (Norway), May 18–20.

Broqua, Christophe. 2012. L'émergence des minorités sexuelles dans l'espace public en Afrique. *Politique Africaine* 126:5–25.

Brown, Karen McCarthy. 1991. *Mama Lola, a Vodou Priestess in Brooklyn*. Berkeley: University of California Press.

Bubandt, Nils. 2013. "The Nautilus Shell: Witchcraft and Aporia in Eastern Indonesia." Unpublished manuscript.

Burnham, Philip, and Thomas Christensen. 1983. Karnu's Message and the "War of the Hoe Handle": Interpreting a Central African Religious Movement. *Africa* 53, no. 4: 3–22.

Butler, K. D. 2001. Africa in the Reinvention of Nineteenth-Century Afro-Bahian Identity. In *Rethinking the African Diaspora: The Making of a Black Atlantic World in the Bight of Benin and Brazil*, edited by K. Mann and E. G. Bay, 135–55. London: Frank Cass.

Buur, Lars, and Helene M. Kyed, eds. 2007. *State Recognition and Democratization in Sub-Saharan Africa: A New Dawn for Traditional Authorities?* New York: Palgrave Macmillan.

Buyandelger, Manduhai. 2013. *Tragic Spirits: Shamanism, Socialism, and the Neoliberal State in Mongolia*. Chicago: University of Chicago Press.

Campbell, C. C., and L. H. Connor. 2000. Sorcery, Modernity and Social Transformation in Banyuwangi, East Java. *Review of Indonesian and Malay Affairs* 34, no. 2: 61–99.

Castillo, Lisa Earl, and Luis Nicolau Parés. 2010. Marcelina da Silva: A Nineteenth-Century *Candomblé* Priestess in Bahia. *Slavery and Abolition* 1 (March): 1–27.

Ceriana Mayneri, Andrea. 2010. La rhétorique de la dépossession, ou L'imaginaire de la sorcellerie chez les Banda de la République centrafricaine. PhD thesis, University of Aix-Marseille I.

Ciekawy, D. M. 1998. Witchcraft and Statecraft: Five Technologies of Power in Colonial and Postcolonial Coastal Kenya. *African Studies Review* 41, no. 3: 119–41.

———. 2001. *Utsai* as Ethical Discourse: A Critique of Power from Mi'jikenda in Coastal Kenya. In *Witchcraft Dialogues: Anthropological and Philosophical Exchanges*, edited by G. C. Bond and D. M. Ciekawy, 158–90. Athens: Ohio University Press.

Ciekawy, D. M., and Peter Geschiere. 1999. Introduction to *African Studies Review* 41, no. 3: 11–14, special issue, *Containing Witchcraft*, edited by Ciekawy and Geschiere.

Cinnamon, John. 2012. Power and Politics in Gabon. *Africa* 82, no. 2: 187–212.

Clifford, J. 1988. *The Predicament of Culture*. Cambridge, MA: Harvard University Press.

Cohn, Norman. 1975. *Europe's Inner Demons: An Enquiry Inspired by the Great Witch-Hunt*. London: Chatto-Heinemann.

Comaroff, Jean. 1997. Consuming Passions: Child Abuse, Fetishism and the "New World Order." *Culture* 1997:7–19.

Comaroff, Jean, and John Comaroff, eds. 1993. *Modernity and Its Malcontents*. Chicago: University of Chicago Press.

———. 1999. Alien-Nation: Zombies, Immigrants and Millennial Capitalism. *Bulletin du Codesria* 1999, nos. 3/4: 17–29.

———. 2000. Millennial Capitalism: First Thoughts on a Second Coming. *Public Culture* 12:291–344, special issue, *Millennial Capitalism and the Culture of Neoliberalism*, edited by Comaroff and Comaroff.

———. 2004. Criminal Justice, Cultural Justice: The Limits of Liberalism and the Pragmatics of Difference in the New South Africa. *American Ethnologist* 31, no. 2: 188–204.

Copet-Rougier, E. 1986. "Le mal court": Visible and Invisible Violence in an Acephalous Society Mkako of Cameroon. In *The Anthropology of Violence*, edited by D. Riches, 50–69. Oxford: Blackwell.

Corten, André. 2001. *Misère, religion et politique en Haïti*. Paris: Karthala.

Crais, C. 2002. *The Politics of Evil: Magic, State Power, and the Political Imagination in South Africa*. Cambridge: Cambridge University Press.

Crick, M. 1979. Anthropologists' Witchcraft: Symbolically Defined or Analytically Undone? *Journal of the Anthropological Society of Oxford* 10:139–46.

Dantas, Beatriz Góis. [1988] 2009. *Nagô Grandma and White Papa: Candomblé and the Creation of Afro-Brazilian Identity*. Chapel Hill: University of North Carolina Press.

Das, Veena. 1998. Specificities: Official Narratives, Rumour and the Social Production of Hate. *Social Identities: Journal for the Study of Race, Nation and Culture* 4, no. 1: 109–30.

Das, Veena, and Deborah Poole. 2004. The State and Its Margins: Comparative Ethnographies. In *Anthropology in the Margins of the State*, edited by Das and Poole, 3–35. Santa Fe, NM: School of American Research Press.

Davies, Owen. 1999. *Witchcraft, Magic and Culture, 1736–1951*. Manchester: Manchester University Press.

De Blécourt, Willem. 1990. *Termen van Toverij: De Veranderende Betekenis van Toverij in Noordoost Nederland tussen de 16de en 20ste Eeuw*. Nijmegen, Netherlands: Socialistiese Uitgeverij Nijmegen.

De Blécourt, Willem, and Owen Davies, eds. 2004. *Witchcraft Continued: Popular Magic in Modern Europe*. Manchester: Manchester University Press.

De Boeck, Filip. 2004. Être *shege* à Kinshasa: Les enfants, la rue et le monde occult. In *Ordre et désordre à Kinshasa: Reponses populaires à la faillite de l'Etat*, edited by T. Trefon, 155–74. Paris: L'Harmattan.

———. 2005. Children, Gift and Witchcraft in the Democratic Republic of Congo. In *Makers and Breakers, Children and Youth in Postcolonial Africa*, edited by F. de Boeck and A. Honwana, 188–215. Oxford: Currey.

———. 2006, Youth, Death and the Urban Imagination: A Case from Kinshasa. *Bulletin des Séances de l'Académie Royale des Sciences d'Outre-mer* 52, no. 2: 113–25.

———. 2009. At Risk, as Risk: Abandonment and Care in a World of Spiritual Insecurity. In *The Devil's Children: From Spirit Possession to Witchcraft; New Allegations That Affect Children*, edited by J. LaFontaine, 129–50. Ashgate, UK: Farnham/Burlington.

———. 2010. *Cemetery State*. Brussels: Filmnatie.

De Boeck, Filip, and Marie-Françoise Plissart. 2004. *Kinshasa: Tales of the Invisible City*. Ghent, Belgium: Ludion.

De Castro, Eduardo Viveiros: see under Viveiros de Castro.

De Certeau, Michel. 1970. *La possession de Loudun*. Paris: Julliard.

———. 1980. *La culture au pluriel*. Paris: Christian Bourgeois.

Deleuze, G. 1990. *Pourparlers 1972–1990*. Paris: Éditions de Minuit.

Delius, Peter.1996. *A Lion amongst the Cattle: Reconstruction and Resistance in the Northern Transvaal*. Johannesburg: Raven.

De Mello e Souza, *see under* Souza.

De Rosny, E. 1981. *Les yeux de ma chèvre: Sur les pas des maîtres de la nuit en pays douala*. Paris: Plon. English translation: 2004. *Healers in the Night*. Eugene, OR: Wipf and Stock.

———. 1992. *L'Afrique des guérisons*. Paris: Karthala.

———. 2004. Étude panoramique des nouveaux mouvements religieux et philosophiques à Douala (Cameroun). In *L'effervescence religieuse: La diversité locale des implan-*

tations religieuses chrétiennes au Cameroun et au Kenya, edited by G. Séraphin, 89–171. Paris: Karthala.

———, ed. 2005. *Justice et sorcellerie*. Yaoundé, Cameroon: Presses de l'Université Catholique de l'Afrique Centrale; Paris: Karthala.

Devisch, René, and Claude Brodeux. 1999. *The Law of the Lifegivers: The Domestication of Desire*. Amsterdam: Harwood.

De Witte, Marleen. 2008. Spirit Media: Charismatics, Traditionalists, and Mediation Practices in Ghana. PhD diss., University of Amsterdam.

Di Simplicio, Oscar. 2002. Witchcraft and Infanticide. *Acta Historiae* 10:411–42.

———. 2009. Giandomenico Fei, the Only Male Witch: A Tuscan or an Italian Anomaly? In *Witchcraft and Masculinity in Early Modern Europe*, edited by Alison Rowlands, 121–48. Houndsmill, UK: Palgrave Macmillan.

Dongmo, J.-L. 1991. *Le dynamisme bamiléké*. Yaoundé, Cameroon: CEPER.

Douglas, Mary. 1963. Techniques of Sorcery Control in Central Africa. In *Witchcraft and Sorcery in East Africa*, edited by John Middleton and E. H. Winter, 123–43. London: Routledge.

———. 1966. *Purity and Danger: An Analysis of Concepts of Pollution and Taboo*. London: Routledge and Kegan Paul.

———. 1970. Introduction to *Witchcraft Confessions and Accusations*, edited by Douglas, xiii–xxxviii. London: Tavistock.

Ellis, S., and G. Ter Haar. 2004. *Words of Power: Religious Thought and Political Practice in Africa*. London: Hurst.

———. 2009. The Occult Does Not Exist: A Response to Terence Ranger. *Africa* 79, no. 3: 399–413.

Englund, Harri. 2002. The Village in the City, the City in the Village: Migrants in Lilongwe. *Journal of Southern African Studies* 28:137–54.

———. 2003. Christian Independency and Global Membership: Pentecostal Extraversions in Malawi. *Journal of Religion in Africa* 33, no. 1: 83–111.

———. 2007a. Pentecostalism beyond Belief: Trust and Democracy in a Malawian Township. *Africa* 77, no. 4: 477–99.

———. 2007b. Witchcraft and the Limits of Mass Mediation in Malawi. *Journal of the Royal Anthropological Institute* 13:295–311.

Englund, Harri, and J. Leach. 2000. Ethnography and the Meta-narratives of Modernity. *Current Anthropology* 41, no. 2: 225–48.

Evans-Pritchard, E. E. 1937. *Witchcraft, Oracles and Magic among the Azande*. Oxford: Clarendon.

Fancello, Sandra. 2011. Pasteurs et sorciers en procès: L'affaire Béhanzin (Côte d'Ivoire). *Politique Africaine* 122:121–45.

———. 2012. D'un guérisseur à l'autre: Diagnostic, délivrance et exorcisme à Bangui. In *Sorcellerie et violence en Afrique*, edited by B. Martinelli and J. Bouju, 55–85. Paris: Karthala.

Favret-Saada, J. 1977. *Les mots, la mort, les sorts*. Paris: Gallimard. English translation: 1980. *Deadly Words: Witchcraft in the Bocage*. Cambridge: Cambridge University Press.

———. 2009. *Désorceler*. Paris: Seuil, Éditions de l'Olivier.

Favret-Saada, J., and Josée Contreras. 1981. *Corps pour corps: Enquêtes sur la sorcellerie dans le Bocage*. Paris: Gallimard.

Ferme, Mariane. 2001. *The Underneath of Things: Violence, History and the Everyday in Sierra Leone*. Berkeley: University of California Press.

Fisiy, Cyprian, and Peter Geschiere. 1990. Judges and Witches, or How Is the State to Deal with Witchcraft? Examples from Southeastern Cameroon. *Cahiers d'Études Africaines* 118:135–56.

———. 1991. Sorcery, Witchcraft and Accumulation: Regional Variations in South and West Cameroun. *Critique of Anthropology* 11, no. 3: 251–78.

———. 1996. Witchcraft, Violence and Identity: Different Trajectories in Postcolonial Cameroon. In *Postcolonial Identities in Africa*, edited by Richard Werbner and Terence O. Ranger, 193–222. London: Zed Books.

———. 2001. Witchcraft, Development and Paranoia in Cameroon: Interactions between Popular, Academic and State Discourse. In *Magical Interpretations, Material Realities: Modernity, Witchcraft and the Occult in Postcolonial Africa*, edited by H. Moore and T. Sanders, 226–47. London: Routledge.

Fondong, J. N. 2008. The American Wanda: Bushfaller Dialectic. Available at http://www.*groups.yahoo.com/group/mkyut_theatre/message/1072* - United States.

Fontein, Joost. 2011. Graves, Ruins and Belonging: Towards an Anthropology of Proximity. *Journal of the Royal Anthropological Institute* 17, no. 4: 706–27.

Forge, A. 1970. Prestige, Influence and Sorcery: A New Guinea Example. In *Witchcraft Confessions and Accusations*, edited by M. Douglas, 257–78. London: Tavistock.

Fortes, M. 1970. *Kinship and the Social Order: The Legacy of Henry Lewis Morgan*. London: Routledge.

Foucault, Michel. 1984. What Is Enlightenment? In *The Foucault Reader*, edited by P. Rabinow. New York: Pantheon.

Freud, Sigmund. [1919] 2003. Das Unheimliche. *Imago* 5, nos. 5–6. English translation: 2003. The Uncanny. In *The Uncanny*, edited by D. McClintock and H. Haughton, 121–61. London: Penguin Classics.

Fukuyama, F. 1995. *Trust: The Social Virtues and the Creation of Prosperity*. New York: Free Press.

Gable, Eric. 2002. Beyond Belief? Play, Scepticism, and Religion in a West African Village. *Social Anthropology* 10, no. 1: 41–56.

Gambetta, Diego, ed. 1988. *Trust: Making and Breaking Cooperative Relations*. Oxford: Blackwell.

Gemmeke, Amber B. 2008. *Marabout Women in Dakar: Creating Trust in a Rural Urban Space*. Zurich: LIT Verlag.

Geschiere, Peter. 1982. *Village Communities and the State: Changing Relations among the Maka of Southeastern Cameroon since the Colonial Conquest*. London: Kegan Paul International.

———. 1984. La paysannerie africaine est-elle captive? Sur la thèse de Goran Hyden et pour une réponse nuancée. *Politique Africaine* 14: 13–34.

———. 1993. Chiefs and Colonial Rule in Cameroon: Inventing Chieftaincy, French and British Style. *Africa* 63, no. 2: 151–76.

———. 1997. *The Modernity of Witchcraft: Politics and the Occult in Postcolonial Africa*. Charlottesville: University of Virginia Press. Shorter version in French: 1995. *Sorcellerie et politique en Afrique: La viande des Autres*. Paris: Karthala.

———. 1998. Sorcellerie et modernité: Les enjeux des nouveaux procès de sorcellerie au Cameroun. *Annales* 53, no. 6: 1251–81.

———. 2000. Sorcellerie et modernité: Retour sur une étrange complicité. *Politique Africaine* 79:17–33.

———. 2005. Funerals and Belonging: Different Patterns in South Cameroon. *African Studies Review* 48, no. 2:45–65.

———. 2006. Witchcraft and the Limits of the Law: Cameroon and South Africa. In *Law and Disorder in the Postcolony*, edited by J. Comaroff and J. Comaroff, 219–47. Chicago: University of Chicago Press.

———. 2009a. Homosexuality in Africa: Identity and Persecution. In *Urgency Required: Gay and Lesbian Rights Are Human Rights*, edited by Ireen Dubel and André Hielkema, 126–32. The Hague: Hivos.

———. 2009b. *Perils of Belonging: Autochthony, Citizenship, and Exclusion in Africa and Europe*. Chicago: University of Chicago Press.

———. 2010. The Self-Reflexive Turn in Ethnography: From Dialogue to Narcissism? *Etnofoor* 22, no. 1: 137–47.

———. 2011. Witchcraft and Modernity: Perspectives from Africa and Beyond. In *Sorcery in the Black Atlantic*, edited by L. Nicolau Parés and R. Sansi, 233–59. Chicago: University of Chicago Press.

———. Forthcoming. African Urbanites and the Funeral in the Villages: Issues of Belonging and Citizenship. In *The Art of Citizenship in African Cities*, edited by Mamadou Diouf and Rosalind C. Fredericks. New York: Palgrave Macmillan.

Geschiere, Peter, B. Meyer, and P. Pels, eds. 2009. *Readings in Modernity in Africa*. Oxford: Currey; Bloomington: Indiana University Press.

Geschiere, Peter, and Francis Nyamnjoh. 2000. Capitalism and Autochthony: The Seesaw of Mobility and Belonging. *Public Culture* 12, no. 2: 423–53, special issue, *Millennial Capitalism and the Culture of Neoliberalism*, edited by J. Comaroff and J. Comaroff.

Giddens, Anthony. 1992. *The Transformation of Intimacy: Sexuality, Love and Eroticism in Modern Societies*. Stanford, CA: Stanford University Press.

Ginzburg, C. 1990. *Ecstasies: Deciphering the Witches' Sabbath*. London: Hutchinson Radius.

Gluckman, Max. 1955. *Custom and Conflict in Africa*. Oxford: Blackwell.

Goldstone, Brian, Juan Obarrio, and Charles Piot, eds. Forthcoming. *African Futures*. Chicago: University of Chicago Press.

Goheen, M. 1996. *Men Own the Fields, Women Own the Crops: Gender and Power in the Cameroon Highlands*. Madison: University of Wisconsin Press.

Goody, Jack. 1973. Bridewealth and Dowry in Africa and Europe. In *Bridewealth and Dowry*, edited by J. Goody and S. J. Tambiah, 1–59. Cambridge: Cambridge University Press.

———. 1976. *Production and Reproduction: A Study of the Domestic Domain*. Cambridge: Cambridge University Press.

———. 2010. *The Eurasian Miracle*. Cambridge: Polity.

Gregory, C. A. 1994. Exchange and Reciprocity. In *Companion Encyclopedia of Anthropology: Humanity, Culture and Social Life*, edited by T. Ingold, 911–40. London: Routledge.

Guyer, Jane I. 1984. *Family and Farm in Southern Cameroun*. Boston: Boston University, African Studies Center.

———. 1993. Wealth in People and Self-Realization in Equatorial Africa. *Man*, n.s., 28, no. 2: 243–65.

———. 2004. *Marginal Gains: Monetary Transactions in Atlantic Africa*. Chicago: University of Chicago Press.

Hayes, J. 1990. *Smart Love*. London: Arrow.

Henry, A. 1991. Vers un modèle de management africain. *Cahiers d'Études Africaines* 31, no. 124: 447–73.

Henry, A., G. H. Tchente, and Ph. Guillerme-Dieumegard. 1991. *Tontines et banques au Cameroun: Les principes de la Société des amis*. Paris: Karthala.

Henry, C., and E. K. Tall. 2008. La sorcellerie envers et contre tous, *Cahiers d'Études Africaines* 189/90:11–35, special issue, *Territoires sorciers*, edited by Henry and Tall.

Herriman, N. 2007. "Sorcerer" Killings in Banyuwangi: A Re-examination of State Responsibility for Violence. *Asian Studies Review* 31, no. 1: 61–78.

———. 2009. A Din of Whispers: The In-Group Manifestation of Sorcery in Rural Banyuwangi. *Anthropological Forum* 19, no. 2: 119–41.

Herzfeld, M. 1997. *Cultural Intimacy: Social Poetics in the Nation-State*. London: Routledge.

———. 2012. Afterword: Reciprocating the Hospitality of These Pages. *Journal of the Royal Anthropological Institute* n.s. 2012:210–17.

Hibou, Béatrice, ed. 1999. *La privatisation des Etats*. Paris: Karthala. English translation: 2004. *Privatising the State*. London: Hurst.

———. 2011. *Anatomie politique de la domination*. Paris: La Découverte.

Hund, J. 2000. Witchcraft and Accusations of Witchcraft in South Africa: Ontological Denial and the Suppression of African Justice. *Comparative and International Law Journal of Southern Africa* 33:369–89.

Hutton, Ronald. 2004. Anthropological and Historical Approaches to Witchcraft: Potential for a New Collaboration? *Historical Journal* 47, no. 2: 413–34.

Hyden, G. 1980. *Beyond Ujamaa in Tanzania: Underdevelopment and an Uncaptured Peasantry*. London: Heinemann.

Ingold, Tim. 1986. *The Appropriation of Nature: Essays on Human Ecology and Social Relations*. Manchester: Manchester University Press.

Jackson, Michael. 2009. Ethnographic Verisimilitude. *Etnofoor* 21, no. 1: 9–21, special issue, *Writing Culture*.

Jankowiak, W. R., ed. 2008. *Intimacies: Love + Sex across Cultures*. New York: Columbia University Press.

Janson, Marloes. i.p. *Young, Modern and Muslim: The Tabligh Jama'at in the Gambia*. Cambridge: Cambridge University Press.

Jewsiewicki, B. 1983. Raison d'état ou raison du capital: L'accumulation primitive au Congo belge. *African Economic History* 12:157–82.

————. 1993. *Naître et mourir au Zaïre: Un demi-siècle d'histoire au quotidien.* Paris: Karthala.

Kapferer, B. 1997. *The Feast of the Sorcerer: Practices of Consciousness and Power.* Chicago: University of Chicago Press.

————. 2002. Introduction: Outside All Reason—Magic, Sorcery and Epistemology in Anthropology. In *Beyond Rationalism,* edited by Kapferer, 1–31. Oxford: Berghahn Books.

Karsenty, A. 1999. Vers la fin de l' Etat forestier? Appropriation des espaces et partage de la rente forestière au Cameroun. *Politique Africaine* 75:147–61.

Laburthe-Tolra, Philippe. 1977. *Minlaaba, histoire et société traditionnelle chez les Běti du Sud Cameroun.* Paris: Champion. Also published as: 1981. *Les seigneurs de la forêt.* Paris: Publications de la Sorbonne; and 1988. *Initiations et sociétés secrètes au Cameroun.* Paris: Karthala.

LaFontaine, Joan. 1998. *Speak of the Devil: Tales of Satanic Abuse in Contemporary England.* Cambridge: Cambridge University Press.

Lallemand, S. 1988. *La mangeuse d'âmes: Sorcellerie et famille en Afrique.* Paris: L'Harmattan.

Landes, Ruth. 1947. *The City of Women.* New York: Macmillan.

Larner, Christina. 1981. *Enemies of God: The Witch-Hunt in Scotland.* Baltimore: Johns Hopkins University Press.

————. 1984. *Witchcraft and Religion: The Politics of Popular Belief.* Oxford: Blackwell.

Lattas, Andrew. 2010. *Dreams, Madness, and Fairy Tales in New Britain.* Durham, NC: Carolina Academic Press.

Le Roy, Ladurie. 1983. *La sorcière de Jasmin.* Paris: Seuil.

Levack, Brian P. 1996–98. State-Building and Witch-Hunting in Early Modern Europe. In *Witchcraft in Early Modern Europe: Studies in Structure and Belief,* edited by J. Barry, M. Hester, and G. Roberts, 96–119. Cambridge: Cambridge University Press.

Lévi-Strauss, Claude. [1949] 1958. Le sorcier et sa magie. *Les Temps Modernes* 4, no. 41: 3–24. Here quoted from 1958. *Anthropologie structurale,* 183–203. Paris: Plon.

————. 1958. Preface to M. Bouteiller, *Sorciers et jeteurs de sorts.* Paris: Plon.

————. [1950] 1987. *Introduction to the Work of Marcel Mauss.* London: Routledge and Kegan Paul. Original: 1950. *Introduction à l'oeuvre de Marcel Mauss.* Paris: Presses Universitaires de France.

Lindenbaum, Shirley. 1981. Images of the Sorcerer in Papua New Guinea. *Social Analysis* 8:119–28, special issue, *Sorcery and Social Change in Melanesia,* edited by M. Zelenietz and S. Lindenbaum.

Lovell, Nadia. 2002. *Cord of Blood: Possession and the Making of Voodoo.* London: Pluto.

Luongo, Katherine, 2011. *Witchcraft and Colonial Rule in Kenya, 1900–1955.* Cambridge: Cambridge University Press.

Macfarlane, Alan. 1978. *The Origins of English Individualism.* Oxford: Blackwell.

Maggie, Yvonne. 1992. *Medo de feitiço: Relações entre magia e poder no Brasil.* Rio de Janeiro: Arquivo Nacional.

————. 2011. The Logic of Sorcery and Democracy in Contemporary Brazil. In *Sorcery in the Black Atlantic,* edited by L. Nicolau Parés and R. Sansi, 145–65. Chicago: University of Chicago Press.

Malaquais, D. 2001a. Anatomie d'un arnaque: Feymen et feymania au Cameroun. *Les Études du CERI* 77.

———. 2001b. Arts de feyre au Cameroun. *Politique Africaine* 82:101–18.

Malinowski, B. 1935. *Coral Gardens and Their Magic: A Study of the Methods of Tilling the Soil and of Agricultural Rites in the Trobriand Islands*. London: Allen and Unwin.

Mandel, J.-J. 2008. Les rétrécisseurs de sexe: Chronique d'une rumeur sorcière. *Cahiers d'Etudes Africaines* 189/90:185–208, special issue, *Territoires sorciers*, edited by C. Henry and E. K. Tall.

Mann, K., and E. G. Bay, eds. 2001. *Rethinking the African Diaspora: The Making of a Black Atlantic World in the Bight of Benin and Brazil*. London: Frank Cass.

Manning, P. 1990. The Slave Trade: The Formal Demography of a Global System. *Social Science History* 14, no. 2: 255–79.

Marrero-Guillamón, I. i.p. Monadology and Ethnography: Gabriel Tarde and the Possibility of Monadic Ethnography. *Ethnography*.

Mars, Kettley. 2010. *Saisons sauvages*. Paris: Éditions Mercure.

Marshall, R. 2006. The War of "Who Is Who?" Autochthony, Nationalism and Citizenship in the Ivorian Crisis. *African Studies Review* 49, no. 2: 9–43.

———. 2009. *Political Spiritualities: The Pentecostal Revolution in Nigeria*. Chicago: University of Chicago Press.

Martinelli, Bruno, and Jacky Bouju, eds. 2012. *Sorcellerie et violence en Afrique*. Paris: Karthala.

Marwick, M. 1964. Witchcraft as a Social Change Gauge. *Australian Journal of Science* 26:263–68. Here quoted from reprint: 1970. *Witchcraft and Sorcery: Selected Readings*, edited by Marwick, 280–95. Harmondsworth, UK: Penguin.

———. 1965. *Sorcery in Its Social Setting*. Manchester: Manchester University Press.

Mary, André. 2009. *Visionnaires et prophètes de l'Afrique contemporaine: Tradition initiatique, culture de la transe et charisme de délivrance*. Paris: Karthala.

Masquelier, Adeline. 2008. Witchcraft, Blood-Sucking Spirits, and the Demonization of Islam in Dogondoutchi. *Cahiers d'Études Africaines* 189/90:131–60, special issue, *Territoires sorciers*, edited by C. Henry and E. K. Tall.

———. 2009. *Women and Islamic Revival in a West African Town*. Bloomington: Indiana University Press.

Matory, J. Lorand. 1994. *Sex and the Empire That Is No More: Gender and Politics of Metaphor in Oyo Yoruba Religion*. Minneapolis: University of Minnesota Press.

———. 2005. *Black Atlantic Religion: Tradition, Transnationalism, and Matriarchy in the Afro-Brazilian Candomblé*. Princeton, NJ: Princeton University Press.

Mauriac, F. 1932. *Le noeud de vipères*. Paris: Grasset.

Mauss, Marcel. [1923–24] 1950. "Essai sur le don: Forme et raison de l'échange dans les sociétés archaiques." *L'année sociologique*, ser. 2,1. Here quoted from Mauss, M. 1950. *Sociologie et antropologie*, 145–285. Paris: Presses Universitaires Françaises. (English translation: 1990. *The Gift*. Translated by W. D. Halls. London: Routledge.)

Mayer, P. 1954/1970. "Witches." In *Witchcraft and Sorcery*, edited by M. Marwick, 45–64. Harmondsworth, UK: Penguin.

Mayneri, Andrea: see under Ceriana Mayneri, Andrea.

Mbembe, Achille. 2006. Le potentat sexuel: À propos de la fellation, de la sodomie et autres privautés postcoloniales. *Le Messager*, February 17.

———. 2010a. Pour l'abolition des frontières héritées de la colonisation: Entretien avec Achille Mbembe. *Buala: Culture Contemporaine Africaine*, October 16, 2010.

———. 2010b. *Sortir de la grande nuit: Essai sur l'Afrique décolonisée.* Paris: La Découverte.

Mbonji, Edjenguèlè. 2000. *Les cultures-vérité, Le soi et l'autre, Ethnologie d'une relation d'exclusion.* Yaoundé, Cameroon: Éditions Étoile.

Mead, Margaret. 1972. *Blackberry Winter: My Earlier Years.* New York: Pocket Books.

Meyer, Birgit. 1992. If You Are a Devil You Are a Witch and If You Are a Witch You Are a Devil: The Integration of "Pagan" Ideas Into the Conceptual Universe of Ewe Christians in Southeastern Ghana. *Journal of Religion in Africa* 22, no. 2: 98–132.

———. 1998a. "Make a Complete Break with the Past": Memory and Postcolonial Modernity in Ghanaian Pentecostalist Discourse. *Journal of Religion in Africa* 28, no. 3: 316–49.

———. 1998b. The Power of Money: Politics, Occult Forces and Pentecostalism in Ghana. *African Studies Review* 4, no. 3: 15–37.

———. 1999. *Translating the Devil: Religion and Modernity among the Ewe in Ghana.* Edinburgh: Edinburgh University Press for IAI.

———. 2002. Christianity and the Ewe Nation: German Pietist Missionaries, Ewe Converts and the Politics of Culture. *Journal of Religion in Africa* 32, no. 2: 167–99.

———. 2009. Response to ter Haar and Ellis. *Africa* 79, no. 3: 413–16.

———. 2010. Aesthetics of Persuasion: Global Christianity and Pentecostalism's Sensational Forms. *South Atlantic Quarterly* 9:741–63.

———. 2013. "Your world is about to change": Videos, Spirits and the Popular Imagination in Ghana. Unpublished manuscript.

Meyer, Birgit, and Peter Geschiere, eds. *Globalization and Identity: Dialectics of Flow and Closure.* Oxford: Blackwell.

Meyer, Birgit, and P. Pels, eds. 2003. *Magic and Modernity: Interfaces of Revelation and Concealment.* Stanford, CA: Stanford University Press.

Middleton, J. 1960. *Lugbara Religion: Ritual and Authority among an East African People.* Oxford: Oxford University Press.

———. 1963. Witchcraft and Sorcery in Lugbara. In *Witchcraft and Sorcery in East Africa*, edited by J. Middleton and E. H. Winter, 257–77. London: Routledge and Kegan Paul.

Midelfort, H. C. Erik. 1972. *Witch-Hunting in South-Western Germany, 1582–1684: The Social and Intellectual Foundations.* Stanford, CA: Stanford University Press.

Miller, Joseph. 1988. *"Way of Death": Merchant Capitalism and the Angolan Slave Trade, 1730–1893.* Madison: University of Wisconsin Press.

Mol, Annemarie. 2002. *The Body Multiple: Ontology in Practice.* Durham, NC: Duke University Press.

———. 2012. Mind Your Plate! The Ontonorms of Dutch Dieting. *Social Studies of Science*, September 13, 2012, http://sss.sagepub.com.

Möllering, G. 2001. The Nature of Trust: From Georg Simmel to a Theory of Expectation, Interpretation and Suspension. *Sociology* 35, no. 2: 403–20.

Monter, William. 1976. *Witchcraft in France and Switzerland: The Borderlands during the Reformation*. Ithaca, NY: Cornell University Press.

Moore, Henrietta. 2011. *Still Life: Hopes, Desires and Satisfactions*. Cambridge: Polity.

Moore, Henrietta, and Todd Saunders, eds. 2001. *Magical Interpretations, Material Realities: Modernity, Witchcraft and the Occult in Postcolonial Africa*. London: Routledge.

Mott, Luiz. 1994. O Calundu-Angolas de Luzia Pinta: Sabará, 1739. *Revista do Instituto de Artes e Cultura* (Universidade Federal de Ouro Preto) 1:73–82.

Muchembled, Robert. 1978a. Avant-propos et sorcières du Cambrésis. In *Prophètes et sorciers dans les Pays-Bas, XVIe–XVIIIe siècles*, edited by M. S. Dupont-Bouchat, W. T. Frijhoff, and R. Muchembled, 13–41, 155–263. Paris: Hachette.

———. 1978b. *Culture populaire et cultures des élites*. Paris: Flammarion.

Nadel, S. F. 1935. Witchcraft and Anti-witchcraft in Nupe Society. *Africa* 8, no. 4: 423–37.

Ndjio, B. 2006. "Feymania": New Wealth, Magic Money and Power in Contemporary Cameroon. PhD diss., University of Amsterdam. (French edition: 2012. *Magie et enrichissement illicite: La feymania au Cameroun*. Paris: Karthala.)

———. 2012. Post-colonial Histories of Sexuality: The Political Invention of a Libidinal African Straight. *Africa* 82, no. 4: 609–31.

Nicolau Parés, Luis: see under Parés, Luis Nicolau.

Niehaus, I. 2001. *Witchcraft, Power and Politics: Exploring the Occult in the South African Lowveld*. London: Pluto.

———. 2012. *Witchcraft and a Life in the New South Africa*. Cambridge: Cambridge University Press.

Noret, Joël, and Pierre Petit. 2011. *Mort et dynamiques sociales au Katanga (République Démocratique du Congo)*. Paris: L'Harmattan.

Nyamnjoh, Francis. 1998. Witchcraft in the "Politics of Belonging." *African Studies Review* 41, no. 3: 69–93.

———. 2011. Cameroonian Bushfalling: Negotiation of Identity and Belonging in Fiction and Ethnography. *American Ethnologist* 38, no. 4: 701–13.

Obarrio, Juan. 2007. The Spirit of the Law in Mozambique. PhD diss., Columbia University.

Offiong, D. A. 1991. *Witchcraft, Sorcery, Magic and the Social Order among the Ibibio of Nigeria*. Enugu, Nigeria: Fourth Dimension.

Palmié, Stephan. 2002. *Wizards and Scientists: Explorations in Afro-Cuban Modernity as Tradition*. Durham, NC: Duke University Press.

Parés, Luis Nicolau. 2004. The "Nagôization" Process in Bahian Candomblé. In *The Yoruba Diaspora in the Atlantic World*, edited by T. Falola and M. Childs, 185–208. Bloomington: Indiana University Press.

———. 2007. Candomblé: Accusations of Sorcery and Struggles for Power. Paper presented at the conference "Culture and the State in the Lusophone Black Atlantic," London, January 17–20, 2007.

———. [2007] 2011. *A formaçao do Candomblé: História e ritual da naçao jeje na Bahia*. Campinas, Brazil: Unicamp. Here quoted from French translation: 2011. *La formation du Candomblé: Histoire et rituel du vodun au Brésil*. Paris: Karthala.

———. 2010. Memories of Slavery in Religious Ritual: Comparing Benin Vodun and Bahian Candomblé. In *Activating the Past: History and Memory in the Black Atlantic World*, edited by A. Apter and L. Derby, 71–97. Cambridge: Cambridge Scholars.

Parés, Luis Nicolau, and Roger Sansi. 2011a. Introduction: Sorcery in the Black Atlantic. In *Sorcery in the Black Atlantic*, edited by L. Nicolau Parés and R. Sansi, 1–19. Chicago: University of Chicago Press.

———, eds. 2011b. *Sorcery in the Black Atlantic*. Chicago: University of Chicago Press.

Pedersen, Morten Axel. 2011. *Not Quite Shamans: Spirit Worlds and Political Lives in Northern Mongolia*. Ithaca, NY: Cornell University Press.

———. 2012. Common Nonsense: A Review of Certain Recent Reviews of the "Ontological Turn." *Anthropology of This Century*, October 31, 2012, http://aotcpress.com/articles/common_nonsense/.

Peel, J. D. Y. 1969. *Aladura: A Religious Movement among the Yoruba*. London: Oxford University Press.

———. 2000. *Religious Encounter and the Making of the Yoruba*. Bloomington: Indiana University Press.

Peires, J. 2004. Frankenstein Visits the Eastern Cape. *South African Historical Journal* 51:224–42.

Pels, P. 2003. Introduction to *Magic and Modernity*, edited by B. Meyer and P. Pels, 1–39. Stanford, CA: Stanford University Press.

Piot, C. 1999. *Remotely Global: Village Modernity in West Africa*. Chicago: University of Chicago Press.

———. 2010. *Nostalgia for the Future: West Africa after the Cold War*. Chicago: University of Chicago Press.

Povinelli, Elizabeth A. 2006. *The Empire of Love: Towards a Theory of Intimacy, Genealogy and Carnality*. Durham, NC: Duke University Press.

Purkiss, Diane. 1996. *The Witch in History: Early Modern and Twentieth-Century Presentations*. London: Routledge.

Ralushai Commission. 1996. Report on the Commission of Inquiry into Witchcraft Violence and Ritual Murders in the Northern Province of the Republic of South Africa. Ministry of Safety and Security, Northern Province, Republic of South Africa.

Ranger, T. 2006. African Religion, Witchcraft and the Liberation War in Zimbabwe. In *Studies in Witchcraft, Magic and War and Peace in Africa*, edited by B. Nicolini, 351–79. New York: Edwin Mellen.

———. 2007. Scotland Yard in the Bush: Medicine Murders, Child Witches and the Construction of the Occult; A Literature Review. *Africa* 77, no. 2: 272–84.

Redding, Sean. 1999. Government Witchcraft: Taxation, the Supernatural, and the Mpondo Revolt in the Transkei, South Africa, 1955–1963. *African Affairs* 95:555–79.

Reis, J. J. 1993. *Slave Rebellion in Brazil: The Muslim Uprising of 1835 in Bahia*. Baltimore: Johns Hopkins University Press.

———. 2001. Candomblé in Nineteenth-Century Bahia: Priests, Followers, Clients. In *Rethinking the African Diaspora*, edited by K. Mann and E. G. Bay, 116–35. London: Frank Cass.

———. 2011 Candomblé and Slave Resistance in Nineteenth-Century Bahia. In *Sorcery and the Black Atlantic*, edited by L. N. Parés and R. Sansi, 55–75. Chicago: University of Chicago Press.

Rey, Pierre-Philippe. 1973. *Les alliances des classes*. Paris: Maspero.

Robbins, J. 2007. Continuity Thinking and the Problem of Christian Culture. *Current Anthropology* 48:5–38.

Robisheaux, Thomas. 2009. *The Last Witch of Langenburg: Murder in a German Village*. New York: W. W. Norton.

Roitman, Janet. 2003. Unsanctioned Wealth, or The Productivity of Debt in Northern Cameroon. *Public Culture* 15, no. 2: 211–38.

Roper, Lyndal. 1994. *Oedipus and the Devil: Witchcraft, Sexuality and Religion in Early Modern Europe*. London: Routledge.

Rosenthal, Judy. 1998. *Possession, Ecstasy, and Law in Ewe Voodoo*. Charlottesville: University Press of Virginia.

Rowlands, Michael. 1985. Notes on the Material Symbolism of Grassfields Palaces. *Paideuma* 31:203–13.

———. 1993. Accumulation and the Cultural Politics of Identity in the Grassfields. In *Itinéraires d'accumulation au Cameroun*, edited by P. Geschiere and P. Konings, 71–97. Paris: Karthala.

Rutherford, B. 1999. To Find an African Witch: Anthropology, Modernity and Witch-Finding in North-West Zambia. *Critique of Anthropology* 19, no. 1: 89–109.

Sabar, Galia. 2010. Witchcraft and Concepts of Evil amongst African Migrant Workers in Israel. *Canadian Journal of African Studies* 44, no. 1: 110–41.

Sabean, David W. 1984. *Power in the Blood: Popular Culture and Village Discourse in Early Modern Germany*. Cambridge: Cambridge University Press.

Sahlins, M. [1965] 1974. On the Sociology of Primitive Exchange. In *The Relevance of Models for Social Anthropology*, edited by M. Banton. London: Tavistock, 1965. Here quoted from later publication in Sahlins, M. 1974. *Stone Age Economics*, 185–277. London: Tavistock.

———. 1974. The Spirit of the Gift. In *Stone Age Economics*, 149–84. London: Tavistock.

———. 2013. *What Kinship Is . . . And Is Not*. Chicago: University of Chicago Press.

Salmon, J. H. M. 1989. History without Anthropology: A New Witchcraft Synthesis. *Journal of Interdisciplinary History* 19, no. 3: 481–86.

Sanders, Andrew. 1995. *A Deed without a Name: The Witch in Society and History*. London: Berg.

Sanders, Todd. 2003. Reconsidering Witchcraft: Postcolonial Africa and Analytic (Un-) certainties. *American Anthropologist* 105, no. 2: 338–52.

Sansi, Roger. 2011. Sorcery and Fetishism in the Modern Atlantic. In *Sorcery in the Black Atlantic*, edited by L. Nicolau Parés and R. Sansi, 19–41. Chicago: University of Chicago Press.

Sansone, Livio. 2003. *Blackness without Ethnicity: Constructing Race in Brazil*. New York: Palgrave Macmillan.

Santos, Jocélio Teles dos. La divinité *caboclo* dans le candomblé de Bahia. *Cahiers d'Etudes Africaines* 125, no. 32–1: 83–107.

Sennett, Richard. 1974. *The Fall of Public Man*. Cambridge: Cambridge University Press.

Séraphin, G. 2000. *Vivre à Douala: L'imaginaire et l'action dans une ville africaine en crise.* Paris: L'Harmattan.

——, ed. 2004. *L'effervescence religieuse: La diversité locale des implantations religieuses chrétiennes au Cameroun et au Kenya.* Paris: Karthala.

Shaw, R. 2002. *Memories of the Slave Trade: Ritual and the Historical Imagination in Sierra Leone.* Chicago: University of Chicago Press.

Shipton, P. 2007. *The Nature of Entrustment: Intimacy, Exchange and the Sacred in Africa.* New Haven, CT: Yale University Press.

Shryock, Andrew, ed. 2004. *Off Stage, On Display: Intimacy and Ethnography in the Age of Public Culture.* Stanford, CA: Stanford University Press.

Siegel, J. 2001. Suharto, Witches. *Indonesia* 71:27–78.

——. 2003. The Truth of Sorcery. *Cultural Anthropology* 18, no. 2: 135–55.

——. 2006. *Naming the Witch.* Stanford, CA: Stanford University Press.

Simmel, G. [1902/3] 1950. The Stranger (Exkurs über den Fremden). In *The Sociology of Georg Simmel*, translated and edited by Kurt H. Wolf. New York: Free Press.

——. [1908] 1950. Das Geheimnis und die Geheime Gesellschaft. In *Soziologie, Untersuchungen über die Formen der Vergesellschaftung*, 257–304. Leipzig: von Duncker & Humblot. Here quoted from the English translation: 1950. *The Sociology of Georg Simmel*, translated and edited by K. H. Wolff. New York: Free Press.

——. [1900] 1989. *Philosophie des Geldes.* Here quoted from the 2nd edition: 1989. Edited by D. P. Frisby and Klaus Christian Köhnke. Frankfurt: Suhrkamp.

——. 1990. *The Philosophy of Money.* 2nd ed. Translated by T. Bottomore and D. P. Frisby. London: Routledge.

Sjørslev, Inger. 1999. Glaube und Besessenheit: Ein Bericht über die Candomble-Religion in Brasilien. Gifkendorf, Germany: Merlin Verlag.

——. 2006. On Leaving the Field: Closure and Continuity as Seen through the Lens of the Candomblé Axexé Ritual. *Folk* 46/47:11–40.

Smith, Daniel Jordan. 2007. *A Culture of Corruption: Everyday Deception and Popular Discontent in Nigeria.* Princeton, NJ: Princeton University Press.

——. 2008. Intimacy, Infidelity, and Masculinity in Southeastern Nigeria. In *Intimacies: Love + Sex across Cultures*, edited by W. R. Jankowiak, 224–44. New York: Columbia University Press.

Smith, J. H. 2008. *Bewitching Development: Witchcraft and the Reinvention of Development in Neoliberal Kenya.* Chicago: University of Chicago Press.

Socpa, Antoine. 2002. *Démocratisation et autochtonie au Cameroun: Variations régionales.* Münster, Germany: LIT Verlag.

Souza, Laura de Mello e. [1986] 2003. *The Devil and the Land of the Holy Cross: Witchcraft, Slavery, and Popular Religion in Colonial Brazil.* Austin: University of Texas Press,

Spierenburg, M. J. 2003. Strangers, Spirits and Land Reforms: Conflicts about Land in Dande, Northern Zimbabwe. PhD diss., University of Amsterdam.

Stephen, Michele, ed. 1987. *Sorcerer and Witch in Melanesia.* Melbourne: Melbourne University Press.

Stoler, Anny. 2005. *Carnal Knowledge and Imperial Power: Race and the Intimate in Colonial Rule.* Berkeley: University of California Press.

Strathern, Marilyn. 1988. *The Gender of the Gift: Problems with Women and Problems with Society in Melanesia*. Berkeley: University of California Press.

Stroeken, K. 2010. *Moral Power: The Magic of Witchcraft*. Oxford: Berghahn Books.

Taliani, Simona. 2012. Coercion, Fetishes and Suffering in the Daily Lives of Young Nigerian Women in Italy. *Africa* 82, no. 4: 579–608.

Tall, Emmanuelle Kadya. 2009. Imaginaire national et mise en patrimoine dans l'Atlantique Sud: Candomblé de Bahia et cultes vodun au Sud Bénin. *Lusotopie* 16, no. 2: 133–55.

Taussig, Michael. 1987. *Shamanism, Colonialism, and the Wild Man: A Study of Terror and Healing*. Chicago: University of Chicago Press.

———.1993. *Mimesis and Alterity*. New York: Routledge.

Tcheuyap, A. 2009. Exclusion et pouvoir: Formes et forces de l'occulte dans les cinémas d'Afrique. *Canadian Journal of African Studies* 43, no. 2: 367–98.

Teles dos Santos, Jocélio: see under Santos.

Ter Haar, Gerrie. 2008. Comment for Review Symposium on Harry G. West's Ethnographic Sorcery. *African Studies Review* 51, no. 3: 140–42.

Thiranagama, Sharika. 2010. In Praise of Traitors: Intimacy, Betrayal and the Sri Lanka Tamil Community. In *Traitors: Suspicion, Intimacy and the Ethics of State-Building*, edited by S. Thiranagama and T. Kelly, 127–50. Philadelphia: Philadelphia University Press.

———. 2011. *In My Mother's House: Civil War in Sri Lanka*. Philadelphia: University of Pennsylvania Press.

Thoden van Velzen, H. U. E. 1997. Dramatization: How Dream Work Shapes Culture. *Psychoanalytic Review* 84, no. 2: 85–118.

Thoden van Velzen, H. U. E., and W. van Wetering. 1988. *The Great Father and the Danger: Religious Cults, Material Forces and Collective Fantasies in the World of the Surinamese Maroons*. Dordrecht: Foris.

———. 1989. Demonologie en de Betovering van het Religieuze Leven. *Sociologische Gids* 36, nos. 3–4: 155–87.

———. 2004. *In the Shadow of the Oracle: Religion as Politics in a Suriname Maroon Society*. Long Grove, IL: Waveland.

Thomas, Keith. 1971. *Religion and the Decline of Magic: Studies in Popular Beliefs in Sixteenth and Seventeenth Century England*. London: Weidenfeld and Nicolson.

Tilly, Charles. 2005. *Trust and Rule*. Cambridge: Cambridge University Press.

Titi Nwel, P. 1986. *Thong Likeng: Fondateur de la religion de Nyambebantu*. Paris: L'Harmattan.

Tonda, Joseph. 2002. *La guérison divine en Afrique centrale (Congo, Gabon)*. Paris: Karthala.

———. 2005. *Le souverain moderne: Le corps du pouvoir en Afrique centrale (Congo, Gabon)*. Paris: Karthala.

Toulabor, C. 1999. Sacrifices humains et politique: Quelques exemples contemporains en Afrique. In *Trajectoires de libération en Afrique contemporaine*, edited by P. Konings, W. van Binsbergen, and G. Hesseling, 207–23. Paris: Karthala.

Turner, S. 2010. Betraying Trust and the Elusive Nature of Ethnicity in Burundi. In

Traitors: Suspicion, Intimacy and the Ethics of State-Building, edited by S. Thiranagama and T. Kelly, 110–27. Philadelphia: University of Philadelphia Press.

Turner, V. W. 1954. *Schism and Continuity in an African Society: A Study of Ndembu Village Life*. Madison: University of Wisconsin Press.

———. 1964. Witchcraft and Sorcery: Taxonomy versus Dynamics. *Africa* 34, no. 4: 314–25.

Van Beek, Walter E. A. 2007. The Escalation of Witchcraft Accusations. In *Imagining Evil: Witchcraft Beliefs and Accusations in Contemporary Africa*, edited by G. ter Haar, 293–315. Trenton, NJ: Africa World Press.

Van Binsbergen, W. M. J. 2001. Witchcraft in Modern Africa as Virtualized Boundary Conditions of the Kinship Order. In *Witchcraft Dialogues*, edited by G. C. Bond and D. M. Ciekawy, 212–64. Athens: Ohio University Press.

Van de Port, M. 2011. *Ecstatic Encounters: Bahian Candomblé and the Quest for the Really Real*. Amsterdam: Amsterdam University Press.

Van Dijk, Rijk. 2001. "Voodoo" on the Doorstep: Young Nigerian Prostitutes and Magic Policing in the Netherlands. *Africa* 71, no. 4: 558–86.

———. 2002. The Soul Is the Stranger: Ghanaian Pentecostalism and the Diasporic Contestation of "Flow" and "Individuality." *Culture and Religion* 3, no. 1: 49–67.

———. 2005. The Moral Life of the Gift in Ghanaian Pentecostal Churches in the Diaspora: Questions of (In-)dividuality and (In-)alienability in Transcultural Reciprocal Relations. In *Commodification: Things, Agency and Identities*, edited by W. M. J. van Binsbergen and P. Geschiere, 201–25. Münster, Germany: LIT Verlag.

Van Dijk, R., Thera Rasing, Nina Tellegen, and W. M. J. van Binsbergen. 2003. *Een Schijn van Voodoo: Culturele Achtergronden van de Handel in Nigeriaanse Meisjes voor de Nederlandse Prostitutie, Een Verkenning*. Leiden: African Studies Centre.

Venkatesan, Soumhya, ed. 2010. Ontology Is Just Another Word for Culture: Motion Tabled at the 2008 Meeting of the Group for Debates in Anthropological Theory, University of Manchester. *Critique of Anthropology* 30, no. 2: 152–200.

Vincent, Jeanne-Françoise. 1976. *Traditions et transition: Entretiens avec des femmes beti du Sud-Cameroun*. Paris: Berger-Levrault.

Viveiros de Castro, Eduardo. 1996. Images of Nature and Society in Amazonian Study. *Annual Review of Anthropology* 25:179–200.

———. 2003. Speech at Anthropology and Science Conference, Manchester, July 14, 2003. *Manchester Papers in Social Anthropology* 7.

———. 2009. *Métaphysiques cannibales: Lignes d'anthropologie structurale*. Paris: Presses Universitaires Françaises.

———. 2010. Intensive Filiation and Demonic Alliance. In *Deleuzian Intersections: Science, Technology and Anthropology*, edited by E. B. Jensen and K. Rödje. 219–55. Oxford: Berghahn Books.

Warnier, J.-P. 1993. *L'esprit d'entreprise au Cameroun*. Paris: Karthala.

———. 2009. *Règner au Cameroun: Le roi-pot*. Paris: Karthala.

Wendl, Tobias. 2005. *Ghanain Video Tales*. Video. Göttingen, Germany: IWF Wissen und Medien.

Werbner, R. 1999. *Tears of the Dead: The Social Biography of an African Family*. Edinburgh: Edinburgh University Press.

West, H. G. 2005. *Kupilikula, Governance, and the Invisible Realm in Mozambique*. Chicago: University of Chicago Press.

———. 2007. *Ethnographic Sorcery*. Chicago: University of Chicago Press.

Whitehead, N. L., and R. Wright, eds. 2004. *In Darkness and Secrecy: The Anthropology of Assault Sorcery and Witchcraft in Amazonia*. Durham, NC: Duke University Press.

Williams, F. E. [1923] 1976. The Vailala Madness. In *"The Vailala Madness" and Other Essays*. London: Hurst.

Yengo, Patrice. 2008a. Le monde à l'envers: Enfance et *kindoki* ou les ruses de la raison sorcière dans le bassin du Congo. *Cahiers d'Études Africaines* 189/90:297–324, special issue, *Territoires sorciers*, edited by C. Henry and E. K. Tall.

———. 2008b. Review of E. de Rosny, ed., *Justice et sorcellerie*. *Cahiers d'Études Aricaines* 189/90:372–78, special issue, *Territoires sorciers*, edited by C. Henry and E. K. Tall.

Yates-Doerr, Emily, and Annemarie Mol. 2012. Cuts of Meat: Disentangling Western Natures-Cultures. *Cambridge Anthropology* 30, no. 2: 48–64.

Ystanes, Margit. 2012. Unfixed Trust: Intimacy, Blood Symbolism, and Porous Boundaries in Guatemala. Paper for workshop "The Entangled Tensions of Intimacy, Trust and the Social," organizers V. Broch-Due and M. Ystanes, Bergen, Norway, May 18–20.

Index

Jackson, M., 10

Jankowiak, W. R., 24, 229n58

Janson, M., 243n42, 262n27

Java, xxiii, xxv, 165, 172, 175, 258n13

Jewsiewicki, B., 237n42, 263n33

Kant, 174–76, 179, 258n15, 259n24

Kapferer, B., 10, 220n16, 222n21, 260n2

Kierkegaard, 32

Kinshasa, 192–97, 201, 229n55, 243n46, 262n25

kinship, and flexibility, 10, 222n21. *See also* reciprocity; witchcraft

LaFontaine, J., 210, 211

Landes, R., 139–44, 151–55, 251nn11–12

Langenburg, 111–15, 118, 124, 178, 206, 249n32

Larner, C., 110, 122, 123, 245n2, 246n7, 247n20

Latour, B., 170, 216n11, 256n8

Lattas, A., xxv, 168, 169, 170, 219–20n14, 256n2

Levack, B., 109

Lévi-Strauss, C., xviii, 175–78, 215n2, 227n43, 258–59n16, 259n22, 260n26

Lindenbaum, S., 167, 256n4

Lovell, N., 161

Luongo, K., 219n14

Mãe Aninha, 144, 145, 148–51

Mãe Stella, 144, 150–52, 155, 252n29, 254n31

Maggie, Y., 138, 153, 251n6

Malaquais, D., 56, 235n24, 235n26

Mammywata, 22, 187

marabout, 82, 83, 160, 241n34, 241n36

Mars, Kettley, 260n1

Marshall, R., xx, 17–20, 90–93, 170, 171, 178, 186, 217n3, 235n22, 242–43n40, 262n26, 265n43

Martinelli, B., 219n14

Martiniano do Bonfim, 140, 144, 145, 151

Marwick, M., 165–69, 215n5, 225n34

Mary, A., 224n30, 225n34, 227n44, 240n19, 241n31, 260n3, 261n11

Masquelier, A., 197–202, 262–63nn27–30

Matory, J. Lorand, 138, 143–46, 150–55, 162, 251n10, 251–52n12, 252n18, 252n20

Mauss, M., xxi, 30, 31, 231nn69–70, 231–32n72

Mayer, P., 16

Mbembe, A., xxi, 216n10, 217n2

Mendouga, 40, 72, 73, 80–88, 101, 240n27

Meyer, B., 67, 191, 217n3, 218–19n11, 223n24, 225n34, 237n43, 240n26, 247n15, 258n15; on Pentecostalism, 90, 91, 178, 207, 226n41, 236n35, 243nn45–46, 256n5; on video-films, 186–88, 224n27, 242n40, 261n9, 261n13–17

Middleton, J., 222n21, 224n29

miedou (charged objects), 5, 220n17

missionaries, 12, 39, 44, 89, 90, 106, 168–70, 186, 220–21n19, 241–42n37, 243n41, 247n15

modernity. *See under* witchcraft

modernization, 2, 88, 162

Mol, A., 256–57n7–8, 257n10

Möllering, G., 32, 70, 232n75, 237n2

Mongolia, 19

Moore, H., 219n14, 226n42

Mott, L., 252n13, 252n20

Mt. Kupé, 15, 45, 63, 64, 242n39

Muchembled, R., 108, 110, 202, 246n7, 246n9, 247n18

multipartyism, 44, 48, 49, 59, 99

ndjaw (house), xvi, 216n7. *See also djambe le ndjaw* (witchcraft of the house)

ndjaw boud (family), 15, 94, 129, 216n7

Ndjio, B., 21, 56–59, 217n2, 228n53, 235n24

ndjobi, 92

neighbors, 16, 108, 123, 248n23, 251n6

neoliberal, 8, 19, 51, 52, 55, 65, 71, 208, 216n9

neotraditional, 52, 55, 102

shaman, 19, 20, 105, 168, 169
Shaw, R., 233n11, 237n41
Shipton, P., 25
Siegel, J., xxv, 165, 172–81, 205, 211,
 215nn1–2, 224n30, 257n11, 258nn13–14,
 258n16, 259–60nn19–25, 264n40
Simmel, G.: on public secret, 240n26; on
 the stranger, xvii, 231n64; on trust,
 xxii, 32, 33, 69–71, 83, 97, 201, 215n1,
 232n75, 238n5, 245n55
sixa, 243n41
Sjørslev, I., 156
sjumbu (witches' sabbath), 4, 241n28
slave trade, 16, 64, 144–46, 161, 162, 169,
 207, 233nn10–11, 252n17, 253n26
Smith, D. J., 229n58, 243–44n46
Smith, J. H., 65, 66, 219n14
sociality, xv, xx, xxi, xxii, 31, 265n43
Socpa, A., 52, 264n38
South Africa, 16, 64–67, 74, 75, 82, 110,
 218n7, 226n38, 259n18, 261n5, 264n42
Souza, Laura de Mello e, 138, 141, 142, 159,
 251n6, 255n40
spirit medium, 12, 109, 224n28
Sri Lanka, 181, 265n43
Stephen, M., 166, 167, 256n4
Stoler, A., 215n1
stranger. *See under* Simmel, G.
Strathern, M., 256n6
Stroeken, K., 219n14, 220n15, 220n17,
 222n21
structural adjustment, 51, 56, 196, 198,
 216n9, 225n33, 235n21
sublime, 174–79, 258n15
Sufi, 197, 198, 262n28
Suharto, xxv, 165, 172–75, 259n19

Taliani, S., 61, 229n56
Tall, E. K., 154, 220n15, 220n17, 261n9
Taussig, M., 217n5, 239n14, 240n26
Tcheuyap, A., 226n37, 261n10
technology, 6, 187, 216n12, 257n10
Ter Haar, G., 11, 224n27

terreiro, xxiv, 17, 138, 141–49, 153, 154, 158,
 160, 207, 255n41
Thiranagama, S., 215n1, 265n43
Thoden van Velzen, H. U. E., 225–26n36,
 231n62, 244n50
Thomas, K., 122, 245n1
Tilly, C., 70, 239n8
Togo, 50, 55, 61, 64, 74, 146, 147, 161,
 225n34, 228n53, 244n48
Tonda, J., 77, 215n3, 233n10, 263n33; on
 (dis)continuity, 17–22, 237n43; on *déparentalisation*, 101, 132, 227n45, 229n55,
 237n37, 262n21, 262n25; on Pentecostalism, 90–92, 169, 219n14, 227nn46–47,
 235n23, 241–42n37, 242–43n40,
 243–44nn45–46, 260n3
Tönnies, 30
torture, 113–20, 142, 178, 248n21,
 248–49n27
Toulabor, C., 74
traitors inside, 215n1, 225n35
tribunals/courts (of justice), 5, 43–46, 86,
 89, 107–10, 114–18, 121, 122, 129, 185,
 205, 260–61n5, 261–62n19
Trier, 109, 261n19
trust: economists on, 29–31, 69, 238n4,
 238n6; and leap of faith, 32, 70, 71,
 232n75; and rational choice, 29–32, 69,
 70, 238, 239; and suspension of doubt,
 32, 33, 181, 201, 202, 211. *See also nganga*
 (healer); reciprocity
Tylor, Edward, 30

uncanny (*unheimlich/heimlich*), xvii, xxii,
 xxv, 23, 26–28, 33–35, 67, 68, 71, 102,
 165, 166, 172–81, 201, 202, 205–7, 210,
 211, 215n1, 231n63, 259n25, 264n41
urban elites, 13, 41–43, 49, 50, 53–55,
 228n54

Van Beek, W., 107
Van Binsbergen, W. M. J., 67, 219n14,
 228n54, 236n33